EITHER/OR
PART II

KIERKEGAARD'S WRITINGS, IV

EITHER/OR
PART II

by Søren Kierkegaard

Edited and Translated
with Introduction and Notes by

Howard V. Hong and
Edna H. Hong

PRINCETON UNIVERSITY PRESS
PRINCETON, NEW JERSEY

Published by Princeton University Press
41 William Street, Princeton, New Jersey
In the United Kingdom: Princeton University Press, Oxford

Library of Congress Cataloging in Publication Data will be
found on the last printed page of this book

ISBN 0-691-07316-3 (cloth)
ISBN 0-691-02042-6 (pbk.)

Third Paperback Printing, with corrections, 1990

10   9   8   7   6   5   4   3

Preparation of this volume has been made possible in part by a grant from.
the Division of Research Programs
of the National Endowment for the Humanities, an independent federal agency

Designed by Frank Mahood

Printed in the United States of America by Princeton
University Press, Princeton, New Jersey

CONTENTS

THE ESTHETIC VALIDITY OF MARRIAGE
3

THE BALANCE BETWEEN THE ESTHETIC AND THE ETHICAL
IN THE DEVELOPMENT OF THE PERSONALITY
155

ULTIMATUM [A FINAL WORD]
THE UPBUILDING THAT LIES IN THE THOUGHT THAT IN
RELATION TO GOD WE ARE ALWAYS IN THE WRONG
339

EITHER/OR

A FRAGMENT OF LIFE

edited by
Victor Eremita

PART II

CONTAINING THE PAPERS OF B,

LETTERS TO A

Les grandes passions sont solitaires, et les trans-
porter au désert, c'est les rendre à leur empire
[The great passions are hermits, and to transport
them to the desert is to hand over to
them their proper domain].

CHATEAUBRIAND

THE ESTHETIC VALIDITY OF MARRIAGE[1]

My Friend,

The lines on which your eye falls first were written last. My intention with them is to attempt once again to compress into the form of a letter the extended exploration that is hereby transmitted to you. These lines correspond to the last lines and together form an envelope, and thus in an external way they evince what the internal evidence will in many ways convince you of—that it is a letter you are reading. This thought—that it was a letter I wrote to you—I have been unwilling to give up, partly because my time has not permitted the more painstaking elaboration that a treatise requires, and partly because I am reluctant to miss the opportunity of addressing you in the more admonishing and urgent tone appropriate to the epistolary form. You are all too skilled in the art of talking in generalities about everything without letting yourself be personally involved for me to tempt you by setting your dialectical powers in motion. You know how the prophet Nathan dealt with King David when he presumed to understand the parable the prophet had told him but was unwilling to understand that it applied to him. Then to make sure, Nathan added: You are the man, O King.[2] In the same way I also have continually tried to remind you that you are the one who is being discussed and you are the one who is spoken to. Therefore, I do not at all doubt that while reading you will continually have the impression that it is a letter you are reading, even if you might be deflected by the fact that the format of the paper is inappropriate for a letter. As a public official, I am accustomed to writing on full sheets; this can perhaps have its good side if it can
contribute to giving my words a certain official quality in your eyes. The letter that you hereby receive is rather long; if it were weighed on a post office scale, it would be an expensive letter; on the troy-weight scale of keen critical analysis, it would perhaps appear to be very negligible. I ask you, therefore, not to

use any of these scales, not the post office scale, for it comes to
you not for forwarding but as a deposit, and not the scale of
critical analysis, since I would be loath to see you make yourself guilty of such a gross and uncongenial misunderstanding.

[3]If anyone other than you were to see this exploration, he
would certainly find it most curious and superfluous; if he
were a married man, he would perhaps exclaim with a certain
paterfamilias-joviality: Yes, marriage is the esthetic in life; if he
were a young man, he would perhaps chime in rather vaguely
and unreflectively: Yes, love, you are the esthetic in life; but
both of them would be unable to comprehend how it could
ever enter my head to want to salvage the esthetic prestige of
marriage. Indeed, rather than earning me the gratitude of actual or prospective husbands, it would probably make me suspect, for he who champions accuses. And for this I would have
you to thank, for I have never had any doubts about it, you
whom I love as a son, as a brother, as a friend, despite all your
bizarre qualities, love with an esthetic love [*Kjærlighed*], because some day you perhaps will find a center for your eccentric behavior, you whom I love for your intensity, for your
passions, for your frailties, love with the fear and trembling of
a religious love because I see the aberrations and because to me
you are something entirely different from a prodigy. When I
see you swerve, see you rear like a wild horse, plunge backward and dash forward again, then, well, then I abstain from
all paltry pedagogics, but I do think of an unbroken horse and
also see the hand that holds the reins, see the harsh fates' lash
raised over your head. And yet when this discussion eventually comes into your hands, you will perhaps say: Yes, it is in-
disputably an enormous task he has undertaken, but now let us
also see how he has carried it out. Perhaps I speak too mildly
to you, perhaps I tolerate too much from you, perhaps I
should have exercised more the authority that I, despite your
pride, have over you, or perhaps I should not have become involved with you in this matter at all, for you are indeed a corrupted person in many ways, and the more one is involved
with you the worse it becomes. That is, you are no enemy of

marriage, but you misuse your ironic look and your sarcastic taunting to ridicule it.

In this connection, I concede that you are not shadow-boxing, that you land some solid blows, and that you are keenly observant, but I also want to say that this is perhaps your error. Your life will amount to nothing but tentative efforts at living. You presumably will answer that this is always better than traveling on the train of triviality and atomistically losing oneself in life's social hordes.[4] To repeat, you cannot be said to hate marriage; as yet your thought has never actually gone that far, at least not without being scandalized by it, and so you must forgive me for assuming that you have not given full consideration to the subject. What you prefer is the first infatuation. You know how to sink down and hide in a dreaming, love-drunk *clairvoyance*. You completely envelop yourself, as it were, in the sheerest cobweb and then sit in wait. But you are not a child, not an awakening consciousness,[5] and therefore your look has another meaning; but you are satisfied with it. You love the accidental. A smile from a pretty girl in an interesting situation, a stolen glance, that is what you are hunting for, that is a motif for your aimless fantasy. You who always pride yourself on being an *observateur* must, in return, put up with becoming an object of observation.

I will remind you of an incident. A pretty young girl whom you by chance (this, of course, must be emphasized; you knew neither her social position nor her name, age, etc.) sat beside at table was too cool to bestow a glance upon you. You were momentarily perplexed as to whether this was merely *Sprödigkeit*[6] [coyness] or whether together with it there was a little embarrassment, which properly illuminated could place her in an interesting situation. She sat directly opposite a mirror in which you could see her. She cast a shy glance in that direction without suspecting that your eyes had already taken quarters there; she blushed when your eyes met hers. You preserve such things as accurately and as swiftly as a daguerreotype, which, as is generally known, takes only a half-minute even in the poorest weather.

Ah, you are a strange fellow, one moment a child, the next

an old man; one moment you are thinking most earnestly about the most important scholarly problems, how you will devote your life to them, and the next you are a lovesick fool. But you are a long way from marriage, and I hope that your good genius will keep you from taking the wrong path, for at times I seem to see in you traces of wanting to play a little Zeus. You are so superior about your love that I daresay you fancy that every girl would count herself lucky to be your sweetheart for one week. And now you may resume for the time being your amorous studies, along with your esthetic, ethical, metaphysical, cosmopolitan, and other studies. One cannot really become angry with you; evil in you, like the Middle Ages' concept of it, has a certain additive of good nature and childishness. As far as marriage is concerned, your relation has always been only that of an observer. There is something treasonable in wanting to be merely an observer. How often you entertained me—yes, I readily admit it—but how often you also tormented me with your stories of how you had stolen your way into the confidence of one and then another married man in order to see how deeply bogged down he was in the swamp of marital life. You are really very gifted at slipping in with people; that I will not deny, nor that it is very entertaining to hear you relate the consequences of it and to witness your hilarity every time you are able to peddle a really fresh observation. But, to be honest, your psychological interest is not in earnest and is more a hypochondriacal inquisitiveness.

But now to the subject. There are two things that I must regard as my particular task: to show the esthetic meaning of marriage and to show how the esthetic in it may be retained despite life's numerous hindrances. In order, however, that you may yield with all the more confidence to the upbuilding that the reading of this little essay can possibly provide you, I always have at the outset a little polemical prologue in which appropriate consideration will be given to your sarcastic observations. But by doing that I also hope to pay appropriate tribute to the pirate cities[7] and then be able to settle down calmly to my calling, for I am still within my calling, I who, myself a married man, battle on behalf of marriage—*pro aris et focis* [on behalf of our altars and hearths].[8] I assure you that this subject is so much on my mind that I, who ordinarily feel only slightly tempted to write books, actually could be tempted to do that if I dared to hope I could save just one single marriage from the hell into which it has perhaps plunged itself or to make a few people more competent to realize the most beautiful task given to a human being.

To be on the safe side, I shall occasionally draw upon my wife and my relation to her, not as if I presumed to represent our marriage as an instance of the norm, but partly because those poetic descriptions seized out of the air usually do not have much convincing power and partly because I consider it is of importance for me to show that it is possible to preserve the esthetic even in everyday life. You have known me for many years; you have known my wife for five. You consider her rather beautiful, exceptionally charming, which I do, too. I know very well, however, that she is not as beautiful in the morning as in the evening, that a certain touch of sadness, almost of ailment, disappears only later in the day, and that it is forgotten by evening when she truly can claim to be appealing. I know very well that her nose is not flawlessly beautiful and that it is too small, but it nevertheless pertly faces the world, and I know that this little nose has provided the occasion for so much teasing that even if it were within my competence I would never wish her one more beautiful. This attaches a much more profound significance to the accidental in life than that which you are so enthusiastic about. I thank God for this good and forget the weak side.

Yet this is of lesser importance, but there is one thing for which I thank God with my whole soul, and that is that she is the only one I have ever loved, the first, and there is one thing for which I pray to God with my whole heart, that he will give me the strength never to want to love any other. This is a family devotion, in which she also shares, because every feeling, every mood, gains a higher meaning for me by having her share in it. All feelings, even the highest religious ones, can take on a certain indolence if one is always alone with them. In

her presence, I am simultaneously priest and congregation.
And if I sometimes should become unloving enough not to
keep this good in mind, uncouth enough not to give thanks for
it, she will remind me of it. You see, my young friend, this is
not the flirting of the first days of infatuation, not a venture in
the imaginary erotic, for example, asking himself and the beloved, as almost everyone does during the engagement period,
the question whether she has been in love before, or whether
he himself has ever loved anyone before, but this is the earnestness of life, and yet it is not cold, unbeautiful, unerotic,
unpoetic. I truly do feel keenly that she really loves me and that
I really love her, not as if over the years our marriage has not
attained just as much stability as that of most other people, but
it still gives me joy to rejuvenate continually our first love, and
in such a way, furthermore, that it has for me just as much religious as esthetic meaning, for God has not become so supra-
mundane for me that he does not concern himself about the
covenant he himself has established between man and woman,
and I have not become so spiritual that the worldly aspect of
life has no meaning for me. All the beauty implicit in the erotic
of paganism has its validity in Christianity insofar as it can be
combined with marriage. This rejuvenation of our first love is
not just a sad looking back or a poetic recollecting of past experience, whereby one is finally enmeshed—all that kind of
thing is exhausting—it is an action. After all, the time when
one must be satisfied with recollecting comes soon enough;
the fresh wellspring of life ought to be kept open as long as
possible.

You, however, actually live by plundering; unnoticed, you
creep up on people, steal from them their happy moment,
their most beautiful moment, stick this shadow picture in your
pocket as the tall man did in *Schlemihl*[9] and take it out whenever you wish. You no doubt say that those involved lose
nothing by this, that often they themselves perhaps do not
know which is their most beautiful moment. You believe that
they should rather be indebted to you, because with your
study of the lighting, with magic formulas, you permitted
them to stand forth transfigured in the supernatural amplitude

of the rare moments. Perhaps they lose nothing thereby, and yet there is the question whether it is not conceivable that they retain a recollection of them that is always painful to them. But you do lose; you lose your time, your serenity, your patience for living, because you yourself know very well how impatient you are, you who once wrote to me that patience to bear life's burdens must indeed be an extraordinary virtue, that you did not even have the patience to want to live.[10] Your life disintegrates into nothing but interesting details like these. If one dared to hope that the energy that kindles you in such moments could take shape in you, distribute itself coherently over your life, well, then something great would certainly come of you, for you yourself are transfigured in such moments.

There is a restlessness in you over which consciousness nevertheless hovers, bright and clear; your whole soul is concentrated upon this single point, your understanding contrives a hundred plans; you arrange everything for the attack, but it miscarries at a single point, and then your almost diabolical dialectic is instantly ready to explain what happened in such a way that it will benefit the new plan of operation. You continually hover over yourself, and no matter how crucial each step, you always keep for yourself a possibility of interpretation that with one word can change everything. Then, in addition, a total incarnation of mood. Your eyes sparkle, or, more correctly, they seem to radiate like a hundred searching eyes at once; a vagrant touch of color crosses your face; you rely confidently on your calculations, and yet you wait with a terrible impatience—yes, my dear friend, when all is said and done, I do believe that you are deceiving yourself, that all this that you tell about catching a man in his happy moment is only your own rare mood that you grasp. You are so intensified that you are creative. This is why I did not think it was very harmful for others; for you it is thoroughly harmful. Is there not indeed some enormous faithlessness underlying this? Presumably you will say that people are no concern of yours, that instead they ought to be grateful that you, by your touch, do not, as Circe did, change them into swine[11] but rather from swine into heroes. You say it would be an entirely different

matter if someone really took you into his confidence, but as
yet you have never met such a person. Your heart is touched;
you melt in fervent emotion at the thought that you would
sacrifice everything for him. I do not deny you a certain good-
natured helpfulness, for example, that the way you help the
needy is truly beautiful, that there is something noble about
the gentleness you manifest at times, but in spite of that I believe this also conceals a kind of aristocratic exclusiveness.

I shall not remind you of specific eccentric expressions of
this; it would be a pity in this way to obscure totally the good
that may be in you, but I do want to remind you of a little incident in your life that can be brought up without being det-
rimental to you. You once told me that on a walk you were
behind two poor women. My description of the situation at
this moment perhaps does not have the animation that yours
had when you rushed up to me, totally absorbed by this idea.
The two women were from the workhouse. They perhaps had
known better days but this was forgotten, and the workhouse
is not exactly the place where hope is loved forth. One of
them, taking and offering the other a pinch of snuff, said: Oh,
if only I had five rix-dollars![12] She herself perhaps was amazed
at this bold wish, which, of course, like the others echoed un-
answered across the embankments. You approached; you had
already taken out your wallet and had removed a five-rix-dol-
lar bank note before you made the crucial step, so that the situation would keep the appropriate tension and so that she
would not prematurely suspect something. You approached
with an almost obsequious courtesy, as befits a serving spirit;
you gave her the five rix-dollars and vanished. You were
tickled pink over the thought of what an impression it would
make on her, whether she would see a divine providence in it
or whether her mind, which through much suffering had already developed a certain defiance, would instead turn almost
with contempt against the divine governance that here assumed the character of chance. You recounted that this provided you with the occasion to ponder whether the altogether
accidental fulfillment of such an accidentally expressed wish
could bring a person to despair, because the reality [*Realitet*][13]

of life was negated at its deepest root. So what you wanted was to play the role of fate; what actually thrilled you was the multiplicity of reflections that could be woven out of this. I readily admit to you that you are well qualified to play the role of fate, insofar as this word combines the conception of the most unstable and most capricious of all; as for me, I am readily satisfied with a less distinctive appointment in life.[14] Moreover, in this event you can see an example that perhaps can throw some light for you on the extent to which your imaginative ventures have a harmful effect on people. You seem to have the advantage on your side; you have given a poor woman five rix-dollars, fulfilled her most extravagant wish, and yet you yourself acknowledge that this could just as well have the effect upon her that she, as Job's wife advised him to do, would curse God.[15] You probably will say that these consequences were not in your power and that if one were to calculate the consequences in this way one would not act at all. But I shall answer: Of course, one can act. If I had had five rix-dollars, I perhaps would also have given them to her, but I would also have been conscious that I was not imaginatively constructing; I would have persisted in the conviction that divine providence, whose humble instrument I felt myself to be at that moment, would certainly guide everything for the best and that I would have had nothing for which to reproach myself.

How insecure and suspended your life is you can ascertain also from your unsureness whether at some time it will weigh heavily upon you that your hypochondriacal keenness and sophistry may bewitch you into a cycle of consequences from which you will try in vain to extricate yourself, and that you will set heaven and earth in motion to find the poor woman again in order to observe what effect it has had upon her, "as well as the best way in which she ought to be influenced," for you always remain the same and never become wiser. Passionate as you are, it was no doubt possible that you, with your passionateness, could decide to forget your great plans, your studies—in short, that everything could become a matter of indifference for you in comparison with the idea of finding that poor woman, who very likely would be long since dead and gone. In this way, you seek to remedy what you have done wrong, and thus your life-task becomes so contentious in itself that one can say that you simultaneously want to be fate and our Lord, a task that our Lord himself cannot carry out, for he is only the one. The zeal you display may very well be praiseworthy, but do you not nevertheless perceive how your zeal makes it more and more clear that what you lack, altogether lack, is faith. Instead of saving your soul by entrusting everything to God, instead of taking this shortcut, you prefer the endless roundabout way, which perhaps will never take you to your destination. You very likely will say: Well, if things are like that, one never needs to act—to which I will answer: Of course, if you are convinced that you have a place in the world that belongs to you, where you ought to concentrate all your activity; but to act as you are doing certainly borders on madness. You will say that even if you folded your hands and let God take care of things, the woman very likely would not be helped—to which I would answer: Very possibly, but you would be helped and the woman also if she likewise entrusted herself to God. Do you not see that if you really put on your traveling boots and wandered out in the world and wasted your time and your energy, then you would miss out on all other activity, something that perhaps would also torment you later. But to repeat—this capricious existence of yours, is it not faithlessness? It certainly does seem *in casu* [in this case] that by wandering all over the world to find the poor woman you would demonstrate an exceptional degree of faithfulness, for there was indeed not the least egotism that moved you; it was not the same as when a lover searches for the beloved; no, it was pure sympathy. I will answer: You certainly should beware of calling that feeling egotism, but it is your usual rebellious insolence. You scorn everything that is established by divine or human laws, and in order to be free of it you snatch at the accidental, which in this case is a poor woman unknown to you. With regard to your sympathy, it very likely was pure sympathy—for your constructing. On all sides, you forget that your existence in the world cannot possibly be calculated solely on the basis of the accidental, and the moment you make this the primary factor, you completely forget what you owe to those closest to you. I know very well that you are not lacking the sophistic shrewdness for glossing over or the ironic adroitness for playing down; therefore you presumably will answer: I am not so haughty as to fancy myself to be one who can act for the whole—that I leave to the distinguished; if I can act just for some particular thing I am content. But basically this is an outrageous lie, for you do not want to act at all; you want to construct imaginatively, and you see everything from this angle, often with much effrontery. Action is always the object of your ridicule, as you once said of a man who had met his death in a ludicrous manner—something you reveled in for many days—that otherwise nothing was known of the significance of his life on the whole, but now it could be said of him that he truly had not lived in vain.[16]

To repeat, what you want to be is—fate. Pause a moment now. I do not intend to preach to you, but there is an earnestness for which I know you have even an unusually deep respect, and anyone who has sufficient power to call it forth in you or sufficient faith in you to let it manifest itself in you will, I know, see in you a quite different person. Imagine, to take the supreme example, imagine that the almighty source of everything, that God in heaven set himself up merely as a riddle for men and would let the whole human race drift in this horrible uncertainty—would there not be something in your innermost being that would rebel against this, would you at any moment be able to endure this torment, or would you at any moment be able to bring your thought to grasp this horror! Yet he might almost say—if I dare use these proud words: Of what concern is man to me? But that is why it is not this way at all, and when I declare that God is incomprehensible, my soul raises itself up to the highest; it is precisely in my most blissful moments that I say it—incomprehensible, because his love is incomprehensible—incomprehensible, because his love passes all understanding.[17] Said about God, this signifies the highest; when one is obliged to say it about a human being, it always signifies a defect, at times a sin. And Christ did not regard it robbery to be equal with God but humbled himself,[18] and you want to regard the intellectual gifts bestowed upon you as a robbery.

Just consider, your life is passing; for you, too, the time will eventually come even to you when your life is at an end, when you are no longer shown any further possibilities in life, when recollection alone is left, recollection, but not in the sense in which you love it so much, this mixture of fiction and truth, but the earnest and faithful recollection of your conscience. Beware that it does not unroll a list for you—presumably not of actual crimes but of wasted possibilities, shadow pictures it will be impossible for you to drive away. You are still young: The intellectual agility you possess is very becoming to youth and diverts the eye for a time. We are astonished to see a clown whose joints are so loose that all the restraints of a man's gait and posture are annulled. You are like that in an intellectual sense; you can just as well stand on your head as on your feet. Everything is possible for you, and you can surprise yourself and others with this possibility, but it is unhealthy, and for your own peace of mind I beg you to watch out lest that which is an advantage to you end by becoming a curse. Any man who has a conviction cannot at his pleasure turn himself and everything topsy-turvy in this way. Therefore I do not warn you against the world but against yourself and the world against you. This much is certain: If I had a daughter of such an age that there could be any possibility of her being influenced by you, I would strongly warn her, especially if she were also highly intelligent. And would there not be grounds for warning against you, since I—who nevertheless fancy that I may match you, if not in agility at least in stability and steadfastness, if not in capriciousness and brilliance then at least in constancy—since I actually at times with a certain reluctance feel that you dazzle me, that I let myself be carried away by your exuberance, by the seemingly good-natured wittiness with which you mock everything, let myself be carried away into the same esthetic-intellectual intoxication in which you live? That is no doubt why I feel a certain degree of unsureness toward you, since I am at times too severe, at times too indulgent. Yet it is not so strange, for you are the epitome of any and every possibility, and therefore at times one must see in you the possibility of your damnation, at times of your salvation. You pursue every mood, every idea, good or bad, happy or sad, to its outermost limit, but in such a way that it happens more *in abstracto* than *in concreto*, so that this pursuit is itself more a mood, from which nothing more results than a knowledge of it, but not so much that it becomes easier or harder for you the next time to surrender to the same mood, for you continually retain the possibility of it. This is why one can almost reproach you for everything and for nothing at all, for it is and yet is not in you. You acknowledge or do not acknowledge, according to the circumstances, having had such a mood, but you are impervious to any attribution of responsibility; for you the point is whether you have had the mood fully, with proper pathos.

It was, as indicated, the esthetic significance of marriage I wished to consider. This might seem to be a superfluous exploration, to be something anyone would concede, since it has been pointed out often enough. Over the centuries have not knights and adventurers experienced incredible toil and trouble in order finally to find quiet peace in a happy marriage; over the centuries have not writers and readers of novels labored through one volume after the other in order to end with a happy marriage, and has not one generation after the other again and again faithfully endured four acts of troubles and entanglements if only there was any probability of a happy marriage in the fifth act? But through these enormous efforts very little is accomplished for the glorification of marriage, and I doubt very much that any person by reading such books has felt himself made competent to fulfill the task he has set for himself or has felt himself oriented in life, for precisely this is the corruption, the unhealthiness in these books, that they end where they should begin. Having overcome the numerous adversities, the lovers finally fall into each other's arms, the curtain falls, the book ends; but the reader is no wiser, for it really is no great art, provided that love in its first flash is present, to have the courage and ingenuity to battle with all one's might for the possession of that good that one regards as the one and only, but on the other hand it certainly takes self-control, wisdom, and patience to overcome the exhaustion that often is wont to follow a fulfilled desire. In the first flash of love, it quite naturally thinks it cannot suffer troubles enough in order to gain possession of the beloved object—indeed, insofar as the dangers are not present, it is inclined to procure such dangers itself merely in order to conquer them. The full attention of this tendency is turned on this, and as soon as the dangers are conquered, the stage manager knows all about it. This is why one seldom sees a wedding or reads about it, except insofar as the opera and ballet have made a provision for this element, which presumably can provide the occasion for some dramatic nonsense or other, for magnificent pageantry, for significant gestures and heavenward glances on the part of a dancer, for the exchange of rings, etc. That which is true in this whole development, the genuinely esthetic, is that love is situated in striving, that this feeling is seen to be battling its way through an opposition. The defect is that this battle, this dialectic, is completely external and that love emerges from this battle just as abstract as when it entered into it. As soon as the idea of love's proper dialectic awakens, the idea of its passionate struggle, of its relation to the ethical, the religious, then in truth there will be no need for hardhearted fathers or maiden bowers or enchanted princesses or trolls and monsters in order to give love an opportunity to show how much it can do. In our day, we seldom encounter such cruel fathers or such horrible monsters, and therefore insofar as modern literature has patterned itself on past literature, it actually is money that has become the medium of opposition through which love moves, and so we again drudge through four acts if there are sound prospects that a rich uncle may die in the fifth.

The occasions when one sees such performances are, however, rare, and on the whole modern literature is totally occupied with ridiculing love in the abstract immediacy in which it is found in the world of the regular novel. For example, in examining Scribe's dramatic works, we find that one of his main themes is that love is an illusion. But I need merely remind you

of this; you have far too much sympathy for Scribe and his polemic. At least I believe that you would make that claim
against the whole world, even though you would reserve
knightly love for yourself, for you are so far from being devoid of feeling that when it comes to feelings you are the most
jealous person I know. I recall that you once sent me a little review of Scribe's *The First Love*[19] that was written with almost
desperate enthusiasm. In it, you claimed that it was the best
Scribe had ever written and that this piece alone, properly
understood, was sufficient to make him immortal. I would
like to mention another piece that, in my opinion, again shows
the defect in that which Scribe substitutes. It is *For Eternity*.[20]
Here he is ironic about a first love. With the aid of a shrewd
mother, who is also a fine lady of the world, a new love is in-
augurated, which she regards as reliable, but the spectator,
who is unwilling to be satisfied that the author has quite arbitrarily put a period here, readily perceives that a third love
could just as well come along. On the whole, it is remarkable
how devouring modern poetry is and how it has lived all this
time on love. Our age reminds one very much of the disintegration of the Greek state; everything continues, and yet there
is no one who believes in it. The invisible spiritual bond that
gives it validity has vanished, and thus the whole age is simultaneously comic and tragic, tragic because it is perishing,
comic because it continues, for it is still always the incorruptible that bears the corruptible, the intellectual-spiritual that
bears the physical, and if it were possible to imagine that an in-
animate body could still perform the usual functions for a little
while, it would be comic and tragic in the same way. But just
let the age go on devouring, and the more it devours of the
substantial content that was intrinsic to romantic love, the
greater the terror, when there is no more pleasure in this annihilation, with which it will eventually become conscious of
what it has lost and in despair feel its misfortune.

We shall now see whether our age, which has annihilated romantic love, has been successful in substituting something
better. But first I shall indicate the characteristics of romantic
love. One could say in a single word: It is immediate. To see

her and to love her would be one and the same, or even though
she saw him but one single time through a crack in the shut-
tered window of a virgin's bower, she nevertheless would love
him from that moment, him alone in the whole world. At this
point, by prearrangement, I really ought to make room for
some polemical effusions in order to promote in you the secre-
tion of gall that is a necessary condition for a sound and beneficial appropriation of what I have to say. But for two reasons
I cannot decide to do this: partly because romantic love is
rather overworked these days and, to be honest, it is inconceivable that in this respect you want to move with the current
since ordinarily you are always against it, and partly because I
actually have preserved a certain faith in the truth of it, a certain respect for it, a certain sadness because of it. Therefore I
mention only the watchword for your polemic on this score,
the title of a little article of yours, "*Empfindsame* [Sensitive] and
Incomprehensible Sympathies, or Two Hearts' *harmonia
præstabilita* [pre-established harmony]."[21] What we are speaking of here is what Goethe in *Wahlverwandtschaften*[22] has so artistically first intimated to us in the imagery of nature in order
to make it real [*realisere*] later in the world of spirit, except that
Goethe endeavored to motivate this drawing power through a
series of factors (perhaps in order to show the difference between the life of the spirit and the life of nature) and has not
emphasized the haste, the enamored impatience and determination with which the two affinities seek each other. And is it
not indeed beautiful to imagine that two beings are intended
for each other! How often do we not have an urge to go beyond the historical consciousness, a longing, a homesickness
for the primeval forest that lies behind us, and does not this
longing acquire a double significance when it joins to itself the
conception of another being whose home is also in that region?
Therefore, every marriage, even one that is entered into after
sober consideration, has an urge, at least in particular moments, to imagine such a foreground. And how beautiful it is
that the God who is spirit also loves the earthly love. That
there is much lying among married people on this score, I
readily admit to you, and that your observations along this

line have frequently amused me, but the truth in it ought not to be forgotten. Perhaps someone thinks it is better to have complete authority in the choice of "one's life-partner," but such an expression as that betrays an extreme narrowness of mind and foolish self-importance of understanding and has no intimation that in its genius [*Genialitet*] romantic love is free and that precisely this genius constitutes its greatness.

II
20

Romantic love manifests itself as immediate by exclusively resting in natural necessity. It is based on beauty, partly on sensuous[23] beauty, partly on the beauty that can be conceived through and in and with the sensuous, yet not in such a way that it becomes visible through deliberation, but in such a way that, continually on the point of manifesting itself, it peeks out through it. Although this love is based essentially on the sensuous, it nevertheless is noble by virtue of the consciousness of the eternal that it assimilates, for it is this that distinguishes all love [*Kjærlighed*] from lust [*Vellyst*]: that it bears a stamp of eternity. The lovers are deeply convinced that in itself their relationship is a complete whole that will never be changed. But since this conviction is substantiated only by a natural determinant, the eternal is based on the temporal and thereby cancels itself. Since this conviction has undergone no ordeal, has found no higher justification, it proves to be an illusion and therefore it is so easy to make it ludicrous. But one should not be so ready to do this, and in modern comedy it is truly disgusting to see these experienced, scheming, silly women who know that love is an illusion. I know no creature so abominable as such a woman. To me no debauchery is so disgusting, and nothing is so revolting to me as to see an amorous young girl in the hands of such a person. It is in truth more terrible than to imagine her in the hands of a club of seducers. It is sad to see a man who has eliminated everything essential in life, but to see a woman on this wrong path is horrible. But, as stated, romantic love has an analogy to the moral [*Sædelige*][24] in the presumed eternity, which ennobles it and saves it from the merely sensuous. That is, the sensuous is momentary. The sensuous seeks momentary satisfaction, and the more refined the sensuous is, the better it knows how to make the moment of enjoyment into a little eternity. Therefore, the true eternity in love, which is the true morality, actually rescues it first out of the sensuous. But to bring forth this true eternity requires a determination of will—but more on that later.

Our age has discerned the weakness in romantic love very well; indeed, at times its ironic polemic against it has been really amusing. Whether it has remedied the defect and what it has substituted in its place, we shall now see. One can say that it has taken two directions, one of which at first glance appears to be a wrong way, that is, immoral; the other one, which is more respectable, nevertheless, in my opinion, misses out on what is more profound in love. If, then, love depends upon the sensuous, anyone easily discerns that this immediate, chivalrous faithfulness is foolishness. No wonder, then, that women wish to be emancipated—in our day one of the many unbeautiful phenomena of which the men are guilty. The eternal in love becomes the object of ridicule; the temporal is retained, but the temporal is also refined in a sensuous eternity, in the eternal moment of the embrace. What I am saying here does not apply only to some seducer prowling about in the world like a beast of prey. No, it fits a goodly chorus of often highly gifted people, and it is not only Byron who declares that love is heaven and marriage hell.[25]

It is plain to see that there is some reflection here, something that romantic love does not have. This can readily take marriage in addition, and take the Church's blessing as one more beautiful celebration, except that as such this nevertheless does not essentially have meaning for it. By reason of that reflection, the love mentioned, with a callousness and a terrible inflexibility of understanding, has invented a new definition of what unhappy love is—namely,[26] to be loved when one no longer loves—it is not to love without having one's love returned. If this attitude really understood the profundity that lies in these few words, it would shrink from them itself, because, in addition to all the experience, sagacity, and refinement, they also contain an intimation that there is a conscience. Consequently, the instant becomes the main thing, and how often have these brazen words been heard from that kind of a lover to the unhappy girl who could love only once: I do not ask for so much, I am satisfied with less; far be it from me to demand that you go on loving me forever if you will just love me in the moment when I desire it. Lovers of that sort know very well that the sensuous is transitory; they also know which is the most beautiful moment, and with that they are satisfied. Such an attitude, of course, is absolutely immoral; theoretically, however, it contains in a way an advance toward our goal, inasmuch as it lodges a veritable protest against marriage. Insofar as this same disposition tries to assume a somewhat more respectable appearance, it restricts itself not only to the particular moment but extends this into a longer period of time, yet in such a way that instead of assimilating the eternal into its consciousness it assimilates the temporal or in this opposition to the eternal entangles itself with the conception of a possible change in time. It thinks that one can probably stand living together for some time, but it wants to keep an escape open in order to make a choice if a happier choice comes along. It makes marriage into a civil arrangement; one needs only to inform the proper authority that this marriage is over and a new one has been contracted, just as one reports that one has moved. Whether the state is served thereby, I shall leave undecided; for the particular individual it must truly be an odd relationship. This is why one does not see it realized in actuality [*Virkelighed*],[27] but the age continually threatens to do so. And it would indeed require a great deal of brazenness for that—I do not feel that this word is too strong—just as it would betray a light-mindedness bordering on depravity, especially on the part of the female participant in this association.

But there is an entirely different spiritual disposition that can easily have a similar idea, and since it is very characteristic of our age, it is this that I shall discuss in detail here. A scheme such as this can have its basis in an *egotistical* or a *sympathetic depression*. Enough has been said about the light-mindedness of the age; it is high time, I think, to say a little about its depression, and I hope that everything will turn out better. Or, is not depression the defect of the age, is it not that which echoes even in its light-minded laughter; is it not depression that has

II
22

robbed us of the courage to command, the courage to obey, the power to act, the confidence to hope? And now when the kind philosophers are doing everything to endow actuality with intensity, shall we not soon become stuffed so full that we choke on it. Everything is cut away but the present; no wonder, then, that one loses it in the constant anxiety about losing it. Now, it is certainly true that one ought not to vanish in a fleeting hope and that it is not in this way that one is going to be transfigured in the clouds, but in order truly to enjoy, one must have air; and it is not only in times of sorrow that it is important to have heaven open, but also in times of joy it is important to have an open prospect and the double doors open wide. To be sure, the enjoyment apparently loses a degree of the intensity that it has with the aid of an alarming limitation such as that, but not much should be lost thereby, since it has something in common with the intense pleasure that costs the Strasbourg geese their lives.[28] Perhaps it would be more difficult to make you perceive this, but I certainly do not need to go into detail about the significance of the intensity one achieves in the other way. In this respect, you are indeed a virtuoso, you, *cui di dederunt formam, divitias, artemque fruendi* [to whom the gods gave beauty, wealth, and the art of enjoyment].[29] If to enjoy were the most important thing in life, I would sit at your feet to learn, for in that you are master. At times you can make yourself an old man in order to imbibe what you have experienced in long, slow draughts through the funnel of recollection;[30] at times you are in your first youth, flushed with hope; at times you enjoy in a masculine way, at times in a feminine way, at times with immediacy; at times [you enjoy] reflection on the pleasure, at times reflection on the pleasure of others, at times abstinence from pleasure; at times you abandon yourself, your mind is open, accessible as a city that has capitulated, reflection ceases, and every step of the aliens echoes in the empty streets, and yet there is always one little observing outpost left; at times you shut your mind, you entrench yourself, inaccessible and brusque. This is how it is with you, and you will also see how egotistical your enjoyment is, and that you never give of yourself, never let others enjoy you. To an extent, you are probably justified in ridiculing the people who are drained by every pleasure—for example, the infatuated people with shredded hearts—since you, on the contrary, understand superbly the art of falling in love in such a way that this love throws your own personality into relief. You know very well that the most intensive enjoyment is in clutching the enjoyment in the consciousness that it may vanish the next moment. This is why the finale in *Don Giovanni* has pleased you so much.[31] Pursued by the police, by the whole world, by the living and the dead, alone in a remote room, he once again gathers together all the powers of his soul, once again raises the goblet, and once again rejoices in the sounds of music.

I turn back, however, to my previous point, that a mixture of egotistic and sympathetic depression can give rise to that view. The egotistic depression naturally fears on its own account and, like all depression, is self-indulgent in enjoyment. It has a certain exaggerated obeisance, a secret horror of any contact with life. "What can one depend upon; everything may change; perhaps even this being I now almost worship can change; perhaps later fates will bring me in contact with another being who for the first time will truly be the ideal of which I have dreamed." Like all depression, it is defiant and is conscious of it; it thinks: Perhaps just this, that I bind myself to one person with an indissoluble bond, will make this being, whom I otherwise would love with my whole soul, become intolerable to me, perhaps, perhaps, etc. Sympathetic depression is more distressing and also somewhat more noble; it fears itself for the sake of the other. Who knows for certain that he cannot be changed; perhaps what I now regard as the good in me can disappear; perhaps what the beloved finds so captivating in me and what I want to keep only for her sake can be taken from me, and now she stands there disappointed, deceived. Perhaps a splendid prospect comes along for her; she is tempted, she perhaps does not withstand the temptation— good lord, to have that on my conscience. I have nothing to reproach her for; it is I who have become changed. I forgive her everything if she can only forgive me, that I was so incau-

II
24

tious as to let her take such a decisive step. I am certainly confident that, far from wheedling her, I instead warned her
against me, that it was her free decision; but perhaps this warning itself tempted her, made her see in me a better being than I
was, etc. One will readily perceive that such a way of thinking
is served as little by a connection for ten years as by one for
five—in fact, not even by a connection such as the one Saladin
made with the Christians for ten years, ten months, ten weeks,
ten days, ten minutes,[32] and as little served by such a connection as by one for a lifetime. One sees very well that such a way
of thinking feels only too deeply the meaning of the saying
that every day has its own troubles.[33] It is an attempt to live
every day as if this day were the decisive day, an attempt to
live as if one were up for examination every day. Therefore,
when in our day there is a great tendency to neutralize marriage, it is not because celibacy is regarded as more perfect, as
in the Middle Ages, but it has its basis in cowardice and self-
indulgence in enjoyment. It will also be obvious that such
marriages, entered into for a specific time, are of no advantage, since they have the same difficulties as those entered into
for a lifetime, and furthermore they are so far from giving the
ones involved the strength to go on living that, on the contrary, they vitiate the innermost power of marital life, relax
the energy of the will, and minimize the blessings of the trust
that marriage possesses. Moreover, it is already clear and later
will be even more so that such associations are not marriages,
since they, although entered into within the sphere of reflection, still have not attained the consciousness of eternity that
morality has and that first makes the connection into marriage.
This is also something on which you will entirely agree with
me, for how often and how surely your ridicule and your
irony have well-deservedly assailed such moods ("the accidental infatuations or love's spurious infinity"[34]), where someone
looks out the window with his fiancée, and at the same time a
girl turns the corner into another street, and it occurs to him
that she is the one he is really in love with—but when he pursues the trail, he is once again frustrated etc.

  The second way out, the respectable way, was the *marriage*

of convenience. One immediately hears in the designation that the sphere of reflection has been entered. Some people, you included, have always taken a dim view of this marriage, which steers a middle course here between immediate love and calculating understanding; for this really ought to be called, if one is to honor the use of language, it ought to be called the marriage based on calculation. In particular, you are always in the habit of very ambiguously recommending "respect" as a solid basis for a marital relation. Having to resort to such a way out as a marriage of convenience shows how thoroughly reflective the age is. Insofar as such a relation renounces real love, it is at least consistent but also shows thereby that it is not a solution of the problem. Therefore, a marriage based on calculation is to be regarded as a capitulation of sorts that the exigencies of life make necessary. But how sad it is that this seems to be almost the only consolation the poetry of our time has left, the only consolation that of despairing; indeed, it obviously is despair that makes such a connection acceptable. Therefore, it is usually entered into by persons who have long since reached their years of discretion and who also have learned that real love is an illusion and its fulfillment at most a *pium desiderium* [pious wish]. Therefore, what is involved is the prose of love, making a living, social status, etc. Insofar as it has neutralized the sensuous in marriage, it seems to be moral, but a question still remains whether this neutralization is not just as immoral as it is unesthetic. Or even though the erotic is not completely neutralized, it is nevertheless daunted by a pedestrian, commonsensical view that one ought to be cautious, not all too hasty to reject, that life never does yield the ideal, that it is a really respectable match, etc. Consequently, the eternal, which, as already indicated above, belongs to every marriage, is not really present here, for a commonsensical calculation is always temporal. Therefore, such a connection is at the same time immoral and fragile. If that which is determinative is somewhat loftier, such a marriage based on calculation can take a more beautiful form. In that case, it is a motive foreign to the marriage itself that becomes the decisive factor—for example, out of love of her family a young girl marries a man who is able to rescue it. But precisely this external teleology readily shows that we cannot seek a solution of the problem here. At this point, I perhaps could appropriately discuss the numerous inducements for entering into a marriage, about which there is frequently sufficient talk. Such deliberation and shrewd consideration belong specifically in the sphere of the understanding. I prefer, however, to stick to the other point, where I also may, if possible, silence it.

It has now become apparent how romantic love was built on an illusion, and that its eternity was built upon the temporal, and that, although the knight remained deeply convinced of its absolute constancy, there nevertheless was no certainty of this, since its trial and temptation had hitherto been in an entirely external medium.[35] To that extent, romantic love was in a very good position to accept marriage with a beautiful piety, but this still did not acquire deeper meaning. It has become apparent how this immediate, beautiful, but also simple love, assimilated in the consciousness of a reflective age, had to become the object of its ridicule and its irony. It has also become apparent what such an age was in a position to substitute for it. An age such as this also assimilated marriage in its consciousness and in part declared itself for love in such a way that marriage was excluded and in part for marriage in such a way that love was relinquished. This is why in a recent play a common-sensical little seamstress also makes the shrewd comment about fine gentlemen's love: They love us but do not marry us; they do not love the fine ladies, but they marry them.[36]

With this, my little exploration (for this is what I am constrained to call what I am writing, even though at first I had thought only of a long letter) has reached the point where marriage can first be properly elucidated. That marriage belongs essentially to Christianity, that pagan peoples have not perfected it, despite the sensuousness of the Orient and all the beauty of Greece, that not even Judaism has been able to do it, despite the truly idyllic marriages found there, this you will no doubt concede to me without my needing to go into it in more detail, and all the more so since it will be sufficient merely to remind you that sex differences were nowhere else so deeply reflected that the other sex thereby attained its full right. But in Christianity, too, love had to undergo many adversities before people came to see the depth, beauty, and truth that lie in marriage. But since the age immediately preceding ours, and to some extent the present one, was so reflective, it is not an easy matter to show this, and since I have found in you such a virtuoso in setting forth the weak sides, the extra task I have assigned myself, to persuade you, if possible, is doubly difficult. I owe it to you, however, to confess that I am very obligated to you for your polemic. If I were to imagine your multifarious, scattered comments, as I have received them, gathered into one, it would be so masterly and ingenious that it would be a good guide for the person who wants to undertake the defense, because your attacks, if you or anyone else ponders them, are not so superficial that they do not in themselves contain the truth, even though neither you nor your opponent is aware of it in the moment of battle.

Inasmuch as it now appeared as a defect in romantic love that it was not reflective, it might seem proper to have true marital love begin with a kind of doubt. This might seem all the more necessary because we come to it out of a world of reflection. That a marriage is artistically feasible after such doubt, I will by no means deny, but the question remains whether the nature of the marriage is not already altered thereby, since it envisages a separation between love and marriage. The question is whether it belongs essentially to marriage to annihilate the first love by doubting the possibility of realizing it, in order through this annihilation to make marital love possible and actual, so that Adam and Eve's marriage would be the only one in which immediate love was kept inviolable, and that again rather for the reason, as Musäus so wittily puts it, that there was no possibility of loving anyone else.[37] The question remains whether the immediate, the first love, by being caught up into a higher, concentric immediacy, would not be secure against this skepticism so that the married love would not need to plough under the first love's beautiful hopes, but the marital love would itself be the first love with the addition of qualifications that would not detract from it but would ennoble it. It is a difficult problem to pose, and yet it is of utmost importance, lest we have the same cleavage in the ethical [*Ethiske*] as in the intellectual between faith and knowledge. And yet, dear friend, it would be beautiful—this you will not deny me (for your heart, too, has a feeling for love, and your head, too, is all too well acquainted with doubts)—yet it would indeed be beautiful if the Christian dared to call his God the God of love in such a way he thereby also thought of that inexpressibly blissful feeling, that never-ending force in the world: earthly love.

Therefore, inasmuch as in the foregoing I have indicated romantic love and reflective love as confrontational positions, it will be clearly apparent here to what extent the higher unity is a return to the immediate, to what extent this contains, in addition to the something more that it contains, that which was implicit in the first. It is now sufficiently clear that reflective love continually consumes itself and that it altogether arbitrarily takes one position and then another; it is clear that it points beyond itself to something higher, but the point is whether this something higher cannot promptly enter into combination with the first love. This something higher is the religious, in which the reflection of the understanding ends, and just as nothing is impossible for God,[38] so also nothing is impossible for the religious individual either. In the religious, love again finds the infinity that it sought in vain in reflective love. But if the religious, as surely as it is something higher than everything earthly, is also not something eccentric in relation to the immediate love but concentric with it, then the unity can indeed be brought about, except that the pain, which the religious certainly can heal but which nevertheless is a deep pain, would not become necessary. It is very seldom that one sees this issue made the subject of deliberation, because those for whom romantic love has an appeal do not care much for marriage, and on the other side, so much the worse, many marriages are entered into without the deeper eroticism that surely is the most beautiful aspect of purely human existence. Christianity is unswervingly committed to marriage. Conse-

quently, if marital love has no place within itself for the eroticism of first love, then Christianity is not the highest
development of the human race; and surely it is a secret anxiety
about such a discrepancy that is largely responsible for the despair that echoes in both modern poetry and prose.

So you see the nature of the task I have set for myself: to
show that romantic love can be united with and exist in marriage—indeed, that marriage is its true transfiguration. No
shadow at all will thereby be cast on the marriages that rescue
themselves from reflection and its shipwreck, nor will it be denied that much can be done; neither shall I be so unsympathetic
that I would withhold my admiration, nor will it be forgotten
that the whole trend of the times can make this a sad necessity.
As for the last, it must nevertheless be remembered that to a
certain degree every generation and every individual in the
generation begins his life from the beginning, and that in this
way it is possible for each one individually to avoid this maelstrom, and nonetheless that one generation is supposed to
learn from the other, and that consequently there is a probability that after reflection has used one generation for this sad
drama a succeeding generation will be more fortunate. No
matter how many painful confusions life can still manifest, I
fight for two things: the enormous task of showing that marriage is the transfiguration of the first love and not its annihilation, is its friend and not its enemy; and for the task—to
everyone else so very insignificant but to me all the more important—of showing that my humble marriage has had this
meaning, whereby strength and courage are gained for the
continual accomplishment of this task.

As I approach this exploration, I cannot help rejoicing that
it is to you I am writing. Indeed, just as surely as I would speak
about my marriage relationship to no other person, just as
surely do I open myself to you in confident joy. When at times
the noise of the struggling and laboring thoughts, of the prodigious mental machinery you carry within you, subsides,
there come quiet moments that no doubt are at first almost
alarming because of their stillness but that also soon prove to
be truly refreshing. I hope that this discussion finds you in

such a moment; and just as one can unconcernedly confide in
you anything one wishes, as long as the machinery is in operation, for then you hear nothing, so can one without surrendering oneself also tell you everything when your soul is still
and solemn. Then I shall also speak about her of whom I ordinarily speak only to silent nature, because I want only to hear
myself—her to whom I owe so much, among other things also
that I dare to discuss with bold confidence the issue of first love
and marriage, for of what, indeed, would I be capable with all
my love and all my effort if she did not come to my aid, and of
what, indeed, would I be capable if she did not inspire me to
want to do it? Yet I know very well that if I said this to her, she
would not believe me—yes, I perhaps would do wrong by
saying this to her; I perhaps would disturb and agitate her deep
and pure soul.

The first thing I have to do is to orient myself and especially
you in the defining characteristics of what a marriage is. Obviously the real constituting element, the substance, is love
[*Kjærlighed*]—or, if you want to give it more specific emphasis, erotic love [*Elskov*].[39] Once this is taken away, married life
is either merely a satisfaction of sensuous appetite or it is an association, a partnership, with one or another object in mind;
but love, whether it is the superstitious, romantic, chivalrous
love or the deeper moral, religious love filled with a vigorous
and vital conviction, has precisely the qualification of eternity
in it.

Every order [*Stand*] of life has its traitors; the order of marriage [*Ægtestand*] also has its traitors. Of course, I do not mean
seducers, for they, after all, have not entered into the holy estate of marriage (I hope that this inquiry will find you in a
mood in which you will not smile at this expression); I do not
mean those who have withdrawn from it by a divorce, for
they nevertheless have had the courage to be flagrant rebels.
No, I mean those who are rebels merely in thought, who do
not even dare let it manifest itself in deed; those wretched husbands who sit and lament that love vanished from their marriage long ago; those husbands who, as you once said of them,
sit like lunatics, each in his marital cubicle, slave away in

chains, and fantasize about the sweetness of engagement and the bitterness of marriage; those husbands who, according to your own correct observation, are among those who with a certain malicious glee congratulate anyone who becomes engaged. I cannot describe to you how contemptible they seem to me and how I relish hearing you say with a sly look, when such a husband makes you his confidant and pours out all his troubles to you, reels off all his lies about the happy first love: Well, I will certainly see to it I don't get out on that thin ice—and it embitters him even more that he cannot pull you into a *commune naufragium* [common shipwreck]. It is those husbands you so frequently refer to when you speak of a fond family man with four wonderful children who he wishes were miles away.

Insofar as there might be anything in what they say, then it would have to be a separation of erotic love and marriage, so that erotic love was placed in one period of time and marriage in another, but erotic love and marriage remained irreconcilable. One also soon found out the period in which erotic love belonged: it was the engagement, the beautiful time of engagement. With a kind of low-comedy excitement and emotion, they know how to chatter up and down about what it is to enjoy the engagement days. I must now confess that I have never cared very much for all that infatuated billing and cooing of the engagement, and the more that is made of this period, the more it seems to me to resemble the time it takes many people to dive into the water when they go swimming, time in which they walk up and down the dock, thrusting now a hand, now a foot, into the water, think that it is now too cold, now too warm. If the period of engagement actually were the most beautiful time, then I really do not see why, if they were right, one marries. But marry they do, and with all the bourgeois precision conceivable when the aunts and cousins, the neighbors and people living across the street find it suitable—something that betrays the same lethargy and slackness as that of regarding the engagement as the most beautiful time. If worst comes to worst, I prefer those foolhardy people who find pleasure only in jumping in. Nevertheless, it is always something, even though the motion never becomes as grand, the shudder of consciousness never as refreshing, the reaction of the will never as energetic, as when a strong masculine arm encloses the beloved firmly and yet tenderly, powerfully and yet in such a way that she feels herself free in this embrace—in order in the sight of God to dive into the sea of existence.

Now if such a separation of erotic love and marriage had any validity—except in the empty heads of a few foolish human beings or, more correctly, of inhuman beings, who know as little of what erotic love is as of marriage—then it would look bad for marriage and for my attempt to show the esthetic in it or that marriage is an esthetic Chladni figure.[40] But then on what grounds is there justification for such a separation? Either it might be because erotic love cannot be preserved at all. Then we would have the same mistrust and cowardliness that so frequently manifests itself in our age, whose distinctive characteristic is that it thinks development is retrogression and annihilation. I will now readily admit that a frail and feeble erotic love like that, equally unmanly and unwomanly (which you with your usual irrepressibleness would call tuppenny love), would not be able to withstand one single puff of life's storm, but nothing would follow from this in regard to erotic love and marriage if both were in a healthy and natural condition. Or it might be because the ethical and the religious, which enter in with marriage, would turn out to be so heterogeneous to erotic love that they cannot be united, so erotic love presumably would be able to battle through life victoriously if it were permitted to be self-contained and to depend upon itself alone. But this point of view would now take the issue back either to the untested pathos of immediate love or to the mood and whim of the particular individual, who would feel able to finish the course under his own power. At first glance, this latter view—that the ethical and the religious in marriage are supposed to be what has the disturbing effect—displays a certain manliness that can easily deceive hasty observation and, even though mistaken, nevertheless has some sublimity in it that is altogether different from all that first wretchedness. I shall

II
32

come back to this later, and all the more since my inquisitorial scrutiny would deceive me considerably if I did not see in you precisely one of these heretics infected to a certain degree by this fallacy.

The substance in marriage is erotic love, but which is first —is the erotic love first, or is the marriage first, so that erotic love follows afterward? This latter point of view has enjoyed no little esteem among people of limited understanding and has been recited frequently by shrewd fathers and even shrewder mothers who themselves think they have had experience and in compensation are unalterable in thinking that their children also ought to have experience. It is the wisdom that pigeon fanciers also have when they shut up in a small cage two pigeons that do not have the least sympathy for each other and think that they surely will learn to get along well together. This whole point of view is so narrow-minded that I have mentioned it merely for the sake of a kind of completeness and also to remind you of all you have abandoned in this regard.

Consequently, erotic love is first. But erotic love, according to what was indicated previously, is also of such a delicate nature—although a nature so unnatural and coddled—that it simply cannot tolerate coming in contact with actuality. Here I am again at the point touched upon earlier. Here, then, the engagement seems to acquire its meaning. It is an erotic love, which has no actuality, which merely lives on the sweet pastry of possibility. The relationship does not have the reality of actuality [*Virkelighedens Realitet*[41]]; its movements are devoid of content, and it continually goes on with the same "meaningless, infatuated gestures." The more unsubstantial the engaged people themselves are, the more even these merely simulated movements cost them in effort and exhaust their strength, the greater the need they will feel to evade the earnest form of marriage. Inasmuch as the engagement as such seems to be devoid of a necessary actuality derived from it, it would indeed be a splendid escape for those who lack the courage for marriage. When about to take the decisive step, they perhaps feel, and in all probability quite soulfully, a need to seek the help of

II
33

a higher power and thus come to terms with themselves and with the higher power—with themselves by pledging themselves on their own responsibility, with the higher power by not avoiding the blessing of the Church, which they then proceed with rather considerable superstition to value too highly. Here again, in its cowardliest, flimsiest, and most unmanly form, we have a schism between erotic love and marriage. But such a monstrosity cannot lead astray; its erotic love is no erotic love: it lacks the sensuous element that has its moral [*sædelig*] expression in marriage; it neutralizes the erotic to such a degree that an engagement such as this could just as well take place between males. However, although it wants to maintain this separation, as soon as it asserts the sensuous it instantly switches over into the previously delineated directions. No matter how one looks at it, such an engagement is unbeautiful; it is also unbeautiful in the religious sense since it is an attempt to deceive God, to sneak into something for which it thinks it does not need his help, and entrusts itself to him only when it feels that things are not going well otherwise.

Marriage, then, ought not to call forth erotic love; on the contrary, it presupposes it not as something past but as something present. But marriage has an ethical and religious element that erotic love does not have; for this reason, marriage is based on resignation [*Resignation*], which erotic love does not have. If one is unwilling to assume that in his life every person goes through the double movement[42]—first, if I may put it this way, the pagan movement, where erotic love belongs, and then the Christian movement, whose expression is marriage—if one is unwilling to say that erotic love must be excluded from Christianity, then it must be shown that erotic love can be united with marriage. Moreover, it occurs to me that if some unauthorized person were to see this paper, he probably would be very amazed that an issue like this could cause me so much trouble. Well, after all, I am writing this just for you, and your development is of such a nature that you fully understand—the difficulties.

First, then, an exploration of erotic love. Here I shall adopt an expression, despite your and the whole world's mockeries, that nevertheless has always had a beautiful meaning for me: the first love (believe me, I will not yield, and you probably will not either; if so, there will be a strange misrelation in our correspondence). When I use this phrase, I think of one of the most beautiful things in life; when you use it, it is the signal that the entire artillery of your observations is firing. But just as for me this phrase has nothing at all ludicrous about it, and just as I, to be honest, tolerate your attack only because I ignore it, so neither does it have for me the sadness that it presumably can have for someone else. This sadness need not be morbid, for the morbid is always something false and mendacious. It is beautiful and healthy if a person has been unfortunate in his first love, has learned to know the pain of it but nevertheless remains faithful to his love, has kept his faith in this first love; it is beautiful if in the course of the years he at times very vividly recalls it, and even though his soul has been sufficiently healthy to bid farewell, as it were, to that kind of life in order to dedicate himself to something higher; it is beautiful if he then sadly remembers it as something that was admittedly not perfect but yet was so very beautiful. And then sadness is far more beautiful and healthy and noble than the prosaic common sense that has long since finished with all such childishness, this devilish prudence of choir director Basil[43] that fancies itself to be health but which is the most penetratingly wasting illness; for what does it profit a man if he gained the whole world but damaged his soul?[44] For me the phrase "the first love" has no sadness at all, or at least only a little admixture of sweet sadness; for me it is a password, and although I have been a married man for several years, I have the honor to fight under the victorious banner of the first love.

For you, however, the concept of the first, its significance, its over- and under-valuation, is an enigmatical undulation. At times you are simply and solely inspired by the first. You are so impregnated with the energy concentrated in it that it is the only thing you want. You are so kindled and inflamed, so amorous, so dreamy and creative, as weighty as a rain cloud, as gentle as a summer breeze—in short, you have a vivid idea of what it means that Jupiter visits his beloved in a cloud or in

rain.[45] The past is forgotten; every boundary is abolished.
[46]You expand more and more, you feel soft and supple, every
joint becomes flexible, every bone a pliant sinew—just as a
gladiator stretches and strains his body in order to have it completely under his control. Everyone must think that in so
doing he dissipates his strength, and yet this voluptuous torture is the very condition that enables him to use his strength
properly. Now, then, you are in the condition in which you
enjoy the sheer voluptuousness of perfect receptivity. The
gentlest touch is enough to make this invisible, expanded,
psychic body tremble. There is a creature about which I fall
into reverie rather often—it is the jellyfish. Have you noticed
how this gelatinous mass can flatten itself into a plate and then
slowly sink, then rise, so still and firm that one would think
one could step on it. Now it notices its prey approaching; then
it funnels into itself, becomes a pouch, and sinks with prodigious speed, deeper and deeper, with this speed snatching in its
prey—not into its pouch, for it does not have a pouch, but into
itself, for it is itself a pouch and nothing else. It is so able to
contract itself that one cannot imagine how it could possibly
extend itself. It is just about the same with you, and you must
forgive me that I have not had a more beautiful creature with
which to compare you and also that you perhaps can hardly
keep from smiling at the thought of yourself as nothing but
pouch. In such moments, then, you are in pursuit of "the
first"; you want only that, without suspecting that it is a self-
contradiction to want the first to recur continually, and that
consequently either you must not have reached the first at all
or you actually have had the first and what you see, what you
enjoy, is continually only a reflection of the first. At this point
it is also to be noted that you are in error when you think that
the first is supposed to be completely present in anything but
the very first if only you seek it properly and that, insofar as
you appeal to your performance, this is also a misunderstanding, since you have never performed in the right way.

At other times, however, you are as cold, as sharp and bit-
ing, as a March wind, as sarcastic as hoarfrost, as intellectually
transparent as the air tends to be in spring, as dry and sterile,

as egotistically astringent as possible. If it so happens that a
person comes to harm in speaking to you in that condition
about the first, about the beauty of the first, perhaps even
about his first love, you become downright ill-tempered.
Now the first becomes the most ludicrous, the most foolish of
all, one of the lies in which one generation reinforces the next.
Like a Herod, you fume from one slaughter of the innocents to
the next.[47] At such a time, you know how to propound at
great length that clinging to the first this way is cowardliness
and unmanliness, that the truth lies in the acquired, not in the
given. I remember that in such a mood you once came up to
visit me. You filled your pipe as was your custom, sat down in
the softest easy chair, put your feet up on another chair, rooted
around in my papers (I also remember that I took them away
from you), and then burst out in an ironic eulogy of the first
love and all the firsts, even "the first thrashing I got in
school,"[48] explaining in an illuminating note that you could
say this with all the more emphasis since the teacher who had
administered it to you was the only one you ever knew who
could hit with emphasis; thereupon you ended by whistling
this student ballad, and the chair on which you had put your
feet you kicked to the other end of the room, and you left.

In you one seeks in vain for an explanation of what is hidden
behind the cryptic phrase: the first, a phrase that has had and
will ever have immense meaning in the world. The meaning
this phrase has for the single individual is actually decisive for
his whole intellectual-spiritual condition, just as the absence of
any meaning whatever for him is sufficient to show that his
soul is not predisposed to be moved or shaken by something
higher. For those, however, for whom "the first" has acquired
meaning, there are two ways. Either the first contains the
promise of the future, is the motivating, the infinite impulse.
These are the happy individuals for whom the first is nothing
but the present, but the present as the continually unfolding
and rejuvenating first. Or the first does not motivate the individual within the individual; the power that is in the first does
not become the propelling but the repelling power within the
individual, becomes that which pushes away. These are the

II
37

unhappy individualities who continually distance themselves
more and more from "the first." The latter, of course, can
never occur totally without the fault of the individual himself.

Everybody who is moved by the idea attaches a solemn
meaning to this phrase "the first," and ordinarily the worst
meaning is applied only to things belonging in a lower sphere.
In this respect, you have plenty of examples: the first printing
proofs, the first time one wears a new outfit, etc. The greater
the probability that something can be repeated, the less meaning the first has; the less the probability, the greater the meaning; and on the other hand, the more meaningful that is which
in its "first" manifests itself for the first time, the less the probability is that it can be repeated. Even if it is something eternal,
then all probability of its being repeated vanishes. Therefore,
if someone has spoken with a tinge of sadness about the first
love, as if it can never be repeated, this is no minimizing of
love but the most profound eulogy on it as the eternal power.
Thus, to make a little philosophical flourish, not with the pen
but with the mind, God became flesh only once, and it is futile
to expect that it could happen more than once. In paganism, it
could happen frequently, but that was simply because it was
not a true incarnation. Thus, a person is born only once, and
there is no probability of a repetition. Transmigration of souls
fails to appreciate the meaning of birth.

With a few examples, I shall illustrate in more detail what I
mean. We greet the first greenness, the first swallow with a
certain solemnity. The reason for this, however, is the conception we attach to it; consequently, here what is heralded in the
first is something other than the first itself, the first particular
swallow. There is an engraving that portrays Cain murdering
Abel. In the background, one sees Adam and Eve. Whether
the engraving itself is valuable I am unable to decide, but the
caption has always interested me: *prima caedes, primi parentes,
primus luctus* [the first killing, the first parents, the first sor-
row]. Here again the first has a profound meaning, and here it
is the first itself that we contemplate, but it is still more with
respect to time than to content, since we do not see the continuity with which the whole is established by the first. (The

whole must naturally be understood as sin propagating itself in the race. The first sin, if by this we think of Adam and Eve's fall, would itself steer thought more to the continuity, but since it is the nature of evil not to have continuity,[49] you will readily perceive why I do not use this example.)

Still another example. As is well known, several strict sects in Christendom have wanted to prove the limitation of the grace of God from the words in the Epistle to the Hebrews[50] about the impossibility for those who have once been enlightened to be restored again to conversion if they fall away. Here, then, the first acquired its whole profound meaning. In this first, the whole profound Christian life proclaimed itself, and then the person who blundered in it was lost. But here the eternal is drawn too much into temporal qualifications. But this example can serve to illustrate how the first is the whole, the whole content. But when that which is foreshadowed in the first depends upon a synthesis of the temporal and the eternal, then everything I have advanced previously seems to remain valid. The whole is *implicite* in the first and is present κατὰ κρύ-ψιν [cryptically].

Now I am not ashamed to mention again the words: the first love. For the happy individualities, the first love is also the second, the third, the last; here the first love has the qualification of eternity; for the unhappy individualities, the first love is the instant; it acquires the qualification of the temporal. For the former, the first love, when it is, is a present. For the latter, it is, when it is, a past. If the fortunate individuals are also reflective and their reflection is directed to the eternal in love, it will be a strengthening of love; insofar as the reflection is on the temporal, it will be a breaking down of love. For the person who reflects temporally, the first kiss, for example, will be a past (just as Byron has put it in a short poem[51]); for the person who reflects eternally, there will be an eternal possibility.

II
39

So much for the predicate we have given to love, the first. I shall now consider more closely *the first love*. But first I beg you to recall the little contradiction we encountered—the first love possesses the whole content; to that extent it seems most sagacious to snatch it and then go on to another first love. But when one empties the first love of its content in this way, it vanishes, and one does not obtain the second love either. But is not the first love only the first? Yes, but, if one reflects on the content, only insofar as one remains in it. Then if one remains in it, does it not nevertheless become a second love? No, precisely because one remains in it, it remains the first love—if one reflects upon eternity.

That such philistines, who think that now they have just about entered the period in which it would be appropriate to look around or to inquire (perhaps even in a newspaper) for a life mate, have shut themselves out once and for all from the first love, and that such a philistine state cannot be regarded as antecedent to the first love—this is certainly evident. No doubt it is conceivable that Eros could be compassionate enough to play also on such a person the trick of making him fall in love—compassionate enough, for it is surely extraordinarily compassionate to bestow upon a person the highest earthly good, and the first love is always that, even if it is unhappy, but this is always an exception, and his previous state remains equally unillustrative.

If we are to believe the priests of music, who in this respect presumably are the most trustworthy, and if among them we also give heed to Mozart, then the state that precedes the first love could probably be best described by recalling that love makes one blind. The individual becomes as if blind; one can almost see it on him: he sinks into himself, intuits within himself his own intuiting, and yet there is a continual striving to look out into the world. The world has dazzled him, and yet he stares out into the world. It is this dreaming and yet seeking state, just as sensuous as it is psychical, that Mozart has portrayed in the Page in *Figaro*.[52]

In contrast to this, the first love is an absolute awakening, an absolute intuiting, and this must be held fixed lest a wrong be done to it. It is directed upon a single specific actual object, which alone exists for it; nothing else exists at all. This one object does not exist in vague outlines but as a specific living being. This first love has an element of the sensuous, an element of beauty, but nevertheless it is not simply sensuous.

The sensuous as such first appears through reflection, but the first love lacks reflection and therefore is not simply sensuous. This is the necessity in the first love. Like everything eternal, it has implicit the duplexity of positing itself backward into all eternity and forward into all eternity. This is the truth in what poets so frequently have celebrated—that to lovers, even the very first moment they see each other, it seems as if they have already loved each other for a long time. This is the truth in the unswerving knightly faithfulness that fears nothing and is not alarmed by the thought of any disjunctive force.

But just as the nature of all love is a unity of freedom and necessity, so also here. The individual feels himself free in this necessity, feels his own individual energy in it, feels precisely in this the possession of everything he is. That is why it is unmistakably observable in every person whether he has truly been in love. There is a transfiguration, an apotheosis in it that endures throughout his whole life. There is a unison in him of everything that otherwise is dispersed; at one and the same moment, he is younger and older than usual; he is an adult and yet a youth, in fact, almost a child; he is strong and yet so weak; he is a harmony, as we said, that resonates in his whole life. We shall celebrate this first love as one of the most beautiful things in the world, but we shall not lack the courage to go further—to let it try itself.

This, however, is not what chiefly occupies us here. It is already possible to have here the same kind of doubt that will arise again later with respect to the relation between the first love and marriage. A religiously developed person makes a practice of referring everything to God, of permeating and saturating every finite relation with the thought of God and thereby consecrating and ennobling it. (This comment is, of course, oblique here.) Consequently, it seems inadvisable to let such feelings appear in the consciousness without taking counsel with God, but insofar as one does take counsel with God, the relation is altered. At this point, it is easier to dismiss the difficulty, for since it is the nature of first love to take by surprise, and because the fruit of surprise is involuntary, it is hard to see how such taking counsel with God would be pos-

sible. Consequently, the only thing there could be any question of would be with regard to a continuing in this feeling,
but this, after all, belongs to a later deliberation. But would it
not be possible to anticipate this first love, inasmuch as in itself
this knows no relation to God?

At this point, I can touch briefly on the marriages in which
that which is decisive is located in someone or something
other than the individual, in which the individual has not yet
reached the qualification of freedom. We encounter the sad
form of this where the individual seeks to evoke the object of
his love through a connection with the forces of nature by
means of witchcraft or other such arts. The nobler form has
what, strictly speaking, must be called religious marriage.
(True marriage, of course, does not lack the religious, but it
also has the erotic element.) Thus when Isaac, for example, in
all humility and trust leaves to God whom he is to choose as
his wife, when in his confidence in God he sends his servant
and does not himself look around,[53] because his fate rests se-
curely in God's hands—this is truly very beautiful, but justice
is not really done to the erotic. But one must keep in mind that
however abstract the Hebrew God was otherwise, he nevertheless was close to the Jewish people and especially to its chosen one in all life situations, and, even though spirit, he was
not so spiritual that he would not concern himself with earthly
matters.[54] For this reason, Isaac presumably dared with a certain degree of assurance to expect that God would surely
choose a wife for him who was young and beautiful and highly
regarded by the people and lovable in every way, but nevertheless we lack the erotic, even if it was the case that he loved
this one chosen of God with all the passion of youth. Freedom
was lacking.

In Christianity we see at times a vague and yet—precisely
because of this vagueness and ambiguity—appealing blend of
the erotic and the religious that has just as much brave and bold
roguishness as it has childlike piety. This is found most often,
of course, in Catholicism, and with us in its purest form
among the common folk. Imagine (and I know you enjoy
doing this, for it is indeed a situation) a young peasant girl with

a pair of eyes audacious and yet modestly hiding behind her eyelashes, healthy, and freshly glowing, and yet there is something about her complexion that is not sickness but a higher healthiness. Imagine her on a Christmas Eve: she is alone in her room; midnight is already past, and nevertheless sleep, which ordinarily visits her so faithfully, is elusive; she feels a sweet, pleasant restlessness; she opens the window halfway and alone with the stars gazes out into the infinite space. A little sigh lightens her heart; she closes the window. With an earnestness that is continually on the verge of roguishness[55] she prays:

> You wise men three,
> Tonight let me see
> Whose bread I shall bake
> Whose bed I shall make
> Whose name I shall carry
> Whose bride I shall be,[56]

and then, hale and hearty, she jumps into bed. To be honest, it would be a disgrace for the three kings if they did not take care of her, and it is no use to say that no one knows whom she wishes—one knows that very well; at least, if not all the omens are wrong, she knows fairly well.

So we turn back to the first love. It is the unity of freedom and necessity. The individual feels drawn by an irresistible power to another individual but precisely therein feels his freedom. It is a unity of the universal and the particular; it has the universal as the particular even to the verge of the accidental. But all this it has not by virtue of reflection; it has this immediately. The more definite the first love is in this respect, the healthier it is, the greater the likelihood that it actually is a first love. By an irresistible force they are drawn to each other, and yet they enjoy therein their complete freedom. Now I have no hardhearted fathers handy, no sphinxes that have to be conquered first; I have adequate means to equip them (but I have not assigned myself the task, as novelists and playwrights do, of spinning out time to the torment of the whole world, of the lovers, the readers, and spectators); so, then, in God's name let

II
42

them come together. You see, I am playing a noble father, and
it is in and by itself truly a very beautiful role, if only we ourselves had not often made it so ridiculous. You perhaps noticed that in the fashion of fathers I added the little phrase: in
God's name. For that you can certainly forgive an old man,
who perhaps never knew what the first love is or has already
long ago forgotten it; but if a younger man, who is still carried
away by the first love, lets himself attach importance to it, you
perhaps are surprised.

The first love, then, has in itself complete spontaneous,
original security; it fears no danger, defies the whole world,
and I wish for it only that it may always have just as easy a time
of it as *in casu* [in this case], for I certainly am placing no hindrances in the way. Perhaps I am doing it no favor thereby,
and, on second thought, I may even fall into disgrace because
of it. In the first love, the individual possesses an enormous
power, and therefore it is just as unpleasant not to meet opposition as it would be for the brave knight who had obtained
a sword that could cut stone if he then found himself placed in
a sandy region where there was not even a twig on which he
could use it. The first love, then, is sufficiently secure, it needs
no support—if it should need a support, the knight would say,
then it is no longer the first love. This also seems to be clear
enough now, but it also becomes obvious that I am making a
circle. We saw above that the defect in romantic love was that
it stopped with love as an abstract *an-sich* [in itself], and that all
the dangers it saw and desired were merely external, completely extraneous to love itself. We would also bring to mind
that if the dangers came from the other side, from the interior,
the matter would then become more difficult. But to that the
knight would naturally reply: To be sure, *if*, but how would
that be possible, and if it were, it would no longer be the first
love. You see, it is not such an easy matter with this first love.

May I now remind you that it is a mistake to assume that
reflection only annihilates [and remind you] that it rescues just
as much. But since the task I have chiefly set for myself is to
show that the first love can continue to exist in marriage, I
shall now emphasize in more detail what I hinted at previ-

ously, namely, that it can be taken up into a higher concentricity and for that doubt is still not needed. I shall show later that it is the essential nature of first love to become historical, that the condition for that is precisely marriage, also that the romantic first love is unhistorical, even though one could fill folios with the knight's exploits.

The first love, then, is in itself immediately certain, but the individuals are also religiously developed. This I certainly have leave to presuppose; yes, this I certainly must presuppose, since I am going to show that the first love and marriage can exist together. It is another matter, of course, if an unhappy first love teaches the individuals to flee to God and to seek security in marriage. Then the first love is altered, even though it becomes possible to establish it again. They are, then, accustomed to bringing everything to God. But bringing everything to God naturally involves a multiplicity of different ways. Now, they do not seek God on the day of trouble, nor is it fear and anxiety that drive them to pray; their hearts, their whole beings are filled with joy—what is more natural for them, then, than to thank him for it? They fear nothing, for external dangers will have no power over them, and internal dangers—well, as a matter of fact, the first love is not acquainted with them at all. But the first love is not changed by this giving of thanks; no disturbing reflection has entered into it; it is caught up in a higher concentricity. But such thanksgiving, like all prayer, is united with an element of work (not in the external but in the internal sense), here the work of willing to hold fast to this love. The nature of the first love is not changed thereby; no reflection is involved; it does not come apart at the joints. It still has all its blessed and confident self-assurance; it is merely caught up in a higher concentricity. In this higher concentricity, it perhaps does not know at all what it has to fear, perhaps imagines no dangers at all, and yet it is drawn up into the ethical by the good intention, which also is a kind of first love. Now please do not charge me with making myself guilty of a *petitio principii* [presupposition of what is to be demonstrated] here by continually using the word "concentricity," since I ought to assume, after all, that these regions

are eccentric. To that I must answer that if I assumed the eccentricity, I would certainly never arrive at concentricity; but
I also beg you to remember that in assuming this I am also
demonstrating it. Thus we have now placed the first love in
relation to the ethical and the religious, and it has become clear
that its nature would not need to be altered thereby; but it was
precisely the ethical and religious that made the union seemingly difficult, and consequently everything appears to be in
order.

But I know you too well to dare hope "to put you off with
anything like this." After all, you know all the difficulties of
the world. With your swiftly penetrating intellect, you have
quickly thought about a multiplicity of scholarly tasks, life situations, etc., but you stop everywhere with the difficulties,
and I believe it is almost impossible for you in any single instance to go beyond them. In one sense, you are like a pilot,
and yet you are just the opposite. A pilot knows the dangers
and steers the ship safely into the harbor; you know the shal-
lows and always run the ship aground. It goes without saying
that you do the best you can and, one must confess, with great
promptitude and familiarity. You have such a practiced eye for
people and channels that you know immediately how far you
have to go with them in order to run them aground. You are
not light-minded either; likewise you do not forget that he is
sitting out there; with a childish malice you are able to remember it until the next time you see him, and you then very solic-
itously ask about his health and how he came afloat. You presumably would not be at a loss for difficulties here either. You
no doubt would recall that I had left it quite vague and indefinite as to which god was being discussed, that it was not a pagan Eros, who was so eager to share the secrets of erotic love
and whose existence ultimately was a reflexion[57] of the lovers'
own mood, but that it was the God of the Christians, the God
of spirit, jealous of everything that is not spirit. You would recall that in Christianity the beautiful and the sensuous are negated; in a trice you would remark that, for instance, it would
be a matter of indifference to the Christians whether Christ
had been ugly or handsome; you would beg me with my or-

thodoxy to stay away from erotic love's secret meetings, and especially to abstain from all attempts to mediate, to which you are more opposed than to even the most stubborn orthodoxy. "Yes, it must be very gratifying to a young maiden to stand before the altar, it must be in perfect harmony with her mood. [58]And the congregation, it would probably look upon her as an imperfect creature who could not withstand the seduction of earthly desire; she would stand there as if she were being chastised in school or making a public confession, and so the pastor would first give her a lecture and after that perhaps lean over the railing and confidentially whisper to her, as a fragment of comfort, that marriage, however, is a state well-pleasing to God. The only aspect of this occasion that has any worth is the pastor's situation, and if she was a beautiful, young girl, I would certainly like to be the pastor in order to whisper that secret in her ear." My young friend! Yes, marriage is truly a state well-pleasing to God; on the other hand, I do not know of any place in the Bible that speaks of a special blessing on bachelors, and yet that is the outcome of all your many love affairs.

But when one has you to deal with, one has no doubt taken on just about the most difficult task, for you are capable of demonstrating anything whatever and in your hands every phenomenon can be made into anything whatever. Yes, indeed, the Christian God is spirit and Christianity is spirit, and there is discord between the flesh [*Kjød*] and the spirit [*Aand*],[59] but the flesh is not the sensuous [*sandselig*]—it is the selfish. In this sense, even the spiritual can become sensuous—for example, if a person took his spiritual gifts in vain, he would then be carnal [*kjødelig*]. And of course I know that it is not necessary for the Christian that Christ must have been physically beautiful; and it would also be very grievous—for a reason different from the one you give—because if beauty were some essential, how the believer would long to see him; but from all this it by no means follows that the sensuous is annihilated in Christianity. The first love has the element of beauty in itself, and the joy and fullness that are in the sensuous in its innocence can very well be caught up in Christianity. But let us guard

against one thing, a wrong turn that is more dangerous than
the one you wish to avoid; let us not become too spiritual. Obviously, neither can an appeal be made to your arbitrariness as
to how you want to interpret Christianity. If your view were
correct, then it certainly would be best that as soon as possible
we begin with all the self-tormenting and annihilation of the
physical we learn about in the excesses of the mystics; indeed,
health itself would become suspect. Yet I doubt very much
that any pious Christian will deny that he may pray to God to
preserve his health, the God who went about healing the sick;
the cripples, then, actually ought to have declined to be healed,
for they were, after all, closest to perfection. The more simple
and childlike a person is, the more he can also pray about; but
since it is also one of the attributes of first love to be childlike,
I see no reason at all why it should not be allowed to pray or,
more correctly—to continue what was stated above—should
not be allowed to thank God, without being altered in its nature.

But you perhaps have even more on your conscience; let it
come out first as well as last. And if with regard to some
comment in the following you should want to say, "You
have never spoken to me this way before," I shall answer,
"Very true, but my good Mr. Observer must forgive a poor
married man for being so bold as to make him an object of his
observation. You are hiding something within you that you
never say right out. Therefore your expression is so very
forceful, is so very resilient, because it indicates something
more you are hinting at, an even more terrible outburst." —
So you have found what your soul hankered for, what it
thought to find in many a mistaken venture. You have found
a girl in whom your whole being finds rest, and even if you
might seem to be a little too experienced, nevertheless this is
your first love—of that you are convinced. "She is beautiful"—of course; "lovely"—oh, by all means; "and yet her
beauty does not lie in that which conforms to the standard but
in a unity of multiplicity, in the accidental, in the self-contra-
dictory"; "she is soulful"—that I can believe; "her abandon-
ment makes such an impression that everything almost goes

black before one's eyes; she is light, can swing like a bird on a branch; she has intelligence [*Aand*]—intelligence enough to illuminate her beauty, but no more."

The day has come that will assure you the possession of all that you own in the world, moreover a possession of which you are adequately sure. You have requested the favor of administering Extreme Unction to her. For some time you have been waiting in the family dining room; a bustling maid, four or five inquisitive cousins, a venerable aunt, and a hairdresser have scurried by you several times. You are already somewhat annoyed by it. Then the door to the living room opens quietly. You quickly glance inside; you are pleased that there is not a soul, that she has had the tact to send all interlopers away even from the living room. She is beautiful, more beautiful than ever. About her there is an animation, a harmony, by whose vibrations she herself is set aquiver. You are amazed; she exceeds even your dreams. You, too, are transformed, but your subtle reflection instantly hides your emotion; your calmness has an even more seductive effect on her, casts a desire in her soul that makes her beauty interesting. You approach her; her splendid attire also lends an air of the unusual to the situation. As yet you have not said a word; you look, and yet as if you were not looking. You do not want to annoy her with amorous clumsiness, but even the mirror comes to your aid. You pin a brooch upon her breast, one you presented to her the very first day you kissed her with a passion that right now is seeking its confirmation; she herself has kept it hidden, no one has known about it. You take a little bouquet containing just one kind of flower, in itself a very insignificant flower. Always, whenever you sent her flowers, there was one little sprig of this flower, but unnoticeable, so that no one suspected but her alone. Today this flower, too, will come into honor and rank; it alone will adorn her, for she loved it. You hand it to her; a tear trembles in her eye. She gives it back to you; you kiss it and pin it on her breast. A certain sadness comes over her. You yourself are moved. She steps back a little, looks at her finery almost with anger; it is an annoyance to her. She throws her arms around your neck. She cannot tear herself away; she embraces you violently as if there were a hostile force that wanted to tear you away from her. Her splendid attire is crushed, her hair has fallen down, and in that very instant she has disappeared. Once again you are left in solitude, which is interrupted only by a bustling maid, four or five inquisitive cousins, a venerable aunt, and a hairdresser. Then the door to the living room opens. She enters; a quiet earnestness is legible in every expression of her countenance. You shake her hand and take your leave to meet her again—before the altar of the Lord.

This you had forgotten. You who have given careful consideration to so much, also to this matter on other occasions, you in your infatuation had forgotten this. You have put up with circumstances that obtain for all, but on this you had not deliberated, and yet you are too mature not to see that a wedding is a bit more than a ceremony. You are seized with anxiety. "This girl, whose soul is pure as the light of day, sublime as the arch of heaven, innocent as the sea, this girl before whom I could kneel in adoration, whose love I feel could tear me out of all my confusion and give me rebirth, she is the one whom I am going to lead up to the altar of the Lord, she is going to stand there as a sinner—it will be said of her and to her that it was Eve who seduced Adam.[60] To her, before whom my proud soul bows, the only one before whom it has bowed, to her it will be said that I am to be her lord and master and she is to be subservient to her husband.[61] The moment has arrived, already the Church is stretching out its arms for her, and before it gives her back to me it will first press a bridal kiss upon her lips, not the bridal kiss for which I surrendered the whole world; already it is stretching out its arms to embrace her, but this embrace will make all her beauty fade, and then it will fling her away to me, and say: Be fruitful and multiply.[62] What kind of authority is it that dares to thrust itself between me and my bride, the bride I myself have chosen and who has chosen me. And this authority will command her to be faithful to me—does she need, then, a command—and what if she would be faithful to me only because a third party, whom she loved more than me, commanded it! And it orders me to be faithful to her—do I need to be ordered, I who belong to her with my whole soul! And this authority determines our relation to each other; it says that I am to order [*byde*] and she to obey [*lyde*]; but what if I do not want to order, what if I feel too inferior for that? No, her I will obey; for me her hint is my command but I will not submit to an alien authority. No, I will flee far, far away with her while there is still time, and I will bid the night to hide us and the silent clouds to tell us fairy tales in bold pictures, which is appropriate for a bridal night, and under the enormous arch of heaven I will become intoxicated with her charms, alone with her, alone in the whole world, and I will plunge down into the abyss of her love; and my lips are silent, for the clouds are my thoughts and my thoughts are clouds; and I will call and invoke all the powers of heaven and earth so that nothing may disturb my happiness, and I will put them on oath and have them swear this to me. Yes—away, far away, so that my soul can be healthy again, so that my chest can breathe again, so that I will not suffocate in this stuffy air—away!"

Yes, away—I, too, would say the same thing: *Procul, O procul este profani* [Away, away, O unhallowed ones].[63] But have you also considered whether she would follow you on this expedition? "Woman is weak"; no, she is humble, she is much closer to God than is man. Moreover, her love is everything, and she certainly will not disdain this blessing and this confirmation that God wants to give her. Moreover, it has never occurred to a woman to have anything against marriage, and never in all eternity will it occur to her if the men themselves do not corrupt her, for an emancipated woman could perhaps hit upon such a thing. The offense always proceeds from the men, for the man is proud; he wants to be all in all, wants to have nothing over him.

That the picture I have just drawn fits you almost perfectly you certainly will not deny, and should you wish to do so, you at least will probably not deny that it fits the spokesmen for this trend. In order to describe your first love, I have deliberately changed the ordinary phrases a bit, for, to be honest, the love described, no matter how passionate it is, with however

II
49

much pathos it proclaims itself, is still much too reflective, much too familiar with the coquettishness of erotic love for one to dare to call it a first love. A first love is humble and is therefore happy that there is an authority higher than itself, if for no other reason, then at least in order to have someone to thank. (This is why a pure first love is found more rarely in men than in women.) Something similar to this is found also in you, for you did say that you would beseech all the powers in heaven and on earth, and you hereby already manifest a need to seek a higher point of departure for your love, except that with you it becomes a fetish with all possible capriciousness.

The first thing, then, that scandalized you was that you should be formally installed as her lord and master. As if you were not that, and perhaps far too much so; as if your words did not sufficiently bear this stamp, but you do not wish to relinquish this idolatry, this coquettishness—that you want to be her slave, although you certainly do feel yourself to be her lord and master.

The second thing was that it shocked your soul that your beloved would be declared a sinful woman. You are an esthete, and I could be tempted to pose it for your idle mind's deliberation whether this very factor would not be able to make a woman even more beautiful; this implies a secret that casts an interesting light over her. The childlike roguishness that sin can have, as long as we dare predicate innocence of it, only heightens the beauty. You certainly can comprehend that I do not seriously maintain this view, since I sense very well and shall later develop what it implies, but, to repeat, if it had occurred to you, perhaps you would have become absolutely enthusiastic about this esthetic observation. Then you would have made a multiplicity of esthetic discoveries, whether it is most fitting, that is, most interesting, to use it almost for provocation by means of the most subtle innuendo, or to let the young innocent girl battle all alone with this dark force, or with a kind of pompous solemnity to seesaw her out of it into irony, etc.—in short, you would certainly have plenty to do in this respect. Eventually you would come to think of the shim-

II
50

mering light that even in the Gospel is shed on the sinner whose many sins were forgiven her because she loved much.[64] What I would say, however, is that again it is your whimsicality that wants her to stand there as a sinner. It is one thing to know sin *in abstracto*, another to know it *in concreto*. But woman is humble, and it has never occurred to a woman really to be offended because the Church's earnest words were spoken to her; woman is humble and trusting, and, also, who can cast down the eyes as a woman does, but who can also raise them up in such a way. If, then, a change should take place in her through the Church's solemn declaration that sin has entered into the world, it would have to be that she would cling even more strongly to her love. But from this it by no means follows that the first love is altered; it is only drawn up into a higher concentricity. It would be very difficult to convince a woman that earthly love is sin at all, since her whole existence would thereby be annihilated at its deepest root. Add to this that she certainly does not go up to the altar of the Lord to deliberate whether or not she is going to love this man who stands by her side. She loves him; in this she has her life, and woe to the one who arouses doubt in her, who will teach her to want to rebel against her nature and refuse to kneel before God but stand upright. Perhaps I should not accommodate you at all, for since you have the fixed idea that in order for first love truly to arise sin must not have entered into the world, you no doubt feel that you are shadow-boxing. (On the whole, by wanting to abstract from sin you show that you are immersed in reflection.) But since the individuals (to whom we attributed the first love) were religious, I do not need to become involved in any way in all this. The sinfulness is not in the first love as such, but in the selfishness in it, but the selfishness first emerges the moment it reflects, whereby it is then annihilated.

It finally shocks you that a third power wants to bind you to faithfulness to her and her to you. To keep things straight, I ask you to remember that this third authority does not force itself, but since the individuals we have in mind are religiously mature they themselves turn to it, and the relevant point is

II
51

whether it puts any obstacle in the way of their first love. You will not deny, however, that it is natural for the first love to seek a confirmation by in one way or another making love an obligation, an obligation they impose upon themselves face to face with a higher power. The lovers swear faithfulness to each other by the moon, the stars, by the ashes of their fathers, by their honor, etc. If to that you say, "Well, such oaths are meaningless; they are merely a reflection of the lovers' own mood, for how would it otherwise occur to them to swear by the moon," then I would answer, "Here you yourself have altered the nature of the first love, for the very beauty of it is that everything acquires reality for it through the power of love; not until the moment of reflection does the meaninglessness of swearing by the moon become apparent; in the time of the oath, it has validity." Is this relation changed through their swearing by a power that actually does have validity? I think not, for it is especially important to love that the oath has genuine meaning. Therefore, if you think that you could readily swear by the clouds and the stars but it disturbs you that you shall swear by God, this proves that you are immersed in reflection. In other words, your love must have no sharer of the secret other than the kind who are not sharers. Now it is indeed true that love is secretive, but your love is so superior that not even God in heaven may know anything about it, although God, to use a somewhat frivolous expression, is an eyewitness who does not cramp one's style. But that God must not know about it, this is selfishness and reflection, for at one and the same time God is in the consciousness and yet he is not supposed to be there. First love is not acquainted with such things.

This need, then, you do not have, the need to let love transfigure itself in a higher sphere, or, more correctly—for the first love does not have the need but does it spontaneously—you do have the need but refuse to satisfy it. If I now turn back momentarily to your imaginary first love, I would say: Perhaps you did succeed in invoking all the powers, and yet there grew a mistletoe[65] nearby. It shot up, wafted coolness upon you, and yet it hid within itself a deeper warmth, and you both rejoiced in it. But this mistletoe is a sign of the feverish restlessness that is the life principle of your love; it cools off and heats up, is continually changing—indeed, you could simultaneously wish that the two of you might have an eternity before you and that this present instant might be the last—and therefore the death of your love is certain.

We saw, then, how the first love could come into relation with the ethical and the religious without having this happen by means of a reflection that altered it—since it is merely drawn up into a higher immediate concentricity. In a certain sense a change has occurred, and it is this that I now wish to consider—something that could be termed the metamorphosis of the lover and the beloved into groom and bride. The way it happens is that in taking their first love to God the lovers thank God for it. Thereby an ennobling change takes place. The man's most besetting weakness is to imagine that he has made a conquest of the girl he loves; it makes him feel his superiority, but this is in no way esthetic. When, however, he thanks God, he humbles himself under his love, and it is truly far more beautiful to take the beloved as a gift from God's hand than to have subdued the whole world in order to make a conquest of her. Add to this that the person who truly loves will find no rest for his soul until he has humbled himself before God in this way, and the girl he loves means too much to him to dare take her, even in the most beautiful and noble sense, as booty. And if he should take delight in conquering and winning her, then he will know that the daily winning throughout a whole lifetime is appropriate, not a brief supranatural power of infatuation. Nevertheless, this does not occur as if it had been preceded by a doubt, but it occurs with immediacy. Consequently, the real life of the first love remains, but the raw spirits, if I may put it this way, are distilled. It is more natural for the opposite sex to feel man's predominance, to submit to it, and even though she feels glad and happy in being nothing, it nevertheless is on the road to becoming something false. Now when she thanks God for the beloved, her soul is safeguarded from suffering; by being able to thank God, she places enough distance between herself and her beloved so that she can, so to speak, breathe. And this does not happen as the result of an alarming doubt—she knows no such thing—but it happens immediately.

I have already suggested above that in first love the eternity, even though illusory, made it moral. Now when the lovers refer their love to God, this thanks will already place an absolute stamp of eternity upon it, upon the intention and the obligation also, and this eternity will then be grounded not on obscure forces but on the eternal itself. The intention also has another significance. Implicit in it is the possibility of a movement in love and consequently also the possibility of being freed from the difficulty that plagues first love as such, namely, that it cannot make any progress. The esthetic consists in its infinitude,[66] but the unesthetic consists in the impossibility of finitizing this infinitude. How it is that the entry of the religious cannot disturb the first love, I shall explain with a metaphorical expression. The religious is really the expression of the conviction that man by the help of God is lighter than the whole world, the same faith as that which is the basis for a person's being able to swim. Now if there were such a swimming belt that could hold one up, it is conceivable that someone who had been in peril of his life would always wear it, but it is also conceivable that a person who had never been in peril of his life would also wear it. The latter instance is the case with the relation between the first love and the religious. The first love girds itself with the religious without having experienced any painful incident or anxious reflection beforehand, but I must beg you not to press this metaphor, as if the religious had a merely external relation to it. In fact, it was shown above that this is not the case.

So let us now once and for all settle the account. You talk so much about the erotic embrace—what is that compared with the marital embrace? How much more richness of modulation there is in the marital "mine" than in the erotic. It resonates not only in the eternity of the seductive moment, not only in the illusory eternity of imagination and idea, but in the eternity of consciousness, in the eternity of eternity. What power there is in the marital "mine," for will, decision, intention, have a far deeper tone;[67] what energy and suppleness, for what is as hard as will, and what so soft. What power of movement there is, not just the confused excitement of dark impulses, for marriage is instituted in heaven, and duty penetrates the whole body of existence to the uttermost extremity and prepares the way and gives the assurance that in all eternity no obstacle will be able to disturb love! So let Don Juan keep his romantic bower, and the knight his nocturnal sky and stars—if he sees nothing beyond them. Marriage has its heaven even higher. So it is with marriage, and if it is not like this, it is not God's fault, or Christianity's fault, not of the wedding ceremony, not of the malediction, not of the benediction, but solely of the people themselves. And is it not really too bad the way books are written that throw people into confusion about life, make them bored with it before they begin it—instead of teaching them to live. And even if they were right, it would be a painful truth, but it is a lie. They teach us to sin, and those who do not have the courage for that are made just as unhappy in some other way. Unfortunately, I myself am too much under the influence of the esthetic not to know that the word "husband" grates on your ears. But it does not matter to me. If the word "husband" has come into discredit and has almost become something ludicrous, then it is high time we again seek to hold it in honor. And if you say, "Although one sees plenty of marriages, a marriage such as this is never seen," this does not upset me, because seeing marriages every day makes one rarely perceive the greatness in marriage, especially since everything is done to belittle it, for have you people not carried it so far that a girl who gives a man her hand before the altar is regarded as inferior to those heroines in your romantic novels with their first love?

After having listened so patiently to you and your outbursts, wilder than you perhaps will properly acknowledge (but when marriage confronts you as an actuality, you will see—even if you perhaps have not completely understood these emotions in yourself—then it will rage within you, although again you probably will not confide in anyone), you must forgive me that I come forward with my little observations. One loves only once in one's life; the heart clings to its first love[68]—marriage. Listen to and admire this harmonious unison of different spheres. It is the same subject, only expressed esthetically, religiously, and ethically. One loves only once. In order to make this real, marriage enters in, and if people who do not love each other take it into their heads to marry, it is not the fault of the Church. One loves only once—this resounds from the most diverse sources, from the happy ones who are reassured every day of this, and from the unhappy ones. Of them there actually are only two classes—those who are always craving for the ideal and those who do not wish to hold fast to it. The latter are the real seducers. They are seldom encountered, because it takes something out of the ordinary to be that. I have known one, but he also admitted that one loves only once—but love had been unable to tame his wild desires. Sure enough, certain people say one loves only once but marries two or three times. Here again the spheres are united, for esthetics says "No" and the Church and Church ethics look dubiously upon the second marriage. This is of utmost importance to me, for if it were true that one loved several times, then marriage would become a dubious matter; then it might appear as if the erotic would suffer damage because of the arbitrariness of the religious, which ordinarily would demand that one should love only once and consequently would treat this matter of the erotic as casually as if it were to say: You can marry once, and with that be finished with the matter.

We have now perceived how the first love entered into relation with marriage without thereby being altered. The same esthetic element implicit in the first love must then also be in marriage, since the former is contained in the latter, but, as developed above, the esthetic consists in the infinitude, the apriority, that the first love has. Thereupon it is implicit in the unity of contrasts that love is: it is sensuous and yet spiritual; it is freedom and yet necessity; it is in the instant, is to a high degree present tense, and yet it has in it an eternity. All this marriage also has; it is sensuous and yet spiritual, but it is more, for the word "spiritual [*aandelig*]" applied to the first love is closest to meaning that it is psychical [*sjælelig*], that it is the sensuous permeated by spirit. It is freedom and necessity, but also more, for freedom applied to the first love is nevertheless actually rather the psychical freedom in which the individuality has not yet purified itself of natural necessity. But the more freedom, the more self-giving, and only he can be prodigal with himself who possesses himself. In the religious, the individuals became free—he from false pride, she from false humility—and the religious pushed in between the two lovers, who held each other so tightly encircled, not to separate them but so that she could give herself with an exuberance that she had not previously suspected and so that he could not only receive but give himself and she receive. Even more than the first love, it has an interior infinitude, for marriage's interior infinitude is an eternal life. Even more than first love it is a unity of contrasts, for it has one more contrast, the spiritual, and thereby the sensuous in an even more profound contrast; but the further away from the sensuous one is, the more esthetic significance it acquires, for otherwise the animal instincts would be the most esthetic. But the spiritual in marriage is higher than that in the first love, and the higher the heaven is over the marriage bed, the better, the more beautiful, the more esthetic it is; and it is not the earthly heaven that arches over marriage but the heaven of the spirit. It is in the instant, sound and powerful; it points beyond itself, but in a deeper sense than the first love, for the abstract character of first love is precisely its defect, but in the intention that marriage has, the law of motion is implicit, the possibility of an inner history. Intention is resignation in its richest form, in which the concern is not for what is to be lost but for what is to be gained by being held fast. In the intention, an other is posited, and in the intention love is placed in relation to that other, but not in the external sense. But the intention [*Forsæt*] here is not the acquired fruit of doubt but the overabundance of the promise [*Forjættelse*]. So beautiful is marriage, and the sensuous is by no means repudiated but is ennobled. Indeed, I confess it—perhaps it is wrong of me—frequently when I think of my own marriage the notion that it will cease to be awakens in me an inexplicable

sadness, as does the thought that—sure as I am that in another
life I will live with her to whom my marriage joined me—this
will give her to me in another way, and the contrast that was a
condition belonging to our marriage will be annulled. Nevertheless it comforts me that I know, and I shall recollect, that I
have lived with her in the most intimate, the most beautiful association that life on this earth provides. If I do have any understanding of the whole subject, the defect in earthly love
[*Kjærlighed*] is the same as its merit—that it is preference
[*Forkjærlighed*]. Spiritual love has no preference and moves in
the opposite direction, continually sheds all relativities.
Earthly love, when it is true, goes the opposite way and at its
highest is love only for one single human being in the whole
world. This is the truth of loving only one and only once.
Earthly love begins with loving several—these loves are the
preliminary anticipations—and ends with loving one; spiritual
love continually opens itself more and more, loves more and
more people, has its truth in loving all. Thus marriage is sensuous but also spiritual, free and also necessary, absolute in itself and also within itself points beyond itself.

Since marriage is an inner harmony in this way, it of course
has its teleology in itself; it is, since it continually presupposes
itself, and thus any question about its "why" is a misunderstanding, which is very easily explained by prosaic common
sense, which, although it usually seems a little more modest
than choir director Basil, who is of the opinion that of all the
ludicrous things marriage is the most ludicrous,[69] nevertheless
readily tempts not only you but also me to say, "If marriage is
nothing else, then of all the ludicrous things it is actually the
most ludicrous."

Just to pass the time, however, let us look a little more
closely at one or another of these. Even if there will be a great
difference in our laughter, we might just as well laugh a little
together. The difference will be approximately the same as the
different tone of voice we would use in answering the question
"Why is there marriage?" with the words: God only knows.
Moreover, when I say that we will laugh a little together it by
no means must be forgotten how much in this respect I owe to

your observations, for which as a married man I really do thank you. That is, if people do not wish to fulfill the most beautiful task, if they want to dance everywhere else but on the island of Rhodes[70] that is assigned to them as a dancing place, then let them be a victim for you and for other rogues who under the mask of a confidant know how to pull their legs. But there is one point that I want to rescue, a point about which I never have and never will allow myself to smile. You have often said that it would be "absolutely superb" to go around and ask every one individually why he got married, and one would discover that usually the deciding factor was a very insignificant circumstance, and you then explore how ludicrous it is that such an enormous effect as a marriage with all its consequences can emerge from such a little cause. I shall not dwell on the mistake implicit in your looking at a little circumstance altogether abstractly, and on the fact that most often it is only because the little circumstance joins a multiplicity of factors that something results from it.

What I want to stress, however, is the beauty in the marriages that have as little "why" as possible. The less "why," the more love—that is, if one perceives the truth in this. To be sure, to the light-minded person it will subsequently appear that it was a little "why"; to the earnest person it will to his joy appear that it was an enormous "why." Indeed, the less "why," the better. Among the lower classes, marriage is ordinarily entered into without any great "why," but for this reason these marriages resound much less frequently with so many "hows"—how are they going to manage, how are they going to take care of the children, etc. Nothing else ever belongs to marriage but marriage's own "why," which is infinite and consequently in the sense in which I take it is no "why"— something of which you, too, will easily convince yourself; for if one were to answer the "why" of such a commonsensical philistine married man with this authentic "therefore," he very likely would respond as did the school teacher in *Alferne*: "Then let us get a new lie."[71] You will also perceive why I do not wish and cannot manage to see a comic side to the lack of this "why," for I fear that the truth will thereby be lost. There is only one true "why," but it also has an intrinsic, infinite energy and power that can quell all "hows." The finite "why" is a sum, a swarm, from which each one picks his own, the one more, another fewer—the whole lot just as foolish, for even if someone could unite all the finite "whys" upon his entrance into marriage, he would simply be the most wretched of all husbands.

One of the ostensibly most respectable answers given to this "why" of marriage is: Marriage is a school for character; one marries in order to ennoble and cultivate one's character. I will turn my attention to a specific circumstance for which I am indebted to you. It involved a public official "you had got hold of"—that was your own phrase and is just like you, for you shrink from nothing when there is an object for your observation, since you believe that you are following your calling. Incidentally, he was a rather intelligent fellow and in particular had considerable linguistic talent. The family gathered at the tea table. He was smoking his pipe. His wife was no beauty, rather plain looking, old in relation to him, and thus one could, as you remarked, immediately think that the "why" had to be an eccentric one. At the tea table sat a young, somewhat pale, newly married woman who seemed to know another "why"; the mistress herself poured the tea, and a young sixteen-year-old girl, not beautiful but buxom and lively, served it; as yet she seemed not to have arrived at any "why." In this worthy company, Your Unworthiness had also found a place. You, who were present *ex officio*, who had already gone there a few times to no avail, of course found the situation far too propitious to dare leave it unutilized. Precisely in those days there was some talk of a broken engagement. As yet the family had not heard this important local news. The case was pleaded from all sides—that is, all were *actores* [plaintiffs]; the case was then taken to judgment and the sinner excommunicated. Feelings were stirred up. You ventured to insinuate a little comment in favor of the one convicted, which naturally was not intended to benefit the person in question but to provide a cue. When it failed, you went on to say, "Perhaps the whole engagement was precipitous; perhaps he did not analyze the important 'why'—one could almost say the *aber* [but] that ought to precede such a decisive step; *enfin* [finally], why does one marry, why, why." Each one of these "whys" was spoken in a different tone of voice but nevertheless just as dubitively. It was too much. One "why" would have been sufficient, but such a complete roll call, a fully mobilized march into the enemy camp, was decisive. The moment had arrived. With a certain good nature, which also bore the marks of prevailing common sense, the host said: Well, my good man, I shall tell you why—one marries because marriage is a school for character. That started everything; partly by opposition, partly by approbation, you made him surpass himself in bizarreness—to the slight edification of his wife, to the offense of the young wife, and to the astonishment of the young girl. I already at that time reproached you for your behavior, not for the sake of the host but for the sake of the women, to whom you were spiteful enough to make the scene as troublesome and protracted as possible. The two women do not need my defense, and for that matter it was just your habitual coquettishness that induced you not to lose sight of them. But his wife—perhaps she nevertheless actually loved him, and must it not therefore have been terrible for her to listen. Add to that the fact that there was something indecent in the whole situation. So far is commonsensical reflection from making marriage moral that it actually makes it immoral. Sensuous love has but one transfiguration, in which it is equally esthetic, religious, and ethical—and that is love; commonsensical calculating makes it just as unesthetic as irreligious, because the sensuous is not within its immediate rights. Consequently, a person who marries for this and that etc. is taking a step that is just as unesthetic as it is irreligious. The goodness of his objective is of no use, for the mistake is precisely that he has an objective. If a woman married—yes, such lunacy has been heard of in the world, a lunacy that seems to give her marriage a prodigious "why"—in order to bear a savior for the world, this marriage would be just as unesthetic as immoral and irreligious. This is something people cannot make clear to themselves often enough. There is a certain group of

II
60

commonsensical men who look down with enormous contempt on the esthetic as trumpery and child's play and who in their wretched teleology consider themselves high above such things, but it is precisely the opposite; in this commonsensicality such people are just as immoral as they are unesthetic. This is why it is always best to look at the other sex, which is both the more religious and the more esthetic. In other respects, the host's discourse certainly was trivial enough, and I do not need to present it. I shall, however, conclude this observation by wishing for every such husband a Xanthippe for a wife[72] and children as depraved as possible—so that he can hope to possess the condition for the attainment of his objective.

That marriage is otherwise actually a school for character or—in order to avoid using so philistine a phrase—is the genesis of character, I will readily concede, although I naturally must continually hold that anyone who married for this reason might rather be relegated to any school whatever except the school of love. Moreover, such a person will never benefit from this schooling. In the first place, he deprives himself of the strengthening, the integration, and the penetrating shiver through every thought and joint that make up marriage, for it truly is a venturesome action; but so it should be, and wanting to calculate is so far from being right that any such calculating is precisely an attempt to enervate it. In the second place, he of course loses out on love's enormous working capital and on the humility that the religious provides in marriage. Naturally he is much too super-sagacious not to bring along a fixed cut-and-dried conception of how he wants to be developed; this, then, becomes the norm for his marriage and the unhappy creature he was shameless enough to select for his guinea pig. But let us forget that and with thankfulness recall how true it is that marriage does educate—that is, if one does not feel superior to it but, as always when it is a question of education, subordinates oneself to that by which one is to be educated. It matures the whole soul by simultaneously giving a sense of meaning and also the weight of a responsibility that cannot be sophistically argued away, because one loves. It ennobles the whole man by the blush of modesty that belongs to the woman but is the man's disciplinarian, for woman is man's conscience. It brings melody into a man's eccentric movement; it gives strength and meaning to the woman's quiet life, but only insofar as she seeks this in the man and thus this strength does not become an unfeminine masculinity. His proud ebullience is dampened by his constant returning to her; her weakness is strengthened by her leaning on him.*

Now for all the minutiae involved in marriage. Yes, here you will surely agree with me—but also pray God to spare you from it. No, there is nothing that educates as much as the mi-

II
62

* Therefore, it is marriage that first actually gives a person his positive freedom, because this relationship can extend over his whole life, over the least as well as the greatest. It frees him from a certain unnatural embarrassment in natural things, which probably can be acquired in many other ways, but then also very easily at the expense of the good; it frees him from stagnating in habit by maintaining a fresh current; it frees him from people precisely by binding him to one human being. I have often noticed that people who are unmarried drudge just like slaves. In the first place, they are slaves to their whims; in their daily lives they dare to indulge themselves in everything, owe no one an accounting, but then they also become dependent on, in fact, slaves of, other people. What a role a servant, a housekeeper, etc. often plays. They are their master's personified whims and inclinations reduced to the stroke of the hour and minute; they know when the master gets up or, more correctly, how long in advance he should be called or, more correctly, how long in advance his study should be warmed before he is called; they know how to lay out his clean linen, to roll his stockings so that he can pull them on easily, to have cold water ready when he has washed himself in warm water,[73] to open the windows when he goes out, to set out his bootjack and house slippers for him when he comes home, etc. etc. The domestic staff, especially if they are somewhat on the bright side, easily make themselves familiar with all this. Now, although all this occurs punctually on the dot, such unmarried people often are not satisfied. After all, they are able to buy the satisfaction of every wish. On occasion, they are ill-tempered and petulant, afterward weak and good-natured. Indeed, a couple of rix-dollars makes everything all right. The servants soon learn how to make use of this; consequently, it is just a matter of doing something a bit wrong at proper intervals, letting the master rage, becoming heartbroken over it, and thereupon receiving a tip. The master and mistress are very charmed by such a person; the master does not know whether he should admire more his scrupulousness or the repentance he shows when he has done wrong. A servant like this becomes invaluable to the master and mistress and is a perfect despot.

II
62

nutiae. There is a period in a person's life when such things
ought to be removed from him, but there is also a period when
they are good. It takes a great soul to save his soul from minutiae, but he can if he will, because to will makes the great
soul, and the person who loves, wills. This can be difficult, especially for the man, and this is why the woman has such great
significance for him in this respect. She is created to deal with
little matters and knows how to give them a meaning, a value,
a beauty that enchants. They rescue from habits, from the tyr-
anny of one-sidedness, from the yoke of whims, and how
would all this evil find time to take shape in a marital union,
which calls itself to account so many times and in so many
ways. Nothing like that can thrive, for "love is patient and
kind, love is not jealous or boastful, it is not arrogant or rude.
Love does not insist on its own way, it is not irritable or re-
sentful, it does not rejoice at wrong but rejoices in the right.
Love bears all things, believes all things, hopes all things, endures all things."[74] Think of these beautiful words by one of
the Lord's apostles; think of them applied to a whole life in
such a way that to them is linked a conception that one enacted
them effortlessly many times, failed many times, forgot many
times, but nevertheless turned back to them again. Think of a
married couple, that they dare to say these words to each other
in such a way that the main impression still remains joyous;
what a blessing there is in this, what a transfiguration of character! In marriage, one makes no headway with great passions.
One cannot give or receive in advance; by being exceedingly
affectionate for one month, one cannot compensate for another time; here it is true that every day has its own troubles,[75]
but also its own blessings. I know that I have subjugated my
pride and my hypochondriacal restlessness to her love; I have
subjugated her vehemence to our love. But I also know that it
has cost many days; I also know that there may be many dangers ahead, but my hope is for victory.

[76]Or a person marries—to have children, to make his small
contribution to propagating the human race on this earth.
Imagine—if he had no children, his contribution would be
very small. In offering rewards to those who married and to

those who had the most male children, countries certainly have allowed themselves to have this purpose for marriage. At times, Christianity has opposed this by offering rewards to those who refrained from marriage. Even if this was a mistake, it nevertheless shows a profound respect for personality to go that far to make the single individual definitive and not just a factor. The more abstractly the state is conceived and the less the individual has fought his way out of this, the more natural is such an offer and such an encouragement. In contrast to this, in our age marriage without children is at times almost extolled. In other words, our age has had a hard time effecting the resignation it takes to enter into a marriage; if one has denied oneself to that extent, one thinks that this is enough and cannot really put up with such tedious difficulties as a flock of children. It is alleged frequently enough in novels, albeit casually but nevertheless as a reason for a particular individual not to marry, that he cannot endure children; in life in the most civilized countries this is expressed by the removal of the children from the parental house as soon as possible and their placement in a boarding school etc. How often have you not been amused by these tragi-comic family men with four darling children whom they secretly wished were far, far away? How often have you not gloated over the outraged sensibilities of such family men at all the petty details that life entails, when the children have to be spanked, when they spill on themselves, when they scream, when the great man—the father— feels frustrated in his venturesomeness by the thought that his children tie him to the earth? How often have you not with well-deserved cruelty brought such noble fathers to the peak of suppressed rage when you, occupied exclusively with his children, dropped a few words about what a blessing it really is to have children?

To marry in order to contribute to the propagation of the human race could seem to be both a very objective and a very natural reason. It would be as if one put oneself in God's position and from this position saw the beauty in the maintenance of the human race; yes, one could place special emphasis on the words: "Be fruitful and multiply and fill the earth."[77]

II
64

And yet such a marriage is just as unnatural as it is arbitrary
and devoid of a stronghold in Holy Scripture. As far as the latter is concerned, we read that God instituted marriage because
it was not good for man to be alone, in order to give him company.[78] Now even if some scoffer at religion might consider
somewhat dubious the company that commenced by plung-
ing the man into corruption, this proves nothing, and I would
rather cite this event as a motto for all marriages, because not
until the woman had done this was the most intimate association strengthened between them. Then, too, we also read
these words: And God blessed them.[79] These words are completely ignored. And when the apostle Paul somewhere quite
severely orders women to receive instruction in silence, in all
humility, and to be silent, and then, having silenced her, to humiliate her still more, adds: She will be saved by bearing children, I truly would never have forgiven the apostle this contempt if he had not redeemed everything by adding: if they
(the children) continue in faith and love and holiness with discipline.[80]

In this connection, it occurs to me that it might seem strange
that I, whose business allows me only little time for studies
and whose lowly studies are ordinarily in an entirely different
direction, seem to be so conversant with the Bible that I could
be qualified for the theological degree. An ancient pagan—I
believe it is Seneca—has said that when a person has reached
his thirtieth year he ought to know his constitution so well that
he can be his own physician;[81] I likewise believe that when a
person has reached a certain age he ought to be able to be his
own pastor. Not as if I would in any way minimize participation in public worship and the guidance given there, but I do
think that one ought to have one's view settled with regard to
the most important life relationships, which, furthermore,
one seldom hears preached about in the stricter sense. To de-
votional books and printed sermons, I have an idiosyncratic
aversion; that is why I resort to Scripture when I cannot go to
church. For information, I then consult some scholarly theologian or some scholarly work where the most important
Scripture passages on the subject in question are to be found,

and then I read them through. So I was already married and had been married for half a year before it occurred to me to deliberate seriously on what the New Testament teaches about marriage. I had attended several weddings prior to my own; consequently I knew the sacred words declared on this occasion. I still wanted, however, a little more thorough knowledge and therefore turned to my friend Pastor Olufsen, who was in town just then. With his instruction, I found the main passages[82] and read them aloud to my wife. I remember very well the impression that particular passage[83] made on her. Moreover, it was a delicate matter. I was not acquainted with the passages in the Bible that I was about to read to her, and I did not wish to look at them in advance. I do not like to prepare the impression I wish to make on her; anything like that is based on misplaced distrust. This you could take to heart; to be sure, you are not married and thus have no human being to whom you are committed in the strictest sense to be open, but your preparation actually verges on the ludicrous. Certainly you can fool people, can appear to do everything very casually, as impromptly as possible, and yet I do not believe you can say "Goodbye" without having deliberated on how you will say it.

But back to marriage and the indefatigable folk married for the multiplication of the human race. This kind of marriage sometimes conceals itself under a more esthetic cover. It is an aristocratic old noble family that is about to die out; there are only two representatives left—a grandfather and his grandson. It is the venerable old man's only wish that the son marry so that the family will not be wiped out. Or it is a man on whose life not so much weight is placed but who thinks back with a certain sadness, if no further back, at least to his own parents, loves them so deeply that he could wish this name might not die out but be preserved in the thankful recollection of living persons. Perhaps he has a vague notion of how beautiful it would be to be able to tell his children about their grandfather long since dead, to fortify their lives with such an ideal image that belongs only to recollection, to inspire them to everything noble and great by this conception; perhaps he will think that in so doing he will be able to repay some of the debt he feels he owes his parents.

Now this is all good and beautiful, but it is still irrelevant to marriage, and a marriage entered into solely for this reason is just as unesthetic as immoral. This might seem a hard saying, but it is nevertheless true. Marriage can be undertaken with only one intention, whereby it is just as ethical as esthetic, but this intention is immanent; any other intention divides what belongs together and thereby makes finitudes of both the spiritual and the sensuous. It may very well happen that by talking this way a person can win a girl's heart, especially if he truly has the feelings described, but it is wrong, and her being is actually altered; it is always an insult to a girl to want to marry her for any other reason than that one loves her.

Even though every stud-consideration (to use your expression) as such is irrelevant to marriage, the family will prove to be a blessing to the person who has not disordered the relationship for himself. For one human being to owe another as much as possible is still a beautiful thing, but nevertheless the highest thing a human being can owe another is—life. And yet a child can owe a father even more, because, after all, it does not receive life bare and blank but receives it with a definite content, and when it has rested on its mother's breast long enough it is laid upon its father's, and he also nourishes it with his own flesh and blood, with the frequently hard-earned experiences of an eventful life. And what possibility there is in a child! I readily agree with you in your hatred of the idolatry that is carried on with children, especially the whole cult of the family and the rite of children circling the table at dinner and supper for the family kiss, the family adulation, the family hopes, while the parents smugly thank each other for the problems surmounted and rejoice over the finished artistic product. Yes, I confess it—I can be just as sarcastic about such odious practices as you are, but I do not let myself be more disturbed by it than that. Children belong to the innermost, hidden life of the family, and to this bright-dark mysteriousness one ought to direct every earnest or God-fearing thought on this subject. But then it will also appear that every child has a halo about its head; every father will also feel that there is more in the child than what it owes to him. Yes, he will feel in humility that it is a trust and that in the most beautiful sense of the word he is only the stepfather. The father who has not felt this has always taken in vain his dignity as a father.

Let us spare ourselves all the misplaced commotion, "all the bowing and scraping with regard to childbirth," but please spare me also your flippancy when, like Holberg's Henrik,[84] you want to pledge yourself to the incredible. A child is the greatest and the most significant thing in the world, the most unimpressive and most insignificant—all according to the way one looks at it, and we have an occasion to gain a deep insight into a person when we find out how he thinks in this regard. An infant can almost have a comic effect on one if one reflects on its pretensions to be a human being; it can have a tragic effect if one reflects on its coming into the world with a cry, that it takes a long time before it forgets to cry, and that no one has explained this infant crying. Thus the child can produce many effects, but the religious viewpoint, which can very well be combined with the others, remains the most beautiful. And now you, you certainly do love possibility, and yet the thought of children will surely not have a joyful effect upon you, for I do not doubt that your inquisitive and vagabond thoughts have peeked into this world also. Naturally this comes from your wanting to have the possibility in your power. You relish being in the situation children are in when they are waiting in the dark room for the revealing of the Christmas tree, but a child, to be sure, is an entirely different kind of possibility, and such an earnest one that you would hardly have the patience to bear it. And yet children are a blessing. It is beautiful and good that a man thinks with deep earnestness about the best for his children, but if he does not sometimes remember that it is not just a duty that is laid upon him, a responsibility, but that they also are a blessing, and that God in heaven has not forgotten what not even men forget, to lay a gift in the cradle, then he has not expanded his heart either to esthetic or to religious feelings. The more a person is able to hold fast to the thought that children are a blessing, the fewer the battles and the less doubt with which he preserves this jewel, the only good that the infant possesses, but also lawfully, for God himself has placed it there, the more beautiful, the more esthetic, the more religious it is.

I, too, stroll the streets at times, lose myself in my own thoughts and in the impressions occasioned by the immediate surroundings. I have seen a poor woman—she had a little business, not in a shop or in a stall, but she stood in the open square; she stood there in rain and wind with a little one in her arms; she herself was neat and clean and her baby was carefully wrapped up. I have seen her many times. A fine lady came along who practically scolded her because she did not leave the child at home, and all the more so because it was just a hindrance to her. A clergyman came along the same street and approached her; he wanted to find a place for the child in an orphanage. She thanked him graciously, but you should have seen the way she looked down and gazed at the child. Had it been frozen, her look would have thawed it; had it been dead and cold, her look would have called it to life; had it been exhausted from hunger and thirst, the benediction of her look would have refreshed it. But the child slept, and not even its smile could reward the mother. You see, this woman perceived that a child is a blessing. If I were a painter, I would never paint anybody but this woman. A sight such as that is a rarity; it is like a rare flower that requires luck for a chance to see it. But the world of spirit is not under the dominion of futility;[85] if one has found the tree, it blossoms continually; I have often seen her. I have pointed her out to my wife; I have not made myself important, have not sent her rich gifts, as if I had a divine carte blanche to pass out rewards; I have humbled myself under her. She really does not need either gold or fine ladies, or orphanages and clergymen, or a poor court-and-city judge and his wife. She needs nothing at all, except that the child will at some time love her with the same tenderness, and she does not need this either, but it is the reward she has deserved, a blessing that heaven will not fail to give her.

You cannot deny that this is beautiful, that it stirs even your calloused heart. Therefore, I shall not, in order to help you ap-

preciate that a child is a blessing, resort to the terror tales people often use when they wish to frighten the unmarried person
with the idea of how lonely he is going to be, how unhappy
not to be surrounded by a flock of children. For one thing, you
probably would not allow yourself to be frightened, at least
not by me—indeed, not by the whole world (when you are
alone with yourself in the dark alcove of heavy thoughts, you
no doubt sometimes become anxious about yourself). Then,
too, it always strikes me as dubious to convince oneself one
has a good thing by making others worried because they do
not have it. So ridicule, then; speak, then, the words that
hover on your lips—the four-seated Holsteiner carriage. Be
amused, then, that the ride is no further than to "Fredsberg."[86]
Drive past us, then, in your comfortable Vienna two-seater,
but guard against indulging too often in your ridicule in this
regard, for in your soul there might secretly develop an ideal
longing that would punish you severely enough.

But children are a blessing in another sense also, for we ourselves learn so indescribably much through them. I have seen
proud men whom no fate has hitherto humbled, who with
such assurance snatched the girl they loved out of the family
life to which she belonged that it was as if they would say:
When you have me, that ought to be enough; I am accustomed
to defy storms—how much more so now when the thought of
you will inspire me, now when I have much more to fight for.
I have seen the same men as fathers: a little mishap occurring
to their children has been able to humble them; a sickness has
been able to bring a prayer to their proud lips. I have seen men
who took pride in practically disdaining the God who is in
heaven, who made a habit of making every one who confessed
him a target of their ridicule—I have seen them as fathers, out
of solicitude for their children, take the most pious people into
their employ. I have seen girls whose proud glance made
Olympus quake,[87] girls whose vain temperaments lived only
for frills and frippery—I have seen them as mothers bear every
humiliation, almost beg for what they believed was best for
the children. I think of a specific instance. She was a very
proud woman. Her child became ill. One of the city physi-

cians was called. He refused to come because of a previous incident. I have seen her go to him, wait in his anteroom in order with her pleas to persuade him to come. But to what end are such intense portrayals, which, although true, still are not as upbuilding as the less emotional examples that are seen every day by the person who has eyes to see?

Then, too, we also learn much from children in another way. In every child there is something original upon which all abstract principles and maxims more or less come to grief. A person must himself begin from the beginning, often with much trouble and effort. There is a profound meaning in the Chinese proverb: Bring up your children well, and you will come to know what you owe your parents. And now the responsibility that is placed on a father. We associate with other people, try to convey to them some conception of what we think is right, perhaps make several attempts; when it all proves futile, we have nothing more to do with them and wash our hands. But when does the moment come when a father dares—or, more correctly, when is a father-heart capable of deciding—to abandon any further attempt? The whole of life is experienced again in the children; only now does one understand one's own life. But it really is futile to speak to you about this; there are things of which one can never have any substantial conception if one has not experienced them, and among these is being a father.

And now, finally, the beautiful way in which through children one makes a connection with a past and a future. Even if a person does not have fourteen noble ancestors and a concern to produce the fifteenth, he has a far greater kinship before him, and it is truly joyous to see how the line seems to take a specific pattern in families. To be sure, the unmarried person can also indulge in such observations, but he will not feel as encouraged or as entitled to do so, inasmuch as to a certain degree he himself is intervening disturbingly.

Or a man marries in order to have a home. He has become bored at home, has taken a trip abroad and become bored, has come home again and is bored. For the sake of company, he keeps an exceptionally beautiful water spaniel and a purebred mare, but he still lacks something. At the restaurant where a few congenial friends gather, he looks long and in vain for an acquaintance. He learns that the man has married. He becomes soft and sentimental about the old days; he feels the emptiness of everything around him—nobody is waiting for him when he is gone. The old housekeeper is really a very good-natured woman, but she knows nothing about cheering up a person and making things a little cozy. So he marries. The neighborhood claps its hands, considers that he has acted wisely and sensibly, and after that he joins in talking about the most important aspect of home management, the greatest earthly good: a good-natured and reliable cook one can allow to go to the market on her own, a handy maid who is so clever that she can be used for everything. Now, if only such a baldheaded old hypocrite would be satisfied with marrying a night nurse—but usually that is not the case. The best is not good enough, and finally he manages to capture a beautiful young girl, who then is forged into a galley slave like this. Perhaps she has never been in love—what a horrible disproportion!

II
71

You see, I am letting you have your say. But you must admit that there are marriages, especially among the simpler classes, that are entered into for the purpose of having a home and are really beautiful. They are people in their earlier years. Not having knocked about in the world very much, they have reached the necessary income level and now consider getting married. It is beautiful, and I also know that it could never occur to you to direct your ridicule against such marriages. A certain noble simplicity gives them both an esthetic and a religious cast. There is nothing at all egotistic in the thought of wanting to have a home; on the contrary, for them the idea of a duty is attached to it, a task that is laid upon them, but which for them is also a pleasant duty.

Frequently enough, married people are also heard to comfort themselves and to alarm the unmarried by saying: Well, we do have a home, and when we grow older a place to stay. At times they add with a singular Sunday tone in the edifying style: Our children and grandchildren will some day close our eyes and grieve for us. The unmarried have the opposite fate.

With a certain envy, it is admitted that they do have a better
time for a while in their younger days; one secretly wishes not
to be married yet oneself, but it comes soon enough. The unmarried are like the rich man:[88] they have taken their share
early in the game.

All marriages of that kind suffer from the mistake of making
a particular feature of the marriage the purpose for marriage,
and therefore they often feel deceived, especially those mentioned first, when they have to admit that marriage means little more than acquiring a comfortable, cozy, suitable home.
But now let us once again disregard what is wrong in order to
see the beautiful and the true. It is not given to everyone to operate on a very large scale, and many of those who imagine
they are working for something great sooner or later find
themselves laboring under a delusion.

This certainly does not mean you, for you, of course, are
too intelligent not to get wind of the illusion at once, and your
ridicule has pilloried it often enough. In that regard, you have
an extraordinary level of resignation and have once and for all
manifested total renunciation [*Renonce*]. You prefer to amuse
yourself. You are a welcome guest everywhere. Your wit,
your ease in company, a certain goodnaturedness, as well as a
certain maliciousness, prompt one to associate with the very
sight of you the idea of a pleasant evening. You have always
been and will always be a welcome guest in my house, partly
because I am not very afraid of you, and partly because I have
a good chance of not needing to begin to be afraid of you—my
only daughter is but three years old, and you do not open your
telegraphic communication with girls that young. You have
sometimes half chided me for withdrawing more and more
from the world, once, I remember, to the tune of "Tell me,
Jeannette—."[89] The reason, of course, as I also replied to you
that time, is that I have a home. In this respect, it is just as hard
to get hold of you as of all the others—that is, you always have
other plans.

If one wishes to strip people of their illusions in order to lead
them to something more true, here as always you are "at your
service in every way." On the whole, you are tireless in track-

ing down illusions in order to smash them to pieces. You talk so sensibly, with such experience, that anyone who does not know you better must believe that you are a steady man. But you have by no means arrived at what is true. You stopped with destroying the illusion, and since you did it in every conceivable direction, you actually have worked your way into a new illusion—that one can stop with this. Yes, my friend, you are living in an illusion, and you are achieving nothing.

Here I have spoken the word that has always had such a strange effect on you. Achieve—"so who is achieving something? That is precisely one of the most dangerous illusions. I do not busy myself in the world at all; I amuse myself the best I can, and I am particularly amused by those people who believe that they are achieving something, and is it not indescribably funny that a person believes that? I refuse to burden my life with such grandiose pretensions."

Every time you talk about this you have a very disagreeable effect on me. It disturbs me because there is in it an implicit brash untruth, which, delivered with your virtuosity, always scores a success, at least always brings the laughter to your side.[90] I remember one occasion when you, after listening for a long time to a man who had been upset by what you said, without answering him a word but merely egging him on with your sarcastic smile, finally responded to the universal delight of those present: Well, if you add this speech to everything else you have achieved, we at least cannot blame you for believing that you are really achieving something in general and in particular. It pains me when you talk that way, because I feel a certain pity for you.[91] If you do not restrain yourself, with you will perish a richly endowed nature. This is why you are dangerous. This is why your sallies and your coldness have a potency I have not seen in anyone else of the many who dabble in the profession of being discontented. As a matter of fact, you do not belong with them; they are the butt of your satire, for you have gone much further. "You are happy and contented, you smile, you wear your hat at a jaunty angle, you do not overstrain yourself on the sorrows of life; as yet you have not become a member of any threefold lamentation society."

But that is precisely why your remarks are so dangerous for young people, because they must be struck by the mastery you have won over everything in the world. Now I am not going to tell you that a person must achieve something in life, but I will ask if there still are not some specific things in your life over which you cast an impenetrable veil; might they not be of the kind in which you wanted to achieve something, even though your depression groans in pain because it is so little? And how altogether different does it not appear within you! Is there not still a profound sorrow over your not achieving anything? I know at least one situation; you dropped a few words about it that did not go unheeded. Undoubtedly you would give everything to be able to achieve something. Whether it is your own fault that you cannot, whether it is your pride that has to be crushed in order to be capable of it, I do not know, and I shall never intrude further upon you, but why do you nevertheless maintain partnership with all that bad lot that really revels in your ability to score a victory every time.

As I said before, one often enough feels how little one achieves in the world. I do not say this despondently. I really have nothing for which to chide myself; I believe that I administer my office conscientiously and cheerfully, and I shall never be tempted to become involved in anything that is none of my business in the hope of achieving more. But nevertheless it is a very circumscribed activity, and it is only in faith that one has the assurance that one is achieving anything. But then along with this I have my home. In this respect, I often think of Jesus Sirach's beautiful words, which I shall also ask you to ponder: "He who acquires a wife begins to acquire his best possessions, for he has acquired a helper and a support to rest upon. Where there is no fence, the property will be plundered; and where there is no wife, a man will sigh and be as one who wanders about. For who will trust an armed robber who skips from city to city? So who will trust a man who has no home, and lodges wherever night finds him?"[92]

I have not married in order to have a home, but I have a home, and this is a great blessing. I am not—and I believe you will not go so far as to call me—a fool of a husband; I am not

my wife's husband in the sense in which the Queen of England
has a husband. My wife is not the slave woman in Abraham's
house, whom I banish with the child,[93] but neither is she a
goddess with whom I wheel around in amorous capers. I have
a home, and this home certainly is not everything to me; but
this I do know, that I have been everything to my wife, partly
because she in all humility has believed it, partly because I personally know that I have been and will be that as far as it is possible for a person to be that to another. Here I am able to enlighten you concerning the beauty in a person's being able to
be everything to another without a reminder of it by any finite
or specific thing whatsoever. I can speak all the more boldly on
this point, for she surely does not stand in the shadows. She
did not need me; the one I married was not a poor girl for
whom I did a good deed—as the world says in all possible contempt for itself. She was not an affected silly whom I married
for other reasons and of whom I have now made something
good through my wisdom. She was independent and, what is
more, so contented that she did not need to let herself be sold;
she was sound, sounder than I, even though more intense. Her
life, of course, could never be as active as mine or as reflective;
with my experience I perhaps could save her from many a mistake, but her soundness made that superfluous. Truly, she
owes me nothing, and yet I am everything to her. She has not
needed me, but I have not therefore been unimportant. I have
guarded her and still sleep, like Nehemiah, with my weapon
at my side[94]—to repeat a phrase that slipped out of my mouth
on a similar occasion and to show you that I have not forgotten
your sarcastic remark that it must be quite a *gêne* [inconveni-
ence] to my wife. My young friend, such remarks do not
bother me, as you can see from the fact that I repeat it and, I
assure you, without anger. Thus I have been altogether nothing and yet everything to her. You, however, have been everything to a goodly number of people, and yet basically you have
been nothing at all to them. And just suppose that in the temporary contacts you have with people you were able to supply
someone or other with such a treasure of the interesting, were
able to prompt so much creativity in himself that he would

II
75

have sufficient for his lifetime, something that, after all, is presumably impossible, but just suppose he really gained through you—you yourself, you would lose, for you nevertheless would have found no individual for whom you could wish to be everything, and even if this is part of your greatness, then this greatness is really so distressing that I pray God to spare me it.

In order to divest oneself of every unsound and despicable idea of comfort, this is the idea one must first and foremost link to the home, that it is a task. Even in the husband's enjoyment there ought to be an element of task,[95] even if this does not manifest itself in a specific external tangible task. In this respect, the husband can be very active although he does not appear to be, whereas the wife's domestic activity is more visible.

But next there is such a concretion of details linked to the idea of a home that it is very difficult to say anything about them in general. In this respect, every household has its distinctiveness, and it might be very interesting to know a number of them. But of course it holds true that every such distinctiveness is permeated by a certain mentality, and I for one am revolted by all this separatistic odious practice in families that deliberately starts right off to show how exclusive everything is with them, which sometimes goes so far that the family speaks its own private language or speaks in such mysterious allusions that one cannot make heads or tails out of them. The point is that the family does possess such a distinctiveness—the art is to know how to hide it.

Those who marry to have a home always plead that there is no one who is waiting for them, no one who welcomes them, etc. This adequately indicates that they actually have a home only when they think of being outside it. Thank God, I never need to go out in order to remember or to forget that I have a home. Often the feeling of having a home comes over me suddenly when I least expect it. I do not need to go into either the living room or the dining room to be sure of it. Often this feeling can come over me when I am sitting all alone in my study. It can come over me when the door of my room opens and a moment later I see a lively face at the door pane and the curtain is closed again, and there is a very soft knock at the door, and after that a head peeks through the door in such a way that one could believe that the head did not belong to any body, and then in a flash she is standing by my side and vanishes again. This home-feeling can come over me late at night when I am sitting all alone as in the old days in my college room; then, I may light my lamp, tiptoe softly into her bedroom to see if she is really sleeping. Of course, this feeling often comes over me when I come home. And when I have rung the doorbell she knows that it is at the time I usually come home (we poor bureaucrats are so handicapped in this way that we are unable to surprise our wives), she recognizes the way I usually ring—then when I hear the noise and clamor of children inside, and of her as well, for she heads this little flock and is herself so childlike that she seems to compete with the children in shouting with joy—then I feel that I have a home. And then if I look serious (you talk so much about being a connoisseur of human nature, but who knows human nature the way a woman does!), how this almost exuberant child changes; she does not become desperate, does not feel bad, but there is a power in her that is not hard but is infinitely flexible, like a sword that could bite stone and yet is coiled around the waist. Or if she can see that I am a bit irritable (good Lord, that also happens), how accommodating she can be, and yet how much superiority there is in this accommodating.

Whatever else I might wish to say to you on this occasion I prefer to link to a particular expression I believe can be properly applied to you, an expression you yourself often use: that you are a stranger and an alien in the world.[96] Younger men, who have no conception of the high price paid for experience, but who also have no intimation of its inexpressible wealth, can easily be sucked into the same whirlpool, can perhaps feel influenced by what you say as by a fresh wind that coaxes them out onto the infinite sea that you show to them. You yourself can become youthfully intoxicated, almost beyond control, by the thought of this infinity that is your element, an element that like the ocean conceals everything unchanged in its depths. Should not you, who already are an experienced man in these waters, know how to tell of disaster and distress at sea?

Of course, on this ocean one person usually does not know much about another. One does not fit out huge vessels such as are launched with difficulty out on the deep. No, one fits out very small boats, jolly boats for one person only. One seizes the moment, unfurls one's sail, sweeps along with the infinite speed of restless thoughts, alone on the infinite ocean, alone under the infinite heaven. This life is dangerous, but one is intimate with the thought of losing it, for it is a real joy to vanish into the infinite in such a way that just enough remains so that one enjoys this vanishing. Seafarers tell that out on the great oceans of the world there is seen a kind of vessel called the Flying Dutchman. It can spread a little sail and with infinite speed sweep over the surface of the ocean. This is just about the way you navigate on the ocean of life.

Alone in his kayak,[97] a person is sufficient unto himself, has nothing to do with any person except when he himself so wishes. Alone in his kayak, a person is sufficient unto himself—but I cannot really understand how this emptiness can be filled, but since you are the only person among my acquaintances about whom this is true to a degree, I also know that you do have a person on board who can help fill up the time. You should say, therefore: Alone in one's boat, alone with one's sorrow, alone with one's despair—which one is cowardly enough to prefer to keep rather than to submit to the pain of healing. Allow me to point out the dark side of your life—not as if I wished to make you fearful; I do not have anything to do with playing the bogeyman, and you are too clever to let yourself be affected by such things. But nevertheless think of the pain, sadness, and humiliation involved in being in this sense a stranger and an alien in the world.

I will not confuse the impression I can possibly make on you by irritating you with the thought of turbid family solidarity, the barn air you detest; but think of family life in its beauty, founded on a deep and intimate community in such a way that what joins it all together is still mysteriously hidden, the one relationship ingeniously entwined with the other so that one has only an intimation of the coherence; think of this family's concealed internal life, clad in such a beautiful external form that one nowhere encounters the hardness of the joints—and now contemplate your relation to such a family. A family like that would appeal particularly to you, and you perhaps would enjoy visiting them often and because of your ease would soon be as if on terms of intimacy with them. I say "as if," for it is clear that you cannot possibly be on such terms, since you will always remain a stranger and an alien. They would regard you as a welcome guest, perhaps would be friendly enough to make everything as pleasant as possible for you; the members of the family would be courteous to you—indeed, they would treat you as one treats a child one likes. And you—you would be inexhaustible in attentiveness, inventive in all ways of delighting the family. It would be very lovely, would it not, and presumably in some odd moment you might be tempted to say that you really did not care to see the family in houserobes, or the daughter in bedroom slippers, or the wife without her cap, and yet, if you look more closely, there is an enormous humiliation for you in the family's correct behavior toward you. Every family would have to behave in this way, and you would become the humiliated one. Or do you not believe that the family conceals a totally different life of its own, which is its shrine; do you not believe that every family still has household gods, even if it does not place them in the front hall? And does not your comment conceal a very refined weakness, for I truly do not believe that you could stand to see your wife—if you ever were to marry—in dishabille, unless this costume were finery designed to please you. You no doubt think that you have done much to entertain the family, to cast a certain esthetic sheen over it, but suppose the family did not think much of this in comparison with the inner life it has. So it would go with you in relation to every family, and no matter how proud you are, there is a humiliation involved here.

No one shares his grief with you; no one confides in you. You no doubt think that it often is the case that you have indeed gained a wealth of psychological observations, but this is often an illusion, for people are quite willing to chat casually

II
78

with you and remotely touch on or drop a hint of a concern, because the interesting that thereby stirs in you soothes the pain and in itself already has a charm that makes one desire this medicine, even without needing it. And if someone approached you precisely because of your isolated position (as you know, people would rather speak with a mendicant friar than with their father confessor), it still would never truly mean anything, neither for you nor for him; not for him because he would sense the arbitrariness implicit in confiding in you; not for you because you would not be able to disregard entirely the ambiguity in which your competence rested. You are undeniably a good operator; you know how to penetrate into the most secret enclosures of sorrow and care, yet in such a way that you do not forget the way back. Well, now, I assume that you succeeded in healing your patient, but you had no genuine and deep joy from it, for the whole thing had an air of arbitrariness and you had no responsibility.

II
79

Only responsibility gives a blessing and true joy, and it does so even if one cannot do it half as well as you; it often gives a blessing when one does nothing at all.[98] But when one has a home, then one has a responsibility, and in itself this responsibility gives security and joy. Precisely because you do not want to have responsibility you must find it entirely in order that people are ungrateful to you—something that you frequently complain about. You, however, rarely have anything to do with healing people; as I told you before, generally your main occupation tends to destroy illusions and occasionally to maneuver people into illusions. When one sees you with one or two young men, how with a few motions you have already helped them a considerable distance beyond all the childish, and in many ways helpful, illusions, how they now become lighter than actuality, how their wings shoot out, while you yourself, like an old and experienced bird, give them an idea of what a wing stroke is, whereby one can fly over all of existence; or when you conduct the same training of young girls and compare the differences in flights, how one hears the wing beat in masculine flight, whereas feminine flight is like rowing dreamily—when one sees this, who then because of your skill

can be angry with you, but who because of your wanton irre-
sponsibility ought not to be angry with you. You can certainly
say of your heart what the old song says:

> *Mein Herz ist wie ein Taubenhaus:*
> *Die Eine fliegt herein, die Andre fliegt heraus*
> [My heart is like a dovecote:
> The one flies in, the other flies out],[99]

except that as far as you are concerned one does not see them
fly in as much as one sees new ones continually flying out. But
a dovecote, no matter how beautiful a symbol of a quiet domestic home it is, must really not be used in this way.

II
80

Is it not painful and sad just to let life go by in this way without ever finding solidity in it; is it not sad, my young friend,
that life never acquires content for you. There is something
sad in the feeling that one is growing older, but it is a much
more profound sadness that comes over a person if he cannot
grow old. At this very moment, I feel how justified I am in
calling you "my young friend." A distance of seven years is
certainly no eternity; I am not going to praise myself for maturity of understanding superior to yours, but I certainly do
for a maturity of life. Yes, I feel that I have really grown older,
but you still continually cling to the initial surprise of youth.
And if at times, even though seldom, I feel world-weary, that,
too, is bound together with a quiet sublimation—I think of
those beautiful words: Blessed are they who rest from their la-
bors.[100] I do not delude myself into thinking that I have had a
great task in life; I have not rejected what was assigned to me.
And even if it was insignificant, it has also been my task to be
happy in it, although it was insignificant. You certainly do not
rest from your labor; for your rest is a curse—you can live only
in restlessness. Rest is your opposite; rest makes you more
restless. You are like a starving man whom eating only makes
more hungry, a thirsty man whom drinking only makes more
thirsty.

But I go back to the preceding discussion, to the finite objectives for which people enter marriage. I have mentioned
only three because they always seem to be of some relevance,

because they do nevertheless reflect upon one or another particular element in marriage, although in their one-sidedness they become just as ludicrous as they are unesthetic and irreligious. I make no mention of a multiplicity of altogether puny objectives, because they are not even laughable. For example, marrying for money, or out of jealousy, or because of the prospects, because there is the prospect that she will soon die—or that she will live a long time but become a well-favored branch that bears much fruit, so that through her one can sweep the property of a whole row of deceased uncles and aunts into one's pocket. I do not care to bring up all such things.

II
81

As a result of this exploration, I can stress here that marriage, in order to be esthetic and religious, must have no finite "why," but this was precisely the esthetic in the first love, and thus here again marriage stands *au niveau* [on a level] with first love. And this is the esthetic in marriage—that it hides in itself a multiplicity of "whys" that life discloses in all its blessedness.

But since I set out primarily to show the esthetic validity of marriage, and since that whereby marriage was distinguished from first love was the ethical and the religious, but in turn the ethical and religious, insofar as they seek their expression in something particular, find this best in the marriage ceremony, I shall dwell on this subject—lest I seem to treat the matter too lightly, lest I make myself the least bit guilty of seeming to be hiding the schism between first love and marriage that you and many others, even though for different reasons, stipulate. You may be right in saying that if a host of people do not take exception to this schism, the reason is that they lack the energy and education to reflect on either the one or the other. Meanwhile, let us take a closer look at the marriage ceremony and its formulations. Perhaps you will discover that I am also well armed in what I am about to say, and of that I can assure you without incommoding my wife, for she quite approves of my holding off freebooters such as you and your ilk. Moreover, I think that, just as a Christian always ought to be able to explain his faith,[101] so also a married man ought to be able to explain his marriage, not simply to anyone who deigns to ask, but to anyone he thinks worthy of it, or even if, as *in casu* [in this case], unworthy, he finds it propitious to do so. And since of late you, having devastated a host of other landscapes, are about to ravage the province of marriage, I feel called upon to challenge you.

That you are acquainted with the formulary of the wedding ceremony, have indeed made a study of it, I assume. On the whole, you are always well armed for war and usually never begin to attack something before you are just as well informed about it as its most tested defenders. This is why it sometimes happens, as you yourself lament, that your attacks are too good and that those who are supposed to defend are not as well informed as you who are attacking. Now we shall see.

But before going to the particular question, let us see if there is anything disturbing in the wedding ceremony itself considered only as ceremony. After all, the wedding ceremony is not something the lovers themselves thought up in an opulent moment, something they could abandon if they thought of something else along the way. Hence, it is a power that we encounter. But does love need to acknowledge any power other than itself? You perhaps are willing to admit that as soon as doubt and concern have taught a person to pray he would put up with bowing to such a power, but first love does not need that. Please remember that we have assumed the individuals under consideration to be religiously developed. Therefore, I am not discussing how the religious can make its way in a person but how it can co-exist with first love, and just as unhappy love can make a person religious, just as surely religious individuals are able to love. The religious is not so alien to human nature that there must first be a break in order to awaken it. But if the individuals involved are religious, then the power that they encounter in the wedding ceremony is not alien, and just as their love unites them in a higher unity, so the religious lifts them up in a still higher unity.

What does the wedding ceremony do, then? First of all, it gives an overview of the genesis of the human race and thereby binds the new marriage in the great body of the human race. It thereby provides the universal, the purely human, calls it forth in the consciousness. This jars on you; you perhaps say: It is distasteful to be reminded, at the very moment one is uniting so intimately with another person, that everything else vanishes, that *es ist eine alte Geschichte* [it is an old story],[102] something that has happened, is happening, and will happen. You wish to delight precisely in that which is unique in your love, you want to have the full passion of love blaze up in you, and you do not want to be disturbed by the thought that every Tom, Dick, and Harry is doing the same thing. "It is extremely prosaic to be reminded of one's statistical significance: In the year 1750, at ten o'clock, Mr. John Doe and demure Miss Jane Doe, and at eleven o'clock the same day, Mr. John Doe and Miss Jane Doe." Now this sounds quite terrible, but hiding in your argument is a reflection that has disturbed first love.

As noted previously, love is a union of the universal and the particular, but to want to enjoy the particular, in the sense in which you do, evidences a reflection that places the particular outside the universal. The more the universal and the particular penetrate each other, the more beautiful the love. The greatness is not in being the particular either in the immediate or in the higher sense but in possessing the universal in the particular. Therefore, to be reminded of the universal cannot be a disturbing introduction to first love. The wedding ceremony also does more than that; namely, in order to refer to the universal it leads the lovers back to the first parents. Consequently, it does not stop with the universal *in abstracto* but shows it as manifested in the first couple of the human race. This is a clue to the nature of every marriage. Like every human life, every marriage is simultaneously this particular and nevertheless the whole, simultaneously individual and symbol. Consequently, it gives the lovers the most beautiful picture of two human beings who are not disturbed by reflection about others; it says to the two individuals: You also are a couple just like them; the same event is being repeated here in you, and you also are standing here alone in the infinite world, alone in the presence of God. Therefore, you see that the wed-

II
83

ding ceremony does provide what you are demanding, but it also provides more in simultaneously providing the universal and the particular.

"But the wedding ceremony declares that sin has entered into the world, and it certainly is discordant to be reminded so emphatically of sin at the very moment one feels most pure. Thereupon it teaches that sin entered the world along with marriage, and this is hardly encouraging to those being married. The Church, of course, can wash its hands of any eventual distressing outcome, for it has not indulged them in any vain hope." That the Church does not indulge in a vain hope certainly ought to be regarded in and by itself as something good. Furthermore, the Church declares that sin came into the world along with marriage and yet permits it; the Church declares that sin came along with marriage, but whether it teaches that this was on account of marriage could still be very problematic. In any case, it proclaims sin only as man's universal lot, does not apply it specifically to the single individual, and least of all does it say: You are now about to commit a sin. To be sure, it is a very difficult matter to explain in what sense sin came along with marriage; here sin and the sensuous might seem to be regarded as identical. But that certainly cannot be the case, inasmuch as the Church allows marriage.[103] Yes, you will say—but not until it has removed all the beauty out of earthly love. To which I would respond: By no means—at least there is not a word about that in the wedding ceremony.

The Church next declares the punishment of sin, that the woman shall bear children in pain and be subservient to her husband. But the first of these consequences is of such a nature that even if the Church did not declare it, it would declare itself. Yes, you answer, but the disturbing thing about it is that it is asserted to be the result of sin. You find it to be esthetically beautiful that a child is born in pain; it shows regard for a human being, is a symbolic mark of the significance it indeed has that a human being comes into the world, in contrast to the animals, which, the lower they are on the scale, bring their young into the world with all the greater ease. Here I must again emphasize that it is declared as the universal destiny of humankind, and that a child is born in sin is the most profound expression of its highest worth, that it is precisely a transfiguration of human life that everything related to it is assigned to the category of sin.[104]

Then it says that the woman shall be subservient to her husband. Here you will perhaps say: Well, now, that is beautiful, and it has always appealed to me to see a woman who in her husband loved her master. But that this is supposed to be a consequence of sin shocks you, and you feel called upon to come forward as the chivalrous champion of the woman. Whether you are doing her a service thereby, I shall leave undecided, but I do believe that you have not grasped in all its inwardness the essence of woman, part of which is that she is simultaneously more perfect and more imperfect than the man. If we wish to characterize the most pure and perfect, we say "a woman"; if we wish to characterize the weakest and most fragile, we say "a woman"; if we want to convey a conception of the spirituality elevated above the sensuous, we say "a woman"; if we want to convey a conception of the sensuous, we say "a woman"; if we wish to characterize innocence in all its uplifting greatness, we say "a woman"; if we wish to characterize the depressing feeling of guilt, we say "a woman." Thus in a certain sense woman is more perfect than man, and Scripture expresses this by saying that she has more guilt.[105] If you recall again that the Church declares only the universal human lot of woman, then I do not discern that anything disquieting can eventuate for first love, although admittedly for the reflection that does not know how to maintain her in this possibility. Moreover, the Church certainly does not make woman a mere slave; it says: "And God said I will make a companion for Adam,"[106] an expression that has just as much esthetic warmth as it has truth. This is why the Church teaches: "Therefore a man shall leave his father and his mother and cleave to his wife."[107] We would rather have expected it to read: The woman shall leave her father and mother and cleave to her husband—for the woman, after all, is weaker than the man. In the expression of Scripture there is an implicit recognition of the woman's significance, and no knight could be more chivalrous toward her.[108]

Finally, with regard to the curse that fell to the man's lot, the circumstance that he must eat his bread in the sweat of his brow certainly seems to chase him, with a single sentence, out of the honeymoon days[109] of first love. That this curse, like all divine curses, as we are often reminded, conceals a blessing proves nothing at this point, inasmuch as the experience of it is always reserved for a future time. I do want to remind you, however, that first love is not cowardly, that it does not fear dangers, and that it will not for that reason see in this curse a difficulty that can terrify it.

What does the wedding ceremony do, then? "It halts the lovers." Not at all—but it allows what was already in motion to appear in the external world. It affirms the universally human, and in this sense sin also, but all the anxiety and torment that wishes that sin had never come into the world is based on a reflection that first love does not know.[110] To wish that sin had never entered the world is to lead mankind back to the more imperfect. Sin has come in, but when the individuals have humbled themselves under this, they stand higher than they stood before.

Then the Church turns to the single individual and addresses some questions to him. This may again prompt a reflection: "Why such questions? Love has in itself its own assurance." But the Church, after all, does not ask these questions in order to shake but to firm up—and to allow what is already firm to express itself. Here, then, the difficulty arises that in its question the Church does not seem to take account of the erotic at all. It asks: Have you counseled with God and your conscience, then with friends and acquaintances? I shall not stress here the great advantage in the profoundly earnest asking of this kind of question by the Church. The Church—to use one of your own phrases—is not a matchmaker. Can this, then, disturb the ones involved? In their gratitude, they have indeed taken their love to God and in this way counseled with him, for, even though indirect, it certainly is taking counsel with God when I thank him. Thus when the Church does not ask them whether they love each other, it is by no means because it wants to do away with earthly love but because it presupposes it.

Then the Church administers a vow. We saw previously how love admirably lets itself be taken up into a higher concentricity. The intention makes the individual free, but, as already explained, the freer the individual is, the more esthetically beautiful is the marriage.

Thus I believe it has become apparent that, insofar as one seeks the esthetic in first love in its present tense, in its immediate infinity, marriage must be regarded as its transfiguration and even more beautiful than first love. I trust that this has been made clear in what I have written previously and also that we have seen in what I have just written that all the talk about the Church's disparagement is baseless and is carried on only by one for whom the religious has caused offense.

But if the situation is as described, the rest follows by itself. The question, namely, is this: Can this love be actualized? After having conceded everything up to this point, you perhaps will say: Well, it is just as difficult to actualize marriage as to actualize first love. To that I must respond: No, for in marriage there is a law of motion. First love remains an unreal *an-sich* [in itself] that never acquires inner substance because it moves only in an external medium. In the ethical and religious intention, marital love has the possibility of an inner history and is as different from first love as the historical is from the unhistorical. This love is strong, stronger than the whole world, but the moment it doubts it is annihilated; it is like a sleepwalker who is able to walk the most dangerous places with complete security but plunges down when someone calls his name. Marital love is armed, for in the intention not only is attentiveness directed to the surrounding world but the will is directed toward itself, toward the inner world.

And now I turn everything around and say: The esthetic is not in the immediate but in the acquired; but marriage is precisely that immediacy which contains mediacy, that infinity which contains finitude, that eternity which contains temporality. Thus, marriage proves to be ideal in a double sense, both in the classical and in the romantic sense.[111] When I say that the esthetic consists in the acquired, it does not at all mean that it lies in the mere striving as such. This is indeed negative, but the merely negative is never esthetic. When, however, it is a striving that in itself has content, a struggle that in itself has the victory, then in this duplexity I have the esthetic.

II
87

This, I believe, ought to be borne in mind in regard to the enthusiasm of despair with which our age hears the acquired recommended in contrast to the immediate, as if it were this it depended upon to destroy everything lock, stock, and barrel in order to build anew. It has really made me uneasy to hear the jubilation with which younger men, just like the terrorists in the French Revolution, shout: *de omnibus dubitandum*.[112] Perhaps I am prejudiced. But I do believe, however, that we must distinguish between personal and scientific doubt.[113] Personal doubt is always a special matter, and such an enthusiasm for destruction, which we hear so much about, has at best the result that a goodly number of men venture out but do not have the power[114] to doubt, and they succumb or become irresolute, which is likewise certain destruction. But if an individual's wrestling in doubt develops the power that in turn overcomes the doubt, such a sight is elevating, since it shows the quality of person, but it is not really beautiful, because to be that requires that it have immediacy within itself. Such a development produced in the highest degree through doubt aims at what in an extreme expression is called: making one into a completely different person. Beauty, however, consists in this, that immediacy is acquired in and with the doubt. I must emphasize this in opposition to the abstraction in which doubt has been affirmed, the idolatry with which people have engaged in it, the rashness with which people have plunged into it, the blind trust with which people have hoped for a glorious result from it.

Then, too, the more spiritual the hoped-for gain, the more doubt can be praised; but love always belongs to a realm in which it is not so much a question of something acquired as of something given, and something given that is acquired. I cannot conceive at all what kind of doubt this would be. Would it

be the right pattern for a married man to have had sorry experiences, to have learned to doubt, and would the marriage
that ensued be truly beautiful if by virtue of this doubt he married with tremendous moral earnestness and was faithful and
constant as a husband? We will praise him but not commend
his marriage except as an example of what a person is able to
do. Or, in order to be a complete doubter, should he also
doubt her love and the possibility of maintaining the beauty of
this relationship and still have the stoicism to will it? I know it
very well; you false teachers are very willing to praise such a
thing precisely in order that your false teaching may find favor
more easily. You praise it when it serves your purpose and say:
Look, this is the true marriage. But you know very well that
this praise conceals a criticism, and that the woman especially
is not served thereby, and in this way you do all you can to
tempt her. Therefore, you divide and separate by the old rule:
divide et impera [divide and rule].[115] You eulogize first love.
When you have your way, it becomes an element that lies outside time, a mysterious something about which any lie can be
told. Marriage cannot hide itself in this way, it takes days and
years to blossom—what an easy opportunity to tear down or
to build up with such traitorous observations that a desperate
resignation is required to endure it.

This much stands established between us: considered as an
element, marital love [*Kjærlighed*] is not only just as beautiful
as the first but even more beautiful, because in its immediacy
it contains a unity in several contrasts. Thus it is not true that
marriage is an exceedingly respectable but tiresomely moral
role and that erotic love [*Elskov*] is poetry; no, marriage is
really the poetic. And if the world has often witnessed with
pain that a first love cannot be sustained, I shall grieve along
with the world but shall also bring to mind that the defect was
not so much in what happened later as in its not beginning
rightly. What the first love lacks, then, is the second esthetic
ideal, the historical.[116] It does not have the law of motion in
itself. If I were to regard faith in personal life as equally immediate, first love would correspond to a faith that in the
power of the promise would believe itself capable of moving

mountains[117] and would then go around and perform miracles. Perhaps it would succeed, but this faith would have no history, for a recitation of all its miracles is not its history, whereas the appropriation of faith in personal life is faith's history. This motion marital love does have, for in the intention the motion is directed inward. In the religious, it lets God, so to speak, take care of the whole world; in the intention, it will fight together with God for itself, will gain itself in patience.[118] In the consciousness of sin, a conception of human frailty is a component, but in the intention it is perceived as surmounted. I cannot emphasize this enough with regard to marital love. I surely have done full justice to first love, and I believe I am even a better extoller of it than you are, but its defect lies in its abstract character.

Marital love, therefore, has something more in it, as you can see also from the fact that it is able to relinquish itself. Suppose that the first love could not be actualized; then, if it was truly a marital love, the individuals would be able to relinquish it and still possess its sweetness, even though in another sense. First love can never do this. But from this it by no means follows that it was doubt that provided marital love with its resignation, as if it were a belittlement of first love. If that was the case, then it was indeed no resignation, and yet perhaps no one knows better how sweet it is than the person who resigns it and yet has the power for it; but in turn this power is just as great when it is a matter of holding on to the love, of actualizing it in life. It takes the same power to relinquish it as to hold on to it, and the true holding on is the power that was capable of relinquishing and now expresses itself in holding on, and only in this lies the true freedom in holding on, the true, secure soaring.

Marital love manifests itself as historical by being a process of assimilation; it tries its hand at what is experienced and refers what it has experienced to itself. Consequently, it is not an uninterested witness to what happens but is essentially participative—in short, it experiences its own development. Romantic love, to be sure, also refers to itself what it experienced—for example, when the knight sends to his beloved the banners etc. won in battle; but even if romantic love could imagine all the time involved in such conquests, it still could never occur to it that love should have a history. The prosaic view goes to the opposite extreme. It can well imagine that love gains a history,[119] but as a rule it is a brief history, and this history is so common and pedestrian that love may soon acquire feet on which to walk. Imaginatively constructing love also acquires a kind of history, but, just as it has no true apriority, it also has no continuity and is confined to the arbitrariness of the experimenting individual who is simultaneously his own world and his own fate in it. Experimenting love is therefore much inclined to inquire into the state of love and so has a double delight—on the one hand, when the outcome corresponds to the reckoning, and on the other, when it appears that something completely different has come out of it. When this happens, it is also satisfied, since it has a task for its inexhaustible composing.

II
90

Marital love, however, has not only apriority in itself but also constancy in itself, and the energizing power in this constancy is the same as the law of motion—it is the intention. In the intention, something else is posited, but this something else is also posited as something surmounted; in the intention, this something else is posited as an internal something else, inasmuch as even the external is seen in its reflection in the internal. The historical consists in the emergence of this something else and the acquiring of its validity, but precisely in its validity it is seen as something that should not have validity. Thus love, tested and purified, issues from this movement and assimilates what is experienced. How this something else emerges does not lie within the power of the individual, who is not related by way of constructing; but in its apriority love has still been victorious also over all this without knowing it.

To be sure, somewhere in the New Testament it reads: Every gift is good if it is received with thanksgiving.[120] The majority of people are willing to be grateful when they receive a good gift, but then they demand that it be left to them to decide which gift is good. This proves their shallowness; but that other thankfulness is truly triumphant and a priori, because it

has an intrinsic eternal soundness that is undismayed even by
a bad gift—not because one knows how to spurn it, but because of the boldness, the high personal courage, that dares to
thank for it. So it also is with love. At this point it would never
enter my head to respond to all the jeremiads you always jo-
cosely have ready for the edification of worried husbands, and
I hope that this time you will restrain yourself, inasmuch as
you are dealing with a married man who simply cannot tempt
you to have the fun of making him even more confused.

But while I am thus tracing love from its cryptogamous
concealment to its phanerogamous life, I encounter along the
way a difficulty that you surely will say has no slight significance. *Posito*, I assume,[121] that I managed to convince you that
the religious and ethical, which in marital love joins first love,
by no means detracts from it, and that you deeply convinced
yourself of this in your innermost being and now by no means
would reject a religious point of departure. Then, alone with
her whom you loved, you would humble yourself and your
love under God. You are really gripped and moved, but now
watch out—I say just one word, "the congregation," and at
once, as it says in the ballad, everything vanishes again.[122] I do
not think you will ever be able to ignore the category of inwardness. "The congregation, the blessed parish, which despite its plurality still is a moral character—yes, even if it had,
just as it has all the boring qualities of moral characters, also
the good quality of having only one head on one neck[123]
. . . . . I know very well what I would do."

You no doubt know of the insane man who had the fixed
idea that his apartment was full of flies[124] so that he was in danger of being smothered by them. In the anxiety of despair and
with the rage of despair, he fought for his life. In the same way
you, too, seem to be fighting for your life against a similar
imaginary swarm of flies, against what you call "the congregation." The matter, however, is not so dangerous; nevertheless I shall first of all go through the most important point of
contact with the congregation. Before doing so, may I recall
that first love simply does not dare reckon to its advantage that
it does not know such difficulties, for this is due to its keeping

itself fixedly abstract and not coming into contact with actuality at all. You know very well how to distinguish among the abstract relationships to the surrounding world, the abstraction of which cancels the relationships. You can even put up with having to pay the clergyman, the parish clerk, and a government official, for money is an excellent means of distancing every relationship. That is also why you let me in on your plan never to do anything and never to accept anything, not the least little thing, without giving or receiving money. By implication, if you ever do get married, you are capable of paying a *douceur* [tip] to everyone who comes to witness to his joy over this step. In that case, it must not surprise you that the congregation increases in number, or if what the man with the flies feared actually does happen to you. What you fear, then, is the personal relationships that by way of inquiries, congratulations, compliments, yes, even through the giving of presents, lay claim to entering into a relationship to you that is incommensurable with money and seek to manifest all possible sharing, although especially on this occasion you would rather be without it for the sake of both you and your beloved. "With money one can avoid a host of ludicrous situations. With money a person can stop the mouth of the church trumpeter who otherwise would trumpet in the national assembly for one; with money he can avoid being proclaimed a married man before the whole congregation, an upright married man, and that despite one's wishing *in casu* [in this case] to limit oneself to being that for one single person."

This is not my invention, this sketch; it is yours. Can you remember how you fumed one time on the occasion of a church wedding? You wished, just as at ordination services all the clergymen present come up and lay their hands upon the ordinand, that similarly all the tenderly participating fraternity present would kiss the bride and bridegroom with a congregational kiss. Indeed, you declared that it was impossible for you to speak the words "bride and bridegroom" without thinking of that impressive moment when a fond father or an old friend rises with his glass to utter with deep emotion those beautiful words: bride and bridegroom. For just as you found the whole church ceremony superbly designed to stifle the erotic, so the subsequent worldliness was as improper as the church ceremony was all too proper, "for it was improper, ludicrous, insipid to place a quasi husband and wife together at a dinner table and thereby prompt the biased and untrue and unbeautiful reflection about whether it is the Church's decree that makes them a married couple." Consequently, you seem to prefer a quiet wedding. I have nothing against that but merely inform you that here you will be pronounced just as fully to be a proper married man. Perhaps you are better able to tolerate the words when no one else hears them. Moreover, may I remind you that the marriage service does not say "before the whole congregation" but [125]"before God and this congregation," a phrase that neither dismays by its limitation nor lacks boldness.

As for anything else you have to say on this, even if said with your customary indiscretion, I can better forgive you because you are still attacking only the social aspects. As far as they are concerned, everyone may have his own opinion, and even though I am a long way from sanctioning your *Sprødigkeit* [coyness], I shall nevertheless be as tolerant as possible. Presumably we will always disagree on them. I regard it as important to live within them, to bring something beautiful out of them if one is capable of it, to submit to them and put up with them if one is incapable of that. I see no danger at all to a person's love in having the banns read from the pulpit; neither do I believe that such an announcement is harmful to the audience, as you with your exaggerated rigidity once made out when you insisted that reading the banns ought to be abolished because so many people, especially women, went to church only to hear them and thus the impact of the sermon was destroyed. There is something untrue in the basis of your apprehensiveness, as if all such trifles could disturb a sound and strong love. With regard to this, it is by no means my intention to come to the defense of every nuisance that is prevalent. When I stand up firmly for the congregation, I do not identify this with an "esteemed public," which, to recall a line by Goethe, "is sufficiently shameless to believe that everything a

II
93

person undertakes he does in order to provide material for conversation."[126]

Another observation, one that for me also accounts for your excessive anxiety about all sociality and commotion, is that you are afraid you will miss out on the erotic moment. You know how to keep your soul as apathetic and motionless as a bird of prey pausing motionless before it plunges down; you know that the moment is not in one's power, and that nevertheless the most beautiful lies in the moment; this is why you understand how to keep watch, do not wish to anticipate anything with the restlessness in which you await the moment. But when such an event is assigned to a specific time that one knows long in advance, when one is perpetually reminded of it by the preparations, then there is the danger of "missing the point." This shows that you have not grasped the nature of marital love and that you harbor a heretical and superstitious belief in first love.

Now let us ponder whether this matter of the congregation is actually so dangerous when it, please note, is not permitted to assume such a terrifying shape as it momentarily assumes in your sick brain. Your life certainly has brought you not merely into contact, no, into intimate connection, with a few individuals, remembrance of whom does not disquiet you, does not disturb the ideality in you, whose names you say aloud to yourself when you want to encourage yourself to the good, whose presence expands your soul, whose personalities are for you a disclosure of the noble and the sublime. Should it now disturb you to have such associates? It is almost as if a person were to declare with regard to religion, "I wish with all my heart to maintain my fellowship with God and Christ, but I cannot bear to have him confess me before all the holy angels."[127]

On the other hand, your life, the outer circumstances of your life, has certainly brought you into contact with others to whom joys and beautiful, significant interruptions are only sparsely allotted in the humdrum routine of daily life. Does not every family know some people like that among its acquaintances, perhaps even in its midst, and is it not beautiful

II
94

that these people, almost forsaken in their loneliness, have a place of resort in a family. For them a marriage would be a significant event, a little poetic island in their everyday life, something they can look forward to long in advance and remember long afterwards. In a family I visit, I frequently see an old spinster who is contemporary with the mistress of the house. She still remembers very vividly the wedding day, alas, perhaps more vividly than the wife herself—how the bride was adorned, every little incidental circumstance. Would you then rob all such people of the opportunity for happiness that you could provide them?

Let us deal lovingly with the frail. Many a marriage has been entered into in all secrecy in order to relish its joy properly, and time perhaps brought something different, so little joy that one could be tempted to say: Well, it still might have had the significance of giving a number of people some joy—then it would nevertheless have been something. You know that I hate, just as much as you, all impertinences about families, but for one thing I know how to keep them out of my life, and, for another, how to rise above them, and you with your bitterness, your polemics, your fire—should you not understand how to clear the area? You do, indeed, but it disturbs you nonetheless. I will not dictate restrictions to you; toss out what disturbs you, but do not forget altogether my principle, do not forget to actualize, if it is possible for you, the even more beautiful; remember that the art is to save such people if it can be done, not to defend yourself. I could enjoin this upon you as a prudential rule, for you know full well that the more a person isolates himself the more almost obtrusive he makes all these idle, gossipy people, you who so often have played your game with them by making them curious and then letting the whole thing dissolve into nothing! I could enjoin this as a prudential rule but shall not, for I have too much respect for the truth of what I am saying to want to degrade it.

Every coming into existence [*Tilblivelse*], the sounder it is, always has an element of the polemic, all the more so the sounder it is, and in the same way every marriage tie also has this. You know very well that I despise laxity in the family, the

vapid *communio bonorum* [joint ownership of property] that can
give a marriage the appearance of one's having married the
whole family.[128] If the marital love is a true first love, then
there is also some concealment about it; it has no desire to
make a display of itself, does not devote its life to appearing on
all festive occasions, does not draw its nourishment from congratulations and compliments or from a divine worship as it
can be arranged in the family. You know that very well; just
let your wit make a game of all this. In many ways, I can agree
with you, and I believe that it would not hurt you and the
good cause if you were to let me, like the experienced, kind
forester, point out the decayed trees to be chopped down, but
then mark a cross in other places also.

I have no hesitation at all in declaring secretiveness to be the
absolute condition for preserving the esthetic in marriage, not
in the sense that one should aim at it, pursue it, take it in vain,
let the only real enjoyment be in the enjoyment of secretiveness. One of the favorite fancies of first love is that it will take
flight to an uninhabited island. Now this has often enough
been made ludicrous, and I shall not take part in the iconoclas-
tic ferocity of our age. The defect in it is that first love believes
it cannot be actualized in any other way than by taking flight.
This is a misunderstanding that is rooted in its unhistorical
character. The art is to remain in the multiplicity and still preserve the secret. Here again I could enjoin it as a prudential rule
that only by remaining among people does the secretiveness
acquire its true energy; only by this opposition does its point
drill in more and more deeply. I shall refrain from doing it for
the same reason as before, and also because I always recognize
a relationship to other people as something that has reality
[*Realitet*]. But this is why it takes artistry, and marital love
does not shun these difficulties but preserves and gains itself in
them. Then, too, marital love has so much else to think about
that it does not have time to become bogged down in a polemic against particulars.

[129]Inwardly this primary condition is as follows: frankness,
uprightness, openness on the largest scale possible; this is the
life-principle of love, and secretiveness here is its death. But

this is not so easily done as said, and it truly takes courage to carry it out consistently, for you presumably do see that in this I am thinking of something more than the frivolous babbling that prevails in complex family-marriages. Of course, there can be the possibility of openness only where there is secretiveness; but to the same degree that this is present, that also becomes more difficult. It takes courage to be willing to appear as one really is; it takes courage not to want to buy oneself off from a little humiliation when one can do this by a certain secretiveness, not to want to buy a little more stature when one can do it by being inclosedly reserved [*indesluttet*]. It takes courage to will to be sound, honestly and sincerely to will the true.

But let us begin with something of lesser significance. A newly married couple who considered themselves obliged "to circumscribe their love within the narrow boundaries of three small rooms" provided you with the occasion for taking a little trip into the kingdom of fantasy, which lies so near to your daily place of sojourn that it is doubtful whether one should call it an excursion. You devoted yourself to decorating, with the greatest solicitude and elegance, a future such as you could wish for yourself. You know that I am not an unwilling participant in little imaginary constructions[130] like that, and, God be praised, I am sufficiently a child so that when a princely carriage with four snorting horses drives by me I can imagine that I am sitting inside it, sufficiently innocent so that when I have convinced myself that this is not the case I am able to be happy that someone else is doing it, sufficiently unspoiled not to want the maximum to be to keep one horse that is both a driving horse and a riding horse because my circumstances allow me only that.

So in your thought you were married, happily married, had kept your love unimpaired in all adversities, and now planned how you could arrange everything in your home so that your love could preserve its fragrance as long as possible. To that end, you needed more than three rooms. I agreed with you on that, since as a bachelor you use five rooms. It would be unpleasant for you if you should be obliged to hand over one of your rooms to your wife; as far as that goes, you would prefer to hand over the four to her and yourself live in the fifth rather than to have one in common. Having considered these inconveniences, you went on to say: Consequently, I proceed from [*gaa ud fra*][131] the three rooms in question, not in the philosophical sense, for I have no intention of coming back to them again, but, on the contrary, of going as far away from them as possible. Indeed, you had such a loathing for three small rooms that if you could not have more than that you would prefer to live like a tramp under the open sky, which at last would be so poetic that it would take a fairly large suite of rooms to compensate for it. By cautioning you that this was one of the common heresies of unhistorical first love, I tried to call you to order and thereupon was really pleased to walk with you through the many spacious, cool, high-ceilinged drawing rooms of your castle in the air, the secret, half-lighted private chambers, the many dining rooms illuminated even in the most remote corners by candles, chandeliers, and mirrors, the little room with folding doors opening out to the balcony, where the morning sun streamed in and the scent of flowers, which exuded only for you and your love, flowed to meet us.

I shall not pursue your bold steps further as you leap from peak to peak like a mountain antelope hunter. I shall discuss in a bit more detail only the principle on which your plan was founded. Obviously the principle was secretiveness, mystification, subtle coquetry. Not only the walls in your great rooms were to be framed in glass,[132] but even your world of consciousness was to be multiplied by similar refractions; you would meet her and yourself, yourself and her, not only everywhere in the room but also in your consciousness.

"But for this to be done, the wealth of the whole world is not adequate; it takes spirit for that, a sagacious moderation by means of which the powers of the spirit are disposed. Therefore they must be such strangers to each other that the intimacy becomes interesting, so intimate that the strangeness becomes a stimulating resistance. Married life must not be a houserobe in which one relaxes, but neither should it be a corset that hinders movement; it must not be a task that requires

exhausting preparation, but neither should it be a dissolute indolence. It must have the stamp of the accidental, and yet one
must have a remote intimation of an artistry; one should not
become quite hypnotized by hooking, day and night, a carpet
that can hide the floor in the great drawing room, but, on the
contrary, the most insignificant attention must have a secret
little mark in the corner; one will not quite have one's mono-
gram on the cake every day they eat together, but yet there can
very well be a little telegraphic signal. It is a matter of staying
as far as possible from the point where one has an intimation
of a circular motion, the point where repetition begins; and
since it cannot be avoided entirely, it is a matter of planning in
such a way that a variation is possible. There is only a set number of texts, and if a person preaches himself out the very first
Sunday, he has nothing to preach about not only the rest of the
year but not even on the first Sunday in the next year. As long
as possible, they ought to remain somewhat mysterious to
each other, and insofar as one gradually discloses oneself, this
must occur through the use of accidental events as much as
possible, so that it becomes so relative that it can be viewed
again from many other sides. One must guard against any sur-
feit and aftertaste.''

You would reside on the first floor of this noble castle,
which would be located in a beautiful region, yet close to the
capital city. Your wife, your consort, would reside in the left
wing of the second floor. That was something you had always
envied people of nobility—the husband and wife had separate
quarters. But then again there was something that took away
the esthetic in this court life, a ceremonial formality that insisted on being ranked above love. One is announced, one
waits a moment, one is received. It was something that in and
by itself was not unbeautiful but acquired its true beauty only
when it became a play in the divine game of love, when it was
credited with validity in such a way that it could just as well be
deprived of validity. Erotic love itself must have many boundaries, but every boundary must also be a voluptuous temptation to step over the boundary.

So you lived on the first floor, where you had your library,

II
98

your billiard room, reception room, study, and bedroom. Your wife lived on the second floor. Here, too, was your *toral conjugale* [conjugal couch], a large room with two small rooms, one on each side. Nothing must remind you or your wife that you are married, and yet again everything must be such that no unmarried person could have it this way. You did not know what your wife was doing, and she did not know what occupied you; but this was not at all in order to be inactive or to forget each other but in order that every contact could be significant, in order to postpone that deadly moment when you would look at each other, and behold—you were bored. You would not trudge around arm in arm in a conjugal procession; with youthful infatuation, you would even watch her for a long time from your window as she walked in the garden, sharpen your eyes in order to follow her, relapse into contemplation of her image when it disappeared from your sight. You would steal after her; yes, at times she would even rest on your arm, for there was indeed always something beautiful in what has become established among people as an expression of a special feeling. You would walk with her on your arm, half doing justice to the beauty in this custom, half joking that you two were walking as proper married folk. But how would I be able to come to an end if I were to follow the shrewd refinements of your ingenious head in this Asiatic luxuriance that almost exhausts me and makes me wish myself back in the three small rooms you so proudly rejected.

Now, if there is otherwise some esthetic beauty in this whole view, no doubt it would be found partly in the erotic shyness of which you permitted an intimation, partly in your wanting at no moment to possess the beloved as acquired but perpetually to acquire her. In and by itself the latter is true and correct, but the task is by no means posed with erotic earnestness and consequently to that extent is not carried out either. You clung continually to an immediacy as such, to a natural disposition, and did not dare let it be transfigured in a shared consciousness, for this is what I have expressed by "sincerity" and "openness." You are afraid that love will cease when the mystery is gone; I think, however, that it does not begin until that is gone. You are afraid that one does not dare to know completely what one loves, you rely upon the incommensurable as an absolutely important ingredient; I maintain that a person does not truly love until he knows what he loves. Furthermore, all your happiness lacks a blessing, for it lacks adversities, and just as this is a defect, insofar as you actually were to instruct anyone with your theory, so it is also fortunate that it is not true.

So let us turn to the way things really are in life. Now, in my insisting that adversity is part of marriage, I by no means permit you to identify marriage with a retinue of adversities. It is already implicit in the resignation contained in the resolution, as previously explained, that there will be accompanying adversities, except that these have not as yet assumed a definite shape and are not alarming, since on the contrary they are already seen as overcome in the resolution. Furthermore, adversity is not seen externally but internally in its reflexion in the individual, but this belongs to the shared history of marital love. Secretiveness itself, as explained above, becomes a contradiction when it has nothing to keep secret, a childishness when it is only amorous bric-à-brac that constitutes its deposit. Not until the individual's love has truly opened his heart, made him eloquent in a much profounder sense than that in which one usually says that love makes one eloquent (for even the seducer may have that kind of eloquence), not until the individual has deposited everything in the shared consciousness, not until then does secretiveness gain its strength, life, and meaning.

But a decisive step is required for this, and consequently courage is also required; yet marital love collapses into nothing if this does not take place, for only thereby does one show that one loves not oneself but another. And how is one to show this except by being only for the other; but how is one to be only for another except by not being for oneself; but to be for oneself is almost the most common expression for the secretiveness that the individual life has when it remains in itself. Love is self-giving, but self-giving is only possible by my going out

II
100

of myself—how then can this be united with the hiddenness that wants expressly to remain in itself?

"But one loses by disclosing oneself this way." Yes, of course, the person who profits by being secretive always loses. But if you want to be consistent, you must work this out much further than this. Then you must advise not only against marriage but against every approach and then see how far your shrewd head would be able to push this in telegraphic signals. The most interesting reading is that in which the reader himself is to a certain degree productive. The true erotic feat would be to make an impression at a distance, which would be very dangerous to the person concerned because she herself would create the object of her love out of nothing and now would love her own creation—nevertheless this is not love but the coquetry of seduction. The person who loves, however, has lost himself in another, but in losing and forgetting himself in the other he is open to the other, and in forgetting himself in another he is remembered in the other. The person who loves will not wish to be confused with another, neither someone better nor inferior, and the person who does not have this respect for himself and for the beloved does not love. Ordinarily, secretiveness is rooted in a small-mindedness that wants to add a cubit to its stature.[133] The person who has not learned to reject such things has never loved, for then he would have sensed that even if he added ten cubits to his stature he would still be too small.

This humility of love is generally believed to belong only in comedies and novels or must be assigned to the convenient lies of the courting days. But this is not at all the case; this humility is a true and helpful and constant disciplinarian whenever anyone wants to measure love with anything else but love. Even though it were the lowliest and most unimportant person in the world who loved the most richly endowed person in the world, the latter, if he had any truth in him, would nevertheless feel that all his gifts still left a chasmic abyss, and that the only way he could satisfy the demand implicit in the other's love would be to love in return. Let us never forget that one cannot reckon with heterogeneous quantities. Therefore, the person who has truly sensed this has loved, but he certainly has not been afraid of depriving himself of something that as such has no value for him. Only the person who has become poor in the world has won the true assurance of ownership, and only the person who has lost everything has gained everything.[134] Hence I say with Fenelon: "Believe in love—it takes everything, it gives everything."[135] Truly it is a beautiful, an uplifting, an indescribably blissful feeling to let all the particulars disappear beneath one, to let them fade and float away like fog images before the infinite power of love. It is an arithmetical process that is just as beautiful in the infinite now in which it happens in one stroke as in the sequence in which one delights in putting out one's hand and letting them disappear one by one. Yes, this is true love's true enthusiasm for annihilation, when it could wish for the whole world—not to score a success thereby but to let it perish as a jest in the diversion of love. In fact, as soon as the door is opened to finite things, then wanting to be loved because one has the best head, the most talent, the highest artistic genius in his generation is just as obtuse and ludicrous as wanting to be loved because one maintains the most beautiful goatee on one's chin. But these manifestations and moods quite naturally belong just as much to first love, and it is only the amazingly unstable attitude you always assume that makes it necessary for me to touch on this again here.

First love can wish with supranatural pathos, but this wishing easily turns into an "if" without content, and we do not live in such a paradise that our Lord gives each and every married couple the whole world with which to wheel and deal as they like. Marital love knows better; its movements are not outward but inward, and here it quickly perceives that it has a wide world before it, but also that every little subjugation of itself has a completely different commensurability with the infinity of love. And even if it feels the pain of having so much with which to struggle, it also feels the courage for this battle. Indeed, it has sufficient boldness to outbid you in paradoxes when it is almost able to rejoice that sin has entered into the world; but also in another sense it has the boldness to outbid you in paradoxes, for it has the courage to resolve them. Marital love, just as first love, knows full well that all these obstacles are conquered in the infinite moment of love. But it also knows, and this is precisely the historical in it, that this victory wills to be gained, and that this gaining is not just a game but also a struggle, yet also not just a struggle but also a game, just as the battle in Valhalla[136] was a struggle to the death, and yet a game, for the warriors always rose up again, rejuvenated by death. And it likewise knows that this skirmish is not a capricious duel but a struggle under divine auspices; it feels no need to love more than one but feels a blessedness in this; and it feels no need to love more than once but feels an eternity in this. And do you think that this love that has no secrets would miss out on something beautiful? Or that it would be unable to withstand time and would necessarily be dulled through daily association? Or that boredom would come more swiftly, as if marital love did not possess an eternal substance of which one never grows weary, an eternal substance that it sometimes gains with a kiss and jest, sometimes with anxiety and trembling, and continually gains?

"But it must renounce all these lovely little surprises." I see no necessity of that at all. It is certainly not my idea that marital love must always stand with open mouth or even talk in its sleep; on the contrary, all these little surprises acquire their significance precisely when there is total openness. This gives, namely, a security and a confidence in which this byplay is seen to best advantage. If, however, one believes that the essence of love and true bliss consists of such a chain of little surprises, that the wretched, refined softness, the restlessness, in which one is prepared at every moment for a little surprise and thinks one up oneself, is something beautiful, then I shall permit myself to say that it is very unbeautiful, and that it is a very dubious sign when a marriage has no other trophies to display than a display cabinet full of bonbons, bottles, cups, embroidered house slippers, trinkets, etc.

It is not uncommon, however, to see marriages in which the secrecy system is in effect. I have never seen a happy marriage in which that was the case. But since this could be purely accidental, I shall run through the reasons for it that are usually given. This is important to me at this point, for an esthetically beautiful marriage is always a happy marriage. Now, if a happy marriage can be built on that basis, my theory will have to be changed. I shall not disregard any outward forms and with all possible justice shall describe every one and dwell especially on one that, in the home where I have seen it realized, has been carried through with a virtuosity that was really imposing.

The secrecy system, I think you will admit, generally comes from the men, and although it is always wrong, it nevertheless is more tolerable than the intolerability of having the woman exercise such a *dominium*. The worst form, of course, is the sheer despotism in which the wife is a slave, the maid-of-all-work in domestic affairs. Such a marriage is never happy, even though the years produce a lethargy that puts up with it. A more beautiful form is the extreme of this—a misplaced solicitude. "Woman is weak," it is said. "She cannot bear troubles and cares—the frail and the weak must be dealt with in love." Falsehood! Falsehood! Woman is just as strong as man, perhaps stronger. And do you really deal with her in love when you humiliate her in this way? Or who gave you permission to humiliate her, or how can your soul be so blind that you regard yourself as a creature superior to her? Just confide everything to her. If she is weak, if she cannot bear it—well, then she can lean on you; after all, you have strength enough. But you cannot tolerate that; you do not have the stamina for that. Therefore, it is you who are lacking in strength and not she. Perhaps she had more strength than you; perhaps she shamed you, and you do not have the strength to bear that. Or have you not promised to share good and evil with her? Is it not unfair to her not to let her in on the evil? Is it not crushing what is most noble in her? Perhaps she is weak; perhaps her grief will make everything harder—*eh bien*, then share this evil with her. But this in turn will save her, and do you have the right to deprive her of a way to salvation, do you have the right to sneak her through the world? And where do you gain your strength—is she not just as close to God as you? Do you want to rob her of the opportunity to find God in the deepest and innermost way—through pain and suffering? Do you know so surely, then, that she has no inkling at all of your secretiveness? Do you know if she does not grieve and sigh in silence, if her soul is not being damaged? Perhaps her weakness is humility; perhaps she believes that it is her duty to bear all this. To be sure, you thereby have been the occasion for developing strength in her, but it was nevertheless not in the way you wished or had promised. Or are you treating her, to put it strongly, like an extra wife—for it is of no help to her that you do not have more. And is it not doubly humiliating to her to discern that you love her not because you are a proud tyrant but because she is a frail creature?

For some time, I was guest in a home where I had opportunity to observe a more skillful and refined practice of the silent system. The husband was a rather young man, unusually gifted, very intelligent, poetic by nature, too lazy to bring himself to produce, yet with an extraordinary perceptiveness and aliveness in making everyday life poetic. His wife was young, not without intellect, but with an unusual character. This captivated him. It was so absolutely amazing how he knew all the ways to awaken and encourage everything youthfully visionary in her. Her whole existence, their married life, was interlaced with poetic magic. He kept his eye on everything; when she looked around, it was not there. He had his finger in everything, but just as figuratively and in the finite sense as unsubstantially as God's finger is in history. Wherever her thoughts might want to turn, he had already been there, had everything ready; like Potemkin,[137] he knew how to conjure up a setting, and precisely one that, after an initial surprise and a little resistance, inevitably pleased her. His domestic life was a little creation story, and just as in the great creation story mankind is that toward which everything strives, so she was the center of a magic circle in which she still enjoyed all her freedom, for the circle conformed to her and had no boundary that might announce: Here and no further.[138] She could rush as fast as she wished and in any direction she wished—the circle adapted itself but nevertheless was there. She walked as if she were in a toddler-walker, but this one was not woven out of willows but was an intertwining of her hopes, dreams, longings, wishes, anxieties—in short, it was formed out of the whole content of her soul. He himself moved in this dream world with consummate assurance, surrendered none of his dignity, asserted and upheld his authority as husband and master. It would have made her uneasy if he had not; it perhaps would have awakened in her a frightening presentiment that might have led her to a dissolution of the secrecy. He did not seem to be so very attentive to the world or even to her, and yet he was secretly aware that she had not received any impressions from him other than those he wanted her to receive, and he knew that he had it in his power to break the spell with a single word. Everything that could have an unpleasant effect on her had been removed; if anything like that came along, she received from him in the form of a forthright communication, either after letting her question him closely or by approaching her frankly, an interpretation that he himself had more or less edited according to the impression he wanted to make. He was proud, fearfully consistent; he loved her but could not abandon, in the deepest stillness of the night or in the moment that lay outside time, the proud thought of presuming to say to himself: Yet she owes everything to me.

Is it not true that you have followed my description with interest, however imperfect my achievement is, because it evokes for your soul a picture that you find congenial, that you perhaps would try to put into practice if you were to be married? This marriage, was it then a happy marriage? Yes, if that is the way you want it—but nevertheless a dark fate hovered over this happiness. Suppose that something went wrong for him, suppose that she suddenly suspected something—I believe that she could never forgive him, for her proud soul was too proud to have it said that he had done it out of love for her.

Here I wish to call to mind an old-fashioned saying about the relation between married people (on the whole I am always happy to support the revolution, or rather the holy war, in which the plain and simple but true and rich expressions of legitimate marriage strive to conquer the kingdom from which

II
105

the novel has displaced them). It is said of married folk that
they should live in good understanding with each other. Most
frequently one hears it expressed negatively. A married couple
is not living in good understanding with each other, and then
ordinarily one supposes that they cannot stand each other, that
they fight and bite etc. Now take the positive version. The
married couple we are talking about living in good understanding—yes, that is what the world would say, but you presumably would not, for how could they live in good understanding when they do not understand each other? But is it not
part and parcel of understanding for the one party to know
how solicitous and affectionate the other is toward him? Or
even if he did not deprive her of anything else, he deprived her
of the occasion to have the degree of gratitude her soul needed
before she could find rest. Is it not a beautiful, a beautiful and
simple phrase: to live in good understanding? It presupposes
that they understand each other clearly and distinctly (you see,
this marital terminology is very well informed and does not
make a big commotion about what nowadays must often be
precisely insisted upon) and assumes this as something self-ev-
ident, as we see from the assignment of an adjective with a special emphasis, for otherwise it would have been sufficient to
say that they should live in understanding. "Good understanding"—what else does it mean but that they should find their
joy, peace, rest, their lives, in this understanding?

You see, therefore, that in no way does the secrecy system
lead to a happy marriage and thus neither to an esthetically
beautiful marriage. No, my friend, honesty, frankness, openness, understanding—this is the life principle in marriage.
Without this understanding, marriage is unbeautiful and actually immoral, for then the sensuous and the spiritual, which
love unites, are separated. Only when the being with whom I
live in the most tender union in earthly life is just as close to
me in the spiritual sense, only then is my marriage moral and
therefore also esthetically beautiful. And you proud husbands,
who perhaps secretly gloat in this conquest over woman, you
forget that in the first place it is a sorry conquest when one
triumphs over the weaker, and that the husband honors him-

self in his wife, and he who does not do so holds himself in contempt.

Understanding, then, is the life principle in marriage. We frequently hear experienced people discussing under what circumstances a person ought to be dissuaded from marrying. Let them discuss the particulars as thoroughly and ruminantly as they wish—what they ordinarily say is of no great significance. For my part, I shall mention only one circumstance— that is, when the individual life is so entangled that it cannot disclose itself. If the history of your inner life has something unspeakable in it or if your life has initiated you into secrets— in short, if in some way or another you have swallowed a secret that cannot be dragged out of you without costing your life—then never marry. Either you will feel bound to a being who has no intimation of what is going on inside you, and in that case your marriage is an unbeautiful misalliance, or you attach yourself to a being who perceives it in frightened anxiety, at every moment sees these silhouettes on the wall. She perhaps will decide never to question you closely, never to come too close to you; she will renounce the curiosity of anxiety that tempts her, but she will never be happy, and you will not either. Whether there are such secrets, whether there is any truth to the inclosing reserve the lock of which not even love can pick, I shall not say; I am carrying through my principle, and as far as I am concerned I have no secrets from my wife. One would think that it would never occur to a person like that to marry, a person who in addition to everything else he had to do also had this daily preoccupation with his painful secret. [139]But still it does happen occasionally, and a person like that is perhaps most dangerously fascinating to a woman.

But since I have now mentioned secretiveness and understanding as the two aspects of the same issue, but this one issue as the most important thing in love, as the absolute condition for preserving the esthetic in marriage, I may very well fear that you will now object that I seem to forget "what I ordinarily adhere to closely like the refrain in a ballad," the historical character of marriage. You still hope, however, to protract the time by means of your secretiveness and your shrewdly cal-

culated relativizing declaration: "But as soon as married people really begin a thorough telling of their more or less short
or long histories, then very soon the moment comes to say:
'Pitty, patty, pat, and that's the end of that.' " My young
friend, you do not perceive that if you can make a charge like
that, it is because you are incorrectly situated. Because of your
secretiveness, you have a time-category within you, and it actually is a matter of protracting the time, whereas love with its
disclosure has an eternity-category within itself, and thus all
competition becomes impossible. Indeed, it is an arbitrary
misunderstanding to interpret this disclosure as if married
people would take a dozen or so days to relate their life story,
and thereupon would follow the silence of the grave, broken
just once by the fairly familiar story: "As it says about the mill
somewhere in a fairy tale, 'And while all this was happening
the mill went klip klap, klip klap.' "[140] The historical character
of marriage makes this understanding something that is all at
once just as much as it continually becomes. It is the same here
as in individual life. When a person has arrived at an understanding of himself, has had the courage to be willing to see
himself, it by no means thereby follows that the story is now
past history, for now it begins, now for the first time it gains
its real meaning, in that every single experienced moment is
led back to this total view. So it is also in marriage. In this disclosure, the immediacy of first love founders, yet it is not lost
but is caught up in the joint marital consciousness, and with
this the history begins, and to this joint marital consciousness
the particular detail is led back, and therein lies its happiness
[*Salighed*], a term in which the historical character of marriage
is preserved and which corresponds to the joy of life or what
the Germans call *Heiterkeit* [serenity], which the first love has.

   To become historical, then, belongs essentially to marital
love, and since the individuals now have the right attitude, the
command "to eat their bread in the sweat of their brow"[141] is
no terrible and unexpected message, and the courage and
power it feels it has is the complement to and the truth in
knightly love's incredible need for incredible deeds. Just as the
knight is without fear, so also is marital love, although the ene-

mies it has to fight against are often far more dangerous. This opens a wide range for contemplation, but one in which I do not plan to set foot; but if the knight has the right to say that the person who does not defy the whole world to save his beloved does not know knightly love, then the married man has the right to say the same. But I must always remind you that every such victory that marital love wins is more esthetically beautiful than the victory the knight wins, for in winning this victory he also wins his love glorified in it. Marital love fears nothing, not even minor mistakes; it does not fear little infatuations—in fact, these, too, only nourish the divine soundness of marital love. Even in Goethe's *Wahlverwandtschaften*,[142] Ottilia is plowed under, as a faint possibility, by the earnest marital love—how much more power, then, a marriage with a deep religious and ethical foundation should have for that. Indeed, Goethe's *Wahlverwandtschaften* demonstrates precisely what secretiveness leads to. That love would not have gained the power if it had not been permitted to grow in stillness. If Edward had had the courage to be open to his wife, it would have been prevented, and the whole story would have become a divertissement in the drama of marriage. The fatefulness was due to both Edward's and his wife's becoming infatuated at the same time, but this again was because of silence. The married man who has the courage to confide to his wife that he loves someone else is saved, and so is the wife. But if he does not have it, he loses confidence in himself and thus what he seeks in another's love is oblivion, just as it is frequently just as much pangs about not having resisted in time as it is genuine love for the other woman that makes a husband surrender. He feels that he has lost himself, and once this is the case, strong opiates are needed as a depressant.

The difficulties with which marital love must struggle I shall discuss only in general in order to show that they are not of such significance that love has anything to fear from them with respect to preserving the esthetic. The objections usually stem from a misunderstanding of the esthetic significance of the historical or from the common practice of having only the classical ideal within romanticism and not the romantic ideal

also. The basis of many other objections is that, while people
always like to think of the first love as dancing on roses, they
are pleased that marital love is cheated in every way and struggles with the most wretched and discouraging difficulties.
Then, too, they secretly think that these difficulties are insur-
mountable, and so they are quickly finished with marriage.

When one is dealing with you, one must always be somewhat cautious. I am not speaking about any particular marriage and thus am free to portray it as I wish; but even if I have
no desire to make myself guilty of any arbitrariness, it does not
mean that you will renounce this urge. If, for example, poverty is cited as a difficulty with which marriage may have to
struggle, I answer: Work, and then everything will be all right.
Since you and I are moving in a poetic world, it perhaps will
please you to assert your poetic license and answer, "They
cannot find work. The decline in business and shipping has put
many people out of work." Or you will permit them to have
a little work, but it is not enough. If I now am of the opinion
that with prudent thriftiness they will manage, you fabricate
the excuse that precisely because of the alarming complex of
circumstances the grain prices are so high that it is utterly impossible to manage with what otherwise would have been
enough for them to pull through. I know you too well. You
take great delight in fabricating the counterthrust, and when
that has amused you long enough, on the basis of some remark
you engage the person with whom you are talking or someone
else present in a long-winded chat that has nothing at all to do
with the original subject. You relish suddenly turning a poetic
caprice into a kind of actuality and then enlarging upon it. If
you had been talking with anyone else but me (for you usually
spare me) in the way described, you probably would have
added to the comment on the high grain prices, "Such high
prices! To think that a pound loaf of bread would cost eight
shillings!" If, as good luck would have it, someone was present who answered that it was utterly unthinkable, you would
inform him that under Olaf Hunger[143] a pound loaf of bread—
and bark bread at that—cost eight and a half shillings in old
Danish currency, and if one considered that people at that time

did not have much money, one would readily perceive etc. Then if you drew out the one to whom you were talking, you would be beside yourself with joy. The one who had originally started the conversation would try in vain to bring you back to reason; everything would be confused, and you would have made a married couple in the world of poetry unhappy.

That is what makes it so difficult to become involved with you. If I were to venture out on what for me certainly could be called thin ice and try to describe fictionally a marriage that victoriously endured in the struggle with a host of such adversities, you would answer very calmly: Well, that is just poetry, and in the world of poetry it is easy to make people happy; that is the least one can do for them. If I took you by the arm and walked around and showed you a real-life marriage that had fought the good fight,[144] then—if you were in the mood—you would answer, "Well, that's all very fine; the outer aspects of temptation can be substantiated, but not the inner ones, and I assume that temptation has not had inner power in them, for otherwise it would not have been endurable." Just as if the true significance of temptation were that people must succumb to it. But enough of that. Once you have a mind to abandon yourself to this demon of arbitrariness, there is no end to it, and just as you are conscious of everything you do, so you are also conscious of this arbitrariness and really revel in shaking all the foundations.

I can divide these difficulties very generally into outer and inner difficulties and continually bear in mind the relativity of such a division with respect to marriage, where of all places everything is inner. First of all, then, the outer difficulties. I have no qualms or fears at all in mentioning all the depressing, humiliating, annoying finite troubles—in short, all those that add up to a *weinerlich* [tearful] drama. You and your kind are extremely arbitrary, here as everywhere. If a play such as this forces you to take such a tour through the caves of misery, you say it is unesthetic, blubbering, and boring. And in that you are right—but why? Because it makes you indignant that something noble and exalted succumbs to such things. But if you and your kind turn to the actual world and there encounter a family that has experienced just half of the adversities that this playwright executioner, in the lascivious pleasure (reserved for tyrants) of tormenting others, thinks up, you tremble, and you think: Goodbye to all esthetic beauty. You feel pity, you are willing to help if for no other reason than to drive off these dark thoughts, but you have long since despaired as far as the unhappy family is concerned. But if it is true in life, then the poet does indeed have the right to portray it and is right in portraying it.

When you are sitting in the theater, intoxicated with esthetic pleasure, then you have the courage to require of the poet that he let the esthetic win out over all wretchedness. It is the only consolation that remains, and, what is even more unmanly, it is the consolation that you take, you to whom life has not provided the occasion to test your strength. You, then, are impoverished and unhappy, just like the hero and the heroine in the play, but you also have pathos, courage, an *os rotundum* [round mouth][145] from which eloquence gushes, and a vigorous arm. You and your kind conquer; you applaud the actor, and the actor is yourselves and the applause from the pit is for you, for you are indeed the hero and the actor. In dreams, in the nebulous world of esthetics, there you are heroes. I do not care very much for the theater, and as far as I am concerned you and your kind can mock as much as you like. Just let the histrionic heroes succumb or let them be victorious, sink through the floor or vanish through the ceiling—I am not greatly moved. But if it is true, as you teach and declaim in life, that it takes far fewer adversities to make a person a slave so that he walks with his head hanging down and forgets that he, too, is created in God's image, then may it be your just punishment, God grant, that all playwrights compose nothing but tearjerking plays, full of all possible anxiety and horror that would not allow your flabbiness to rest on the cushioned theater seats and let you be perfumed with supranatural power but would horrify you until in the world of actuality you learn to believe in that which you want to believe in only in poetry.

In my own marriage, I admittedly have not experienced many adversities of that kind—that I readily concede—and therefore I cannot speak from experience, but I nevertheless have the conviction that nothing is able to crush the esthetic in a human being, a conviction so powerful, so blessed, so fervent that I thank my God for it as for a gift of grace. And when we read in the Bible about the many gifts of grace, I would actually count this among them—the cheerful boldness, the trust, the belief in actuality and in the eternal necessity whereby the beautiful triumphs, and in the blessedness implicit in the freedom with which the individual offers God his assistance. And this conviction is a component of my whole mental disposition, and for that reason I do not let myself palpitate enervatingly and voluptuously with artificial stimulations in a theater. The one and only thing I can do is thank God for this imperturbability in my soul, but in so doing I also hope to have saved my soul from taking it in vain.

You know how I hate all imaginary constructing [*Experimenteren*],[146] but all the same it may be true that a person can have experienced in thought much that he never comes to experience in actuality. Moments of dejection come sometimes, and if the individual does not himself evoke them in order voluntarily to test himself, this, too, is a struggle and a very earnest struggle, and through this an assurance can be gained that is very significant, even if it does not have the reality [*Realitet*] it would have had if acquired in a real life situation. There are occasions in life when it is a mark of something great and good in a person that he is as if mad, that he has not separated the world of poetry and the world of actuality but sees the latter *sub specie poeseos* [under the aspect of poetry].[147] Luther says somewhere in one of his sermons, where he speaks of poverty and need: One has never heard of a Christian dying of hunger.[148] And for Luther that ends the matter, and he thinks, surely with justification, that he has spoken on this with much pathos and unto true upbuilding.

Now insofar as marriage involves outer trials of this nature, the thing to do, of course, is to make them inner trials. I say "of course" and speak rather boldly about the whole matter, but I am addressing this only to you, after all, and we two are more or less equally experienced in this kind of adversity. If one wishes to preserve the esthetic, it is a matter of transforming the outer into an inner trial. Or does it disturb you that I still use the word "esthetic"; or do you think it is almost a kind of childishness on my part to want to look for the esthetic among the poor and the suffering; or have you demeaned yourself with that scandalous division that gives the esthetic to the aristocratic and powerful, the wealthy, the cultured, and gives, at most, the religious to the poor? Well, I do not happen to believe that the poor suffer by this division, and do you not perceive that the poor, if they truly possess the religious, also have the esthetic, while the rich, insofar as they do not have the religious, do not have the esthetic either? Then, too, I have mentioned only the extreme here, and it probably is not rare that those who cannot be classified as poor have trouble making ends meet. Moreover, other temporal cares, illness, for example, are common to all classes. But I am convinced that the person who has the courage to transform the outer trial into an inner trial has already virtually surmounted it, since by faith a transubstantiation takes place even in the moment of suffering.

II
113

The married man who has enough memory for his love and enough courage in the time of need to say, "The primary question is not one of where I am going to find the money and at what percent but first and foremost is of my love, whether I have kept a pure and faithful covenant of love with her to whom I am united." The man who forces himself to do this in his not too numerous inner struggles, who either in the youthful vigor of his first love or in the assurance gained by experience, makes this movement—that person has triumphed; he has preserved the esthetic in his marriage, even if he did not have three small rooms in which to live. It is by no means denied (something your sly intellect will soon light upon) that the very internalizing of the outer spiritual trial can make it even harder, but then, too, the gods do not sell greatness for nothing,[149] and precisely therein lies the educative and the idealizing aspects of marriage.

So often it is said that it is easier to bear all such things if one stands alone in the world. It is probably true, up to a point, but in this kind of talk a huge falsehood is often hidden, for why can a person bear it more easily—because he can throw himself away more easily, can do damage to his soul without involving anyone else, can forget God, can let the storms of despair drown out the shrieks of pain, can become dulled within, can almost take pleasure in living among human beings as a ghost. To be sure, everyone, even if he stands alone, ought to pay attention to himself; but only the person who loves has the proper conception of who he is and what he can do, and only marriage gives the historical faithfulness that is every bit as beautiful as the knightly kind. In other words, a married man can never conduct himself this way, and no matter how much the world goes against him, even if he momentarily forgets himself and already feels so light because despair is about to set him adrift, feels so strong because he has sipped the anesthetizing drink blended by defiance and despondency, cowardice and pride, feels so free because the bond that binds him to truth and justice seems to be loosened and he now experiences the speed that is the transition from good to evil—he nevertheless will soon turn back to the old paths and as a married man [*Ægtemand*] prove himself to be an authentic [*ægte*] man.

So much, then, for these outer trials. I write briefly about them because I do not feel the authority to discuss them and because to do so adequately would require a complicated development. But this is my conclusion: If love can be preserved—and that it can, so help me God!—then the esthetic can be preserved also, for love itself is the esthetic.

The other objections are due primarily to a misunderstanding of the significance of time and of the esthetic validity of the historical. Consequently, they touch every marriage and may be discussed in general. This I shall now do, and in my generalizing I shall try not to overlook the point in the attack and the point in the defense.

The first thing you will name is "habit, the unavoidable habit, this dreadful monotony, the everlasting *Einerlei* [sameness] in the alarming still life of marital domesticity. I love nature, but I am a hater of the second nature." It must be granted that you know how to describe with seductive fervor and sadness the happy time when one is still making discoveries and how to paint with anxiety and horror the time when it is over. You know how to elaborate to the point of ridiculousness and loathsomeness a marital uniformity that not even nature can match, "for here, as Leibniz has already shown, nothing is exactly the same; such uniformity is reserved only for rational creatures, either as the fruit of their lassitude or of their pedantry."[150] I have no intention whatsoever of denying that it is a beautiful time, an eternally unforgettable time (please note in what sense I am able to say this), when the individual is astounded and made happy in the world of erotic love by things long since discovered, of which, of course, he probably has often heard and read, but which he now for the first time appropriates with the total enthusiasm of surprise and the full depth of inwardness. It is a beautiful time, from the very first intimation of love, the first glimpse and the first disappearance of the beloved object, the first chord of this voice, the first glance, the first handshake, the first kiss—right up to the first perfect assurance of its possession. It is a beautiful time—the first restlessness, the first longing, the first pain because she did not come, the first joy because she came unexpectedly— but this by no means implies that the ensuing time is not just as beautiful. You who fancy yourself to have such a knightly mentality—examine yourself. When you say that the first kiss is the sweetest, the most beautiful, you are insulting the beloved, for then it is time and its qualification that give the kiss absolute worth.

But now, lest harm be done to the cause I am defending, you must first give me a little accounting. That is, if you do not wish to proceed altogether arbitrarily, you must attack the first love in the same way as you attack marriage. That is, if it is to last in life, it must be exposed to the same calamities and will be far from having the resources to combat them that marital love has in the ethical and the religious. To be consistent, you must therefore hate all love that wants to be an eternal love. You must therefore stop with the first love as a moment. But in order for this to have its true meaning, it must have an intrinsic naive eternity. Once you have learned that it was an illusion, it is all over for you, except insofar as you work to enter into the same illusion once again, which is a self-contradiction. Or could it be that your brilliant intellect has conspired with your lust to such a degree that you could completely forget what you owe to others? Even if it can never be repeated like the first time, do you think that there would still be a tolerable way of escape, that one would be rejuvenated by experiencing the illusion in others, so that one would enjoy the infinity and novelty in the originality of the individual whose virginal girdle of illusion was not as yet undone? Such things betray just as much desperation as corruption, and since they betray desperation, it will indeed be impossible to find any enlightenment about life here.

The first thing I must now protest against is your right to use the word "habit" for the recurring that characterizes all life and therefore love also. "Habit" is properly used only of evil, in such a way that by it one designates either a continuance in something that in itself is evil or such a stubborn repetition of something in itself innocent that it becomes somewhat evil because of this repetition. Thus habit always designates something unfree. But just as one cannot do the good except in freedom, so also one cannot remain in it except in freedom, and therefore we can never speak of habit in relation to the good.

Next I must also protest against your declaration, in your characterization of marital uniformity, that nothing like it is to be found in nature. That is indeed quite true, but that uniformity can be precisely the expression of something beautiful, and to that extent man can be very proud of being the inventor of it; thus in music the uniform rhythm can be very beautiful and of great effect.

Finally, I would like to say that if a monotony like that were unavoidable in the life together in marriage, then you must perceive, if you are honest, that the task would be to surmount it, that is, to preserve love [*Kjærlighed*] in the midst of it, not to despair, for that can never be a task; it is an easy way out, seized upon, I readily admit, only by those who perceive the task.

But now let us examine more closely the case of this much

publicized uniformity. Your mistake, and also your misfortune, is that you think too abstractly about everything and
thus also with regard to love. You think of a little summation
of the elements of love; you think, as you yourself perhaps
would say, of the categories of love. In that respect, I readily
concede to you an unusual categorical completeness. You
think every category concretely in one element, and this is the
poetic. Then when you think of the long duration of marriage
alongside this, there is for you an alarming disparity. Your
mistake is that you do not think historically. If a systematician
were to think of the category of interaction and elaborate it
fully and with expert logic, but if he were also to add, "It will
take an eternity before the world can complete its eternal interaction," you surely cannot deny that one would have the
right to laugh at him. Well, this is indeed the meaning of time,
and it is the fate of humankind and of individuals to live in it.
So if you have nothing else to say than that it is unendurable,
then you had better look for another audience. Now, this
would be a perfectly adequate response, but lest you find occasion to say, "Basically you agree with me but deem it best to
submit to what cannot be changed," I shall try to show that it
is not only best to submit to it since it is a duty, but that to submit to it is truly the best.

But let us begin with a point that can be regarded as a point
of contact. You certainly do not fear the time that precedes the
culmination; on the contrary, you love it and by a multiplicity
of reflections you often strive to make the moments of reproduction even longer than they were originally, and if someone
at this point wanted to reduce life for you to a category, you
would be most indignant. In that time preceding the culmination, it is not just the major, momentous encounters that interest you, but every little triviality, and then you know how
to speak beautifully enough about the secret that remains hidden from the wise[151]—that the least is the greatest. But once
the point of culmination has been reached, then, indeed,
everything changes, then everything shrivels together into an
impoverished and unrefreshing abbreviation. Well, so be it;
this is supposed to be rooted in your nature, which is merely

conquestive and cannot possess anything. Now, if you do not, in all arbitrariness and one-sidedness, insist that, after all, this is the way you are, then you really will have to declare a temporary armistice and open the ranks so that I can come and see to what extent it is true and, if that is the case, to what extent there is truth in it. If you are unwilling, then I shall, without troubling myself about you, imagine a person just like you and now calmly proceed with my vivisection. But I do hope, nevertheless, that you will have sufficient courage to submit personally to the operation, sufficient courage actually to let yourself be executed—and not merely *in effigie.*

By persisting that this, after all, is the way you are, you do thereby admit that others could be different. More I do not yet dare to assert, for it might be possible that you are the normal human being, although the anxiety with which you cling to yourself as that which, after all, you now are does not seem to indicate it. But how do you conceive of others? When you see a married couple whose life together, so it seems to you, drags on in the most dreadful boredom, "in the most insipid repetition of the sacred institutions and sacraments of erotic love," then, yes, then a fire rages within you, a fire that wants to consume them. And this is not something arbitrary on your part; you are indeed justified; you are indeed entitled to let the lightning of irony strike them and the thunder of anger terrify them. As a matter of fact, you do destroy them not because you have a liking for it but because they have deserved it. You pass judgment on them, but what does it mean "to judge" except to require something of them; and if you cannot require it and it is a contradiction to require the impossible, then it certainly is a contradiction to pass judgment on them. Is it not true that you have blundered, that you have suggested a law that you do not wish to acknowledge and that you nevertheless have enforced against others? Yet you are not devoid of composure; you say, "I do not censure them, do not reproach them, do not judge them—I feel sorry for them."

But suppose that those involved did not find it at all boring. A self-contented smile crosses your lips; a bright idea has taken you by surprise and no doubt will certainly also surprise the

II
118

person you are talking with: "As I said, I feel sorry for them, for either they feel the full weight of boredom, and in that case I feel sorry for them, or they are not aware of it, and in that case I also feel sorry for them, for then they are in a very regrettable illusion." This is approximately the way you would answer me, and if there were several people present, your self-confidence would not fail in its effect. But no one is listening to us now, and consequently I can continue this exploration. So you feel sorry for them in both instances.

Now there is only a third possibility, namely, that one knows that this is the way it is with marriage and fortunately has not entered into it. But this situation is clearly just as regrettable for the person who has felt love and then understands that it cannot be realized. And, finally, the situation of the person who has done his best to extricate himself from this shipwreck by the egotistical means described above is also regrettable, for he has indeed cast himself in the role of a robber and bully. Consequently it seems that just as a marriage has become a universal expression for a happy ending to something, so the ending of marriage itself is not very happy. This brings us to a universal regret as the true result of this whole exploration, but such a result is a self-contradiction and is equivalent to saying that the result of the development of life is that one is going backward. Ordinarily you are not afraid of going along and perhaps will say here, "Well, it does happen sometimes; when the going is slippery and the wind is against you, the result of going forward is often a going backward."

But I return to the consideration of your psychical [*aandelig*] disposition. You say that you have a conquering nature and cannot possess. In saying this, you presumably do not think you have said anything disparaging about yourself; on the contrary, you feel superior to others instead. Let us scrutinize this more closely. What takes more strength—to ascend or to descend a hill? Assuming the same steepness, it obviously takes more strength to do the latter. Almost everyone is born with a penchant for climbing a hill, whereas most people have a certain anxiety about going down a hill. Similarly, I believe also that there are far more conquering natures than possessing ones, and if you feel superior to many married people and "their dull brutish contentment," that certainly can be true up to a point, but of course you are not supposed to learn from your inferiors. For the most part, true art goes in the direction opposite to that of nature, without therefore annihilating it, and likewise true art manifests itself in possessing and not in making a conquest; in other words, possessing is an inverse conquering. In this phrase you already perceive to what extent art and nature struggle against each other. The person who possesses has indeed also something that has been taken in conquest—in fact, if the expressions are to be used strictly, one can say that only he who possesses makes a conquest. Now, very likely you also suppose that you do have possession, for you indeed have the moment of possession, but that is no possession, for that is not appropriation in the deeper sense. For example, if I imagine a conqueror who subjugated kingdoms and countries, he would indeed possess these subjugated provinces, he would have great possessions, and yet one would call such a prince a conquering and not a possessing prince. Only when he guided these countries with wisdom to what was best for them, only then would he possess them. This is rarely found in a conquering nature; ordinarily such a person lacks the humility, the religiousness, the genuine humanity needed in order to possess. That, you see, was why I stressed the religious factor when I explained the relation of marriage to first love, because the religious factor will dethrone the conqueror and allow the possessor to come forth; that was why I commended the marital pattern as designed precisely for the highest, for lasting possession.

Here I may remind you of a phrase you fling around often enough: "It is not the given that is great, but the acquired," for the conquering nature in a man and his making conquests are actually the given, but his possessing and wanting to possess are the acquired. To conquer takes pride, to possess takes humility; to conquer takes violence, to possess, patience; to conquer—greed, to possess—contentment with little; to conquer requires eating and drinking, to possess, prayer and fasting. But all the predicates I have used here, and indeed justifiably, to describe the conquering nature can all be applied to and are absolutely appropriate to the natural man, but the natural man is not the highest. To be specific, a possessing is not a spiritually dead and invalid *Schein* [appearance], even though with legal status, but a constant acquiring. Here you see again that the possessing nature has the conquering nature intrinsically. In other words, he conquers like a farmer who does not place himself at the head of his hired men and drives his neighbor away but conquers by digging in the earth. Thus true greatness is not in making conquest but in possessing. Now, if at this point you say: "I am not about to decide which is greater, but I readily admit that there are two large classes of people; each one must decide for himself to which he belongs and take care not to let himself be radically converted by some proselyting apostle." I certainly feel that with this last remark you have your eye on me a little. In response to that, however, I say that the one is not only greater than the other, but there is meaning in the one that is not in the other. The one has both a subordinate clause and a main clause; the other is only a subordinate clause and instead of a main clause has a problematic dash, the significance of which I shall explain to you some other time if you do not already know it.

Now, if you keep on declaring that you, for better or for worse, are indeed conquestive by nature, it makes no difference to me, for you must nevertheless grant me that it is greater to possess than to conquer. When a person conquers, he is continually forgetting himself; when he possesses, he recollects himself—not as a futile pastime but in all possible earnestness. When he goes up a hill, he just keeps his eye on the goal, but when he goes down a hill he has to keep watch on himself, on the proper relationship between the center of gravity and the point of support.

But to go on. You perhaps will admit that it is more difficult to possess than to conquer and that to possess is greater than to conquer: "If only I am permitted to conquer, I will not be so stingy but, on the contrary, very generous with my compliments to those who have the patience to possess, especially if they turn out to be willing to work hand in hand with me by being willing to possess my conquests. All right, it is greater, but more beautiful it is not; more ethical it is, all honor to ethics, but it is also less esthetic."

Let us try to achieve a little more mutual understanding on this point. It is quite true that there is a misunderstanding among many people that confuses what is esthetically beautiful with what can be presented with esthetic beauty. This is very easily explained by the fact that most people seek esthetic satisfaction, which the soul needs, in reading, in viewing works of art, etc.; whereas there are relatively few who themselves see the esthetic as it is in existence, who themselves see existence in an esthetic light and do not enjoy only the poetic reproduction.

II
121

But an esthetic representation always requires a concentration in the moment [*Moment*], and the richer this concentration is, the greater the esthetic effect. In this way, and only in this way, the happy, the indescribable, the infinitely rich moment—in short, *the moment*—gains its validity. Either this is a predestined moment, as it were, that sends a shudder through the consciousness by awakening the idea of the divineness of existence, or the moment presupposes a history. In the first case, it takes hold by surprising one; in the second case, it certainly is a history, but the artistic representation cannot linger on this, at best can only suggest it and then hasten on to the moment. The more it can put into it, the more artistic it becomes. Nature, as some philosopher has said, takes the shortest path;[152] it could be said that it takes no path at all, that in one stroke it is all there at once, and if I want to lose myself in gazing at the arch of heaven, I do not need to wait for the countless heavenly bodies to form, for they are all there at once. But the way of history, just like the way of the law, is very long[153] and arduous. So art and poetry intervene and shorten the way for us and delight us in the moment of consummation; they concentrate the extensive in the intensive. But the greater the significance of that which is to advance, the slower the course of history; but the more significant also the course itself, the more it will be evident that all that is the goal is also the way.

With respect to individual life, there are two kinds of history—the outer and the inner. It has two currents that flow in opposite directions. The first, in turn, has two sides. The individual does not have that for which he strives, and history is the struggle in which he acquires it. Or the individual has it but nevertheless cannot take possession of it, because there is continually something external that prevents him. History, then, is the struggle in which he overcomes these obstacles. The other kind of history begins with possession, and history is the process by which he acquires it. Since in the first case the history is external and what it strives for lies outside, history does not have true reality [*Realitet*],[154] and the poetic and artistic representation consists altogether properly in foreshortening it and hastening on to the intensive moment.

To hold to the subject we are most concerned with, let us imagine a romantic love. Imagine, then, a knight who has slain five wild boars, four dwarfs, has freed three princes from a spell, brothers of the princess he adores. To the romantic mentality, this has its perfect reality. But to the artist and poet it is of no importance whatever whether there are five or only four. On the whole, the artist is more limited than the poet, but even the latter has no interest in punctiliously describing what happened in the slaying of each particular wild boar. He hastens on to the moment. Perhaps he curtails the number, focuses the hardships and dangers in poetic intensity, and speeds on to the moment, the moment of possession. To him the entire historical sequence is of minor importance.

But when it is a matter of inner history, every single little moment is of utmost importance. Inner history is the only true history, but the true history struggles with that which is the life principle in history—with time—but when one struggles with time, the temporal and every single little moment thereby has its great reality. Wherever the individuality's inner blossoming has not yet begun, wherever the individuality is still closed up, it is a matter of outer history. As soon, however, as this bursts into leaf, so to speak, inner history begins.

Think now of our point of departure, the difference between the conquering and the possessing natures. The con-

quering nature is continually outside itself, the possessing nature is within itself; therefore the first gains an outer history,
and the second an inner history. But since outer history can be
concentrated without any damage, it is natural for art and poetry to choose it and thus in turn choose for representation the
unopened individuality and what pertains to him. To be sure,
it is said that love opens the individuality, but not if love is
understood as it is in romanticism, since it is brought only to a
point where he is supposed to open, and there it ends, or he is
about to open but is interrupted. But just as outer history and
the closed individuality, if anything, will be the most immediate subject of artistic and poetic portrayal, so everything that
constitutes the content of such an individuality will also be
their subject. But all this is basically what belongs to the natural man.

A few examples. Pride can be portrayed very well, because
what is essential in pride is not sequence but intensity in the
moment. Humility is hard to portray precisely because it is sequence, and whereas the observer needs to see pride only at its
climax, in the second case he really needs to see something that
poetry and art cannot provide, to see its continuous coming
into existence, for it is essential to humility to come into existence continuously, and if this is shown to him in its ideal moment, he misses something, for he senses that its true ideality
consists not in its being ideal at the moment but in its being
continuous. Romantic love can be portrayed very well in the
moment; marital love cannot, for an ideal husband is not one
who is ideal once in his life but one who is that every day. If I
wish to portray a hero who conquers kingdoms and countries,
this can be done very well in the moment, but a cross-bearer
who takes up his cross every day can never be portrayed in
either poetry or art, for the point is that he does it every day.
If I imagine a hero who loses his life, this can be concentrated
very well in the moment, but the daily dying cannot, because
the point is that it goes on every day. Courage can be concentrated very well in the moment; patience cannot, precisely because patience contends against time. You will say that art
nevertheless has portrayed Christ as the image of patience, as

bearing all the sin of the world, that religious poems have concentrated all the bitterness of life in one cup and had one individual empty it at one moment. That is true, but that is because they have concentrated it almost spatially. But anyone
who knows anything about patience knows very well that its
real opposite is not intensity of suffering (for then it more ap-
proximates courage) but time, and that true patience [*Taal-
mod*] is that which contends against time or is essentially long-
suffering [*Langmod*]; but long-suffering cannot be portrayed
artistically, for the point of it is incommensurable with art;
neither can it be poetized, for it requires the protraction of
time.

What more I want to say here you may regard as a poor
married man's trivial offering on the altar of esthetics, and if
you and all the priests of esthetics disdain it, I certainly know
how to console myself, and so much more so because what I
bring is not shew-bread, which only the priests can eat,[155] but
homemade bread, which like all homemade food is plain and
unspiced but healthful and nourishing.

If one traces dialectically and just as much historically the
development of the esthetically beautiful, one will find that the
direction of this movement is from spatial categories to temporal categories, and that the perfecting of art is contingent
upon the possibility of gradually detaching itself more and
more from space and aiming toward time. This constitutes the
transition and the significance of the transition from sculpture
to painting, as Schelling early pointed out.[156] Music has time
as its element but has no continuance in time; its significance is
the continual vanishing in time; it sounds in time, but it also
fades and has no continuance. Ultimately poetry is the highest
of all the arts and therefore also the art that best knows how to
affirm the meaning of time. It does not need to limit itself to
the moment in the sense that painting does; neither does it disappear without a trace in the sense that music does. But despite
all this, it, too, is compelled, as we have seen, to concentrate
in the moment. It has, therefore, its limitation and cannot, as
shown above, portray that of which the truth is precisely the
temporal sequence. And yet this, that time is affirmed, is not a

disparagement of the esthetic; on the contrary, the more this occurs, the richer and fuller the esthetic ideal becomes.

How, then, can the esthetic, which is incommensurable even for portrayal in poetry, be represented? Answer: by being lived.[157] It thereby has a similarity to music, which is only because it is continually repeated, is only in the moment of being performed. That is why in the foregoing I called attention to the ruinous confusing of the esthetic and that which can be esthetically portrayed in poetic reproduction. Everything I am talking about here certainly can be portrayed esthetically, but not in poetic reproduction, but only by living it, by realizing it in the life of actuality. In this way the esthetic elevates itself and reconciles itself with life, for just as poetry and art in one sense are precisely a reconciliation with life, yet in another sense they are enmity to life, because they reconcile only one side of the soul.

Here I am at the summit of the esthetic. And in truth, he who has humility and courage enough to let himself be esthetically transformed, he who feels himself present as a character in a drama[158] the deity is writing, in which the poet and the prompter are not different persons, in which the individual, as the experienced actor who has lived into his character and his lines is not disturbed by the prompter but feels that he himself wants to say what is being whispered to him, so that it almost becomes a question whether he is putting the words in the prompter's mouth or the prompter in his, he who in the most profound sense feels himself creating and created, who in the moment he feels himself creating has the original pathos of the lines, and in the moment he feels himself created has the erotic ear that picks up every sound—he and he alone has brought into actual existence the highest in esthetics.

But this history that proves to be incommensurable even for poetry is the inner history. This has the idea within itself and precisely therefore is the esthetic. Therefore it begins, as I expressed it, with the possession, and its progress is the acquiring of this possession. It is an eternity in which the temporal has not disappeared as an ideal element, but in which it is continually present as a real element. Thus, when patience acquires itself in patience,[159] it is inner history.[160]

Let us now consider the relation between romantic and marital love, for the relation between the conquering and the possessing natures presents no difficulties at all. Romantic love continually remains abstract in itself, and if it can find no outer history, death is already lying in wait for it, because its eternity is illusory. Marital love begins with possession and gains an inner history. It is faithful—and so also is romantic love, but now mark the difference.

The faithful romantic lover waits, let us say for fifteen years; then comes the moment [*Øieblikke*] that rewards him. Here poetry very properly perceives that the fifteen years can easily be concentrated; now it hastens to the moment [*Moment*]. A married man is faithful for fifteen years, and yet during these fifteen years he has had possession; therefore in this long succession he has continually acquired the faithfulness he possessed, since marital love has in itself the first love and thereby the faithfulness of the first love. But an ideal married man of this sort cannot be portrayed, for the point is time in its extension. At the end of the fifteen years, he seems to have come no further than he was in the beginning, and yet to a high degree he has been living esthetically. For him his possession has not been inert property, but he has been continually acquiring its possession. He has not fought with lions and trolls but with the most dangerous enemy, which is time. But now eternity does not come afterward, as for the knight, but he has had eternity in time, has preserved eternity in time. Therefore only he has been victorious over time, for it may be said of the knight that he has killed time, just as one to whom time has no reality always wishes to kill time, but this is never the right victory. Like a true victor, the married man has not killed time but has rescued and preserved it in eternity. The married man who does this is truly living poetically;[161] he solves the great riddle, to live in eternity and yet to hear the cabinet clock strike in such a way that its striking does not shorten but lengthens his eternity, a contradiction that is just as profound as, but far more glorious than, the one in the familiar situation described in a story from the Middle Ages about a poor wretch who woke up in hell and shouted, "What time is it?"—whereupon the devil answered, "Eternity!"[162] And although this cannot be portrayed artistically, then let your consolation be, as it is mine, that we are not to read about or listen to or look at what is the highest and the most beautiful in life, but are, if you please, to live it.

Therefore, when I readily admit that romantic love lends itself much better to artistic portrayal than marital love, this does not at all mean that it is less esthetic than the other—on the contrary, it is more esthetic. In one of the most brilliant stories from the romantic school,[163] there is a character who, unlike the others with whom he is living, has no desire to write poetry, because it is a waste of time and deprives him of genuine pleasure; he, on the contrary, wants to live. Now, if he had had a more valid idea of what it is to live, he would have been my man.

Marital love, then, has its enemy in time, its victory in time, its eternity in time—therefore, even if I were to imagine away all its so-called outer and inner trials, it would always have its task. Ordinarily it does have them, but if one is to view them properly one must pay attention to two things: that they are always inner qualifications and that they always have in them the qualification of time. For this reason, too, it is obvious that this love cannot be portrayed. It always moves inward and spends itself (in the good sense) in time, but that which is to be portrayed by reproduction must be lured forth, and its time must be foreshortened. You will be further persuaded of this by pondering the adjectives used to describe marital love. It is faithful, constant, humble, patient, long-suffering, tolerant, honest, content with little, alert, persevering, willing, happy. All these virtues have the characteristic that they are qualifications within the individual. The individual is not fighting against external enemies but is struggling with himself, struggling to bring his love out of himself. And these virtues have the qualification of time, for their veracity consists not in this, that they are once and for all, but that they are continually. And by means of these virtues nothing else is acquired; only they themselves are acquired. Therefore, marital love is simultaneously commonplace—as you have often mockingly called it—and also divine (in the Greek sense), and it is divine by virtue of being commonplace. Marital love does not come with external signs, not like that bird of fortune with rustling and bustling,[164] but is the inviolable nature of a quiet spirit.[165]

Of the latter, you and all conquering natures have no idea. You are never in yourselves but continually outside. Indeed, as long as every one of your nerves is palpitating, whether you are stealthily reconnoitering or you are advancing and internal Janizary music drowns out your consciousness, well, then it seems to you that you are living. But when the battle is won, when the last echo of the last shot has died away, when the swift thoughts, like orderly officers rushing back to G.H.Q. to report that the victory is yours—yes, then you are at a loss, then you do not know how to begin, for now for the first time you are standing at the real beginning.

Therefore, what you abhor under the name of habit as inescapable in marriage is simply its historical quality, which to your perverse eyes takes on such a terrifying look.

But what is it that you are accustomed to regard as being not only destroyed but, worse yet, profaned by the habit that is inseparable from marital life? Ordinarily you mean "the visible, sacred symbols of the erotic, which, like all visible symbols, in and by themselves certainly do not have meaning, but whose meaning depends on the energy, the artistic bravura and virtuosity—which are indeed also a natural genius—with which they are executed. How disgusting it is to see the dullness with which all such things are done in marital life, how superficially, how apathetically they take place, almost on the stroke of a clock, much as in the tribe the Jesuits discovered in Paraguay, a tribe so apathetic that the Jesuits found it necessary to have a bell rung at midnight as a pleasant reminder to all married men to attend to their marital duties. In this way, because of discipline, everything takes place at the right time."

Let us now agree that in our consideration we shall not allow ourselves to be at all disturbed by the presence of ever so much that is ludicrous and wrong in the world but only see whether it is necessary and, if so, learn from you deliverance. In this respect, I certainly dare not expect much from you, because you are continually fighting, even though in quite another sense, yet just like that Spanish knight,[166] for a bygone time. Since you are in fact fighting for the moment against time, you actually are always fighting for what has disappeared.

Let us take an idea, an expression from your world of poetry, or from the actual world of first love. The lovers "see" one another. This word "s e e"—you are very adept at spacing[167] it, at endowing it with an infinite reality, an eternity. Now, a married couple who have lived together for ten years and have seen each other daily may not see each other in that sense, but should they not be able to look upon each other lovingly? Here again I come to your old heresy. You happen to restrict your love to a certain age, and love for one person to a very brief time, and thereupon, like all conquering natures, you have to recruit in order to carry out your experiment, but this is the very deepest profaning of the eternal power of erotic love. It is indeed despair. However you twist and turn at this point, you must admit that the task is to preserve love in time. If this is impossible, then love is an impossibility. The source of your unhappiness is that you locate the essence of love simply and solely in these visible symbols. If these are to be repeated again and again and, please note, in the morbid thought whether they continually have the reality they had through the accidental circumstance that it was the first time, then it is no wonder that you are uneasy and that you classify these symbols and "gesticulations" with the things about which one does not dare to say: *decies repetita placebunt* [they will please even when repeated ten times],[168] for if what gave them validity was the condition of being the first time, then a repetition is indeed an impossibility. But true love has an utterly different value; it does its work in time and therefore will be able to renew itself in these external signs and has—this is my main point—a completely different idea of time and of the meaning of repetition.

In the foregoing, I have developed the idea that marital love has its struggle in time, its victory in time, its benediction in time. There I considered time merely as simple progression; now it will become evident that it is not just a simple progression in which the original is preserved but is a growing progression in which the original is increased. You, with your capacity for observation, will certainly agree with me in the general remark that people are divided into two great classes: those who live predominantly in hope and those who live predominantly in recollection.[169] Both indicate an improper relation to time.

The healthy individual lives simultaneously in hope and in recollection, and only thereby does his life gain true and substantive continuity. Thus he has hope and therefore does not wish to go backward in time, as do those who live only in recollection. What, then, does recollection do for him, for it certainly must have some influence? It places a sharp on the note of the moment; the further back it goes, the more often the repetition, the more sharps there are. For example, if in the present year he experiences an erotic moment, this is augmented by his recollection of it in the previous year etc.

This has also found expression in a very beautiful way in marital life. I do not know what age the world happens to be in at present, but you know as well as I do that we customarily say that first came the Golden Age, then the Silver Age, then the Copper Age, then the Iron Age.[170] In marriage it is the reverse—first the silver wedding, and then the golden wedding. Or is recollection not the real point in such a wedding—and yet the terminology of marriage declares them to be even more beautiful than the first wedding. But this must not be misinterpreted, as would be the case if you were inclined to say, "Then it would be best to be married in the cradle in order to begin at once with one's silver wedding and have a chance to be the first to coin a brand new term in the dictionary of marital life." You yourself probably perceive what constitutes the falsity in your jest, and I will not linger further on it. What I do wish to call to mind, however, is that the individuals do not live only in hope; at all times they have hope and recollection together in the present. At the first wedding, hope has the same effect as recollection at the last. Hope hovers over it as a hope of eternity that fills out the moment. You, too, will perceive the justification of this if you consider that if a person married only in the hope of a silver wedding and consequently hoped and hoped again for twenty-five years, when the twenty-fifth year came around he would have no right to celebrate a silver wedding, for he would have nothing to remember, since everything would have fallen apart in this continual hoping. Incidentally, I have frequently wondered why it is that, according to the common way of speaking and thinking, the single state has no such prospects at all, that on the contrary a bachelor who celebrates an anniversary is held up to ridicule instead. The reason surely must be that it is ordinarily assumed that the single state can never really comprehend the truly present time, which is a unity of hope and recollection, and therefore is usually based on hope or on recollection. But this in turn suggests the right relation to time that marital love has, also as commonly understood.

But there is also something else in marital life you designate with the word "habit": "its uniformity, its complete lack of events, its continuance in emptiness, which is death and worse than death." You know that there are neurotic people who are upset by the least noise, who are unable to think if someone is tiptoeing across the floor. Have you noticed that there is also another kind of neuroticism? There are people who are so enervated that they need loud noise and diverting surroundings in order to work. What is the reason for this if it is not that they lack self-control, except in the inverse sense? When they are alone, their thoughts wander into the wild blue yonder; when, however, there is noise and confusion around them, they are required to set their wills in opposition. This is why you are afraid of peace and quiet and rest. You are inside yourself only when there is opposition, but therefore you actually are never inside yourself but always outside yourself. In other words, the moment you assimilate the opposition there is quiet again. Therefore you dare not do so, but then the result will be that you and the opposition stand there face to face, and consequently you are not inside yourself.

Here, of course, the same thing holds as earlier with regard
to time. You are outside yourself and therefore cannot do
without the other as opposition; you believe that only a restless spirit is alive, and all who are experienced believe that only
a quiet spirit is truly alive. For you, a turbulent sea is a symbol
of life; for me it is the quiet, deep water. I have often sat beside
a little running stream. It is always the same, the same gentle
melody, on the bottom the same green vegetation that undu-
lates with the quiet ripples, the same tiny creatures that move
down there, a little fish that slips in under the cover of the
flowers, spreads its fins against the current, hides under a
stone. How uniform, and yet how rich in change! So it is with
the domestic life of marriage—quiet, modest, humming. It
does not have many *changements* [variations], and yet it is like
that water, running, and yet, like that water, it has melody,
dear to the one who knows it, dear to him precisely because he
knows it. It is not showy, and yet at times it has a sheen that
nevertheless does not interrupt its usual course, just as when
the moon shines on that water and displays the instrument on
which it plays its melody.

So it is with the domestic life of marriage. But to be perceived in this way and to be lived in this way, it presupposes a
quality to which I shall now refer. There is a poem by Oehlenschläger that I know you, at least at one time, prized very
highly. For the sake of completeness I will copy it:

> To guarantee the zest complete of love,
> How many things must be on earth combined!
> First, two hearts which a mutual passion prove:
> Then grace and beauty, with a soul refined:
> Then the moon shining through the beechen grove,
> When the spring greets the earth with zephyrs kind:
> Then meeting without danger or suspense:
> Then the embrace; and with that—innocence.[171]

You, too, are given to praising erotic love [*Elskov*]. I have no
desire to deprive you of what certainly is not your property,
for, after all, it is the poet's, but something you nevertheless
have appropriated; but since I, too, have appropriated it, let us

share it—you receive the whole poem, I the last phrase: and then innocence.

Finally, there is one more aspect of marital life that has frequently provided you with an occasion for attack. You say, "Within itself, marital love is hiding something completely different; it seems so gentle and beautiful and tender, but as soon as the door is shut on the married couple and before one can say Jack Robinson, out comes Master Erik; then the tune is changed to duty. And now you can decorate this scepter for me as much as you please, turn it into a Shrovetide birch switch; it is still a Master Erik."[172] I shall discuss this objection here because it is based essentially on a misunderstanding of the historical in marital love. You want to have either mysterious forces or caprice be the constituents in love [*Kjærlighed*]. As soon as an awareness enters in, this witchcraft vanishes, but marital love has this awareness. To put it quite crudely, instead of the orchestra director's baton, the motions of which mark the time for the graceful dance positions of first love, you show us duty's unpleasant policeman's stick. First of all, you must concede to me that as long as the first love, which, as we have agreed, marital love does indeed have, remains unchanged, there can be no question of the rigorous necessity of duty. So you do not believe in the eternity of first love. Here, you see, we have your old heresy; it is you who so often set yourself up as its knight, and yet you do not believe in it—indeed, you profane it. Consequently, because you do not believe in it, you do not dare become involved in a relation that will force you *nolens* [unwilling] to remain in it when you are no longer *volens* [willing]. Love is obviously not supreme for you, for otherwise you would be happy if there were a power capable of constraining you to remain in it. Perhaps you will reply that this means is no means, but to that comment I shall point out that it all depends on how one looks at the matter.

This turns out to be one of the points to which we continually return—you, seemingly against your will and without being entirely clear how it comes about, I, in full awareness—the point that the illusory or naive eternity of the first love or romantic love must cancel itself in one way or another. Pre-

II
132

cisely because you now seek to maintain it in this immediacy, seek to delude yourself that true freedom consists in being outside yourself, intoxicated with dreams, you fear this metamorphosis. And this is why it does not manifest itself as such but as something altogether alien that contains the death of the first love, and thus your abhorrence of duty. For if this has not already existed in embryo in the first love, then its appearance is naturally very disturbing. But such is not the case with marital love, which in the ethical and the religious already has duty within itself, and when duty manifests itself to them it is not a stranger, a shameless outsider, who nevertheless has such an authority that by virtue of the secrecy of love one does not dare to show him the door. No, he comes as an old intimate, as a friend, as a confidant whom the lovers both know in the deepest secrecy of their love. And when duty speaks it is not something new that he says, but something familiar, and when he has spoken the individuals humble themselves under it but are also lifted up by it, since they are assured that what he bids them to do is what they themselves wish, and that his bidding them to do it is only a more majestic, a more elevated, a divine way of expressing that their wish can be realized. To them it would not be sufficient for duty to say encouragingly, "It can be done, love can be preserved"; but because he says: "It shall be preserved," there is an implicit authority that corresponds to the inwardness of their wish. Love casts out fear,[173] but if love nevertheless fears for itself a moment, for its own salvation, then duty is precisely the divine nourishment love needs, for duty says, "Fear not; you shall [*skal*] conquer"—says it not just in the future tense, for then it is only a hope, but in the imperative mood, and therein rests a conviction that nothing can shake.

So, then, you regard duty as the enemy of love, and I regard it as its friend. Perhaps you will be satisfied with this explanation and with your usual sarcasm will congratulate me on having a friend who is just as interesting as he is unusual. I am not, however, at all satisfied with that and feel free to carry the battle over into your territory. If duty, once it has entered into consciousness, is the enemy of love, then love must indeed see to conquering it, for you certainly do not want love to be such a weak thing that it cannot get the better of every opposition. Yet on the one hand you think that if duty puts in its appearance it is all over with love and also think that sooner or later duty will inevitably show up, not only in marital love but also in romantic love, and the reason you essentially fear marital love is that it has duty in it to such a degree that when it does put in its appearance you cannot run away from it. But you think it is quite in order in romantic love, for the moment duty is mentioned, love is finished and duty's arrival is your signal to take your leave with a polite bow, or, as you once expressed yourself, that you regard it as your duty to take your leave.

Here again you see what happens with your eulogies on love. If duty is the enemy of love, and if love cannot conquer this enemy, then love is not the true triumpher. Then as a result of this you must leave love helpless. Once you have adopted the desperate idea that duty is the enemy of love, your defeat is sure, and you have disparaged love and robbed it of its majesty just as much as you have done the same with duty, and it was only the latter that you wished to do. You see, this is again despair, whether you feel the pain that is in it or in despair you try to forget it. If you cannot manage to see the esthetic, the ethical, and the religious as the three great allies, if you do not know how to preserve the unity of the different manifestations everything gains in these different spheres, then life is without meaning and one must completely agree with your pet theory that of everything it can be said: Do it, or do not do it—you will regret it either way.[174]

II
134

Unlike you, I do not have the sad necessity of being obliged to begin a campaign against duty that invariably ends unhappily. For me, duty is not one climate, love another, but for me duty makes love the true temperate climate, and for me love makes duty the true temperate climate, and this unity is perfection. But in order that your false theory may become properly obvious to you, I shall pursue this a bit further and ask you to ponder the various ways in which a person could feel that duty is the enemy of love.

Imagine a person who has married without ever rightly

coming to terms with the ethical, which is implicit in marriage. He loved with all the passion of youth and suddenly was prompted by an external circumstance to the doubt that the one he loved, but to whom he was also bound by the bond of duty, might possibly think that in reality he nevertheless loved her only because it was his duty. He was indeed in a situation similar to the one mentioned above; for him, too, duty seemed to manifest itself as antagonistic to love, but he did love, and for him his love was truly supreme, and consequently his efforts would be aimed at vanquishing this enemy. Consequently, he would love her—not because duty commanded it, not by the meager standard of a *quantum satis* [sufficient amount] that duty could provide—no, he would love her with his whole soul, with all his strength, and all his might;[175] he would love her even at that moment—if that were possible—when duty permitted him to stop.

You readily perceive the confusion in his thinking. What did he do? He loved her with his whole soul, but that is precisely what duty commands, for let us not be confused by the talk of those who think that in relation to marriage one's duty is nothing but a compendium of ritualistic stipulations. The duty is only one thing: it is to love in truth, in one's inmost heart; and duty is just as protean as love itself and pronounces everything holy and good if it is of love and inveighs against everything, however beautiful and deceptive it is, that is not of love. You see, therefore, that he, too, had taken a wrong position; but precisely because there was truth in him, he does neither more nor less than what duty commands, since he does not wish to do only what duty commands. Essentially, the more that he does is that he does it, for the more that I can do is always that I can do what duty commands. Duty commands; more it cannot do. The more I am capable of doing is to do what it commands, and the moment I do that I can in a certain sense say that I am doing more; I translate duty from the outer to the inner, and I am thereby beyond duty.

From this you perceive what infinite harmony and wisdom and consistency there are in the world of spirit. If one proceeds from a specific point and quite calmly pursues it with truth and energy, it must always be a disappointment if everything else seems to be in contradiction with it; and if one thinks that one is exhaustively attesting to the disharmony, one is attesting to the harmony. Therefore the married man of whom we have been speaking came out of it unscathed, and really the only punishment he had to suffer was that duty teased him a little about his little faith. Duty is always consonant with love. If you separate them as he did and want to make one part the whole, you are continually in self-contradiction. It is as if someone were to separate the letters "b" and "e" in the syllable "be" and then want to discard the "e" and insist that "b" is the whole. The moment he enunciates it, he says the "e" also. So it is with true love; it is not a dumb, abstract inexpressible something, but neither is it a weak, wavering indeterminate. It is an articulated sound, a syllable. If duty is hard, *eh bien,* then love pronounces it, actualizes it, and thereby does more than the duty; if love is about to become so soft that it cannot be kept stable, duty sets boundaries to it.

Now, if your position that duty is the enemy of love was like that, if it was merely an innocent misunderstanding, then it would go with you as with the man of whom we speak; but your view is a misunderstanding and also a guilty misunderstanding. That is why you disparage not only duty but also love; that is why duty appears to be an unconquerable enemy, precisely because duty loves true love and has a mortal hatred for the false kind—indeed, kills it. When the individuals are in the truth, they will see in duty only the eternal sign that the road to eternity is prepared for them and is the road they are eager to take; they are not only permitted to take it but are commanded to take it; and over this road there watches a divine providence that continually shows them the prospect and places signposts at all the danger spots. Why should the person who truly loves be unwilling to accept a divine authorization because it expresses itself divinely and does not say only "You may" but says "You shall"? In duty the road is all cleared for the lovers, and therefore I believe that in language the expression of duty is in the future tense in order thereby to indicate the historical.

Now I have finished this little exposition. Presumably it has really made an impression upon you; you feel that everything is upside down, and yet you cannot completely steel yourself against the consistency with which I have spoken. Nevertheless, if I had expressed all this in a conversation, you would undoubtedly find it hard to refrain from the sarcastic comment that I am sermonizing. But still you cannot actually blame my presentation for suffering from this fault or for being just what it perhaps ought to be when one speaks to a hardened sinner such as you are; and as for your lecturing and your wisdom, they often remind me of Ecclesiastes [*Prædikers Bog*, Book of the Preacher], and one would actually think that you occasionally chose your text from it.

I shall, however, allow you yourself to give me an occasion to throw light on this matter. Ordinarily you are not disdainful of ethics, and you really have to be driven to a particular point before you throw it overboard. As long as you are in some measure able to keep it on your side, you do so. "I do not in any way hold duty in contempt"—that is how the more temperate lecture, the more subtle assassination of duty, usually begins. "Far be it from me, but above all let's not scramble the eggs—duty is duty and love is love, and that's that, and, above all, no commingling. Or is not marriage the only monstrosity that has this nature, this hermaphroditic equivocation? Everything else is either duty or love. I acknowledge that it is a person's duty to seek a particular employment in life, I regard it as his duty to be faithful to his occupation; and on the other hand, when he violates his duty, then let him suffer his well-deserved punishment.

"Here is duty. I take it upon myself to do a specific something; I can stipulate exactly what it is I promise dutifully to fulfill. If I do not do it, then I am faced with an authority that can compel me. On the other hand, if I form a close friendship with another person, love is everything here. I acknowledge no duty; if love is over, then the friendship is finished. To base itself on something unreasonable like that is reserved solely for marriage. But what does it mean to commit oneself to love? Where is the boundary? When have I fulfilled my duty? In what, more closely defined, does my duty consist? In case of doubt, to what council can I apply? And if I cannot fulfill my duty, where is the authority to compel me? State and Church have indeed set a certain limit, but even though I do not go to the extreme, can I not therefore be a bad husband? Who will punish me? Who will stand up for her who is the victim?"

Answer: you yourself. However, before I proceed to untangle the jumble into which you have lured yourself and me, I must make a comment. In your statements there is often a certain degree of ambiguity, which for you is essential and characteristic. What you say could be said equally well by the most light-minded and heavy-hearted of men. You yourself are well aware of this, for it is one of the means you use to deceive people. You say the same thing at different times, place the tonal emphasis at different points, and look—the whole thing is different. If you are accused of saying something different from before, you very calmly respond: Isn't it literally the same?

But enough of that. Let us now analyze your division of duty and love. There is a proverb that has survived through the centuries and has been used to designate the shrewd politics of the Romans: *divide et impera* [divide and conquer].[176] In a much more profound sense, this can be said of the process of the understanding, for its cunning politics is expressly to divide and to secure dominion by means of this division, inasmuch as the powers that in alliance are invincible, now separated and alien, cancel one another, and the understanding retains dominion. Consequently, you think that all the rest of life can be construed within the category of duty or its opposite and that it has never occurred to anyone to apply another criterion; marriage alone has made itself guilty of this self-contradiction. You cite as an example the duty to one's occupation and think that this is a very appropriate example of a pure duty-relationship. This is by no means the case. If a person were to view his occupation merely as the sum total of assignments he carries out at specific times and places, he would demean himself, his occupation, and his duty. Or do you believe that such a view would make for a good public official? Where, then, is there room for the enthusiasm with which a

person devotes himself to his occupation, where is there room
for the love with which he loves it? Or what tribunal would
supervise him? Or is this not required of him precisely as duty,
and would not the state regard anyone who became a civil servant without this as a jobholder, as one whose drudgery it
could well use and pay for, but yet who in another sense was
an unworthy public servant? Now, even if the state does not
explicitly say this, it is because that which it requires is something external, something palpable, and if this is done, then it
presupposes the rest. In marriage, however, the internal is primary, something that cannot be displayed or pointed to, but
its expression is precisely love. Therefore, I see no contradiction in its being required as duty, for the circumstance that
there is no one to supervise is irrelevant, since he can indeed
supervise himself. Now, if you keep on making this demand,
then it is either because you want to use it to sneak out of duty,
or because you are so fearful for yourself that you would willingly be declared incapable of managing your own affairs, but
that certainly is equally wrong and equally reprehensible.

II
138

If you adhere to what I have developed in the foregoing discussion, just as I have developed it here, you will readily perceive that in maintaining the inwardness of duty in love I am
not doing it with the wild anxiety with which it sometimes is
done by people whose prosaic prudence has first annihilated
the immediate and who now in their old age have resigned
themselves to duty, people who in their blindness do not
know how to ridicule the purely natural violently enough, to
praise duty stupidly enough, as if in this way duty were anything other than what you call it. Thank God I know no such
gap. I have not fled with my love out into the wilderness and
the desert, where in my solitude I could not find my way; neither have I consulted my neighbors and next-door neighbors
about what I should do; such isolation and such particularism
are equally wrong. In the universally valid itself, which is
duty, I have continually had *impressa vestiga* [footprints] before
me. I have also felt that there are moments when the only salvation is to let duty speak, that it is sound and healthful to let
it carry its own punishment, not with the gloomy unmanliness

of a *heautontimoroumenos* [self-tormentor],[177] but in all earnestness and firmness. But I have not been afraid of duty; it has not
appeared to me as an enemy that would disturb the fragment
of joy and happiness I had hoped to rescue in life, but it has appeared to me as a friend, the first and only confidant in our
love. But this capacity to have open prospects at all times is the
benediction of duty, whereas romantic love goes astray or
comes to a standstill because of its unhistorical character.

Dixi et animam meam liberavi [I have spoken and un-
burdened my soul],[178] not as though up to now my soul
had been ensnared and just now has relief in this protracted expectoration[179]—no, this is merely healthy breathing in
which my soul has enjoyed its freedom. As you know, the
Latin for "breathing" is *r e spiratio*, a word that signifies the in-
haling of what was first exhaled. In respiration the organism
enjoys its freedom, and thus I, too, have enjoyed my freedom
in this writing, the freedom that is mine every day.

II
139

Accept now in well-prepared anticipation what is here offered to you as well tested. If you find it far too trivial to satisfy
you, then see if it is not possible to prepare yourself better, see
if you have not forgotten some precautionary measure. [180]The
Serbs have a legend that tells about an enormous giant who has
an equally enormous appetite. He comes to a poor peasant and
wants to share his noon meal. The peasant sets out the humble
best his house can manage. The giant's greedy eyes have already devoured it and have correctly surmised that he would
be just as hungry if he actually had eaten it. They sit down to
the table. It never occurs to the peasant that there would not be
enough for both of them. The giant reaches for the dish; the
peasant stops him with the words: It is the custom in my house
to begin with a prayer. The giant acquiesces, and lo, there is
enough for both of them.[181]

Dixi et animam meam liberavi, for her also, whom I still love
continually with the youthfulness of first love; her also I have
made free—not as though she were bound beforehand, but she
has rejoiced together with me in our freedom.

In accepting my fond greeting, please accept also, as you usually do, a greeting from her, friendly and sincere as always.

It is a long time since I have seen you here with us. This I can say in both a literal and a figurative sense, for although during the two weeks I have spent my evenings on this letter *instar omnium* [that stands for all], I have in a way continually seen you here with me; nevertheless I have not seen you even figuratively in my house, in my room, but outside my door, from which I have almost tried to drive you with my sweeping. I am not sorry to perform this task, and I know that you will not take offense at my behavior either. But as always I would like even more to see you, both in the literal and the figurative sense, here with us. I say this with all the pride of a husband who feels entitled to use the formal phrase "with us"; I say it with all the cordial respect any individual "with us" can always be sure of meeting. Please accept an invitation for next Sunday, not a family invitation "for ever," that is, for a whole day. Come when you will—you are always welcome; stay as long as you want to—you are always an engaging guest; go when you please—always with our best wishes.[182]

II
140

THE BALANCE BETWEEN THE ESTHETIC AND THE ETHICAL IN THE DEVELOPMENT OF THE PERSONALITY[1]

My Friend,

What I have said so often to you I say once again, or, more exactly, I shout it to you: Either/Or, *aut/aut*, for the introduction of a single corrective *aut* does not clarify the matter, inasmuch as the subject under discussion is too significant for anyone to be satisfied with just a part of it and in itself too coherent to be capable of being possessed in part. There are conditions of life in which it would be ludicrous or a kind of derangement to apply an Either/Or, but there are also people whose souls are too dissolute to comprehend the implications of such a dilemma, whose personalities lack the energy to be able to say with pathos: Either/Or.

These words have always made a great impression on me and still do, especially when I say them this way plainly and by themselves; therein lies the possibility of setting in motion the most terrifying contradictions. They act upon me like an incantation formula, and my soul becomes exceedingly earnest, at times is almost in a state of shock. I think of my early youth, when without really comprehending what it is to make a choice in life I listened with childish trust to the talk of my elders, and the moment of choice became a very solemn and momentous matter, although in choosing I only followed someone else's directions. I think of moments later in life when I stood at the crossroads, when my soul was made ripe in the hour of decision. I think of the many less important but for me not trivial incidents in my life when it was a matter of choosing, for even if there is only one situation in which these words have absolute meaning—namely, every time truth, justice, and sanctity appear on one side and lust and natural inclinations, dark passions and perdition on the other side. Nevertheless, even in matters that in and by themselves are innocent, what a person chooses is always important. It is important that he choose properly, test himself, so that eventually he does not have to begin a painful retreat to the point where he started and thank God if he has no more for which to upbraid himself than having wasted his time.

In daily conversation, I use these words as others use them; indeed, it would be a foolish pedantry to stop using them that way; but at times it may occur to me that I have used them about utterly trivial matters. They take off their humble clothes; I forget the insignificant ideas they separated; they appear before me in all their dignity, in their vestments. Just as a magistrate wears civilian clothes in everyday life and mingles with the crowd without any distinction, so also these words go about in everyday conversation; but when he appears in his authority, he separates himself from all the others. These words, then, appear before me like a magistrate I am accustomed to seeing only on solemn occasions, and my soul always becomes earnest. And even though my life has its Either/ Or behind it to a certain degree, I know very well that there will still be many a time when it will have its full significance. Meanwhile, I hope that when these words halt me on my way they will at least find me appropriately disposed, and I hope that I will make the right choice. But in any case I will try to choose with unfeigned earnestness; I may then at least dare to take comfort in the thought that I shall leave my wrong path sooner.

And now you, you certainly do use these words often enough—indeed, they have almost become a byword to you. What meaning do they have for you? None whatsoever. For you, to remind you of your own expression, they are a wink, a turn of the hand, a *coup de mains* [sudden attack], an abracadabra. You know how to apply them on any occasion, and they are not without effect either. On you they work like strong drink on a high-strung person; you become completely intoxicated in what you call the higher madness.

"Therein is contained the whole wisdom of life, but no one has ever rendered them as impressively—as if he were a god in the shape of a scarecrow who spoke to suffering humanity—as that great thinker and genuine philosopher of life who said to a man who had hurled his hat to the floor: Pick it up, and you will get a beating; leave it there, and you will also get a beating; now you may choose." You have your great joy "comforting" people when they turn to you in crucial situations; you listen to their expositions and then say: Yes, now I see it all perfectly; there are two possible situations—one can do either this or that. My honest opinion and my friendly advice is this: Do it or do not do it—you will regret both. But the person who mocks others mocks himself, and it is not meaningless but is rather a profound mockery of yourself, a tragic proof of how flabby your soul is, that your view of life is concentrated in one single sentence: "I say simply Either/Or." Now, if you actually meant that in all earnestness, then there would be nothing to be done with you. One would have to let you be what you are and lament that heaviness of heart or lightness of mind had debilitated your spirit. But since we know that is not the case, we are not tempted to feel sorry for you but to wish that your life situation might tighten its screws on you and force you to let what resides in you come out, might begin that more rigorous examination that is not satisfied with chatter and witticisms. Life is a masquerade, you explain, and for you this is inexhaustible material for amusement, and as yet no one has succeeded in knowing you, for every disclosure is always a deception. Only in this way can you breathe and prevent people from crowding too close upon you and making it difficult for you to breathe. Your occupation consists in preserving your hiding place, and you are successful, for your mask is the most enigmatical of all; that is, you are a nonentity and are something only in relation to others, and what you are you are only through this relation. You hold out a lovesick hand to an affectionate shepherdess and at once are masked in all possible Arcadian sentimentality; a venerable clergyman you deceive with a brotherly kiss etc. You yourself are a non-entity, an enigmatical figure on whose brow stands Either/Or. "This is my motto, and these words are not, as grammarians think, disjunctive conjunctions; no, they belong inseparably together and therefore ought to be written together in one word, since in union they form an interjection that I shout at mankind just as one shouts 'hip, hip' to a Jew."

II
145

Although every such remark from you has no effect on me or, if it does, at most arouses righteous indignation, I nevertheless shall answer you for your own sake. Are you not aware that there comes a midnight hour when everyone must unmask; do you believe that life will always allow itself to be trifled with; do you believe that one can sneak away just before midnight in order to avoid it? Or are you not dismayed by it? I have seen people in life who have deceived others for such a long time that eventually they are unable to show their true nature. I have seen people who have played hide-and-seek so long that at last in a kind of lunacy they force their secret thoughts on others just as loathsomely as they proudly had concealed them from them earlier. Or can you think of anything more appalling than having it all end with the disintegration of your essence into a multiplicity, so that you actually became several, just as that unhappy demoniac became a legion,[2] and thus you would have lost what is the most inward and holy in a human being, the binding power of the personality?

You really should not be facetious about something that is not only earnest but is also dreadful. In every person there is something that up to a point hinders him from becoming completely transparent to himself, and this can be the case to such a high degree, he can be so inexplicably intertwined in the life-relations that lie beyond him, that he cannot open himself.[3] But the person who can scarcely open himself cannot love, and the person who cannot love is the unhappiest of all. And you flippantly do the same; you practice the art of being mysterious to everybody. My young friend, suppose there was no one who cared to guess your riddle—what joy would you have in it then? But above all for your own sake, for the sake of your salvation—for I know no condition of the soul that can better be described as damnation—halt this wild flight, this passion for annihilation that rages within you, for that is what you want: you want to annihilate everything; you want to satisfy the hunger of your doubt by consuming existence. For this you fashion yourself, and for this you toughen your mind. You readily admit that you are good for nothing, that your only diversion is to march around existence seven times, blow the trumpet,[4] and then let the whole thing collapse so that your soul can be soothed, indeed, become sad, so that you can call forth echo, for echo sounds only in emptiness.

But by this road I probably will come no further along with you. Besides, my head, if you so please, is too weak to be able to endure this and, if I so please, too strong to take pleasure in this continual dizziness before my eyes. Therefore I shall embark on the subject from another side. Imagine a young man at the age when life really begins to have some meaning for him; he is healthy, pure, happy, brilliant, himself rich in hope, and the hope of everyone who knows him. Imagine—indeed, it is hard for me to have to say this—imagine that he made a mistake in you, that he believed you were an earnest, tested, experienced person to whom one could safely turn for enlightenment about the enigmas of life. Imagine that he turned to you with that lovable confidence that is the ornament of youth, with the undeniable exaction that is the prerogative of youth—what would you reply to him? Would you reply: Well, I simply say Either/Or? You certainly would hardly do that. Would you, as you are wont to say when you want to show your abhorrence of being burdened by others with their affairs of heart, would you poke your head out the window and say, "Go to the next house [*Huus forbi*]";[5] or would you treat him as you treat others who desire your counsel or seek enlightenment from you, whom you turn away as one does a tithe collector with the words that you are only a renter in life and not a householder and family man? This you probably would not do either. A brilliant young man is something you value far too much.

But your relation to him was not entirely what you ordinarily wished a relation to be; it was not an accidental encounter that put you in contact with him; your sense of irony was not tempted. Although he was the younger and you the older, yet he in his noble youthfulness made the moment earnest. Is it not true that you yourself would become young, that you would feel that there is something beautiful in being young but also something very earnest, that it is by no means unimportant how one uses one's youth, that one is faced with a choice, an actual Either/Or? You would feel that what matters is not so much the cultivating of one's mind as the maturing of one's personality. Your kindness, your sympathy, was set in motion, and on that basis you would speak with him. You would strengthen his soul, vindicate him in the confidence he had in the world; you would assure him that there is a power in a human being that can defy the whole world; you would urge him very strongly to use his time. All this you can do—and, when you want to, you do it very beautifully.

But note well what I am about to say to you, young man, for although you are not young, one is nevertheless always constrained to call you that. What did you do in this case? You admitted—something you otherwise are unwilling to admit—the importance of an Either/Or. Why? Because your soul was moved by love for the young man. And yet you deceived him in a way, for he perhaps will meet you at other times when it will not be at all convenient for you to admit it. There you see a sad consequence of a person's inability to disclose his nature harmoniously. You thought you were doing the best thing, and yet you perhaps have harmed him; perhaps he would have been able to hold out against your mistrust of life instead of finding rest in the subjective, fraudulent trust you instilled in him. Suppose that after some years you meet that young man again; he is lively, witty, brilliant, bold in his thought, spirited in his speech, but your sensitive ears easily detect the doubt in his soul. You have a suspicion that he, too, has arrived at the dubious wisdom: I simply say Either/Or. Is it not true that you would feel sorry for him, feel that he had lost something, and something very essential? But you will not grieve over yourself; you are satisfied, indeed, even proud of your dubious wisdom, yes, so proud of it that you cannot let another person share it since you want it all to yourself. And yet in another respect you find it regrettable—and it is your honest opinion that it is regrettable—that this young man arrived at the same wisdom. What an enormous contradiction! Your whole being contradicts itself. But only with an Either/Or can you extricate yourself from this contradiction; and I who love you more sincerely than you loved that young man, I who in my life have experienced the significance of choice, I congratulate you for being still so young that even though you will always miss out on something, you nevertheless—if you have the energy or, more accurately, will to have the energy for it—can win what is the main concern in life, you can win yourself, gain yourself.

Now, if a person could continually keep himself on the spear tip of the moment of choice, if he could stop being a human being, if in his innermost being he could be nothing more than an ethereal thought, if personality meant nothing more than being a nisse who admittedly goes through the motions but nevertheless always remains the same—if that were the situation, it would be foolish to speak of its being too late for a person to choose, since in a deeper sense there could be no question of a choice at all. The choice itself is crucial for the content of the personality: through the choice the personality submerges itself in that which is being chosen, and when it does not choose, it withers away in atrophy. For a moment that between which the choice is to be made lies—for a moment it seems to lie—outside the person who is choosing; he stands in no relation to it, can maintain himself in a state of indifference toward it. This is the moment of deliberation, but, like the Platonic [moment],[6] it actually is not at all, and least of all in the abstract sense in which you wish to hold onto it; and the longer one stares at it, the smaller it is. That which is to be chosen has the deepest relation to the one who is choosing, and when the choice is about an issue of elemental importance to life, the individual must at the same time continue to live, and this is why the longer he puts off the choice, the more easily he comes to alter it, although he goes on pondering and pondering and thereby believes that he is really keeping separate the two alternatives of the choice.

If one views life's Either/Or in this way, one is not easily tempted to trifle with it. One sees that the inner working of the personality has no time for imaginary constructions in thought, so that it continually speeds ahead and in one way or another posits either the one or the other, whereby the choice is made more difficult in the next moment, for that which has been posited will be withdrawn. Imagine a captain of a ship the moment a shift of direction must be made; then he may be able to say: I can do either this or that. But if he is not a mediocre captain he will also be aware that during all this the ship is ploughing ahead with its ordinary velocity, and thus there is but a single moment when it is inconsequential whether he does this or does that. So also with a person—if he forgets to take into account the velocity—there eventually comes a moment where it is no longer a matter of an Either/Or, not because he has chosen, but because he has refrained from it, which also can be expressed by saying: Because others have chosen for him—or because he has lost himself.

From the discussion so far, you will also see how my view of a choice is essentially different from yours, provided that I can speak of such a thing, for the difference in yours is precisely that it prevents a choice. For me, the moment of choosing is very earnest, not so much because of the rigorous thinking through of what appears separated in the choice, not because of the multiplicity of thoughts linked to each particular element, but because there is danger involved, that in the very next moment a choice may not be at my disposal, that something has already been experienced that must be done again. If one believes that at some moment a person can keep his personality completely blank and bare or that in the strictest sense one can halt and discontinue personal life, one certainly is mistaken. Already prior to one's choosing, the personality is interested in the choice, and if one puts off the choice, the personality or the obscure forces within it unconsciously chooses. Then when a choice is eventually made—provided, as I said before, one has not become completely volatilized—one discovers that there is something that must be done over again, must be withdrawn, and this is often very difficult. There are stories about human beings whom mermaids or mermen have subjected to their power with their demonic music.[7] To break the spell, so says the story, it was necessary for the person under the spell to play the same piece backward without making a single mistake. This is a very profound thought but very difficult to do, and yet this is the way it is. The error one has absorbed has to be rooted out in this way, and every time one makes a mistake one must begin all over again. As you see, this is why it is important to choose and to choose in time.

You, however, have another method, for I know full well that the polemical side you turn to the world is not your true nature. Yes, if deliberating were the task for human life, then you would be close to perfection. I shall illustrate. To be appropriate to you, the alternatives must naturally be bold: either a pastor—or an actor. Here is the dilemma. Now all your passionate energy is aroused; reflection with its hundred arms seizes the idea of becoming a pastor. You find no rest; day and night you think about it; you read all the books you can find, go to church three times every Sunday, make the acquaintance of pastors, write sermons yourself, deliver them to yourself, and for half a year you are dead to the whole world. Now you are ready; you can speak with more insight and seemingly with more experience about being a pastor than many a one who has been a pastor for twenty years. When you meet them, it arouses your exasperation that they do not know how to expectorate[8] with a completely different eloquence. You say: Is this enthusiasm? Compared with them, I, who am not a pastor, who have not dedicated myself to being a pastor, I speak with the voice of angels. That may very well be true, but you nevertheless did not become a pastor. Now you conduct yourself the same way with the other alternative, and your enthusiasm for art almost exceeds your ecclesiastical eloquence. Then you are ready to choose.

One thing is certain, however, that in the enormous mental activity you have gone through, much has dropped to the side, a host of minor reflections and observations. Therefore, at the moment you are to choose, these remnants come to life and into motion, and a new Either/Or turns up: a lawyer, perhaps a trial lawyer—that has something in common with both sides. Now you are lost. At that very moment, you are enough of a trial lawyer to be able to demonstrate the rightness of including the third. Your life goes on in this way. After

wasting a year and a half on these deliberations, after having
strained with amazing energy all the powers of your soul, you
have not advanced a single step. Then the thread of thought
snaps. You become impatient, emotional; you burn and dev-
astate, and now you continue: Either hairdresser or bank
teller—I simply say Either/Or.

No wonder that these words have become an offense and a
foolishness[9] to you, "that they appear to you to be like the
arms of the virgin whose embrace was death."[10] You look
down on people, make them objects of ridicule, and you have
become what you most abominate—a critic, a universal critic
in all the branches of learning. At times I cannot help smiling
at you, and yet it is sad that your truly remarkable intellectual
capacities have been dispersed in this way. But here again is the
same contradiction in your nature, for you discern the ludicrous very well, and God help the person who falls into your
hands if he is in the same situation. And yet the entire difference is that he perhaps becomes bowed down and crushed,
whereas you become erect and more jocular than ever and
make yourself and others happy with the gospel *vanitas vanitatum vanitas* [vanity of vanities all is vanity],[11] hurrah![12] But
this is no choice; it is what we say in Danish: *Lad gaae* [Let it
pass]! Or it is a compromise like making five an even number.
Now you feel yourself to be free; tell the world "Farewell."

II
151

> So zieh' ich hin in alle Ferne,
> Ueber meiner Mütze nur die Sterne
> [So I move on to places afar,
> Above my cap only the stars].[13]

With that you have chosen—not, of course, as you yourself
will probably acknowledge, the better part; but you have not
actually chosen at all, or you have chosen in a figurative sense.
Your choice is an esthetic choice, but an esthetic choice is no
choice. On the whole, to choose is an intrinsic and stringent
term for the ethical. Wherever in the stricter sense there is a
question of an Either/Or, one can always be sure that the ethical has something to do with it. The only absolute Either/Or

is the choice between good and evil, but this is also absolutely ethical.

The esthetic choice is either altogether immediate, and thus no choice, or it loses itself in a great multiplicity. For example, when a young girl follows her heart's choice, this choice, however beautiful it is otherwise, is no choice in the stricter sense, because it is altogether immediate. If a man esthetically ponders a host of life tasks, then he, as is the case with you in the preceding portion, does not readily have one Either/Or but a great multiplicity, because the self-determining aspect of the choice has not been ethically stressed and because, if one does not choose absolutely, one chooses only for the moment and for that reason can choose something else the next moment.

Therefore, the ethical choice is in a certain sense much easier, much simpler, but in another sense it is infinitely more difficult. The person who wants to decide his life task ethically does not ordinarily have such a wide range; the act of choosing, however, is much more meaningful to him. Now, if you are to understand me properly, I may very well say that what is important in choosing is not so much to choose the right thing as the energy, the earnestness, and the pathos with which one chooses. In the choosing the personality declares itself in its inner infinity and in turn the personality is thereby consolidated. [14]Therefore, even though a person chose the wrong thing, he nevertheless, by virtue of the energy with which he chose, will discover that he chose the wrong thing. In other words, since the choice has been made with all the inwardness of his personality, his inner being is purified and he himself is brought into an immediate relationship with the eternal power that omnipresently pervades all existence [*Tilværelse*]. The person who chooses only esthetically never reaches this transfiguration, this higher dedication. Despite all its passion, the rhythm in his soul is only a *spiritus lenis* [weak aspiration].[15]

Like a Cato,[16] then, I shout my Either/Or to you, and yet not like a Cato, for my soul has not yet attained the resigned coldness that he had. But I know that this adjuration alone, if

I have sufficient strength, will be able to arouse you, not to the activity of thinking, for in that you are not deficient, but to earnestness of spirit. Without it, you may succeed in accomplishing a great deal, even in astounding the world (for I am not stingy), and yet you will miss out on the highest, on the only thing that truly gives life meaning; you may win the whole world and lose yourself.[17]

What, then, is it that I separate in my Either/Or? Is it good and evil? No, I only want to bring you to the point where this choice truly has meaning for you. It is on this that everything turns. As soon as a person can be brought to stand at the crossroads in such a way that there is no way out for him except to choose, he will choose the right thing. Therefore, if it should so happen that before you finish reading this somewhat lengthy exploration, which again is being sent to you in the form of a letter, you feel that the moment of choice has arrived, then throw away the remainder—do not bother with it; you have lost nothing. But choose, and you will see the validity inherent in so doing; indeed, no young girl can be as happy with her heart's choice as a man who has known how to choose. Consequently, either a person has to live esthetically or he has to live ethically. Here, as stated, it is still not a matter of a choice in the stricter sense, for the person who lives esthetically does not choose, and the person who chooses the esthetic after the ethical has become manifest to him is not living esthetically, for he is sinning and is subject to ethical qualifications, even if his life must be termed unethical. You see, this is, so to speak, the *character indelebilis*[18] of the ethical, that the ethical, although it modestly places itself on the same level as the esthetic, nevertheless is essentially that which makes the choice a choice.

And this is what is sad when one contemplates human life, that so many live out their lives in quiet lostness; they outlive themselves, not in the sense that life's content successively unfolds and is now possessed in this unfolding, but they live, as it were, away from themselves and vanish like shadows. Their immortal souls are blown away, and they are not disquieted by the question of its immortality, because they are already disintegrated before they die. They do not live esthetically, but neither has the ethical become manifest to them in its wholeness; nor have they actually rejected it, and therefore they are not sinning either, except insofar as it is a sin to be neither one thing nor the other. Nor do they doubt their immortality, for the person who deeply and fervently doubts it on his own behalf is sure to find what is right. I say "on his own behalf," and it certainly is high time that someone warns against the magnanimous, gallant objectivity with which many thinkers think on behalf of all others and not on their own. If anyone calls what I am claiming here self-love, then I shall answer: That comes from having no idea of what this "self" is and from the futility of a person's gaining the whole world but losing himself, and also it is bound to be a poor argument that does not first and foremost convince the person who presents it.

Rather than designating the choice between good and evil, my Either/Or designates the choice by which one chooses good and evil or rules them out. Here the question is under what qualifications one will view all existence and personally live. That the person who chooses good and evil chooses the good is indeed true, but only later does this become manifest, for the esthetic is not evil but the indifferent. And that is why I said that the ethical constitutes the choice. Therefore, it is not so much a matter of choosing between willing good or willing evil as of choosing to will, but that in turn posits good and evil. The person who chooses the ethical chooses the good, but here the good is altogether abstract; its being is thereby merely posited, and this by no means precludes that the one choosing cannot in turn choose evil even though he chose the good. Here you see again how important it is that a choice is made and that it does not depend so much upon deliberation as on the baptism of the will, which assimilates this into the ethical. The more time that passes by, the more difficult it becomes to choose, for the soul is continually in one part of the dilemma, and hence it becomes more and more difficult to work itself free. And yet this is necessary if a choice is to be made, and consequently extremely important if a choice means anything, and that this is the case I shall point out later.

II
154

As you know, I have never passed myself off as a philosopher, least of all when I am conversing with you. Partly to tease you a little, partly because it actually is my most cherished, precious, and in a certain sense most meaningful occupation in life, I usually appear as a married man. I have not sacrificed my life to art and science; compared with them, that to which I have sacrificed my life is but a trifle. I sacrifice myself to my work, my wife, my childen, or, to be more accurate, I do not sacrifice myself to them but find my joy and satisfaction in them. These are trifles compared with what you are living for; nevertheless, my young friend, take care that the great things to which you are really sacrificing your life do not deceive you. Now, although I am not a philosopher, I nevertheless am constrained at this point to venture into a little philosophical deliberation, which I beg you not so much to criticize as to take *ad notam* [note of] for yourself.

The polemical conclusion, from which all your paeans over existence resonate, has a strange similarity to modern philosophy's pet theory that the principle of contradiction is canceled.[19] I am well aware that the position you take is anathema to philosophy, and yet it seems to me that it is itself guilty of the same error; indeed, the reason this is not immediately detected is that it is not even as properly situated as you are. You are situated in the area of action, philosophy in the area of contemplation. As soon as it is to be moved into the area of practice, it must arrive at the same conclusion as you do, even though it does not express it the same way. You mediate the contradictions in a higher lunacy, philosophy in a higher unity. You turn toward the future, for action is essentially future tense; you say: I can either do this or do that, but whichever I do is equally absurd—*ergo*, I do nothing at all. Philosophy turns toward the past, toward the totality of experienced world history; it shows how the discursive elements come together in a higher unity; it mediates and mediates.[20] It seems to me, however, that it does not answer the question I am asking, for I am asking about the future. In a way you do answer, even though your answer is nonsense.

Now, I assume that philosophy is right, that the principle of contradiction is actually canceled or that philosophers at every moment elevate it into the higher unity that is for thought. Yet this cannot, after all, apply to the future, for the contradictions certainly must be present before I can mediate them. But if the contradiction is present then it is an Either/Or. The philosopher declares: This is the way it was up until now. I ask: What am I supposed to do if I do not want to be a philosopher, for if I want to be a philosopher, I am well aware that I like other philosophers will have to mediate the past. For one thing, this is no answer to my question "What am I supposed to do?" for even if I had the most brilliant philosophic mind there ever was, there must be something more I have to do besides sitting and contemplating the past. Second, I am a married man and far from being a philosophic brain, but in all respect I turn to the devotees of this science to find out what I am supposed to do. But I receive no answer, for philosophy mediates the past and is in the past—philosophy hastens so fast into the past that, as a poet says of an antiquarian, only his coattails remain in the present.[21] See, here you are at one with the philosophers. What unites you is that life comes to a halt. For the philosopher, world history is ended, and he mediates. This accounts for the repugnant spectacle that belongs to the order of the day in our age—to see young people who are able to [22]mediate Christianity and paganism, who are able to play games with the titanic forces of history, and who are unable to tell a simple human being what he has to do here in life, nor do they know what they themselves have to do.

You are very prolific in coining phrases for your favorite conclusion. I shall single out one of them, because in it you are strikingly similar to the philosopher, even if his actual or assumed earnestness forbids him to participate in the obligato flight in which you delight. If someone asks you whether you will sign a petition to the king, or whether you desire a constitution or the right to impose taxes, or whether you want to join this or that charitable cause, you answer, "My esteemed contemporaries, you misunderstand me. I am not a participant at all; I am outside; like a little silent Spanish 's' I am outside."

So it is also with the philosopher. He is outside; he is not a participant. He sits and grows old listening to the songs of the past; he has an ear for the harmonies of mediation. I respect scholarship, and I honor its devotees, but life, too, has its demands. And even though I, if I saw one single extraordinarily endowed intellect one-sidedly lose himself in the past, would be perplexed about how I should form a judgment, about what opinion I should have alongside the respect I would hold for his intellectual competence—I am not perplexed today when I see a host of young people, not all of whom could possibly be philosophic minds, lost in today's favorite [*yndling*] philosophy, or what I am somewhat tempted to call the adolescent [*yngling*] philosophy of our day.

I have a valid claim against philosophy, as does anyone whom it does not dare to dismiss on the grounds of total incompetence. I am a married man; I have children. What if I now ask in their name what a human being has to do in life. You will perhaps smile; in any case the philosophical young people will smile at the family man, and yet I think it is truly an enormous argument against philosophy if it has nothing to answer. Has the movement of life come to a standstill? If the present generation can perhaps live on contemplation, what will the next generation live on? On contemplation of the same thing? After all, the last generation accomplished nothing, left nothing behind to be mediated. See, here again I can put you together with the philosophers and say to all of you: You are missing out on the highest. My position as a married man makes me better able to explain what I mean. If a married man were to say that the perfect marriage is the childless marriage, he would be guilty of the same mistake that the philosophers make. He makes himself into the absolute, and yet any married man will consider that this is untrue and unbeautiful and that his becoming himself a moment,[23] as he does by having a child, is much truer.

But I may already have gone too far; I have become involved in investigations I perhaps ought not to be making, partly because I am not a philosopher, partly because it is not at all my intention to converse with you about some phenomenon of the day but rather to address you, to make you feel in every way that you are the one addressed. But since I have come this far, I want to give a little closer consideration to the philosophical mediation of contradictions. If what I say should lack stringency, then perhaps it has a little more earnestness, and it is for that reason alone that it is set forth here. I do not aim to compete for any philosophical status, but certainly, since I have once taken up my pen, I aim to defend with it what I generally defend in other and better ways.

II
157

As truly, then, as there is a time to come, so truly there is an Either/Or. The time in which the philosopher lives is not absolute time; it is itself a moment.[24] It is always a dubious circumstance when a philosopher is barren; indeed, it must be regarded as a disgrace for him, just as in the Orient barrenness is regarded as a dishonor. Therefore, time itself becomes a moment, and the philosopher himself becomes a moment in time. Then in turn our age will appear to a later age as a discursive moment,[25] and in turn a philosopher of a later age will mediate our age, and so on. To that extent, then, philosophy is in the right, and it would be regarded as an incidental error on the part of the philosophy of our age to confuse our time with absolute time.

Yet it is easy to perceive that the category of mediation thereby has suffered a considerable blow and that absolute mediation is not possible until history is finished, in other words, that the system is in a continual process of becoming. What philosophy has retained, however, is the acknowledgment that there is an absolute mediation. This is, of course, extremely important for it, because if one abandons mediation, then one abandons speculation.

On the other hand, it is a dubious matter to admit this, for if one admits mediation, then there is no absolute choice, and if there is no such thing, then there is no absolute Either/Or. This is the difficulty; yet I believe it is due partially to a confusion of the two spheres with each other, the spheres of thought and of freedom. For thought, the contradiction[26] does not exist; it passes over into the other and thereupon together with the other into a higher unity. For freedom, the contradiction does exist, because it excludes it. I am by no means confusing *liberum arbitrium* [the freedom of indifference][27] with true, positive freedom, because even this has evil forever outside itself, even though it is only as a weak possibility. It does not become perfect by more and more assimilating evil but by more and more excluding it, but exclusion is the very opposite of mediation. That I do not thereby assume a radical evil[28] will be shown later.

II
158
The spheres with which philosophy properly has to deal, the spheres proper to thought, are logic, nature, and history. Here necessity rules, and therefore mediation has its validity. That this is true of logic and nature, no one will deny, but with history there is a difficulty, for here, it is said, freedom prevails.[29] But I think that history is incorrectly interpreted and that the difficulty arises from the following: History, namely, is more than a product of the free actions of free individuals. The individual acts, but this action enters into the order of things that maintains the whole of existence. What is going to come of his action, the one who acts does not really know. But this higher order of things that digests, so to speak, the free actions and works them together in its eternal laws is necessity, and this necessity is the movement in world history; it is therefore quite proper for philosophy to use mediation—that is, relative mediation. If I am contemplating a world-historical individual,[30] I can make a distinction between the deeds of which Scripture says "they follow him"[31] and the deeds by which he belongs to history. Philosophy has nothing at all to do with what could be called the inner deed, but the inner deed is the true life of freedom. Philosophy considers the external deed, yet in turn it does not see this as isolated but sees it as assimilated into and transformed in the world-historical process. This process is the proper subject for philosophy and it considers this under the category of necessity. Therefore it rejects the reflection that wants to point out that everything could be otherwise; it views world-history in such a way that there is no question of an Either/Or.

It seems, to me at least, that there is much foolish and incompetent talk mixed up in this point of view. I do not deny that the young necromancers who want to conjure up the spirits of history are especially ludicrous to me, but I also genuflect deeply to the magnificent accomplishments our age has to exhibit. As stated, philosophy sees history under the category of necessity, not under the category of freedom, for even though the world-historical process is said to be free, this is in the same sense as one speaks of the organizing process in nature.[32] For the historical process there is no question of an Either/Or, but nevertheless no philosopher can think of denying that for the acting individual there is such a question. This in turn explains the carelessness, the placability, with which philosophy regards history and its heroes, for it sees them under the category of necessity. This in turn accounts for its incapacity for having a person act, its inclination to let everything come to a standstill, for what it actually demands is that one must act necessarily, which is a contradiction.

So even the lowliest of individuals has a double existence. He, too, has a history, and this is not simply a product of his own free acts. The interior deed, on the other hand, belongs to him and will belong to him forever; history or world history cannot take it from him; it follows him, either to his joy or to his despair. In this world there rules an absolute Either/Or, but philosophy has nothing to do with this world. If I imagine an older man looking back over an active life, he has also a mediation of it in thought, for his history was interwoven in time's history, but deep within he has no mediation. There an Either/Or still continually separates what was separated when he chose. If there is any question of a mediation here, it could be said to be repentance. But repentance is no mediation; it does not look longingly at what must be mediated. Its wrath consumes it, but this is similar to exclusion, the opposite of mediation. Here it is also obvious that I am not assuming a radical evil, for I am positing the reality [*Realitet*] of repentance; but repentance, to be sure, is an expression for reconciliation, but it is also an absolutely irreconcilable expression.

Perhaps, however, you concede all this to me—you who nevertheless in so many ways make common cause with the philosophers, except insofar as you on your own account undertake to scoff at them. Perhaps you think that as a married man I can be satisfied with that and put it to use in my domestic life. To be honest, I ask no more, but I would still like to know which life is higher—the philosopher's or the free man's. If the philosopher is only a philosopher, absorbed in philosophy and without knowing the blessed life of freedom, then he misses a very important point, he wins the whole world and he loses himself—this can never happen to the person who lives for freedom, even though he lost ever so much.

It is for freedom, therefore, that I am fighting (partly in this letter, partly and chiefly in myself), for the time to come, for Either/Or. This is the treasure I intend to leave to those I love in this world. Indeed, if my little son at this moment were old enough to be able to understand me rightly and my last hour had come, I would say to him: I am not leaving you a fortune, nor titles and honors, but I know where a treasure is buried that can make you richer than the whole world, and this treasure belongs to you, and you must not even thank me for it, lest you damage your soul[33] by owing everything to a human being. This treasure is stored in your own inner being. There is an Either/Or there that makes a human being greater than the angels.[34]

Here I shall cut short this line of thought. It perhaps does not satisfy you; your greedy eye devours it without being satisfied, but that is because the eye is the last to be satisfied,[35] especially when one, like you, is not hungry but merely suffers a lust of the eye that cannot be appeased.

What takes precedence in my Either/Or is, then, the ethical. Therefore, the point is still not that of choosing something; the point is not the reality[36] of that which is chosen but the reality of choosing. This, however, is what is crucial, and it is to this that I shall strive to awaken you. Up to that point, one person can help another; when he has reached that point, the significance the one person can have for the other becomes more subordinate. In my previous letter, I noted that to have loved gives a person's being a harmony that is never entirely lost. Now I will say that to choose gives a person's being a solemnity, a quiet dignity, that is never entirely lost.

There are many who attach great importance to having seen

some extraordinary world-historical individuality face to face. They never forget this impression; it has given their souls an ideal image that ennobles their natures, and yet, however significant this very moment can be, it is nothing compared with the moment of choice. When around one everything has become silent, solemn as a clear, starlit night, when the soul comes to be alone in the whole world, then before one there appears, not an extraordinary human being, but the eternal power itself, then the heavens seem to open, and the *I* chooses itself or, more correctly, receives itself. Then the soul has seen the highest, which no mortal eye can see[37] and which can never be forgotten; then the personality receives the accolade of knighthood that ennobles it for an eternity. He does not become someone other than he was before, but he becomes himself. The consciousness integrates, and he is himself. Just as an heir, even if he were heir to the treasures of the whole world, does not possess them before he has come of age,[38] so the richest personality is nothing before he has chosen himself; and on the other hand even what might be called the poorest personality is everything when he has chosen himself, for the greatness is not to be this or that but to be oneself, and every human being can be this if he so wills it.

That in a certain sense the point is not a choice of something, you will perceive from this—that what appears on the other side is the esthetic, which is the indifferent. And yet the point here is a choice, indeed, an absolute choice, for only by choosing absolutely can one choose the ethical. Consequently, the ethical is posited by the absolute choice, but it by no means follows that the esthetic is excluded. In the ethical, the personality is brought into a focus in itself; consequently, the esthetic is absolutely excluded or it is excluded as the absolute, but relatively it is continually present. In choosing itself, the personality chooses itself ethically and absolutely excludes the esthetic; but since he nevertheless chooses himself and does not become another being by choosing himself but becomes himself, all the esthetic returns in its relativity.

The Either/Or I have advanced is, therefore, in a certain sense absolute, for it is between choosing and not choosing.

II
161

But since the choice is an absolute choice, the Either/Or is absolute. In another sense, the absolute Either/Or does not make its appearance until the choice, because now the choice between good and evil appears. I shall not concern myself here with this choice posited in and with the first choice; I wish only to force you to the point where the necessity of making a choice manifests itself and thereafter to consider existence under ethical qualifications. I am no ethical rigorist, enthusiastic about a formal, abstract freedom. If only the choice is posited, all the esthetic returns, and you will see that only thereby does existence become beautiful, and that this is the only way a person can save his soul and win the whole world, can use the world without misusing it.

But what does it mean to live esthetically, and what does it mean to live ethically? What is the esthetic in a person, and what is the ethical? To that I would respond: the esthetic in a person is that by which he spontaneously and immediately is what he is; the ethical is that by which he becomes what he becomes. The person who lives in and by and from and for the esthetic that is in him, that person lives esthetically.

It is not my intention here to go into a detailed consideration of all that is contained in the proposed definition of the esthetic. It also seems superfluous to want to tell you what it means to live esthetically, you who have practiced it with such virtuosity that I would need your help instead. But I do nevertheless want to outline a few stages in order to make our way to the point where your life really belongs, which is a matter of importance to me lest you give me the slip too soon by one of your much favored digressions. Then, too, I do not doubt that I shall be able to tell you a good deal about what it means to live esthetically. Although I would direct anyone who wants to live esthetically to you as the most reliable guide, I would not direct him to you if he in a higher sense wished to understand what it means to live esthetically, for you would be unable to inform him precisely, because you yourself are trapped in it; the only person who can explain it to him is the one who stands on a higher level, or the one who lives ethically. You might be tempted momentarily to vex me by saying that I, too, would not be able to provide a reliable explanation of what it means to live ethically, since I myself am trapped in it. But this would only give me an occasion for more information. The reason the person who lives esthetically can in a higher sense explain nothing is that he is always living in the moment, yet is always cognizant of it only in a certain relativity, within a certain limitation. It is not at all my intention to deny that in order to live esthetically, when such a life is at its highest, a multiplicity of intellectual gifts may be necessary, indeed, that these may even be intensively developed to an unusual degree, but they are still enslaved and lack transparency.[39] For example, there are animal species that possess much sharper, much more powerful senses than human beings do, but they are in bondage to animal instinct.

I would like to take you yourself as an example. I have never denied that you have extraordinary intellectual gifts, as you yourself can see from my having frequently reproached you for misusing them. You are witty, ironic, observant, a dialectician, experienced in enjoyment. You know how to calculate the moment; you are sentimental, heartless, all according to the circumstances; but during all this you are at all times only in the moment, and for that reason your life disintegrates, and it is impossible for you to explain it. Now if someone desires to learn the art of enjoyment, it is altogether right to go to you; but if he wishes to understand your life, then he is turning to the wrong person. Perhaps with me he is more likely to find what he is looking for, although I by no means have all your intellectual gifts. You are trapped and have, so to speak, no time to extricate yourself; I am not trapped in my judgment of either the esthetic or the ethical, for in the ethical I am raised above the moment, I am in freedom, but it is a contradiction for anyone to be able to become trapped by being in freedom.

Every human being, no matter how slightly gifted he is, however subordinate his position in life may be, has a natural need to formulate a life-view, a conception of the meaning of life and of its purpose. The person who lives esthetically also does that, and the popular expression heard in all ages and from various stages is this: One must enjoy life. There are, of

II
163

course, many variations of this, depending on differences in the conceptions of enjoyment, but all are agreed that we are to enjoy life. *But the person who says that he wants to enjoy life always posits a condition that either lies outside the individual or is within the individual in such a way that it is not there by virtue of the individual himself.* I beg you to keep rather fixed the phrases of this last sentence, for they have been carefully chosen.

Let us now very briefly run through these stages in order to arrive where you are. Perhaps you are already slightly irritated by the popular expression for living esthetically that I have stated, and yet you will scarcely be able to deny its accuracy. Often enough you have been heard ridiculing people, saying that they do not know how to enjoy life, while you yourself, on the other hand, think that you have studied it from the bottom up. Admittedly, it is possible that they do not understand it, but they nevertheless agree with you on the expression itself. You may now have a suspicion that in this deliberation you are going to end up joining hands with people who ordinarily are an abomination to you. You may be thinking that I ought to be sufficiently courteous to treat you as an artist and tacitly ignore the bunglers who are enough of a nuisance to you in life and with whom you in no way wish to have anything in common. But I cannot be of any assistance to you, for you do nevertheless have something in common with them, and something very essential—namely, a life-view—and what distinguishes you from them is in my eyes something unessential. I cannot help but laugh at you. It is a curse, you see, my young friend, that follows you: all those brother artists you have whom you have no intention of acknowledging. You are running the risk of getting into bad and vulgar company, you who are so distinguished. I do not deny that it must be disagreeable to share a life-view with every toper or *Jagtliebhaber* [hunting buff]. Nor is that exactly the case, for, as I shall show later, you do lie somewhat beyond the esthetic realm.

[40]However great the differences within the esthetic may be, all stages still have the essential similarity that spirit is not qualified as spirit but is immediately qualified. The differences can be extreme, all the way from total absence of spirit to the high-

est level of brilliance; but, even in the stage where brilliance manifests itself, spirit is still not qualified as spirit but as gift.

May I just very briefly single out each stage and dwell on only that which in some way or other could be applicable to you or which I would like you to apply to yourself. The personality is immediately qualified, not mentally-spiritually but physically. Here we have a life-view that teaches that health is the most precious good, is that around which everything revolves. A more poetic expression of the same view reads: Beauty is the ultimate. Now, beauty is a very frail good, and therefore we seldom see this life-view sustained. Frequently enough we encounter a young girl or young man who for a short time plumes herself or himself on her or his beauty, but it soon deceives them. But I do remember once having seen it sustained with rare good fortune. During vacations in my student days, I sometimes visited at a count's residence in one of the provinces. In his younger days, the count had had a diplomatic appointment; now he was old and was living in rural tranquillity at his manor house. As a young girl, the countess had been extraordinarily lovely; even in her advancing years she was the most beautiful woman I have seen. With his masculine beauty, the count in his youth had made a great hit with the fair sex. At court, the handsome royal gentleman-in-waiting was still remembered. Age had not broken him, and a noble, genuinely distinguished dignity made him still more handsome. Those who had known them in their younger days swore that they were the handsomest couple they had seen, and I who had the good luck to become acquainted with them in their advanced years found this entirely fitting, for they were still the handsomest couple around. The countess and also the count were very well educated and yet the countess's life-view centered in the idea that they were the handsomest couple in the whole country.

I still recall vividly an event that convinced me of this. It was a Sunday forenoon; there was a little festival in the church lying near the manor house. The countess had not felt well enough to go out and be present. The count, however, went out there that morning, dressed in all his glory, wearing his

royal court uniform adorned with medals and ribbons. The
windows in the great hall faced an avenue that led to the
church. The countess stood at one of them; she was dressed in
an attractive morning dress and was very lovely. I had in-
quired about her health and had engaged in a conversation
with her about a sailing party that was to take place the next
day, when the count appeared far down the avenue. She became silent; she became more beautiful than I had ever seen
her; her face became almost a little sad. The count had come so
near that he could see her at the window; with grace and dignity she threw him a kiss and then turned to me and said,
"William, my dear friend, isn't it true that my Ditlev is the
handsomest man in the whole kingdom! Oh, yes, I do see that
he sags a little on one side, but no one can see that when I am
walking beside him, and when we go walking together we are
still the handsomest couple in the whole land." No little miss
of sixteen years could be more ecstatic about her fiancé, the
handsome gentleman-in-waiting, than her ladyship over the
already superannuated lord chamberlain.

Both life-views are in agreement that we are supposed to enjoy life; the condition for this lies in the individual himself, but
in such a way that it is not posited by the individual himself.

We proceed. We encounter life-views that teach that we are
to enjoy life but place the condition for it outside the individual. This is the case with every life-view in which wealth, honors, noble birth, etc. are made life's task and its content. Here,
again, I would like to mention a certain kind of falling in love.
If I imagine a young girl in love with all her soul, whose eyes
have no delight except in seeing her beloved, whose soul has
no thought except of him, whose heart has no desire except to
belong to him, for whom nothing, nothing, neither in heaven
nor on earth, has any meaning except him, then this, too, is an
esthetic life-view in which the condition is placed outside the
individual. You, of course, think that it is foolish to love this
way; you think that it is something that happens only in novels. But it can be imagined, and this much is certain: In the eyes
of many people a love such as that would be regarded as some-

thing extraordinary. Later I shall explain to you why I cannot approve of it.

We proceed. We encounter life-views that teach that we are to enjoy life, but the condition for it lies within the individual himself, yet in such a way that it is not posited by himself. Here the personality is ordinarily defined as talent. It is a talent for practical affairs, a talent for business, a talent for mathematics, a talent for writing, a talent for art, a talent for philosophy. Satisfaction in life, enjoyment, is sought in the unfolding of this talent. Perhaps one does not stop with the talent in its immediacy but refines it in every way, but the condition for satisfaction in life is the talent itself, a condition that is not posited by the individual himself. People with this life-view frequently are among those who are usually the butt of your constant ridicule because of their unflagging activity. You believe that you yourself are living esthetically and will by no means acknowledge that they are. That you have another view of enjoying life is undeniable, but that is not the essential point; the essential point is that one wants to enjoy life. Your life is much more distinguished than theirs, but theirs is also much more innocent than yours.

Just as all these life-views have their esthetic nature in common, so they also resemble one another in having a certain unity, a certain coherence, the one particular thing around which everything revolves. What they build their lives upon is something simple, and therefore this life-view is not fragmented as is the life-view of those who build upon something intrinsically multiple.

This is the case with the life-view on which I shall now dwell a bit longer. It teaches "Enjoy life" and interprets it as "Live for your desire." But desire per se is a multiplicity, and thus it is easy to see that this life splits up into a boundless multiplicity except insofar as desire in a particular individual has from childhood been limited to one specific desire, which then might rather be called an inclination, for example, a bent toward fishing or hunting or keeping horses etc. Insofar as this life-view splits up into a multiplicity, it is easy to see that it is within the sphere of reflection; yet this reflection is always

II
166

only a finite reflection, and the person remains in his immediacy. In the desire itself, the individual is immediate, and however refined and sophisticated, however artfully devised it is, the individual is still in it as immediate. In the enjoyment, he is in the moment, and however multiple he is in this respect, he nevertheless is continually immediate because he is in the moment.

To live in order to satisfy one's desire is a very distinguished appointment in life, and thank God one rarely sees it put into practice completely because of the trials and tribulations in life that give a person something else to think about. If this were not the case, we no doubt would often enough be witnesses to this terrible spectacle, for we certainly too frequently hear people complain that they feel cramped by their prosaic life, which unfortunately all too often means nothing else than that they would like to fling themselves into all the wildness into which desire can spin a person. In order for this life-view to be carried out, the individual must possess a variety of external conditions, and this fortune, or more correctly, misfortune, is rarely one's lot—this misfortune, for it certainly is not from the gracious gods but from the angry gods that this fortune comes.

II
167

We rarely see this life-view put into practice on any significant scale, but we not infrequently see people who dabble in it, and when the conditions are no longer present, they feel that they surely would have attained the joy and happiness they craved in life if only the conditions had been at their disposal. In history, however, we find an occasional example of this, and since I believe there may be some benefit in seeing where this life-view leads when everything is in its favor, I shall present such a character, and to that end I choose that omnipotent man, the emperor Nero, before whom a whole world bowed, who was perpetually surrounded by a countless host of the accommodating messengers of desire. With your usual rashness, you once said that Nero could hardly be blamed for burning Rome in order to get an idea of the conflagration of Troy,[41] but one might question whether he actually had enough artistry to understand how to enjoy it.

Now, it is one of your imperial desires never to step aside for any thought, never to be terrified by it. For this, one does not need an imperial guard, nor gold and silver, nor all the treasures of the world; one can do this all by oneself and decide privately; it is not thereby less terrible but is more prudent. You presumably did not mean to mount a defense of Nero, and yet there is a kind of defense in fixing one's gaze not on what he does but on the *how*. Yet I am well aware that this rashness in thoughts is something often found in young people, who at such moments try them out, as it were, on the world and then are easily tempted to exalt themselves, especially when they have an audience. I know full well that you and I and every other human being, indeed, Nero himself, flinch at such ferociousness, and yet I should never advise anyone to attribute to himself, in the strictest sense, strength enough not to become a Nero.

To be specific, if in order to describe Nero I were to mention what in my opinion constituted his nature, to you the word would perhaps seem all too lenient, and yet I certainly am no lenient judge, even though in another sense I never judge any human being. But believe me, the word is not too lenient; it is the legitimate word, but it can also show how close such ferociousness can be to a person; indeed, it may be said that to every human being who does not remain a child all his life there comes a moment when he has a presentiment, even though remote, of this perdition. Nero's nature was *depression* [*Tungsind*]. In our day, it has become somewhat prestigious to be depressed; as far as that goes, I can well understand that you find this word too lenient; I hold to an ancient doctrine of the Church that classifies depression among the cardinal sins.[42] If I am correct, this is certainly a very unpleasant bit of information for you, for it turns your whole outlook on life upside down. By way of precaution, I shall promptly point out that a person can have sorrow and care—indeed, this can be so deep that it may follow him his whole life, and this can even be beautiful and true—but only through his own fault does a person become depressed.

I picture, then, that imperial sensualist. Not only when he

II
168

ascends his throne or goes to the council meeting is he surrounded by lictors, but also and mainly when he sets out to
satisfy his appetites—so that they can clear the way for his pirate expeditions. I imagine him as a somewhat older person;
his youth is past, his buoyant disposition has drained away,
and he is already familiar with every imaginable pleasure, already sated with them. But no matter how corrupted that life
may be, it nevertheless has ripened his soul, and despite all he
knows about the world, despite all his experience, he is still a
child or a young man. The immediacy of the spirit cannot
break through, and yet it requires a breakthrough; it requires
a higher form of existence. But if this is to happen, there will
come a moment when the splendor of the throne, his power
and his might, will pale, and for that he does not have the
courage. Now he snatches at pleasure; all the ingenuity of the
world must devise new pleasures for him, because only in the
moment of pleasure does he find rest, and when that is over,
he yawns in sluggishness. The spirit continually wants to
break through, but it cannot achieve a breakthrough; it is continually being swindled, and he wants to offer it the satiation
of pleasure.

Then the spirit masses within him like a dark cloud; its
wrath broods over his soul, and it becomes an anxiety that
does not cease even in the moment of enjoyment. This, you
see, is why his eyes are so dark that no one can bear to look into
them, his glance so flashing that it alarms, for behind the eyes
the soul lies like a gloomy darkness. This is called the imperial
look and the whole world quakes before it, and yet his innermost being is anxiety. A child who looks at him in a way different from what he is used to, an incidental glance, can terrify
him. It is as if that person owned him, for the spirit wants to
come through in him, wants him consciously to possess himself, but that he cannot do, and the spirit is pressed back and
accumulates new wrath. He does not possess himself; only
when the world quakes before him does he calm down, for
then there is no one who dares to seize him. That is the reason
for the anxiety about people that Nero has in common with
every such personality. He is as if possessed, inwardly unfree,

and that is why it seems to him as if every glance would bind him. He, the emperor of Rome, can be afraid of the look of the lowliest slave. He catches such a look; his eyes dispatch the person who dares to look at him that way. A miscreant stands at the emperor's side, comprehends this wild glance, and that person is no more.

But Nero has no murder on his conscience; yet the spirit has a new anxiety. Only in the moment of desire does he find diversion. He burns up half of Rome, but his agony is the same. After a while, such things do not give him pleasure any more. There is a still greater pleasure; he will make people anxious. He is a riddle to himself, and anxiety is his nature; now he will be a riddle to everybody and rejoice over their anxiety. Hence that imperial smile that no one can comprehend. They approach his throne; he smiles at them in a friendly way, and yet they are seized by a dreadful anxiety. Perhaps this smile is their death sentence; perhaps the floor will open and they will plunge down into the abyss. A woman approaches his throne; he smiles graciously at her, and yet she almost faints from anxiety. Perhaps this smile is already selecting her as a sacrifice to his lust. And this anxiety amuses him. He does not want to impress; he wants to cause anxiety. He does not make his entrance proudly in all his imperial dignity; weak, feeble, he sneaks in, for this infirmity is even more alarming. He looks like a dying man, his breathing is faint, and yet he is Emperor of Rome and holds people's lives in his hand. His soul is sluggish; only witticisms and puns are able to revive him momentarily. But what the world has is exhausted, and yet he cannot breathe if this is silenced. He could have a child cut down before its mother's eyes to see if her despair could provide passion a new expression capable of amusing him. If he were not the Roman emperor, he perhaps would end his life with suicide, for, indeed, they are just different expressions of the same thing when Caligula wishes that the heads of all people were on one neck so that the whole world could be annihilated with one stroke[43] and when a person takes his own life.

Whether this was the case with Nero, I do not know, but a certain good-naturedness is sometimes found in personalities like this, and if Nero had had it I do not doubt that the people around him would have been willing to call it graciousness. Incongruous as it is, it does, however, provide new evidence of the immediacy that in being repressed is the main constituent of the actual depression. Then it happens that when all the treasures and glory of the world are scarcely adequate to amuse them, a single word, an odd little something, a person's external appearance, or any such intrinsically trifling thing can provide extraordinary delight to them. A Nero can be happy as a child over such things. As a child—this is exactly the right term for it, because here it is the child's total immediacy that manifests itself unaltered and unclarified. A matured personality cannot enjoy in this way, for although he has retained his childlikeness he nevertheless has ceased to be a child. Usually, then, Nero is an old man; on occasion he is a child.

Here I shall terminate this little sketch, which on me, at least, has made a very sobering impression. Even after his death Nero causes anxiety, for however corrupt he is, he is still flesh of our flesh and bone of our bone, and there is something human even in an inhuman wretch. I have not presented this in order to engage your imagination; I am not an author who curries a reader's favor, least of all yours, and, as you know, I am not an author at all and am writing only for your sake. Neither have I presented this in order to give you and me an opportunity to thank God along with that Pharisee that I am an altogether different kind of man.[44] In me it arouses other thoughts, even though I thank God that my life has been so uneventful that I have only a faint intimation of this horror and am now a happily married man. As far as you are concerned, I am glad that you are still young enough to learn something from this. Let each one learn what he can; both of us can learn that a person's unhappiness never lies in his lack of control over external conditions, since this would only make him completely unhappy.

What, then, is depression? It is hysteria of the spirit. There comes a moment in a person's life when immediacy is ripe, so to speak, and when the spirit requires a higher form, when it wants to lay hold of itself as spirit. As immediate spirit, a person is bound up with all the earthly life, and now spirit wants to gather itself together out of this dispersion, so to speak, and to transfigure itself in itself; the personality wants to become conscious in its eternal validity. If this does not happen, if the movement is halted, if it is repressed, then depression sets in. One can try a great many things to consign it to oblivion; one can work, can snatch at more innocent remedies than a Nero, but the depression continues.

II
171

There is something unexplainable in depression [*Tungsind*]. A person with a sorrow or a worry knows why he sorrows or worries. If a depressed person is asked what the reason is, what it is that weighs [*tynge*] on him, he will answer: I do not know; I cannot explain it. Therein lies the limitlessness of depression. This answer is altogether correct, because as soon as he knows what it is, it is eliminated, whereas sorrow in the sorrowing one is not eliminated by his knowing why he sorrows. But depression is sin, is actually a sin *instar omnium* [that stands for all], for it is the sin of not willing deeply and inwardly, and this is a mother of all sins. This sickness, or more correctly this sin, is very prevalent in our day, and it is under this same sin that all of young Germany and France are now groaning.

I have no desire to irritate you; I deal with you as considerately as possible. I readily concede that in one sense being depressed is not a bad sign, for generally it happens only with the most endowed natures. Neither shall I badger you by assuming that anyone who suffers from indigestion has the right to call himself depressed, something we see quite frequently in our age, since being depressed has almost become the status that everyone covets. But the person who wants to be eminently endowed will have to tolerate my placing the responsibility upon him and his capacity to be more at fault than other people. If he looks at this in the proper light, he will not see this to be a disparaging of his personality, even though it will teach him to bow in true humility before the eternal power.

As soon as this movement has occurred, the depression is essentially canceled, although the same individual may suffer many sorrows and troubles in his life, and as far as that is con-

cerned you know full well that I am the last person to expound
the paltry commonsensical notion that it is futile to sorrow,
that one should cast the sorrows away. I would be ashamed of
myself if I dared to come to a sorrowing person with those
words. But even the person in whose life this movement occurs most calmly and peacefully and at the right time will still
always retain a little depression, but this is linked to something
much deeper, to hereditary sin, and is rooted in this, that no
human being can become transparent to himself.

But the persons whose souls do not know this depression
are those whose souls have no presentiment of a metamorphosis. I have nothing to do with them here, because I am writing
only about and to you, and I believe that this explanation will
satisfy you, for you scarcely assume, as do many physicians,
that depression inheres in the physical, and, strangely enough,
physicians nevertheless are unable to eliminate it. Only the
spirit can eliminate it, for it inheres in the spirit, and when it
finds itself all the little afflictions vanish, all the causes that produce depression in some people, according to their view—
such as not feeling at home in the world, coming too early or
too late into the world, not finding one's place in life—because
the person who possesses himself eternally comes into the
world neither too early nor too late, and the person who possesses himself in his eternal validity certainly does find his
meaning in this life.

This, however, was a digression for which I hope you will
forgive me, inasmuch as it was done primarily for your sake.
I return to the life-view that holds that one is to live to satisfy
desire. A shrewd common sense easily discerns that this cannot be carried out, and for that reason it is not worth the trouble to embark on it; a sophisticated egotism discerns that it
misses the point in enjoyment. Here, then, is the life-view that
teaches "Enjoy life" and in turn expresses it this way: "Enjoy
yourself; in enjoyment you are to enjoy yourself." This is a
higher reflection but still does not, of course, penetrate the
personality itself, which remains in its accidental immediacy.
Here, too, the condition for enjoyment is still an external condition that is not within the individual's power; for although

he, as he says, enjoys himself, yet he enjoys himself only in the enjoyment, but the enjoyment itself is linked to an external condition. Thus the entire difference is that he enjoys reflectively, not immediately. To that extent, even this Epicureanism is dependent on a condition that he does not have within his power. A certain case-hardening of the understanding now teaches a way out; it teaches: Enjoy yourself by continually discarding the conditions.[45] But it obviously follows that he who enjoys himself by discarding the conditions is just as dependent on them as one who enjoys them. His reflection is continually reverting to himself, and since his enjoyment is a matter of his enjoyment having as little content as possible, he is hollowing himself out, so to speak, since a finite reflection such as that is of course unable to open the personality.

With these observations, I trust I have given an outline (adequately recognizable at least by you) of the territory of the esthetic life-view. All the stages have this in common, that the reason for living is that whereby one immediately is what one is, because reflection never reaches so high that it reaches beyond this. What I have done is just a very rough sketch, but then I did not wish to do more; for me the various stages are not important, but only the movement that is inescapably necessary, such as I shall now indicate, and it is to this that I now bid you to give your attention.

I assume, then, that the man who lived for his health was, to use one of your expressions, just as hale and hearty as ever when he died, that the count and his wife danced at their golden wedding, and that a whisper ran through the great hall, exactly as it did when they danced on their wedding day; I assume that the rich man's gold mines were inexhaustible, that honors and status signalized the lucky man's pilgrimage through life; I assume that the young girl married the one she loved, that the man with the talent for business spread his connections over the five continents of the world and controlled all the stock exchanges in the world, that the man with the talent for mechanics connected heaven and earth—I assume that Nero never yawned but that new enjoyment took him by surprise at every moment, that that crafty Epicurean could delight in himself at every moment, that the Cynic continually had conditions to discard in order to rejoice in his lightness—I assume all this, and so all these people were indeed happy. You presumably will not say that; the reasons for it I shall explain later. But you certainly will admit that many people would think this way—indeed, that one or two of them would fancy he had said something very clever if he added that what they lacked was that they did not appreciate it.

I shall now make the opposite movement. Nothing of all this happens. What then? Then they despair. Presumably you will not do this either; you will perhaps say that it is not worth the trouble. Why you are unwilling to admit despair, I shall explain later; at this point I merely ask that you acknowledge that certainly a great many people would find it fitting to despair. Let us now see why they despaired. Because they discovered that they had built their lives on something that was transient? But is that a reason to despair; has an essential change taken place in that on which they built their lives? Is it an essential change in the transitory that it manifests itself as transitory, or is it not rather something accidental and inessential about it that it does not manifest itself this way? Nothing new has supervened that could cause a change. Consequently, when they despair, the basis of it must be that they were in despair beforehand. The difference is only that they did not know it, but this is indeed an entirely accidental difference. Consequently, it is manifest that every esthetic view of life is despair, and that everyone who lives esthetically is in despair, whether he knows it or not. But when one knows this, and you certainly do know it, then a higher form of existence is an imperative requirement.

With just a few words I shall explain in a little more detail my judgment concerning the young girl and her love. As you know, in my capacity as a married man I make it a practice on every occasion to affirm against you, both orally and in writing, the reality [*Realitet*] of love, and in order to prevent a misunderstanding, I therefore want to express my opinion here also. A worldly-wise person would perhaps be a little dubious about such love; he would perhaps see through its frailty and in contrast express his paltry wisdom as follows: Love me little and love me long. As if all his sagacity about life were not still more frail and at least far more paltry than her love! You will then easily discern that I could not take exception to it in that way.

In the sphere of erotic love, I find it very difficult to make imaginary constructions in thought. I have loved only once and am still continually and indescribably happy in this love, and I find it difficult to imagine myself loved by anyone else than the one to whom I am united and in any other way than the way by which she makes me so happy, but I shall risk it here. Let us suppose, then, however it came about, that I have become the object of such a love. It would not make me happy, and I would never accept it, not because I would spurn it—by God, I would rather have a murder on my conscience than to have spurned a girl's love, but for her own sake I would not allow it. I wish to be loved, if I had my way, by everyone. I wish to be loved by my wife as much as one human being can be loved by another, and it would pain me if I were not. But I do not desire more. I would not allow a person to damage her soul[46] in order to love me; I would love her too much to allow her to demean herself. For the arrogant mind there is something seductive in being loved this way, and there are men who know the art of infatuating a girl so that she forgets everything else because of them—let them take care how they defend this! Usually a girl like that is punished harshly enough for it, but the dastardly thing is to let it happen. This, you see, is why I told you and tell you again that the girl was just as much in despair whether she got her beloved or not, for it would indeed be incidental if the one she loved was such an upright man that he helped her out of her heart's delusion, and if the means he used to do it were ever so severe I would still say that he acted honestly, uprightly, faithfully, and nobly toward her.

It has become apparent, then, that every esthetic life-view is despair; therefore it might seem proper to make the movement by which the ethical appears. But there is still a stage, an esthetic life-view, the finest and the most distinguished of them

all, which I shall discuss most carefully, for now your turn
comes. You can calmly go along with everything I have developed in the foregoing, and in a sense it is not to you that I
have been speaking, and it would also be of little help to speak
this way to you or to inform you that life is vanity. You know
that very well and have tried in your own way to shift for
yourself. The reason I propounded it is that I wanted to keep
my rear line open, wanted to prevent you from suddenly leap-
ing back. This last life-view is despair itself. It is an esthetic
life-view, because the personality remains in its immediacy; it
is the final esthetic life-view, for up to a point it has absorbed
the consciousness of the nothingness of such a life-view. But
there is a difference between despair and despair. If I imagine
an artist, for example a painter who goes blind, he perhaps—
unless there is something more profound in him—will despair.
He despairs over this particular matter, and if his sight is restored again, the despair would terminate. This is not the case
with you; you are much too brilliant, and in a certain sense
your soul is too profound for this to happen to you. In an external sense this has not happened to you either. You still have
in your power all the elements for an esthetic life-view. You
have financial means, independence; your health is undimin-
ished; your mind is still vigorous; and you have never been unhappy because a young girl would not love you. And yet you
are in despair. It is not a despair involving something actual
but a despair in thought. Your thought has rushed ahead; you
have seen through the vanity of everything, but you have not
gone further. Occasionally you dive into it, and when for a
single moment you abandon yourself to enjoyment, you are
also aware that it is vanity. Thus you are continually beyond
yourself—that is, in despair. Therefore, your life lies between
two enormous contradictions: at times you have colossal energy, at times an equally great indolence.

Frequently I have noticed in life that the costlier the liquid
on which a person becomes intoxicated, the more difficult the
cure becomes; the intoxication is more beautiful and the consequences apparently not as pernicious. The person who becomes intoxicated on aquavit is soon aware of the pernicious

consequences, and there is hope for rescue. It is more difficult for a champagne drinker to be cured. And you—you have chosen the very finest, for what intoxication is as beautiful as despair, as elegant and as fetching, especially in the eyes of the girls (about that you have firsthand knowledge), especially if one also has the ingenuity to be able to repress the wildest outbursts, to let the despair, like a fire in the distance, be vaguely sensed and be only reflected externally. It gives a slight flourish to the hat and to the whole body; it gives a proud, defiant look. The lips smile haughtily. It provides an indescribable lightness to life, a regal outlook on everything. And then when a character like that approaches a young girl, when this proud head bows down only to her, to her alone in the whole world, it is flattering, and unfortunately there might be someone innocent enough to believe this false bowing. Is it not disgraceful for a person to—but, no, I shall not deliver a thundering oration; it would only incite you. I have other more powerful resources. I have that young hopeful person—perhaps he is in love. He comes to you; he is mistaken about you; he believes that you are a trustworthy, honest man; he seeks your advice. You can in fact shut your door to any such unfortunate young man, but your heart you cannot shut. Even if you do not wish him to be a witness to your humiliation, it will not fail to occur, for you are not that ruined, and when you are all alone by yourself, your good-naturedness is perhaps even greater than anyone believes.

Here, then, I have your view of life, and, believe me, much in your life will become clear to you if you will consider it along with me as thought-despair. You are a hater of activity in life—quite appropriately, because if there is to be meaning in it life must have continuity, and this your life does not have. You keep busy with your studies, to be sure; you are even diligent; but it is only for your own sake, and it is done with as little teleology as possible. Morever, you are unoccupied; like the laborers in the Gospel standing idle in the marketplace,[47] you stick your hands in your pocket and contemplate life. Now you rest in despair. Nothing concerns you; you step aside for nothing; "If someone threw a roof tile down I would still not step aside." You are like a dying person. You die daily,[48] not in the profound, earnest sense in which one usually understands these words, but life has lost its reality [*Realitet*] and "You always count the days of your life from one termination-notice day to the next." You let everything pass you by; nothing makes any impact. But then something suddenly comes along that grips you, an idea, a situation, a young girl's smile, and now you are "involved," for just as on certain occasions you are not "involved," so at other times you are "at your service" in every way. Wherever there is something going on, you join in. You behave in life as you usually do in a crowd. "You work yourself into the tightest group, see to it, if possible, to get yourself shoved up over the others so that you come to be above them, and as soon as you are up there you make yourself as comfortable as possible, and in this way you also let yourself be carried through life." But when the crowd is gone, when the event is over, you again stand on the street corner and look at the world.

A dying person, as is known, has a supranatural energy, and so it is also with you. If there is an idea to be thought through, a work to be read through, a plan to be carried out, a little affair to be experienced—yes, a hat to be purchased—then you tackle it with enormous energy. According to the circumstances, you work undauntedly for a day, a month; you feel a gratification in assuring yourself that you still have the same vigor as before. You do not pause to rest. "No devil can keep up with you." If you are working together with others, you work them to smithereens. But when the month, or what you regard as the maximum, the half year, is over, then you cut short, then you say, "That is that"; you withdraw and leave the whole thing to the other person or, if you have been alone in it, you speak to no one about the matter. Then you pretend to yourself and to others that you have lost interest and flatter yourself with the vain thought that you could have gone on working with the same intensity if you had cared to do so. But this is an enormous delusion. Like most people, you would have managed to finish if you had patiently willed it, but then you would also have learned that it takes a persistence quite different from the kind you have. So you have quickly deceived yourself, and you have learned nothing for your later life.

Here I can favor you with a little information. I am not ignorant of how deceitful one's own heart is, how easy it is to deceive oneself, to say nothing of when one possesses the disjunctive power of dialectic to the extent that you do, the power that not only gives dispensation to everything but disintegrates and wipes it out. So when I have encountered something in life, when I have decided on something that I was afraid would take on another aspect for me in the course of time, when I have done something I was afraid I would interpret differently in the course of time, I often wrote down briefly and clearly what it was that I wanted or what it was that I had done and why. Then when I felt that I needed it, when my decision or my action was not as vivid to me, I would take out my charter and judge myself.

II
178

You may think that this is pedantic, that it is too prolix and not worth the trouble of making such a fuss. To that I have no other answer than this: If you feel no need for that, if your mind is always so unerring and your memory so faithful, then leave it alone. But I do not really believe that, for the capacity of soul that is actually wanting in you is memory, that is, not of this or of that, not of ideas, witticisms, or dialectical intricacies—far be it from me to make that claim—but memory of your own life, of what you have experienced in it. If you had that, the same phenomenon would not be repeated so frequently in your life, it would not display so many of what I would call half-hour jobs, for I can readily call them that even if you took half a year for them, because you did not finish. But you like to deceive yourself and others. If you were always as powerful as you are in the moment of passion, then you—yes, that I shall not deny—then you would be the strongest person I have known. But you are not, and you know that very well yourself. That is why you withdraw, hide yourself almost from yourself and relax again in indolence. To my eyes, whose attentiveness you cannot always escape, you become almost ludicrous with your momentary zeal and the justification you seek in it for the ridiculing of others.

Once there were two Englishmen who journeyed to Arabia to purchase horses. They even brought along some English race horses and wanted to test their excellence against the Arabs' horses. They proposed a race, and the Arabs were willing and let the Englishmen choose the horse they wanted from among the Arabian horses. This they did not want to do right away, for they explained that they would first take forty days for training. They waited the forty days, the prize was determined, the horses saddled, and now the Arabs asked how long they were to ride? "One hour," was the answer. This amazed the Arabs, and they answered quite tersely: We thought we were going to ride for three days.

You see, so it is with you. If one wants to run a race with you for one hour, then "the devil himself cannot keep up with you"; three days and you get the worst of it. I recall that I told you this story once, and I also recall your answer—that it was a dubious matter to run a race for three days; one took the risk of working up such momentum that one could never stop, and therefore you wisely refrained from all such violence. "Once in a while I take a ride, but I wish neither to be a cavalryman nor to have any other unremitting activity in life." Indeed, this is entirely true up to a point, for you are always afraid of continuity, chiefly because it deprives you of the chance to delude yourself. The energy you possess is the energy of despair; it is more intense than ordinary human energy, but it also has a shorter span.

You continually hover above yourself, but the higher atmosphere, the more refined sublimate, into which you are vaporized, is the nothing of despair, and you see down below you a multiplicity of subjects, insights, studies, and observations that nevertheless have no reality for you but which you very whimsically utilize and combine to decorate as tastefully as you can the sumptuous intellectual palace in which you occasionally reside. No wonder that existence [*Tilværelse*] for you is a fairy tale, that you frequently are tempted to begin every story thus: "Once upon a time, there was a king and a queen who could have no children," and that you thereupon forget everything else in order to make the comment that, curiously enough, in the fairy tale this is always a reason for a king and a queen's grief, whereas in everyday life we hear instead about grief over having children, which orphan asylums and all such institutions bear out. At present you have the notion that "Life is a fairy tale." You are able to employ a whole month just for reading fairy tales. You make a thorough study of them; you compare and examine, and your study is not without a yield—but for what use? To entertain your mind; you shoot it all off in a brilliant firework display.

You hover above your self, and what you see down below you is a multiplicity of moods and conditions that you make use of in order to find interesting contacts with life. You can be sentimental, heartless, ironic, witty, and when it comes to this it must be admitted that you have been well trained. As soon as something is able to wrest you out of your indolence, you are up and doing with all your passion, and your doing is not lacking in skill, since you are much too well equipped with wit, cunning, and all the seductive gifts of the mind. As you put it with such self-satisfied pretentiousness, you are never so ungallant as to show up without bringing with you a small, fragrant, freshly plucked bouquet of wit. The better one knows you, the more one must be almost astonished at the calculating sagacity that pervades everything you do in the short time when you are moved by passion, for passion never blinds you but only makes you see better. Then this chance contact with someone occupies you absolutely, and you forget your despair and anything else that otherwise rests on your soul and mind.

II
180

I want to recall for you a little incident that took place in my own house. I probably have to thank the two young Swedish girls who were present for the speech you delivered. The conversation had taken a more serious turn and had arrived at a point that was not pleasing to you. I had expressed myself somewhat against the misplaced respect for intellectual gifts that is so prevalent in our day; I had pointed out that the essential matter was something entirely different, an inwardness in one's whole being, for which language had no other word than faith [*Tro*]. You perhaps were thereby placed in a less favorable light, and you perceived that you could not make any progress along the road taken, and so you felt called upon to try your hand at what you yourself call the higher madness in the sentimental key.

"Do I not believe [*tro*]? I believe that deep in the solitariness of the forest, where the trees are mirrored in the dark waters, in its dark secrecy, where there is twilight even at midday, there lives a creature, a nymph, a maiden; I believe that she is more beautiful than can be imagined; I believe that in the morning she braids garlands, at noon she bathes in the cool waters, that in the evening she sadly plucks the leaves from the garlands. I believe that I would be happy, the one and only human being who would deserve to be called happy, if I could capture her and possess her. I believe that there is a longing in my soul that searches the whole world; I believe that I would be happy if my longing were satisfied. [49]I believe that there is indeed meaning in the world if only I could find it—now, do not tell me that I am not strong in faith or ardent in spirit!"

You perhaps think that a speech like that could be a trial piece that would qualify you as worthy of membership in a Greek symposium,[50] because that, among other things, is indeed what you are grooming yourself for, and you would deem it the most beautiful life to join some young Greek men every night, to sit with a garland in your hair and deliver eulogies on love or whatever might occur to you—yes, you would devote yourself completely to delivering eulogies. To me this speech seems to be gibberish, even though it is ever so ingenious, and even though it makes an impression at the moment, especially when you yourself are allowed to deliver it with your feverish eloquence. And it also seems to me to be an expression of your confused state of mind, for if someone does not believe in anything that others believe in, it is quite appropriate for him to have faith in such mysterious beings; as so often happens in life, someone who is not afraid of anything either in heaven or on earth is afraid of spiders. You are smiling; you are thinking that I have fallen into the trap, that I believed that you believed what you are further from believing than any other human being. Quite right, for your speeches always end in absolute skepticism, but however clever and however calculating you are, you simply cannot deny that for a moment you warm yourself with the sickly heat implicit in an overwrought state like that. Perhaps your intention is to deceive people, and yet there is a moment when you—even if you do not know it—deceive yourself.

What holds for your studies holds for every one of your activities; you are in the moment, and in the moment you are a supranatural magnitude. You put your whole soul into it, even with the energy of your will, because for one moment you have your being absolutely in your power. Anyone who sees you only in such a moment is very easily deceived, whereas anyone who waits until the next moment can easily have a chance to triumph over you. You perhaps recall the familiar folk tale by Musäus about Roland's three squires. From the old witch whom they visited in the forest, one of the squires obtained a thimble that made him invisible. With the aid of the thimble, he made his way into the apartment of the beautiful princess Urraca and professed his love for her, which made a strong impression on her, inasmuch as she could not see anyone and therefore presumed that he was at least a fairy prince who was honoring her with his love. But she insists on a revelation. Here was the difficulty: as soon as he himself appeared, the magic charm would vanish, and yet he would have no joy from his love if he could not reveal himself. I have Musäus's folk tale right at hand and will copy a short passage from it and bid you read it through for your own benefit. "Er willigte dem Anscheine nach ungern ein, und die Phantasie der Prinzessin schob ihr das Bild des schönsten Mannes vor, den sie mit gespannter Erwartung zu erblicken vermeinte. Aber welcher Contrast zwischen Original und Ideal, da nichts als ein allgemeines Alltagsgesicht zum Vorschein kam, einer von den gewöhnlichen Menschen, dessen Physiognomie weder Genie-Blick noch Sentimental-Geist verrieht [He consented reluctantly to the appearance, and the imagination of the princess placed before her the image of the most handsome man whom she with tense expectation thought she would see. But what a contrast between the original and the ideal, since nothing but an everyday face became visible, the face of an ordinary man whose physiognomy disclosed neither the glance of genius nor the sentimental spirit]!"[51] What you wish to achieve by these contacts with people you do in fact achieve, for you are a good deal more clever than that squire; you readily perceive that it does not pay to become open. When you have conjured up an ideal image for somebody—and here it must be conceded that you are able to appear ideal in any direction whatever—you carefully withdraw and then have the gratification of having duped someone. What you also achieve is that the coherence in your view is broken and you have obtained one more factor, which makes you start all over again.

From a theoretical point of view, you are finished with the world; the finite cannot survive in your thought; from a practical point of view, you are also finished with it up to a point—that is, in the esthetic sense. All the same, you have no lifeview. You have something that resembles a view, and this gives your life a kind of composure that must not, however, be confused with a secure and revitalizing confidence in life. You have composure only by contrast with the person who is still pursuing the phantoms of enjoyment, *per mare pauperiem fugiens, per saxa, per ignis* [fleeing poverty through sea, through rocks, through flame].[52] As far as enjoyment goes, you have an absolutely aristocratic pride. This is entirely appropriate, for, after all, you are finished with the finite altogether. And yet you cannot give it up. Compared with those who are chasing after satisfaction, you are satisfied, but that in which you find your satisfaction is absolute dissatisfaction. To see all the glories of the world is no concern of yours, for in thought you are beyond them, and if they were offered to you, you would very likely say, as always: Well, maybe one could spend a day on that. You do not care that you have not become a millionaire, and if the chance were offered to you, you would very likely answer: Well, it could really be interesting to have been a millionaire, and one could probably spend a month on it. If you could be offered the love of the most beautiful of girls, you would nevertheless answer: Yes, it would be all right for half a year. At this point I shall not add my voice to the frequently heard lament about you that you are insatiable; I shall rather say: In a certain sense you are right, for nothing that is finite, not even the whole world, can satisfy the soul of a person who feels the need of the eternal. If someone could offer you honors and distinctions, the admiration of your contemporaries—and yet that is the point at which you are weakest—you would reply: Well, it would be all right for a short time. You do not really crave it, and you would not take one step for it. You would discern that for it to have any meaning you would actually have to be so remarkably endowed that it was really true; even in that case your mind would regard the highest degree of intellectual endowment as transitory. Therefore, your polemic provides you with an even higher expression when in your deep resentment against all of life you could wish that you were the most foolish of all human beings and still were admired by your contemporaries as the wisest of all, for that would hold all existence up to ridicule much more profoundly than if a genuinely most competent person were honored as such. Therefore, you crave nothing, wish [ønske] for nothing, because the only thing you could wish for would be a divining rod [Ønskeqvist, wishing twig] that could provide you with everything, and you would then use it for cleaning out your pipe. So you are finished with life "and do not need to make a will, for you will leave nothing behind you."

But you cannot stay on that apex, for it is true that your thought has taken everything away from you, but it has provided you with nothing in its place. At the next moment, a mere trifle fascinates you. Admittedly, you do not look upon it with all the superiority and pride that your supercilious thought gives you; you spurn it as a trivial plaything. You are almost bored with it even before you pick it up, but nevertheless it engages you, and even if it is not the thing itself that engages you—and that is never the case—that you are willing to condescend to it does nevertheless engage you. In this regard, as soon as you become involved with people, your nature has a high degree of perfidiousness, for which you nevertheless cannot be reproached ethically, for you reside outside the ethical categories. Fortunately for others, you do not join in very much, and therefore it is not noticed. You come frequently to my house, and you know that you are always welcome, but you also know that it never occurs to me to invite you to take part in the least little thing. I would not even go for a drive in the forest with you, not because you cannot be very lively and entertaining but because your participation is always a lie, for if you are really happy, one can always be sure that it is not over something that makes the rest of us happy or over the excursion but over something you have *in mente* [in mind]. And if you are not happy, it is not because of encountering annoyances that put you in a bad mood, for that could happen to the rest of us, but because by the moment you get into the carriage you have already seen through the emptiness of this amusement. I readily forgive you, for your mind is always too active, and what you often say of yourself is true, that you are like a woman in labor, and under such circumstances it is no wonder that one is a little different from others.

II
184

But the spirit does not allow itself to be mocked;[53] it avenges itself on you and binds you in the chains of depression. My young friend, here is the path to becoming a Nero—if there were not an original earnestness in your soul, if there were not an innate profundity in your thought, if there were not a magnanimity in your soul—and if you had become emperor in Rome. Yet you are taking another path. Now there looms up before you a life-view that seems to you to be the only one that can satisfy you—it is to submerge your soul in sadness and sorrow. Your thought, however, is too sound for this life-view to pass its test, because for such an esthetic sorrow existence is just as empty as it is for every other esthetic life-view; if a person cannot sorrow more profoundly than that, then there is truth in my saying that sorrow passes away just as well as joy, for everything that is only finite passes away. And if many find that it is a consolation that sorrow passes away, this thought seems just as unconsoling to me as the thought that joy passes away. So then in turn your thought annihilates this life-view, and if one has annihilated sorrow one retains the joy; instead of sorrow, you choose a joy that is sorrow's changeling. This joy you have now chosen, the laughter of despair. You come back to life again; under this light, existence acquires a new interest for you. Just as you take great pleasure in talking with children in such a way that they superbly and easily and naturally understand what you are saying, and yet for you yourself it means something entirely different, so you take pleasure in deceiving people with your laughter. If you can make people laugh, be jubilant, and rejoice with you, then you triumph over the world, then you say to yourself: If you people only knew what you are laughing at!

But the spirit does not allow itself to be mocked, and the gloom of depression thickens around you, and the lightning flash of a demented witticism only shows you yourself that it is even more dense, even more terrible. And there is nothing to divert you; all the worldly pleasures are meaningless to you, and even if you envy the simple their foolish joy in life, you do not go in pursuit of it. Pleasure tempts you not. And however sad your situation is, it is truly a blessing that it does not. It is not my intention to praise the pride in you that scorns it but to praise the grace that keeps your thought firm, for if pleasure tempted you, you would be lost. But your not being tempted shows the road you must take, that you must go forward and not back. There is another wrong road, no less terrible, and here again I do not rely on your pride but on the grace that continually keeps you afloat. It certainly is true that you are proud and that it is better for a person to be proud than to be vain; it is certainly true that there is a terrible passion in your thought, that you regard it as a debt you do not intend to cancel, "that you would rather consider yourself as a creditor in the world who has not been paid than to wipe out the debt"— and yet all human pride is only a flimsy security.

II
185

You see, my young friend, this life is despair; if you conceal it from others, you cannot conceal it from yourself that it is despair. And yet in another sense this life is not despair. You are too light-minded [*letsindig*] to despair, and you are too heavy-minded [*tungsindig*] not to come in contact with despair. You are like a woman in labor, and yet you are continually holding

off the moment and continually remain in pain. If a woman in
her distress were to have the idea that she would give birth to
a monstrosity or were to ponder just what would be born to
her, she would have a certain similarity to you. Her attempt to
halt the process of nature would be futile, but your attempt is
certainly possible, for in a spiritual sense that by which a person gives birth is the *nisus formativus* [formative striving][54] of
the will, and that is within a person's own power. What are
you afraid of, then? After all, you are not supposed to give
birth to another human being; you are supposed to give birth
only to yourself.

And yet I am fully aware that there is an earnestness about
this that shakes the entire soul; to become conscious in one's
eternal validity[55] is a moment that is more significant than
everything else in the world. It is as if you were captivated and
entangled and could never escape either in time or in eternity;
it is as if you lost yourself, as if you ceased to be; it is as if you
would repent of it the next moment and yet it cannot be undone. It is an earnest and significant moment when a person
links himself to an eternal power for an eternity, when he accepts himself as the one whose remembrance time will never
erase, when in an eternal and unerring sense he becomes conscious of himself as the person he is. And yet one can refrain
from doing it!

You see, there is an Either/Or here. Let me speak to you as
I would never speak to you if someone else heard it, because in
one sense I do not have the right to do so and because if I say
anything I speak almost solely about the near future. If you do
not want this, if you want to go on amusing your soul with the
trifling of wittiness and the vainglory of the intellect, then do
so. Leave your home, emigrate, go to Paris, devote yourself to
journalism, court the smiles of languid women, cool their hot
blood with the chill of your wit, let it be your life's proud task
to dispel an idle woman's boredom or the gloomy thoughts of
a burned-out sensualist; forget that you were a child, that there
was piety in your soul and innocence in your thoughts; muffle
every lofty voice in your heart, loaf your life away in the glittering wretchedness of social gatherings; forget that there is an

immortal spirit within you, torture the last farthing out of your soul; and when your wittiness lapses into silence, there still is water in the Seine and gunpowder in the shop and traveling company for every time of the day.

But if you cannot do that, if you do not want to do that—and that you neither can nor will—then pull yourself together, stifle every rebellious thought that would have the audacity to commit high treason against your better nature, disdain all that paltriness that would envy your intellectual gifts and desire them for itself in order to put them to even worse use; disdain the hypocritical virtue that is unwilling to carry the burden of life and yet wants to be eulogized for carrying it; but do not therefore disdain life, respect every decent effort, every modest activity that humbly conceals itself, and above all have a little more respect for woman. Believe me, as surely as corruption comes from man, salvation comes from woman. I am a married man and thus I am partial, but it is my conviction that even though a woman corrupted man, she has honestly and honorably made up for it and is still doing so, [56]for of a hundred men who go astray in the world, ninety-nine are saved by women, and one is saved by an immediate divine grace. And since I also think that it is the nature of a man to go astray either in one way or in another and that it holds just as truly for the life of the man as it holds for the life of the woman that she ought to remain in the pure and innocent peace of immediacy, you readily perceive that in my opinion woman makes full compensation for the harm she has done.

What do you have to do, then? Someone else might say: Marry, and then you will have something else to think about. Certainly, but it is still a question whether it is beneficial to you, and however you think of the opposite sex, you are still too chivalrous of mind to want to marry for that reason. Furthermore, if you cannot control yourself, you will scarcely find anyone else who is able to do it. Or someone might say: Seek a career, throw yourself into the world of business; it takes your mind off yourself, and you will forget your depression; work—that is the best thing to do. Perhaps you will succeed in bringing yourself to the point where it seems to have been forgotten. But forgotten it is not; it will still break out at certain moments, more terrible than ever; perhaps it will be able to do what it has not been able to do previously—take you by surprise. Moreover, whatever you may think of life and its task, you will still be too chivalrous of mind about yourself to choose a career for that reason, for there is still the same falseness here as in marrying for that reason. What, then, is there to do? I have only one answer: Despair, then!

I am a married man; my soul is firmly and imperturbably attached to my wife, to my children, and to this life, whose beauty I shall always praise. So when I say "Despair," it is no overexcited youth who wants to whirl you into the maelstrom of passions, no mocking demon who shouts this consolation to the shipwrecked. But I shout it to you not as a consolation, not as a state in which you are to remain, but as an act that takes all the power and earnestness and concentration of the soul. I do this just as certainly as it is my conviction, my victory over the world,[57] that any human being who has not tasted the bitterness of despair has fallen short of the meaning of life, even if his life has been ever so beautiful, ever so abundantly happy. You do not perpetrate a deception on the world in which you live; you are not lost to it, for you have vanquished it, just as certainly as I take comfort in being an upright married man, although I, too, have despaired.

When I consider your life in this way, I shall count you happy, for in truth it is extremely important that a person does not look at life in the wrong way in the moment of despair. That is just as dangerous for him as for the woman in labor to do something wrong. The person who despairs about something in particular runs the risk that his despair will not be authentic and deep, that it is an illusion, a distress over the particular. You are not to despair in this way, for no particular thing has been taken from you, you still have it all. If the despairing person errs and thinks that the trouble is somewhere in the multiplicity outside himself, then his despair is not authentic and it will lead him to hate the world and not love it, for however true it is that the world is an oppression to you because it seems to want to be something different for you than it can be, so is it also true that when in despair you have found yourself you will love it because it is what it is. If it is guilt and wrongdoing, an oppressed conscience, that bring a person to despair, he perhaps will have difficulty in regaining his happiness. Therefore, despair with all your soul and all your mind; the longer you postpone it the harder the conditions will be, and the requirement remains the same. I shout it to you, just like that woman who offered to sell Tarquinius a collection of books,[58] and when he would not pay the price she demanded, she burned a third of the books and asked the same price; and when he again refused to pay the price she demanded, she burned the second third of the collection and asked the same price, until finally he did pay the original price for the last third.

Your condition of despair is propitious, and yet there is one even more propitious. Imagine a young man as gifted as you. Have him love a girl, love her just as much as he loves himself. Have him ponder sometime in a peaceful hour what he has built his life upon and upon what she can build hers. Love they do have in common, but nevertheless he will feel that there are differences. Perhaps she is endowed with beauty, but this has no significance for him and then, too, is so fragile; perhaps she has the cheerful disposition of youth, but her cheerfulness has no real meaning for him; but he has power of mind and spirit and feels its strength. He wants truly to love her, and therefore it will not occur to him to give her this, and her humble soul will not demand it; yet there is a difference and he will feel that it must be removed if he is to love her truly. Then he will let his soul sink into despair. He does not despair for his own sake but for hers, and yet it is for his sake also, for he loves her just as much as himself. Then the power of despair will consume everything until he finds himself in his eternal validity, but then he has found her also, and no knight will come back happier and more joyful from the most dangerous feats than he from this battle against flesh and blood and the vain distinctions of the finite, because the one who despairs finds the eternal human being, and in that we are all equal. The foolish idea of blunting his mind and spirit or neglecting to improve them, and in that way to achieve equality, will not occur to him; he wants to keep his mental-spiritual gifts, but in his innermost heart he will be secretly aware that he who has them is as one who does not have them.[59] Or imagine someone with a deeply religious disposition, who out of a true and sincere love for his fellow men threw himself into the sea of despair until he found the absolute, the point where it makes no difference whether a forehead is flat or whether it overarches more proudly than the sky, the point that is not the point of indifference but of absolute validity.

You have various good ideas, many droll fancies, many foolish ones. Keep them all; I do not ask for them. But you do have one idea I beg you to hold onto firmly, an idea that convinces me that my mind has kinship with yours. You have often said that you would prefer to be anything in the world to being a poet,[60] since as a rule a poet-existence is a human sacrifice. As far as I am concerned, it must in no way be denied that there have been poets who had found themselves before they began to write or who found themselves through writing, but on the other hand it is also certain that the poet-existence as such lies in the darkness that is the result of a despair that was not carried through, the result of the soul's continuing to quake in despair and of the spirit's inability to achieve its true transfiguration. The poetic ideal is always an untrue ideal, for the true ideal is always the actual. So when the spirit is not allowed to rise into the eternal world of spirit, it remains in transit and delights in the pictures reflected in the clouds and weeps over their transitoriness. Therefore, a poet-existence as such is an unhappy existence; it is higher than the finite and yet is not the infinite. The poet sees the ideals, but he must run away from the world in order to delight in them. He cannot carry these idols within him[61] in the midst of life's confusion, cannot calmly go his way unmoved by the caricature that appears around him, to say nothing of his having the strength to put on the ideals. For this reason the poet's life is often the object of a shabby pity on the part of people who think they have their own lives safe and sound because they have remained in the finite. Once, in a discouraged moment, you said that no doubt there were even some people who had secretly settled their accounts with you and were willing to give a receipt on the following conditions: you would be acknowledged to be a brilliant fellow and in return you would drop out of sight and not be an officious member of society. Yes, beyond a doubt there is such a shabbiness in the world that in this way wants to gain the upper hand over anything that so much as sticks a finger ahead. But do not let it bother you; do not defy them, do not disdain them—here I shall say as you are in the habit of saying: It is not worth the trouble. But if you do not want to be a poet, then there is no other way for you than the one I have pointed out to you: Despair!

Choose despair, then, because despair itself is a choice, because one can doubt [*tvivle*] without choosing it, but one cannot despair [*fortvivle*] without choosing it. And in despairing a person chooses again, and what then does he choose? He chooses himself, not in his immediacy, not as this accidental individual, but he chooses himself in his eternal validity.[62]

This point I shall attempt to explain in a little more detail with reference to you. There has been more than sufficient talk in modern philosophy about all speculation beginning with doubt [*Tvivl*],[63] but insofar as I have been able on occasion to be occupied by such deliberations, I sought in vain for some enlightenment on how doubt is different from despair [*Fortvivlelse*]. At this point I will try to explain this difference, in the hope that it will help orient and situate you properly. Far be it from me to credit myself with any real philosophic competence. I do not have your virtuosity in playing with categories, but what in the most profound sense is the meaning of life must be capable of being grasped even by a more simple person.

Doubt is thought's despair; despair is personality's doubt. That is why I cling so firmly to the defining characteristic "to choose"; it is my watchword, the nerve in my life-view, and that I do have, even if I can in no way presume to have a system. Doubt is the inner movement in thought itself, and in my doubt I conduct myself as impersonally as possible. I assume that thought, when doubt is carried through, finds the absolute and rests therein; therefore, it rests therein not pursuant to a choice but pursuant to the same necessity pursuant to which it doubted, for doubt itself is a qualification of necessity, and likewise rest.

This is the grandeur of doubt; this is why it so often has been recommended and promoted by people who hardly understood what they were saying. But its being a qualification of necessity indicates that the whole personality is not involved in the movement. That is why there is much truth in a person's saying "I would like to believe, but I cannot—I must doubt." Therefore, we often also see that a doubter can nevertheless have in himself a positive substance that has no communication at all with his thinking, that he can be an extremely conscientious person who by no means doubts the validity of duty and the precepts for his conduct, by no means doubts a host of sympathetic feelings and moods. On the other hand, especially in our day, we see people who have despair in their hearts and yet have conquered doubt. This was especially striking to me when I looked at some of the German philosophers. Their minds are at ease; objective, logical thinking has been brought to rest in its corresponding objectivity, and yet, even though they divert themselves by objective thinking, they are in despair, for a person can divert himself in many ways, and there is scarcely any means as dulling and deadening as abstract thinking, for it is a matter of conducting oneself as impersonally as possible.

Doubt and despair, therefore, belong to completely different spheres; different sides of the soul are set in motion. But I am not at all satisfied with this, because then doubt and despair would become coordinate, and that is not the case. Despair is precisely a much deeper and more complete expression; its movement is much more encompassing than that of doubt. Despair is an expression of the total personality, doubt only of thought. The supposed objectivity that doubt has, and because of which it is so exalted, is a manifestation precisely of its imperfection. Thus doubt is based on differences among people, despair on the absolute. It takes a natural aptitude to doubt, but it does not at all take a natural aptitude to despair; but a natural aptitude as such is a difference, and whatever requires a difference to validate itself can never be the absolute, because the absolute can be as the absolute only for the absolute. The lowliest, least endowed person can despair; a young girl who is anything but a thinker can despair—whereas everyone readily senses the foolishness of saying that such people are doubters. The reason a person's doubt can be set at ease and he can still be in despair and go on being in despair is that in a deeper sense he does not will despair. Generally speaking, a person cannot despair at all without willing it, but in order truly to despair, a person must truly will it; but when he truly wills it, he is truly beyond despair. When a person has truly chosen despair, he has truly chosen what despair chooses: himself in his eternal validity. The personality is first set at ease in despair, not by way of necessity, for I never despair necessarily, but in freedom, and only therein is the absolute attained. In this respect, I think that our age will advance, provided I may have any opinion at all about our age, inasmuch as I know it only from reading the papers and a book or two or from talking with you. The time is not far off when we shall experience— quite likely at a high price—that the true point of departure for finding the absolute is not doubt but despair.

But I go back to my category—I am not a logician, and I have only one category, but I assure you that it is the choice of both my heart and my thought, my soul's delight and my salvation—I go back to the significance of choosing. When I choose absolutely, I choose despair, and in despair I choose the absolute, for I myself am the absolute; I posit the absolute, and I myself am the absolute. But in other words with exactly the same meaning I may say: I choose the absolute that chooses me; I posit the absolute that posits me—for if I do not keep in mind that this second expression is just as absolute, then my category of choosing is untrue, because it is precisely the identity of both. What I choose, I do not posit, for if it were not posited I could not choose it, and yet if I did not posit it by choosing it then I would not choose it. It is, for if it were not I could not choose it; it is not, for it first comes into existence through my choosing it, and otherwise my choice would be an illusion.

But what is it, then, that I choose—is it this or that? No, for I choose absolutely, and I choose absolutely precisely by having chosen not to choose this or that. I choose the absolute, and what is the absolute? It is myself in my eternal validity. Something other than myself I can never choose as the absolute, for if I choose something else, I choose it as something finite and consequently do not choose absolutely. Even the Jew who chose God did not choose absolutely, for he did indeed choose the absolute, but he did not choose it absolutely, and thereby it ceased to be the absolute and became something finite.

But what is this self of mine? If I were to speak of a first moment, a first expression for it, then my answer is this: It is the most abstract of all, and yet in itself it is also the most concrete of all—it is freedom. Let me make a little psychological observation. We frequently hear people vent their dissatisfaction in a complaint about life; often enough we hear them wishing. Imagine a poor wretch like that; let us skip over the wishes that shed no light here because they involve the utterly accidental. He wishes: Would that I had that man's intellect, or that man's talent etc. Indeed, to go to the extreme: Would that I had that man's steadfastness. Wishes of that sort are frequently heard, but have you ever heard a person earnestly wish that he could be someone else? It is so far from being the case that it is particularly characteristic of people called unfortunate individualities that they cling most of all to themselves, that despite all their sufferings they still would not wish to be anybody else for all the world. That is because such people are very close to the truth, and they feel the eternal validity of the personality not in its blessing but in its torment, even if they have retained this totally abstract expression for the joy in it, that they prefer to go on being themselves. But the person with many wishes is nevertheless continually of the opinion that he would be himself even if everything were changed. Consequently, there is something within him that in relation to everything else is absolute, something whereby he is who he is even if the change he achieved by his wish were the greatest possible.

That he is mistaken, I shall show later, but at this point I merely want to find the most abstract expression for this "self" that makes him who he is. And this is nothing other than freedom. By this route it is actually possible to present a very plausible demonstration of the eternal validity of the personality. Indeed, even a suicide does not actually will to do away with his self; he, too, wishes—he wishes another form for his self, and this is why we certainly can find a suicide who is very convinced of the immortality of the soul, but whose whole being was so ensnared that he believed he would by this step find the absolute form for his spirit.

The reason, however, it may seem to an individual as if he could be changed continually and yet remain the same, as if his innermost being were an algebraic symbol that could signify anything whatever it is assumed to be, is that he is in a wrong position, that he has not chosen himself, does not have a concept of it, and yet there is in his folly an acknowledgment of the eternal validity of the personality. But for him who is in a proper position things take another course. He chooses himself—not in the finite sense, for then this "self" would indeed be something finite that would fall among all the other finite things—but in the absolute sense, and yet he does choose himself and not someone else. This self that he chooses in this way is infinitely concrete, for it is he himself, and yet it is absolutely different from his former self, for he has chosen it absolutely. This self has not existed before, because it came into existence through the choice, and yet it has existed, for it was indeed "himself."

The choice here makes two dialectical movements simultaneously—that which is chosen does not exist and comes into existence through the choice—and that which is chosen exists; otherwise it was not a choice. In other words, if what I chose did not exist but came into existence absolutely through the choice, then I did not choose—then I created. But I do not create myself—I choose myself. Therefore, whereas nature is created from nothing, whereas I myself as immediate personality am created from nothing, I as free spirit am born out of the principle of contradiction or am born through my choosing myself.

Now he discovers that the self he chooses has a boundless multiplicity within itself inasmuch as it has a history, a history in which he acknowledges identity with himself. This history is of a different kind, for in this history he stands in relation to other individuals in the race and to the whole race, and this history contains painful things, and yet he is the person he is only through this history. That is why it takes courage to choose oneself, for at the same time as he seems to be isolating himself most radically he is most radically sinking himself into the root by which he is bound up with the whole. This makes him uneasy, and yet it must be so, for when the passion of freedom is aroused in him—and it is aroused in the choice just as it presupposes itself in the choice—he chooses himself and struggles for this possession as for his salvation, and it is his salvation. He can give up nothing of all this, not the most painful, not the hardest, and yet the expression for this struggle, for this acquiring, is—repentance. He repents himself back into himself, back into the family, back into the race, until he finds himself in God. Only on this condition can he choose himself. And this is the only condition he wants, for only in this way can he choose himself absolutely.

II
194

Yet what is a human being without love? But there are many kinds of love. I love my father and my mother differently, my wife, in turn, in another way, and each different love has its different expression. But there is also a love with which I love God, and this love has only one expression in language—it is "repentance." If I do not love him in this way, then I do not love him absolutely, out of my innermost being. Any other love of the absolute is a fallacy, for (to take what is ordinarily so highly prized and what I myself esteem) when thought with all its love holds fast to the absolute, then it is not the absolute I love, then I do not love absolutely, for I love out of necessity. As soon as I love freely and love God, then I repent. And if there were no other basis for repentance as the expression of my love of God, it is this—that he has loved me first.[64] And yet this is an imperfect designation, for only when I choose myself as guilty do I absolutely choose myself, if I am at all to choose myself absolutely in such a way that it is not identical with creating myself. And even though it was the father's guilt that was passed on to the son by inheritance, he repents of this, too, for only in this way can he choose himself, choose himself absolutely. And if his tears would almost wipe out everything for him, he continues to repent, for only in this way does he choose himself. His self is, so to speak, outside him, and it has to be acquired, and repentance is his love for it, because he chooses it absolutely from the hand of the eternal God.

What I have expressed here is not academic wisdom; it is something every person can express who wants to, something every person can will if he so wills. I have not learned it in lecture halls; I have learned it in the living room or, if you like, in the nursery, for when I see my little son running across the floor, so joyful, so happy, I think to myself: Who knows whether I may not have had much harmful influence on him? God knows that I take all possible care of him, but this thought does not put me at ease. Then I tell myself that there will come a moment in his life when his spirit, too, will be matured in the moment of choice; then he will choose himself, then he will also repent of whatever guilt may rest upon him from me. It is beautiful that a son repents of his father's guilt, and yet he will not do it for my sake, but because only in this way can he choose himself. Let happen what will happen; frequently what one regards as the best can have the most harmful consequences for a person, but still all this amounts to nothing. I can be very beneficial to him, and that I shall strive to do, but only he himself can make himself do what is the highest. This, you see, is why it is so hard for individuals to choose themselves, because the absolute isolation here is identical with the most profound continuity because as long as one has not chosen oneself there seems to be a possibility in one way or another of becoming something different.

So here you have my humble view of what it is to choose and to repent. It is improper to love a young girl as if she were one's mother or one's mother as if she were a young girl; every love has its distinctiveness; love of God has its absolute distinctiveness, and its expression is repentance. Compared with this, what is all other love; it is nothing more than children's babbling. I am not a young fanatic who tries to put forward his theories; I am a married man, and I certainly dare to let my wife hear that all love in comparison with repentance is but children's babbling. Nevertheless I know that I am a good husband, "I, who even as a married man am still struggling under the triumphant banner of first love." I know that she shares my point of view, and therefore I love her even more, and therefore I would not wish to be loved by that young girl, because she would not share this view.

That wrong paths, new and terrible, appear again here, that the person who creeps along the ground does not so readily run the risk of falling as does the one who climbs the mountain top, that the person who sits in the chimney corner does not so readily run the risk of going astray as does the one who ventures out into the world—that I know, but nevertheless I stick just as cheerfully to my choice.

Now, at this point a theologian would find a starting point for a multiplicity of observations; since I am a layman, I shall not go into it any further. I shall try only to throw some light on the previous discussion by saying that in Christianity repentance has first found its true expression. The pious Jew felt the guilt of his fathers resting upon him, and yet he did not feel it nearly as profoundly as the Christian, for the pious Jew could not repent of it because he could not absolutely choose himself. The guilt of the forefathers was heavy upon him, brooded over him; he sank under the burden, he sighed, but he could not lift it up; only the person who absolutely chooses himself with the aid of repentance can do that. The greater the freedom, the greater the guilt, and this is the secret of salvation. If it is not cowardice, it is a faintheartedness of the soul not to will to repent of the guilt of the forefathers; if it is not abject meanness, it still is smallness of mind and lack of magnanimity.

Despair's choice, then, is "myself," for it certainly is true that when I despair, I despair over myself just as over everything else. But the self over which I despair is something finite like everything else finite, whereas the self I choose is the absolute self or my self according to its absolute validity. This being so, you will perceive again here why I said previously and go on saying that the Either/Or I erected between living esthetically and living ethically is not an unqualified dilemma, because it actually is a matter of only one choice. Through this choice, I actually do not choose between good and evil, but I choose the good, but when I choose the good, I choose *eo ipso* the choice between good and evil. The original choice is forever present in every succeeding choice.

Despair, then, and your light-mindedness will never more make you wander like a fitful phantom, like a ghost, among the ruins of a world that is lost to you anyway; despair, and your spirit will never sigh in despondency, for the world will once again become beautiful and happy for you, even if you look at it with other eyes than before, and your liberated spirit will vault up into the world of freedom.

Here I could stop, for I have now brought you to the point I wanted—for you are there if you yourself are willing. I wanted you to tear yourself loose from the illusions of the esthetic and from the dreaming of a half-hearted despair, in order to become awakened to the earnestness of the spirit. But it is not my intention at all to stop here, for I want to go on from here and give you a view of life, an ethical life-view. What I have to offer you is only something simple, partly because my gift is by no means proportionate to the task, partly because simplicity is the primary characteristic of everything ethical, a quality that can be rather striking to one who comes from the overabundance of the esthetic. Here it is a matter of *nil ad ostentationem, omnia ad conscientiam* [nothing for show, everything for conscience]. To stop here could be dubious for another reason also, for it could easily look as if I ended in a kind of quietism in which the personality would settle down with the same necessity as thought does in the absolute. What, then, would be the good of having gained oneself, what would be the good of acquiring a sword that could conquer the whole world, if one had no other use for it than to put it away in the scabbard?

But before proceeding to present more explicitly such an ethical view of life, I shall suggest in a few words the danger that faces a person in the moment of despair, the reef on which he can be stranded and utterly shipwrecked. The Bible says: For what would it profit a person if he gained the whole world but damaged his own soul; what should he have in return?[65] Scripture does not state the antithesis to this, but it is implicit in the sentence. The antithesis would read something like this: What damage would there be to a person if he lost the whole world and yet did not damage his soul; what would he need in return? There are expressions that in themselves seem simple and yet fill the soul with a strange anxiety, because they almost become more obscure the more one thinks about them. In the religious sphere, the phrase "sin against the Holy Spirit" is such an expression. I do not know whether theologians are able to give a definite explanation of it; I do not regard myself as capable of it, but then I am only a layman. But the phrase "to damage one's soul" is an ethical expression, and the person who thinks he has an ethical life-view must also think he is able to explain it. We often hear the words used, and yet anyone who wants to understand them must have experienced deep movements in his soul—indeed, he must have despaired, for it is actually the movements of despair that are described here: on the one side the whole world, on the other side one's own soul.

You will readily perceive, if we pursue this expression, that we arrive at the same abstract definition of "soul" at which we arrived earlier in the definition of the word "self" in the psychological consideration of wishing, without, however, wanting to become someone else. In other words, if I can gain the whole world and yet damage my soul, the phrase "the whole world" must include all the finite things that I possess in my immediacy. Then my soul proves to be indifferent to these things. If I can lose the whole world without damaging my soul, the phrase "the whole world" again includes all the finite qualifications that I possess in my immediacy, and yet if my soul is undamaged it is consequently indifferent toward them. I can lose my wealth, my honor in the eyes of others, my intellectual capacity, and yet not damage my soul; I can gain it all and yet be damaged. What, then, is my soul? What is this innermost being of mine that is undismayed by this loss and suffers damage by this gain?

For the person in despair, this movement is evident; it is no rhetorical expression but is the only adequate one when he sees on the one side the whole world and on the other side himself, his soul. In the moment of despair, the separation is evident, and now it is a matter of how he despairs, because, as I pointed out above with regard to every esthetic life-view, it is despair to gain the whole world and in such a way that one damages one's soul, and yet it is my deep conviction that to despair is a person's true salvation. Here again the significance of willing one's despair is evident, of willing in an infinite sense, in an absolute sense, for a will such as that is identical with absolute self-giving. But if I will my despair in a finite sense, then I damage my soul, for then my innermost being does not attain the breakthrough in despair; it locks itself in it. It becomes hardened, so that finite despair is a hardening, absolute despair an infinitizing. When I in my despair gain the whole world, I damage my soul by making myself finite, since I have my life in the finite. When I despair over losing the whole world, I damage my soul, for I make it finite in the very same way, since here again I see my soul as established by the finite. That a person can gain the whole world by means of crimes and yet damage his soul is obvious, but there is an apparently far more innocent way in which it can happen. This is why I said that that young girl was just as much in despair whether she got the one she loved or not. Every finite despair is a choice of the finite, for I choose it just as much when I attain it as when I lose it, for my attaining it is not under my control, but choosing it certainly is. Finite despair is, therefore, an unfree despair; it does not actually will despair, but it wills the finite, and this is despair.

A person can stay at this point, and as long as he stays there I cannot really decide to dare to say of him that he has damaged his soul. He stands at an extremely dangerous point. At every moment there is a possibility of it. Despair is there, but as yet it has not attacked his innermost being; not until he finitely hardens himself in it has he damaged his soul. His soul, so to speak, is anesthetized in despair, and not until he, when he awakens, chooses a finite way out of the despair, not until then has he damaged his soul, for then he closes up, then his rational soul is smothered and he is changed into a beast of prey who shrinks from no expedient, since to him everything is self-defense. There is a terrible anxiety in the thought that a person has damaged his soul, and yet anyone who has despaired will have had intimations of this wrong way, this lostness.

That a person can damage his soul in this manner is certain; to what extent it is the case with the particular individual can never be ascertained, and with regard to this let no one dare to judge another. Someone's life may seem strange, and one may be tempted to think that this is the case with him, and yet he may have quite another interpretation that makes him feel sure of the very opposite; on the other hand, a person can damage his soul without anyone's suspecting it, for this is not an external damage; it lies within a person's innermost being. It is like the rot at the heart of fruit, while the outside can look very delectable; it is like the inner hollowness of which the shell gives no hint.

Now, when you choose yourself absolutely, you will easily discover that this self is not an abstraction or a tautology. At most it may appear to be so during the time of orientation when one differentiates until one finds the most abstract expression for this self. And even then it is nevertheless an illusion that it is completely abstract and devoid of content, for this is still not the consciousness of freedom in general (this is a category of thought), but it has resulted from a choice and is the consciousness of this specific free being who is himself and no other. This self contains in itself a rich concretion, a multiplicity of qualities, of characteristics—in short, it is the total esthetic self that is chosen ethically. Therefore, the more you absorb yourself in yourself, the more you will perceive the significance even of the insignificant, not in the finite but in the infinite sense, because it is posited by you. When a person chooses himself ethically in this way, this is not only a sober reflecting about oneself, but in describing this act one could recall the words of Scripture about rendering an account of every careless word that is spoken.[66] In other words, when the passion of freedom is awakened, it is jealous of itself and by no means allows what belongs to a person and what does not to remain unspecified and confused. Therefore, at the first moment of choice the personality seemingly emerges as naked as the infant from the mother's womb; at the next moment it is concrete in itself, and a person can remain at this point only through an arbitrary abstraction. He remains himself, exactly the same that he was before, down to the most insignificant feature, and yet he becomes another, for the choice penetrates everything and changes it. Thus his finite personality is now made infinite in the choice, in which he infinitely chooses himself.

II
200

Now he possesses himself as posited by himself—that is, as chosen by himself, as free—but in possessing himself in this way, an absolute difference becomes manifest, the difference between good and evil. As long as he has not chosen himself, this difference is latent. How does the difference between good and evil come to light at all? Can it be thought—that is, is it something for thought? No. I have hereby again arrived at the point where I was before, and therefore it might seem as if philosophy had actually canceled the principle of contradiction, but that means only that it has not arrived there yet. As soon as I think, I am related necessarily to what I think, but that is the very reason the difference between good and evil does not exist. Think what you will, think the most abstract of all categories, think the most concrete—you never think in the categories of good and evil. Think of history in its totality—you think the necessary movement of the idea, but you never think in the categories of good and evil. You continually think relative differences, never the absolute difference. In my opinion, it can readily be acknowledged that philosophy is right in being unable to think an absolute contradiction, but from this it by no means follows that this does not exist. When I think, I also infinitize myself, but not absolutely, for I vanish in the absolute. Not until I absolutely choose myself do I absolutely infinitize myself, because I myself *am* the absolute, because only I myself can choose absolutely; and this absolute choice of myself is my freedom, and only when I have absolutely chosen myself have I posited an absolute difference: namely, the difference between good and evil.

In order to stress the element of self-determination in thinking, philosophy declares: The absolute is because I think it. But since philosophy itself perceives that free thinking is thereby designated, not the necessary thinking it usually celebrates, it substitutes another expression: namely, that my thinking of the absolute is the absolute's thinking-itself in me.[67] This expression is by no means identical with the one preceding; it is, however, very suggestive. That is to say, my thinking is an element in the absolute, and therein lies the necessity of my thinking, therein lies the necessity with which I think it. It is otherwise with the good. The good is because I will it, and otherwise it is not at all. This is the expression of freedom, and the same is also the case with evil—it is only inasmuch as I will it. This in no way reduces or lowers the categories of good and evil to merely subjective categories. On the contrary, the absolute validity of these categories is declared. The good is the being-in-and-for-itself, posited by the being-in-and-for-itself, and this is freedom.

It might seem dubious for me to use the expression "to choose oneself absolutely," because this might seem to imply that I chose both the good and the evil just as absolutely and that both the good and the evil belonged to me just as essentially. It was to prevent this misunderstanding that I used the expression "I repent myself out of the whole of existence." Repentance specifically expresses that evil essentially belongs to me and at the same time expresses that it does not essentially belong to me. If the evil in me did not essentially belong to me, I could not choose it; but if there were something in me that I could not choose absolutely, then I would not be choosing myself absolutely at all, then I myself would not be the absolute but only a product.

Here I shall interrupt these deliberations in order to show how an ethical life-view regards the personality and life and its significance. For the sake of order, I shall go back to a couple of comments made earlier on the relation between the esthetic and the ethical. It was said that every esthetic view of life is despair; this was due to its having been built upon that which can both be and not be. This is not the case with the ethical life-view, for it builds its life upon that which "to be" essentially belongs. The esthetic, it was said, is that in a person whereby he immediately is the person he is; the ethical is that whereby a person becomes what he becomes. This by no means says that the person who lives esthetically does not develop, but he develops with necessity, not in freedom; no metamorphosis takes place in him, no infinite internal movement by which he comes to the point from which he becomes the person he becomes.

When an individual considers himself esthetically, he becomes conscious of this self as a complex concretion intrinsically qualified in many ways; but despite all the internal variety, all these together are nevertheless his nature, have equal right to emerge, equal right to demand satisfaction. His soul is like soil out of which grow all sorts of herbs, all with equal claim to flourish; his self consists of this multiplicity, and he has no self that is higher than this. Now, if he has what you so often speak of—esthetic earnestness and a little common sense about life—he will perceive that it is impossible for everything to flourish equally. Then he will choose, and that which determines him is a more and less, which is a relative difference.

Suppose that a person could live without coming in touch with the ethical. He would then be able to say: I have a natural capacity to be a Don Juan, a Faust, a robber chief;[68] I will now train this natural capacity, for esthetic earnestness demands that I become something specific, that I allow it to develop to the fullness for which the seed has been planted within me. Esthetically, such a view of the personality and its development would be entirely correct. From this you see what esthetic development signifies; it is a development just like that of a plant, and although the individual becomes, he becomes that which he immediately is.

Someone who views the personality ethically has at once an

absolute difference: namely, the difference between good and evil. And if he finds more of evil in him than of good, this still does not mean that it is the evil that is to advance, but it means that it is the evil that is to recede and the good that is to advance. When the individual develops ethically, he becomes that which he becomes, for even when he lets the esthetic within him (which for him means something different from what it means for one who lives only esthetically) have its validity, it is nevertheless dethroned. Like all earnestness, even esthetic earnestness is beneficial for a person, but it can never rescue him entirely.

I believe that up to a point this has been the case with you; for just as the ideal has always done you harm because you have been hypnotized by staring at it, so it has also been beneficial for you insofar as the bad ideal has had just as repelling an effect upon you. Of course, esthetic earnestness cannot cure you, for you never go any further than to leave the bad alone, but you do leave it alone not because it is bad or because you abhor it but because it cannot be accomplished ideally. Thus you have come no further than the feeling that you are just as powerless for the good as for evil. Moreover, evil is perhaps never as seductively effective as when it steps forth in esthetic categories this way. It takes a high degree of ethical earnestness never to want to conceive of evil in esthetic categories. Such a view of it slyly sneaks into every human being, and the predominantly esthetic culture of our day contributes not a little to this. Therefore we not infrequently hear even moralizers rant against evil in such a way that we perceive that the speaker, although he praises the good, nevertheless relishes the satisfaction that he himself could very well be the most cunning and wily of men but has rejected it on the basis of a comparison with being a good man. But this betrays a secret weakness that shows that to him the difference between good and evil is not clear in all its earnestness. So much of the good still remains in everyone that he senses that to be a good person is the highest, but in order to have a little distinction from the common herd he demands a high degree of recognition because he, who had so many capacities for being bad, nevertheless became good. It is just as if having many capacities for becoming bad were a good point and just as if dwelling on these capacities in this way did not betray a preference for them.

We frequently also find people who in their heart of hearts actually are good but do not have the courage to acknowledge it because it seems that they thereby fall into all too trivial categories. Such people also recognize the good as the highest but do not have the courage to admit evil to be what it is. We often hear the expression: That was a poor end to the story. Ordinarily, one can be sure that what is greeted and advertised in this way is the ethical. When a person has in one way or another become a riddle to others, and then the explanation comes and shows that he was not, as people had hoped and happily anticipated, a sly and underhanded deceiver but a kind and good person, then we say: No more than that? Is that the whole story? Indeed, it truly takes considerable ethical courage to acknowledge the good as the highest, because one thereby falls into altogether universal categories. People are very reluctant to do that; they much prefer to have their lives in differences. For everyone who wills it can be a good person, but to be bad always takes talent. This is why many a person prefers to be a philosopher, not a Christian, because to be a philosopher takes talent, to be a Christian humility, and anyone who so wills can have that. You, too, can bear in mind what I am saying here, because in your innermost being you are not a bad person. Now, do not be angry; I do not mean to insult you. You know that I have had to make a virtue of necessity, and since I do not have your gifts, I must take care to maintain a little respect for being a good person.

There are also other ways in which people in our day have tried to enervate the ethical view. That is, although to be a good person is regarded as an exceedingly poor employment in life, people still have even a certain respect for it and do not like to have it stressed. In no way do I mean that a person is supposed to wear his virtue on his sleeve and take every opportunity to fling in people's faces the fact that he is a good person, but on the other hand he is not to hide it or be afraid of owning up to his own striving. If he does, an outcry is

promptly raised against him: He wants to put on airs; he wants
to be better than others. They join in the flippant locution: Let
us be human; before God we are all sinners.[69] This I need not
tell you, but I certainly do need to warn you against the excessive activity into which your mockery often carries you.
Therefore it is quite all right that in modern drama the bad is
always represented by the most brilliantly gifted characters,
whereas the good, the upright, is represented by the grocer's
apprentice.[70] The spectators find this entirely appropriate and
learn from the play what they already knew, that it is far beneath their dignity to be classed with a grocer's apprentice.

Yes, my young friend, it takes considerable ethical courage
to will in earnest to have one's life not in differences but in the
universal. In this respect our age needs a jolt, and this is bound
to happen, for the moment is certainly coming when it will see
how the most outstanding first-rate individuals in the esthetic
sense, those whose lives are based on differences, will despair
over them in order to find the universal. This can be good for
us small people [*Smaa-Folk*], inasmuch as we, too, at times are
dismayed at not being able to have our lives in differences because we are too insignificant for that—not because we have
been sufficiently great to reject [*forsmaa*] them.

Every person who lives only esthetically therefore has a secret horror of despairing, for he knows very well that what despair brings is the universal, and he also knows that what he
has his own life in is differences. The higher an individual
stands, the more differences he has exterminated or despaired
over, but he always retains one difference that he is unwilling
to exterminate—that in which he has his life. It is remarkable
to see how even the simplest people discover with admirable
proficiency that which could be called their esthetic difference,
however insignificant it is, and one of the afflictions of life is
the foolish conflict about which difference is more important
than the other.

The estheticists signify their antipathy toward despair also
by saying that it is a break. This word is quite correct insofar
as life's development is supposed to consist of a necessary unfolding of the immediate. If that is not the case, then despair is

no break but a transfiguration. Only the person who despairs over something in particular experiences a break, but that is because he does not despair completely. The estheticists are also afraid that life will lose the entertaining multiplicity it has as long as every particular individual is regarded as living within esthetic categories. This is again a misunderstanding, prompted, no doubt, by various rigoristic theories. In despair nothing perishes; all the esthetic remains in a person except that it is made an auxiliary and precisely thereby is preserved. Yes, it is certainly true that one does not live in it as before, but from that it by no means follows that one has lost it; perhaps it can be used in another way, but from that it does not follow that it is gone. The ethicist only carries through the despair that the more advanced estheticist has already begun but has arbitrarily interrupted, for however great the difference, it is still only relative. And when the estheticist himself admits that the difference that gives his life meaning is also transitory, but adds that it is still always best to rejoice in it as long as one has it, this actually is a cowardliness that loves a certain kind of low-ceilinged coziness and is unworthy of a human being. It is as if a person wanted to rejoice in a relationship based on a mis-understanding that sooner or later would come to light, but he did not have the courage to be aware of it or to admit it and wanted to take delight in the relationship as long as possible. But this is not the case with you; on the contrary, you are like someone who has admitted the misunderstanding, broken off the relationship, and nevertheless now continually wants to take leave of it.

The esthetic view also considers the personality in relation to the surrounding world, and the expression for this in its re-currence in the personality is enjoyment. But the esthetic expression for enjoyment in its relation to the personality is mood. That is, the personality is present in the mood, but it is dimly present. The person who lives esthetically tries as far as possible to be engrossed completely in mood. He tries to bury himself completely in it so that nothing remains in him that cannot be modulated into it, because a remainder like that al-ways has a disturbing effect; it is a continuity that will hold him back. The dimmer the presence of the personality in the mood, the more the individual is in the instant, and this in turn is the most adequate expression for the esthetic existence—it is in the instant. This accounts for the enormous fluctuations to which one who lives esthetically is exposed.

The person who lives ethically is also familiar with mood, but for him it is not the highest; because he has chosen himself infinitely, he sees his mood beneath him. The "more" that refuses to be absorbed in mood is precisely the continuity that to him is the highest. The person who lives ethically has a memory of his life (to recall an earlier expression); the person who lives esthetically does not have it at all. The person who lives ethically does not exterminate the mood. He looks at it for a moment, but this moment saves him from living in the instant; this moment gives him supremacy over the desire, for the art of mastering desire is not so much in exterminating it or utterly renouncing it as in determining the moment.

Take whatever desire you please—the secret in it, the power in it, is in its being absolutely in the instant. It is often said that the only way is to refrain altogether. This is a very wrong method, which also succeeds only for a time. Imagine a person who has become addicted to gambling. Desire awakens in all its passion; it is as if his life would be at stake if his desire is not satisfied. If he is able to say to himself: At this moment I will not do it; I will not do it for an hour—then he is cured. This hour is the continuity that saves him. The mood of the person who lives esthetically is always eccentric, because he has his center in the periphery. The personality has its center in itself, and the person who does not have himself is eccentric. The mood of the person who lives ethically is centralized. He is not in the mood, and he is not mood, but he has mood and has the mood within himself.[71] What he works for is continuity, and this is always the master of mood. His life does not lack mood—indeed, it has a total mood. But this is acquired; it is what would be called *aequale temperamentum* [even disposition]. But this is no esthetic mood, and no person has it by nature or immediately.

But can the person who has chosen himself infinitely say:

Now I possess myself; I ask for no more, and I meet all the ups and downs of the world with the proud thought: I am the person I am?[72] By no means! If a person were to talk this way, it would be easy to see that he had gone astray. His basic error would really be that he had not, strictly speaking, chosen himself; he had, no doubt, chosen himself, but outside himself; he had conceived of choosing altogether abstractly and had not grasped himself in his concretion; he had not chosen in such a way that in the choice he remained in himself, arrayed himself in himself; he had chosen himself according to his necessity and not in his freedom; he had taken the ethical choice esthetically in vain. The more significant the truth of that which is to emerge, the more dangerous the aberrations, and here, too, a terrible wrong path appears.

When the individual has grasped himself in his eternal validity, this overwhelms him with all its fullness. Temporality vanishes for him. At the first moment, this fills him with an indescribable bliss and gives him an absolute security. If he now begins to stare at it one-sidedly, the temporal asserts its claims. These are rejected. What temporality is able to give, the more or less that appears here, is so very insignificant to him compared with what he possesses eternally. Everything comes to a standstill for him; he has, so to speak, arrived in eternity ahead of time. He sinks into contemplation, stares fixedly at himself, but this staring cannot fill up time. Then it appears to him that time, temporality, is his ruination; he demands a perfect form of existence, and here in turn there appears a weariness, an apathy, that resembles the lethargy that accompanies enjoyment. This apathy can so engulf a person that suicide seems the only escape for him. No power is able to tear him from himself; the only power is time. It certainly cannot tear him from himself either, but it stops him and delays him; it retards the embrace of the spirit with which he grasps himself. He has not chosen himself; like Narcissus,[73] he has become infatuated with himself. Such a condition has not infrequently ended in suicide.

His mistake is that he has not chosen in the right way, not simply in the sense that he has had no eye at all for his flaws, but he has regarded himself within the category of necessity; himself, this personality with all the multiplicity of its qualifications, he has regarded as belonging to the world process; he has seen it before the eternal power whose fire has penetrated it without consuming it.[74] But he has not seen himself in his freedom, has not chosen himself in freedom. If he does that, then at the very moment he chooses himself he is in motion. However concrete his self is, he nevertheless has chosen himself according to his possibility; in repentance he has ransomed himself in order to remain in his freedom, but he can remain in his freedom only by continually realizing [*realisere*] it. He who has chosen himself on this basis is *eo ipso* one who acts.

This may be the place to discuss briefly a life-view that is so very pleasing to you, especially as a tutor and sometimes as a practitioner. It amounts to nothing less than this, that to sorrow is indeed the real meaning of life, and to be the unhappiest one is the supreme happiness.[75] At first sight, this view does not seem to be an esthetic view of life, because enjoyment surely cannot really be its watchword. But it is not ethical either; it is situated at the perilous point at which the esthetic is to pass over into the ethical, where the soul is so easily entangled in some formulation of a theory of predestination.

You entertain several false doctrines; this is almost the worst, but you are also aware that it is most useful when it is a matter of sneaking up to people and sucking them to yourself. You can be more heartless than anyone; you can make a jest of everything, even a person's pain. That this is tempting to the young, you are not unaware, and yet this conduct does alienate you somewhat from the young, for such treatment is just as repellent as it is appealing. If it is a young woman you want to deceive in this way, it by no means escapes you that a womanly soul has too much depth to be fascinated by such conduct for any length of time. Indeed, even if you have engrossed her for a moment, it will soon end with her becoming weary of it and almost taking a dislike to you, because her soul does not require such titillations. Now the method is altered; with a few enigmatic exclamations, which only she can understand, you let a detached melancholy be suspected as the explanation of

II
209

the whole thing. You open yourself only to her, but so circumspectly that she still never does come really to know any more; you leave it to her imagination to paint the deep sadness you are hiding in your innermost being. You are clever—that cannot be denied—and what a young girl said of you is true: you will probably end up becoming a Jesuit.[76] The more cunningly you know how to play for them the line that leads deeper and deeper into the secret recesses of sadness, the happier you are, the more sure of drawing them to yourself. You do not make long speeches; you do not proclaim your pain by a sincere handshake or "by gazing romantically into a kindred soul's romantic eyes"—you are too clever for that. You avoid witnesses and only for a single moment do you let yourself be taken unawares. There is an age at which there is no more dangerous poison for a young girl than sadness, that you know; and this knowledge, like any other knowledge, in and by itself can be rather good, but the use you make of it I shall not commend.

Since you have hardened your mind to interpret all existence in esthetic categories, it is taken for granted that sorrow has not escaped your attention, for sorrow in and by itself is at least as interesting as joy. The imperturbability with which you everywhere cling to the interesting wherever it appears is a constant occasion for those around you to misunderstand you and sometimes to regard you as absolutely heartless and sometimes as a really good-natured person, although you actually are neither. The very circumstance that you are seen just as often in search of sorrow as in the company of joy can prompt such a misunderstanding—that is, please note, if there is an idea in the sorrow as well as in the joy, for only thereby is your esthetic interest aroused. If you could be frivolous enough to make a person unhappy, you would be capable of providing the occasion for the most singular deception. Unlike others who perfidiously seek only joy, you would not withdraw and pursue it down some other road again. No, sorrow in this same individual would become even more interesting to you than joy; you would stay with him; you would become absorbed in his sorrow. You have experience, fer-

vency, command of language, the pathos of tragedy. You
know how to offer the sufferer the relief that the esthetic sorrower alone craves: expression. It delights you to see how the
sorrowing one rests in the music of mood when you are playing it. Soon you become indispensable to him, for your words
lift him up out of the dark abodes of sorrow. He, however,
does not become indispensable to you, and very soon you are
weary. For to you it is not merely joy that

> Is like a casual friend
> One meets when traveling,[77]

but sorrow also, since you are at all times a traveler. Then
when you have consoled the sorrowing one and by way of
compensation for your trouble have distilled the interesting
out of it, you leap into your carriage and shout: Let us be off!
If you are asked "Where to?" you answer with the hero Don
Giovanni, "To pleasure and merriment."[78] In other words,
now you are bored with sorrow, and your soul demands the
opposite.

   You do not, presumably, behave quite as badly as I have pic-
tured it, and I do not deny that you often have a genuine interest in the sorrowing one, that you really do wish to heal him,
to win him for joy. Then you harness yourself, as you yourself
say, like a spirited horse, and try to work him out of the snares
of sorrow. You do not spare time and energy, and at times you
succeed. Even then I cannot praise you, for something is hiding under all this. You are, namely, envious of sorrow; you do
not like it that any other person has sorrow or a sorrow that
cannot be surmounted. When you heal a person in sorrow,
you relish the satisfaction of saying to yourself: But my own
sorrow, no one can heal that. That is a conclusion you always
keep *in mente* [in mind]; whether you are seeking the diversion
of joy or of sorrow, you are firmly convinced that there is a
sorrow that cannot be dispelled.

   So I have now arrived at the point where you think that the
meaning of life is to sorrow. The whole modern trend is
marked by a greater inclination to want to sorrow than to
want to be happy. This is regarded as a loftier view of life, and

so it is, insofar as wanting to be happy is natural and to sorrow is unnatural. Then, too, being happy carries with it a certain obligation upon the individual to be grateful, even though his thoughts are too confused for him to know clearly whom he should thank. Sorrowing exempts one from this, and vanity is all the more satisfied. Moreover, our age has experienced the vanity of life in so many ways that it does not believe in joy, and in order nevertheless to have something in which to believe, it believes in sorrow. Joy, says our generation, passes away, but sorrow lasts,[79] and therefore the person who builds his view of life on this builds on a firm foundation.

If you are asked more explicitly what kind of sorrow you are talking about, you are clever enough to bypass ethical sorrow. It is not repentance you have in mind—no, it is esthetic sorrow, especially reflective sorrow.[80] It is based not on guilt but on misfortune, on fate, on a mournful disposition, on the influence of others, etc. All this is something you have learned to know very well from novels. If you read it there, you laugh at it; if you hear others talking about it, you make fun of it, but when you yourself are discoursing on the subject, then there is meaning and truth in it.

Although the view that makes sorrowing in and by itself the meaning of life might seem lamentable enough, I cannot refrain from showing you, from a side you perhaps did not expect, that it is a dreary view. To repeat what I have said before, sorrow passes away in the same sense in which it is said that joy passes away. This is something to which I do not need to call your attention, for this you can learn from your master, Scribe, who has frequently made fun of the sentimentality that believes in an eternal sorrow.[81] The person who says that to sorrow is the meaning of life has joy outside himself in the same way as the person who wants to be happy has sorrow outside himself. Joy can then take him by surprise in exactly the same way as sorrow can the other. Thus his life-view is linked to a condition that is not in his power, for it is not in one's power to stop being happy any more than to stop being distressed. But every life-view that has a condition outside itself is despair. Thus, wanting to sorrow is despair in exactly the same sense as wanting to seek happiness, since it is always despair to have one's life in something whose nature is that it can pass away. So, then, be as sagacious and ingenious as you wish, scare joy away with a lachrymose outward appearance, or, if you prefer, deceive it by your outward appearance in order to hide your sorrow—joy can nevertheless surprise you, for time consumes the children of time,[82] and such a sorrow is a child of time, and the eternity it falsely ascribes to itself is a deception.

The deeper the basis of the sorrow, the more it may seem that it would be able to last an entire lifetime, indeed, that nothing would need to be done, but that it would keep on as a matter of course. If it is a specific event, it will already appear to be very difficult. You are well aware of that, and thus if you are going to speak about the meaning of sorrow for an entire lifetime, then you are thinking rather of unhappy individualities and tragic heroes. The whole psychic disposition of the unhappy individuality is of such a nature that he cannot be happy or glad; a fate broods over him, and likewise over the tragic hero. Here it is perfectly correct that to sorrow is the meaning of life, and here we have a pure and simple fatalism, which always has something seductive about it. Here, too, you come with your pretension, the gist of which is neither more nor less than that you are the unhappiest one. And yet it is undeniable that this thought is the proudest and the most defiant that can arise in the mind of a human being.

Let me answer you as you deserve to be answered. First and foremost: you are not sorrowing. You know that very well, for your favorite expression is that the unhappiest person is the happiest. But this is a falsification, more terrible than any other; it is a falsification directed against the eternal power who rules the world. It is mutiny against God, like laughing when one ought to cry, and yet there is a despair that is capable of this, there is a defiance that stands up to God himself. But this is also treason against the human race. To be sure, you also distinguish between sorrows, but you nevertheless believe that there is a difference so vast that it is impossible to bear this sorrow as such. But if there is such a sorrow, it is not up to you to decide which it is; one difference is just as good as the other, and you have betrayed humankind's deepest and most sacred right or grace. It is treason against greatness, a base envy, for it ends up saying that great men have not been tried in the most dangerous testing, that they have slipped easily into their honors, and that they, too, would have been overwhelmed if the superhuman temptation of which you speak had come upon them. Is this, then, the way you intend to honor greatness, by disparaging it; is this the way you intend to give the testimonial, by disavowing it?

Now, do not misunderstand me. I am not one who thinks that a person is not supposed to sorrow; I despise this miserable common-sensicality, and if I have a choice between them, then I choose sorrow. No, I know that to sorrow is beautiful, and that there is substance in tears, but I also know that one is not to sorrow as someone who has no hope.[83] There is an absolute contradiction between us that can never be canceled. I cannot live within esthetic categories; I feel that what is most sacred in my life will perish. I require a higher expression, and the ethical provides me with that. And here sorrow first acquires its true and deep meaning. Do not be upset by what I am saying here; do not take exception if I, when speaking of the sorrow that requires heroes to endure, speak of children. It is a sign of a well brought up child to be inclined to say it is sorry without too much pondering whether it is in the right or not, and it is likewise a sign of a high-minded person and a deep soul if he is inclined to repent, if he does not take God to court but repents and loves God in his repentance. Without this, his life is nothing, only like foam on water. Indeed, I assure you that if my life through no fault of my own were so interwoven with sorrows and sufferings that I could call myself the greatest tragic hero, could divert myself with my affliction and shock the world by naming it, my choice is made: I strip myself of the hero's garb and the pathos of tragedy; I am not the tormented one who can be proud of his sufferings; I am the humbled one who feels my offense; I have only one word for what I am suffering—guilt, only one word for my pain— repentance, only one hope before my eyes—forgiveness. And

II
213

if this proves to be difficult for me to do—oh, then I have only
one prayer. I would throw myself upon the earth and appeal
from morning till night to the heavenly power who rules the
world for one favor, that it might be granted me to repent, for
I know only one sorrow that could bring me to despair and
plunge everything into it—that repentance is an illusion, an illusion not with respect to the forgiveness it seeks but with respect to the imputation it presupposes.

And do you think that the way I am going about this does
not give sorrow its due, that I am running away from it? By
no means! I lay it away in my being and therefore never forget
it. On the whole, it is disbelief in the validity of the spirit not
to dare believe that I can possess something within me without
looking at it every moment. In daily life, what we want to
keep safest we put away in a place where we do not go every
day, and so it is also in the spiritual sense. I have the sorrow
within me, and I know that it will be part of my being; I know
it much more certainly than the one who in his anxiety about
losing it takes it out every day.

II
214

My life has never been so turbulent that I have felt tempted
to confuse chaotically all existence, but in my daily life I have
often experienced how beneficial it is to give sorrow an ethical
expression, not to wipe out the esthetic in sorrow but to control it ethically. As long as the sorrow is quiet and humble, I
am not afraid of it; if it becomes violent, passionate, and so-
phistical and deludes me in despondency, I rise up. I tolerate
no mutiny; I do not want anything in the world to trick me out
of what I have received as a gift of grace from the hand of God.
I do not chase sorrow away, do not try to forget it, but I repent. And even if the sorrow is of such a nature that I myself
have no guilt in it, then I repent that I let it gain power over
me; I repent that I did not immediately take it to God, and if
that had happened, it would not have gained the power to delude me.

Forgive me for speaking of children again here. If a child
goes around whining and does not want either this or that, we
say: Perhaps you are looking for something to cry about—and
this method is supposed to be excellent. So it is also with me,

for however much one has reached the age of discretion, one always retains something of the child. So when I whine, I say to myself: You certainly want something to cry about, and then I carry out the transformation. And that, I can assure you, is very beneficial for a person, for the tears the esthetic sorrower sheds for himself are nevertheless hypocritical tears and are of no avail; but to feel one's own guilt is actually something to cry about, and there is an eternal benediction in the tears of repentance.

When the Savior went up to Jerusalem and wept over the great city that did not know what was best for it,[84] it is certainly possible that he also could have moved it to weep along with him, but if the tears had been esthetic tears, they would have been of only little use. Yet the world surely has not seen many tragedies like the one when the chosen people were rejected. If they had been tears of repentance, there would indeed have been substance to them, and yet here it was a matter of repenting of more than their own guilt, for it was not only the generation living just then that was guilty; there was the guilt of the forefathers that rested upon it. Here repentance appears in all its profound meaning, for while in one way it isolates me, in another way it binds me indissolubly to the whole human race, because my life does not begin now and with nothing, and if I cannot repent of the past, then freedom is a dream.

II
215

You perhaps see now why I am discussing this life-view here. The personality is again seen here within the categories of necessity, and there is left only enough freedom to be able, like a restless dream, to keep the individual continually half-awake and to lead him astray into the labyrinth of sufferings and vicissitudes, where he sees himself everywhere and yet cannot come to himself. It is unbelievable how light-mindedly such issues are often treated. Even systematic thinkers treat it as a natural oddity about which they have nothing more to say beyond a mere description, and yet it never occurs to them that if there were such a natural oddity, then all the rest of their wisdom is nonsense and illusion. This is why one feels helped in an entirely different way by the Christian view than by all the wisdom of the philosophers. The Christian view attributes everything to sin, something the philosopher is too esthetic to have the ethical courage to do. And yet this courage is the only thing that can rescue life and humankind, unless one according to whim interrupts one's skepticism and joins some others who are likeminded about what truth is.

The first form the choice takes is complete isolation. That is, in choosing myself, I separate myself from my relations to the whole world, until in this separation I end in an abstract identity. Since the individual has chosen himself according to his freedom, he is *eo ipso* [precisely thereby] acting. Yet his action has no relation to anything in the surrounding world, for the individual has completely exterminated this and is only for himself. The life-view that appears here is, however, an ethical view.

It found expression in Greece in a single individual's efforts to develop himself into a paragon of virtue.[85] Like the anchorites later in Christendom, he withdrew from active life, not in order to lose himself in metaphysical speculations but in order to act—not outwardly but within himself. This internal action was simultaneously his task and his satisfaction, for it certainly was not his intention to discipline himself to serve the state all the better at some later time. No, in this disciplining he was to himself enough, and he abandoned civic life never to return to it. In the strict sense, he did not actually withdraw from life; on the contrary, he remained in its multiplicity, because contact with it was in pedagogical respects necessary for his own sake. But civic life as such had no meaning for him; by some magic formula, he had rendered it harmless, indifferent, meaningless for himself. Thus the virtues he developed were not the civic virtues (and they really were the true virtues in paganism that correspond to the religious virtues in Christianity), they were the personal virtues: courage, gallantry, abstinence, contentment, etc.

In our day, of course, we seldom see this life-view actualized, for everyone is too influenced by the religious to stop with such an abstract definition of virtue. The deficiency of this life-view is easy to see. The error was that the individual had chosen himself altogether abstractly, and therefore the perfection he coveted and attained was just as abstract. This was my reason for emphasizing that choosing oneself is identical with repenting oneself, because repentance places the individual in the closest connection and the most intimate relation with an outside world.

Analogies to this Greek life-view have often been seen and in the Christian world are sometimes still seen, except that in Christianity it becomes more beautiful and more copious through the addition of the mystical and the religious. A Greek individual who developed himself into a perfect epitome of all the personal virtues may attain as high a degree of masterliness as he wishes; nevertheless his life is no more immortal than the world whose temptation his virtue conquered; his bliss is a solitary self-satisfaction, as transitory as everything else. The life of a mystic is much more profound. He has chosen himself absolutely, for even though a mystic is rarely heard to express himself this way, even though he usually uses the apparently opposite expression, that he has chosen God, yet, as shown above, it is the same, for if he has not chosen himself absolutely he is not in any free relationship to God, and it is precisely in freedom that the distinctive characteristic of Christian piety lies. In the language of the mystic, the expression for this free relationship often is that he is the "absolute thou." The mystic has chosen himself absolutely, and consequently according to his freedom, and consequently is *eo ipso* acting, but his action is internal action. The mystic chooses himself in his perfect isolation; for him the whole world is dead and exterminated, and the wearied soul chooses God or himself. This expression, "the wearied soul," must not be misunderstood, must not be misused to the disparagement of the mystic, as if it were a dubious matter that the soul did not choose God until it was weary of the world. By this expression, the mystic undoubtedly means his repentance over not having chosen God before, and his weariness must not be regarded as identical with boredom with life. Already here you will perceive how little the mystic's life is ethically structured, since the supreme expression of repentance is to repent that he did not choose God earlier, before he became concrete in the world, while his soul was only abstractly defined, consequently as a child.

The mystic, having chosen, is *eo ipso* one who is acting, but his action is internal action. Insofar as he is acting, his life has a movement, a development, a history. But a development can be metaphysical or esthetic to the point where it becomes doubtful whether it can properly be called a history, since that implies a development in the form of freedom. A movement can be so erratic that it can be doubtful to what extent one dares to call it a development. For example, when the movement consists of the return of a feature again and again, undeniably there is motion—in fact, one can perhaps discover a law for the movement—but there is no development. Repetition in time is without meaning, continuity is lacking. To a great extent this is the case with the mystic's life. It is frightful to read a mystic's laments over the flat moments. Then when the flat moment is over comes the luminous moment, and thus his life is continually alternating; it certainly has movement, but not development. His life lacks continuity. It is a feeling, namely a longing, that really constitutes the continuity in a mystic's life, whether this longing is directed to the past or to the future. But the very fact that a feeling constitutes the intervening period in this way proves that coherence is lacking. A mystic's development is metaphysically and esthetically qualified to such a degree that one does not dare to call it history except in the same sense that one speaks of the history of a plant.

For the mystic the whole world is dead; he has fallen in love with God. Now the development of his life is the unfolding of this love. Just as there are examples of lovers who have a certain resemblance to each other, also outwardly in mien and facial form, so the mystic is absorbed in contemplation of the divine, whose image is reflected more and more in his loving soul, and thus the mystic renews and revives the lost image of God in humankind. The more he contemplates, the more clearly this image is reflected in him, the more he himself comes to resemble this image. Thus his internal action does not consist in the acquiring of the personal virtues but in developing the religious or contemplative virtues.

But even this is too ethical an expression for his life, and therefore prayer is essentially his life. That prayer also belongs to an ethical life, I do not deny, but the more ethically a person lives, the more his prayer has the character of purpose, so much so that even in his prayer of thanksgiving there is an element of purpose. It is different with the mystic's prayer. For him prayer is more meaningful the more erotic it is, the more it is fired by a burning love. Prayer is the expression for his love, the only language in which he can address the deity, with whom he has fallen in love. Just as in earthly life lovers long for the moment when they are able to breathe forth their love for each other, to let their souls blend in a soft whisper, so the mystic longs for the moment when in prayer he can, as it were, creep into God. Just as the lovers feel most blissful in this whispering when they actually have nothing at all to talk about, so for the mystic his prayer is all the more blessed, his love all the happier, the less content his prayer has, the more he in his sighing almost vanishes from himself.

Perhaps it might not be out of the way here to emphasize more explicitly the falsity in such a life, all the more so because every deeper personality always feels moved by it. You yourself by no means lack the elements for becoming a mystic, at least for a time. Generally speaking, the most extreme opposites meet in this domain, the purest and most innocent souls and the most guilty of men, the most richly endowed and the most simple-minded.

First of all, may I quite simply state what it really is that jars me in such a life. This is my private judgment. Later I shall try to show the correctness of it with regard to the abuses I pointed out, and also the reason for them and the terrifying wrong paths that lie so very close.

In my opinion, the mystic cannot be absolved of a certain obtrusiveness in his relationship to God. That a person is supposed to love God with all his soul and all his mind—indeed, not only that he is supposed to do it but that doing it is bliss itself—who would deny this? But it by no means follows that the mystic is supposed to reject the existence, the actuality, in which God has placed him, because he thereby actually rejects God's love or demands another expression for it than that which God wills to give. Samuel's sober words are relevant here: Obedience is dearer to God than the fat of rams.[86] But this obtrusiveness can sometimes take an even more dubious form—for example, if a mystic bases his relationship to God on his being precisely who he is, regards himself by virtue of some accidental characteristic as the object of God's preference. He thereby debases God and himself: himself, because to be essentially different from others by virtue of something accidental is always a debasement; God, because he makes him an idol and himself a favorite in his court.

The second aspect of a mystic's life that is unpalatable to me is the softness and weakness of which he cannot be absolved. That a person wishes to be convinced in his innermost heart that he loves God in truth and honesty, that he often feels prompted really to make sure of it, that he can pray God to let his Spirit witness with his spirit,[87] that he does this—who would deny the beauty and truth in this? But it by no means follows that he will repeat this attempt every moment, test his love at every moment. He will have sufficient greatness of soul to believe in God's love, and then he will also have the cheerful boldness to believe in his own love, and rejoicing abide in the circumstances assigned to him simply because he knows that this abiding is the surest expression of his love, of his humility.

Finally, a mystic's life is displeasing to me because I regard it as a deception of the world in which he lives, a deception of the persons to whom he is bound or with whom he could establish a relationship if it had not pleased him to become a mystic. Ordinarily the mystic chooses the solitary life, but with that the issue is not clarified, because the question is whether he has the right to choose it. Insofar as he has chosen it, he does not deceive others, for he indeed says thereby: I do not want a relationship with you. But the question is whether he has the right to say that, the right to do that. It is especially as a married man and as a father that I am an enemy of mysticism. My domestic life also has its ἄδυτον [inner sanctum], but if I were a mystic I would have to have still another one for myself alone, and then I would be a poor husband. Since in my view, which I shall develop later, it is a duty for every person to marry, and since it cannot possibly be my view that a person should marry in order to become a poor husband, you readily perceive that I must have an animosity toward all mysticism.

The person who devotes himself one-sidedly to a mystical life eventually becomes so alienated from all people that every relationship, even the tenderest and most intimate, becomes a matter of indifference to him. It is not in this sense that one is to love God more than father and mother;[88] God is not that self-ish. Neither is he a poet who wishes to torment people with the most horrible conflicts, and if there actually were a conflict between love of God and love of human beings, the love of whom he himself has implanted in our hearts, it would be hard to imagine anything more horrible.

Presumably you have not forgotten young Ludvig Black-feldt, with whom both of us, I in particular, had considerable contact a few years ago. He most certainly was a very brilliant mind; his misfortune was that to the exclusion of everything else he lost himself one-sidedly in a mysticism not so much Christian as Indian. If he had lived in the Middle Ages, he un-doubtedly would have found a place of resort in a monastery. Our age does not have such resources. If a person goes astray today, he must of necessity perish if he is not completely healed; we have no such relative salvation to offer him. As you know, he ended with suicide. He had a kind of confidence in me and this violated his pet theory that one should not place oneself in relationship to any human being, but directly to God. But his confidence in me was not great either, and he never entirely opened himself to me. In the last half year of his life, I was with anxiety a witness to his eccentric movements. It is quite possible that I stopped him several times, but since he never opened himself to anyone I cannot know that for sure. He had an unusual gift for hiding the state of his soul and for giving one passion the appearance of another.

Finally he ended his life without anyone's being able to ex-plain the reason for it. His physician thought it was a partial derangement; the physician's opinion was very sensible. In one sense, his mind did not deteriorate until the last moment. You may not know that there exists a letter he wrote to his brother, the councilor, in which he informed him of his intention. I enclose a copy of it. It has a shocking veracity and is a very objective expression of the final agony of complete isolation.*

Poor Ludvig certainly was not religiously motivated, but nevertheless he was mystically motivated, because the distinctiveness of the mystical is not the religious but the isolation in which the individual, without regard for any relation to the given actuality, wants to place himself in immediate rapport with the eternal. The reason one promptly and specifically thinks of something religious as soon as the word "mysticism" is mentioned is that the religious has a tendency to isolate the individual, something of which the simplest observation can convince you. You perhaps go to church very seldom but undoubtedly are all the more observant. Have you not noticed that even though in a certain sense one receives the impression of a congregation, yet the individual feels isolated;

---

* Most Honorable Mr. Councilor:

    I am writing to you because in one way you are the one closest to me; in another way you are no closer than other people. When you receive these lines, I am no more. If anyone should ask you the reason, you may say that once upon a time there was a princess whose name was Morning Glory or something like that, for this is the way I myself would answer if I could have had the joy of surviving myself. If anyone should ask you the occasion, you may say that it was on the occasion of the great fire. If anyone asks you the time, you may say that it was the month of July, so very special to me. Should no one ask you any of these questions, you are to answer nothing.

    I do not regard a suicide as something commendable. It is not out of vanity that I decided on it. On the contrary, I believe in the correctness of the thesis that no human being can endure seeing the infinite. It once appeared to me in the intellectual sense, and the expression for this is ignorance. Ignorance is precisely the negative expression for infinite knowledge. A suicide is the negative expression for infinite freedom. It is a form of infinite freedom, but the negative form. Fortunate is the one who finds the positive.

                                          With deepest respect,
                                          Yours faithfully

people become strangers to one another, and they are united again only by way of a long detour, as it were. And what is the reason for this except that the individual feels his God-relationship so powerfully in all its inwardness that beside it his earthly relationships lose their significance? For a sound person this moment does not last long and a momentary distancing like this is so far from being a deception that instead it augments the inwardness of the earthly relationships. But that which as an element can be sound and healthy becomes a very grave sickness if it is developed one-sidedly.

II
222

Since I do not have a theological education, I do not regard myself as competent to deal with religious mysticism in greater detail. I have considered it only from my ethical point of view, and therefore, legitimately I believe, have given the word "mysticism" a much greater range than it usually has. I do not doubt that there is very much that is beautiful in religious mysticism, that the many profound and earnest natures who have devoted themselves to it have experienced much in their lives and thus have become qualified to serve with advice, guidance, and clues others who want to venture out on this dangerous road; but nevertheless this road is not only a dangerous road but a wrong road. There is always an inconsistency in this. If on the whole the mystic does not esteem actuality, it is not clear why he does not regard with the same mistrust that moment in actuality when he was stirred by something higher.

The mystic's error, then, is not that he chooses himself, for in so doing he does well, in my opinion, but his error is that he does not choose himself properly; he chooses according to his freedom, and yet he does not choose ethically. But a person can choose himself according to his freedom only when he chooses himself ethically, but he can choose himself ethically only by repenting himself, and only by repenting himself does he become concrete, and only as a concrete individual is he a free individual. Therefore, the mystic's error does not lie in something that comes later; it lies in the very first movement. If that is deemed to be right, then every distancing from life, every ascetic self-torture, is only a further and proper consequence. The mystic's error is that in the choice he does not become concrete either to himself or to God; he chooses himself abstractly and therefore lacks transparency. In other words, a person makes a mistake if he believes that abstractions are transparent; the abstract is the dim, the misty. Therefore, his love for God has its highest expression in a feeling, a mood; at twilight, in the time of mist, he blends with his God in indeterminate movements. But to choose oneself abstractly is not to choose oneself ethically. Not until a person in his choice has taken himself upon himself, has put on himself, has totally interpenetrated himself so that every movement he makes is accompanied by a consciousness of responsibility for himself— not until then has a person chosen himself ethically, not until then has he repented himself, not until then is he concrete, not until then is he in his total isolation in absolute continuity with the actuality to which he belongs.

II
223

To this stipulation that to choose oneself is to repent oneself, however simple it is in and by itself, I cannot return frequently enough. In other words, everything revolves around this. The mystic also repents, but he repents himself out of himself, not into himself; he repents metaphysically, not ethically. To repent esthetically is loathsome, because it is flabbiness; to repent metaphysically is an unseasonable superfluity, for the individual certainly did not create the world and does not need to become so upset if the world should actually prove to be vanity. The mystic chooses himself abstractly, and therefore he has to repent himself abstractly. This can best be seen in the verdict the mystic pronounces on existence, the finite actuality in which he nevertheless is living. The mystic expressly teaches that it is vanity, illusion, sin, but every such judgment is a metaphysical judgment and does not ethically determine my relation to it. Even when he declares that finiteness is sin, he is saying just about the same thing he says when he calls it vanity. On the other hand, if he wants to claim the word "sin" ethically, he does not determine his relation to it ethically but metaphysically, because the ethical expression would not be to flee from it but to enter into it, to annul it or to bear it. Ethical repentance has only two movements—it either annuls its object or bears it. These two movements also imply a concrete relation between the repenting individual and the object of his repentance, whereas fleeing from it expresses an abstract relationship.

The mystic chooses himself abstractly; one can therefore say that he is continually choosing himself out of the world, but as a result he cannot choose himself back into the world again. The true concrete choice is the one by which I choose myself back into the world the very same moment I choose myself out of the world. That is, when repenting I choose myself, I collect myself in all my finite concretion, and when I have thus chosen myself out of the finite in this way, I am in the most absolute continuity with it.

Since the mystic chooses himself abstractly, his trouble is that he finds it very difficult to begin to move or, to put it more correctly, that it is an impossibility for him. The same thing happens to the mystic in his religious first love as happens to you in your earthly first love. He has tasted it in all its blessedness and now has nothing to do except to wait for it to come again in just as much glory as before, and about that he can easily be tempted to harbor a doubt, which is the point I have frequently made, that development is retrogression, a falling off. For a mystic, actuality is a delay, yes, of such precarious nature that he almost runs the risk that life will rob him of what he once possessed. Therefore, if a mystic were asked what the meaning of life is, he perhaps would answer: The meaning of life is to learn to know God and to fall in love with him. But this is not an answer to the question, for here the meaning of life is understood as an instant, not as succession.

If I were to ask him what meaning it has for life that life has had this meaning or, in other words, what is the meaning of temporality, he would not have much to say, in any case not much that is joyful. If he says that temporality is an enemy that has to be vanquished, one might ask him more specifically whether the vanquishing of this enemy would have no meaning. The mystic does not really think so, and yet he would rather be all through with temporality. Therefore, just as he failed to appreciate actuality and metaphysically viewed it as

II
224

vanity, so he now fails to appreciate the historical and meta-physically views it as futile toil. The highest meaning he can ascribe to temporality is that it is a period of testing in which one undergoes the test again and again, yet without really having any results or going any further than one was in the beginning. This, however, is a failure to appreciate temporality, for it is true that it always retains in itself an element of an *ecclesia pressa* [oppressed church], but it is also the possibility of the glorification of the finite spirit. The particular beauty of temporality is that the infinite spirit and the finite spirit in it are separated, and it is the particular greatness of the finite spirit that temporality is assigned to it. Therefore, temporality does not exist, if I dare speak this way, for the sake of God, in order that he, to put it in mystical terms, can test and try the one who loves, but it exists for the sake of humankind and is the greatest of all the gifts of grace.

A human being's eternal dignity lies precisely in this, that he can gain a history. The divine in him lies in this, that he himself, if he so chooses, can give this history continuity, because it gains that, not when it is a summary of what has taken place or has happened to me, but only when it is my personal deed in such a way that even that which has happened to me is transformed and transferred from necessity to freedom. What is enviable about human life is that one can assist God, can understand him, and in turn the only worthy way for a human being to understand God is to appropriate in freedom everything that comes to him, both the happy and the sad. Or do you not think so? This is the way it appears to me—indeed, I think that to say this aloud to a person is all one needs to do to make him envy himself.

The two positions touched on here could be regarded as attempts to actualize an ethical life-view. The reason that they do not succeed is that the individual has chosen himself in his isolation or has chosen himself abstractly. To say it in other words, the individual has not chosen himself ethically. He therefore has no connection with actuality, and when that is the case no ethical view of life can be put into practice. But the person who chooses himself ethically chooses himself con-

cretely as this specific individual, and he achieves this concretion because this choice is identical with the repentance, which
ratifies the choice. The individual, then, becomes conscious as
this specific individual with these capacities, these inclinations,
these drives, these passions, influenced by this specific social
milieu, as this specific product of a specific environment. But
as he becomes aware of all this, he takes upon himself responsibility for it all. He does not hesitate over whether he will take
this particular thing or not, for he knows that if he does not do
it something much more important will be lost. In the moment of choice, he is in complete isolation, for he withdraws
from his social milieu, and yet at the same moment he is in absolute continuity, for he chooses himself as a product. And
this choice is freedom's choice in such a way that in choosing
himself as product he can just as well be said to produce himself. At the moment of choice, he is at the point of consummation, for his personality is consummating itself, and yet at
the same moment he is at the very beginning, because he is
choosing himself according to his freedom. As a product he is
squeezed into the forms of actuality; in the choice he makes
himself elastic, transforms everything exterior into interiority.
He has his place in the world; in freedom he himself chooses
his place—that is, he chooses this place. He is a specific individual; in the choice he makes himself into a specific individual: namely, into the same one, because he chooses himself.

An individual thus chooses himself as a complex specific
concretion and therefore chooses himself in his continuity.
This concretion is the individual's actuality, but since he
chooses it according to his freedom, it may also be said that it
is his possibility or, in order not to use such an esthetic expression, it is his task. In other words, the person who lives esthetically sees only possibilities everywhere; for him these
make up the content of future time, whereas the person who
lives ethically sees tasks everywhere. Then the individual sees
this, his actual concretion, as task, as goal, as objective. But in
seeing his possibility as his task, the individual expresses precisely his sovereignty over himself, something he never sur-
renders, even though on the other hand he does not relish the

very unconstrained sovereignty that a king without a country always has. This gives the ethical individual a security that the person who lives only esthetically lacks altogether. The person who lives esthetically expects everything from the outside. This accounts for the sickly anxiety with which many people speak of the dreadfulness of not having found their place in the world. Who will deny the joy in having made a good catch in this respect, but such an anxiety always indicates that the individual expects everything from the place, nothing from himself. The person who lives ethically will also be careful about choosing his place properly, but if he detects that he has made a mistake, or if obstacles are raised that are beyond his control, he does not lose heart, for he does not surrender sovereignty over himself. He promptly sees his task and therefore is in action without delay.

We frequently see men who fear that when they fall in love someday they will not find a girl who is precisely the ideal, who is just right for them. Who will deny the joy in finding a girl like that, but on the other hand it is indeed a superstition to think that something that lies outside a person is what can make him happy. The person who lives ethically also wishes to be happy in his choice, but if the choice proves to be not entirely according to his wish, he does not lose heart; he immediately sees his task and that the art is not to wish but to will.

Many who still have a conception of what human life is wish to be contemporary with great events, to be involved in meaningful life situations. Who will deny that such things have their validity, but on the other hand it is indeed a superstition to think that events and life situations as such make a person amount to something. The person who lives ethically knows that what counts is what one sees in each situation, and the energy with which he considers it, and that the one who thus disciplines himself in the most insignificant life situations can experience more than the one who has been a witness to— indeed, been a participant in—the most noteworthy events. He knows that there is a dancing place everywhere,[89] that even the lowliest of men has his, and that if he himself so wills his dancing can be just as beautiful, just as gracious, just as mimetic, just as dramatic as the dancing of those to whom a place has been assigned in history. This is the fencer's skill, this litheness that is really the immortal life in the ethical. The old saying "to be—or not to be"[90] holds for the person who lives esthetically, and the more esthetically he is allowed to live, the more conditions his life requires, and if only the least of them is not satisfied, he is dead. The person who lives ethically always has a way out when everything goes against him; when the darkness of the storm clouds so envelops him that his neighbor cannot see him, he still has not perished, there is always a point to which he holds fast, and that point is—himself.

There is only one thing I do not want to fail to stress, that as soon as the ethical person's gymnastics become an imaginary constructing he has ceased to live ethically. All such imaginary gymnastic constructing is equivalent to sophistry in the realm of knowledge.

Here I now want to call to mind the definition of the ethical I gave before—that it is that whereby a person becomes what he becomes. It does not want to make the individual into someone else but into the individual himself; it does not want to destroy the esthetic but to transfigure it. For a person to live ethically it is necessary that he become conscious of himself, so thoroughly that no accidental element escapes him. The ethical does not want to wipe out this concretion but sees in it its task, sees the material with which it is to build and that which it is to build. Ordinarily we view the ethical altogether abstractly and therefore have a secret horror of it. In that case the ethical is viewed as something alien to the personality, and we shrink from devoting ourselves to it, since we cannot be really sure what it will lead to in the course of time. In the same way, many people fear death, because they harbor obscure and confused notions that the soul in death has to cross over into another order of things where the established laws and conventions are completely different from the ones they have learned to know in this world. The reason for such a fear of death is the individual's aversion to becoming transparent to himself, for if he is willing to do this, he readily perceives the unreasonableness of this fear. So it is with the ethical also; if a person fears transparency, he always avoids the ethical, because the ethical really does not want anything else.

In contrast to an esthetic life-view, which wants to enjoy life, we often hear about another life-view that places the meaning of life in living for the performance of one's duties. This is supposed to signify an ethical view of life. But the formulation falls far short, and one could almost believe that it was devised to discredit the ethical. One thing is sure, that in our day we often see it used in such a way that it almost makes us smile, for example, when Scribe has this thesis recited with a certain farcical solemnity that makes a very disparaging contrast to the joy and mirth of enjoyment.[91] The mistake is that the individual is placed in an external relation to duty. The ethical is defined as duty, and duty in turn as a multiplicity of particular rules, but the individual and duty stand outside each other. Of course, a life of duty such as that is very unlovely and boring, and if the ethical did not have a much deeper connection with the personality it would always be very difficult to champion it against the esthetic. That there are many people who do not advance beyond this, I shall not deny, but that is not owing to duty but to the people themselves.

It is curious that the word "duty" can prompt one to think of an external relation, since the very derivation of the word[92] suggests an internal one; for that which is incumbent upon [*paaligge*] me, not as this individual with accidental characteristics but in accordance with my true being, certainly has the most intimate relation with myself. That is, duty is not something laid upon [*Paalæg*] but something that lies upon [*paaligge*]. When duty is regarded in this way, it is a sign that the individual is oriented within himself. Then duty will not split up for him into a multiplicity of particular stipulations, for this always indicates that he has only an external relation to duty. He has put on duty; for him it is the expression of his innermost being. When he is thus oriented within himself, he has immersed himself in the ethical, and he will not run himself ragged performing his duties. Therefore, the truly ethical person has an inner serenity and sense of security, for he does not have duty outside himself but within himself. The more deeply a man has structured his life ethically, the less he will feel compelled to talk about duty every moment, to worry every moment whether he is performing it, every moment to seek the advice of others about what his duty is. When the ethical is viewed properly, it makes the individual infinitely secure within himself; when it is viewed improperly, it makes the individual utterly insecure, and I cannot imagine an unhappier or more tormented life than when a person has his duty outside himself and yet continually wants to carry it out.

If the ethical is regarded as outside the personality and in an external relation to it, then one has given up everything, then one has despaired. The esthetic as such is despair; the ethical is the abstract and as such is without the means for accomplishing the least thing. That is why it is both comic and tragic to see at times people with a kind of honest zeal working their fingers to the bone in order to carry out the ethical, which like a shadow continually evades them as soon as they try to grasp it.

The ethical is the universal and thus the abstract. That is why in its perfect abstraction the ethical is always interdictory. Thus the ethical takes the form of law. As soon as the ethical is prescriptive, it already has something of the esthetic. The Jews were the people of the law. Therefore they understood most of the commandments in the Mosaic law splendidly, but the commandment they did not seem to have understood was the commandment to which Christianity attached itself most of all: You shall love God with all your heart. This commandment is neither negative nor abstract; it is highly positive and highly concrete. When the ethical becomes more concrete, it crosses over into the category of morals. But in this respect the reality of it lies in the reality of a national individuality, and here the ethical has already assimilated an esthetic element.

But the ethical is still abstract and cannot be fully actualized because it lies outside the individual. Not until the individual himself is the universal, not until then can the ethical be actualized. This is the secret that lies in the conscience; this is the secret the individual life has with itself—that simultaneously it is an individual life and also the universal, if as such not immediately, then nevertheless according to its possibility. The person who views life ethically sees the universal, and the person who lives ethically expresses the universal in his life. He makes himself the universal human being, not by taking off [*afføre*] his concretion, for then he becomes a complete nonentity, but by putting it on [*iføre*] and interpenetrating it with the universal. The universal human being is not a phantom, but every human being is the universal human being—that is, every human being is shown the way by which he becomes the universal human being. The person who lives esthetically is an accidental human being; he believes he is the perfect human being by being the one and only human being. The person who lives ethically works toward becoming the universal human being. When, for example, a person is esthetically in love, the accidental aspects play an enormous role, and it is important to him that no one has loved this way, with the nuances that are his; when the person who lives ethically marries, he actualizes the universal. That is why he is no hater of the concrete, but he has one expression in addition, deeper than every esthetic expression, inasmuch as he sees in love a revelation of the universally human. Thus he who lives ethically has himself as his task. His self in its immediacy is defined by accidental characteristics; the task is to work the accidental and the universal together into a whole.

II
230

The ethical individual, then, does not have duty outside himself but within himself. This comes to light at the moment of despair and now works itself forward through the esthetic in and with this. Of the ethical individual it may be said that he is like the still waters that have a deep source, whereas the one who lives esthetically is only superficially moved. Therefore, when the ethical individual has completed his task, has fought the good fight,[93] he has come to the point where he has become the unique human being—that is, there is no other human being like him—and he has also become the universal human being. To be the unique human being is not so great in and by itself, for every human being shares this with every product of nature, but to be that in such a way that he is thereby also the universal—that is the true art of living.

So the personality does not have the ethical outside itself but within itself and it bursts forth from this depth. It is not, as said before, a matter of exterminating the concrete in an abstract and contentless assault but of assimilating it. Since the ethical lies so deep in the soul, it is not always visible, and the person who lives ethically may do exactly the same as one who lives esthetically, and thus it may deceive for a long time, but eventually there comes a moment when it becomes manifest that the person who lives ethically has a boundary that the other does not know. The individual rests with confident security in the assurance that his life is ethically structured, and therefore he does not torment himself and others with quibbling anxiety about this or that.

I find it quite in order that the person who lives ethically has a whole territory for inconsequentials, and being unwilling to force it into every triviality is precisely a veneration for the ethical. Any effort to do so, which always fails, is made only by those who do not have the courage to believe in the ethical and who in a deeper sense lack inner security. There are people whose pusillanimity is known simply by their never being able to finish with the totality because for them this is a multiplicity. But these people lie outside the ethical, for no other reason, of course, than weakness of will, which like any other psychical weakness can be regarded as a kind of madness. The lives of such people are given to straining at gnats.[94] They have no notion either of the beautiful and pure earnestness of the ethical or of the carefree joy of the inconsequential. But, of course, for the ethical individual the inconsequential is dethroned, and he can set the limit at any moment. Thus one also believes that there is a providence, and the soul rests confidently in this conviction, and yet one would never think of venturing to interpenetrate every contingency with this thought or to be conscious of this faith every minute. To will the ethical without being disturbed by inconsequentials, to believe in a providence without being disturbed by contingency, is a healthiness that can be acquired and preserved if a person himself wills it. Here, too, it is a matter of seeing the task, that this, insofar as one has an inclination to be diverted this way, is to offer resistance, to hold fast to the infinite, and not run off on a wild goose chase.

The person who chooses himself ethically has himself as his task, not as a possibility, not as a plaything for the play of his arbitrariness. Ethically he can choose himself only if he chooses himself in continuity, and then he has himself as a multiply defined task. He does not try to blot out or evaporate this multiplicity; on the contrary, he repents himself firmly in it, because this multiplicity is himself, and only by penitently immersing himself in it can he come to himself, since he does not assume that the world begins with him or that he creates [*skabe*] himself. The latter has been branded with contempt by language itself, for we always speak contemptuously of a man when we say: He is putting on airs [*skabe sig*]. But in choosing himself penitently he is acting—not in the direction of isolation but in the direction of continuity.

Let us now compare an ethical and an esthetic individual. The primary difference, the crux of the matter, is that the ethical individual is transparent to himself and does not live *ins Blaue hinein* [in the wild blue yonder], as does the esthetic individual. This difference encompasses everything. The person who lives ethically has seen himself, knows himself, penetrates his whole concretion with his consciousness, does not allow vague thoughts to rustle around inside him or let tempting possibilities distract him with their juggling; he is not like a "magic" picture[95] that shifts from one thing to another, all depending on how one shifts and turns it. He knows himself. The phrase γνῶθι σεαυτόν [know yourself][96] is a stock phrase, and in it has been perceived the goal of all a person's striving. And this is entirely proper, but yet it is just as certain that it cannot be the goal if it is not also the beginning. The ethical individual knows himself, but this knowing is not simply contemplation, for then the individual comes to be defined according to his necessity. It is a collecting of oneself, which itself is an action, and this is why I have with aforethought used the expression "to choose oneself" instead of "to know oneself."

When the individual knows himself, he is not finished; but

this knowing is very productive, and from this knowing emerges the authentic individual. If I wanted to be clever, I could say here that the individual knows himself in a way similar to the way Adam knew Eve, as it says in the Old Testament.[97] Through the individual's intercourse with himself the individual is made pregnant by himself and gives birth to himself. The self the individual knows is simultaneously the actual self and the ideal self, which the individual has outside himself as the image in whose likeness he is to form himself, and which on the other hand he has within himself, since it is he himself. Only within himself does the individual have the objective toward which he is to strive, and yet he has this objective outside himself as he strives toward it. That is, if the individual believes that the universal human being lies outside him, so that it will come to him from the outside, then he is disoriented, then he has an abstract conception, and his method will always be an abstract annihilating of the original self. Only within himself can the individual become enlightened about himself. That is why the ethical life has this duplexity, in which the individual has himself outside himself within himself. Meanwhile the exemplary self is an imperfect self, for it is only a prophecy and thus is not the actual self. But it escorts him at all times; yet the more he actualizes it, the more it vanishes within him, until at last, instead of appearing before him, it is behind him as a faded possibility. This image is like a person's shadow. In the forenoon he casts his shadow before him; at noon it walks almost unnoticed beside him; in the afternoon it falls behind him. When the individual has known himself and has chosen himself, he is in the process of actualizing himself, but since he is supposed to do that freely, he must know what it is he wants to actualize. What he wants to actualize is certainly himself, but it is his ideal self, which he cannot acquire anywhere but within himself. If he does not hold firmly to the truth that the individual has the ideal self within himself, all of his aspiring and striving becomes abstract. Both the one who wants to copy another person and the one who wants to copy the normative person become equally affected, although in different ways.

The esthetic individual considers himself in his concretion and makes distinctions *inter et inter* [between the one and the other].[98] He sees something as belonging to him in an accidental way, something else as belonging essentially. Yet this distinction is very relative, for as long as a person lives only esthetically, everything really belongs to him equally accidentally, and when an esthetic individual maintains this distinction, it merely shows a lack of energy.

The ethical individual has learned this in despair and thus has another distinction, for he also makes a distinction between the essential and the accidental. Everything that is posited in his freedom belongs to him essentially, however accidental it may seem to be; everything that is not posited in his freedom is accidental, however essential it may seem to be. But for the ethical individual this distinction is not a product of his arbitrariness so that he might seem to have absolute power to make himself into what it pleased him to be. To be sure, the ethical individual dares to employ the expression that he is his own editor, but he is also fully aware that he is responsible, responsible for himself personally, inasmuch as what he chooses will have a decisive influence on himself, responsible to the order of things in which he lives, responsible to God. Regarded in this way, the distinction is correct, I believe, for essentially only that belongs to me which I ethically take on as a task. If I refuse to take it on, then my having refused it essentially belongs to me.

When a person considers himself esthetically, he may make distinctions as follows. He says: I have a talent for painting— this I regard as an accidental trait; but I have a keen wit and a keen mind—this I regard as the essential that cannot be taken away from me without my becoming somebody else. To that I would answer: This whole distinction is an illusion, for if you do not take on this keen wit and keen mind ethically, as a task, as something for which you are responsible, then it does not belong to you essentially, and primarily because as long as you live merely esthetically your life is totally inessential. To a certain degree, the person who lives ethically cancels the distinction between the accidental and the essential, for he takes responsibility for all of himself as equally essential; but it comes back again, for after he has done that, he makes a distinction, but in such a manner that he takes an essential responsibility for excluding what he excludes as accidental.

Insofar as the esthetic individual, with "esthetic earnestness," sets a task for his life, it is really the task of becoming absorbed in his own accidental traits, of becoming an individual whose equal in paradoxicality and irregularity has never been seen, of becoming a caricature of a human being. The reason we rarely meet such characters in life is that we rarely meet people who have a notion of what it is to live. But since many people have a decided penchant for chattering, we encounter on the street, at parties, and in books a great amount of chatter that has the unmistakable stamp of the *Originalitets-Wuth* [mania for originality] that, carried over into life, would enrich the world with a host of artificial products, one more ridiculous than the other.

The task the ethical individual sets for himself is to transform himself into the universal individual. Only the ethical individual gives himself an account of himself in earnest and is therefore honest with himself; only he has the paradigmatic decorum and propriety that are more beautiful than anything else. But to transform himself into the universal human being is possible only if I already have it within myself κατα δύναμιν [potentially]. In other words, the universal can very well continue in and with the specific without consuming it; it is like that fire that burned without consuming the bush.[99] If the universal human being is outside me, there is only one possible method, and that is to take off my entire concretion. This striving out in the unconstraint of abstraction is frequently seen. There was a sect of Hussites who thought that in order to become a normal human being one had to go around naked like Adam and Eve in Paradise.[100] In our day we not infrequently encounter people who in the spiritual sense teach the same thing—that one becomes a normal human being by going stark naked, which can be done by taking off one's entire concretion. But that is not the way it is. In the act of despair, the universal human being came forth and now is behind the concretion and emerges through it. There are many more paradigmatic verbs in a language than the one presented as the paradigm in the grammar book. It is accidental that this one is presented; all the other regular verbs could serve just as well— so also with human beings. Every person, if he so wills, can become a paradigmatic human being, not by brushing off his accidental qualities, but by remaining in them and ennobling them. But he ennobles them by choosing them.

By now you have easily seen that in his life the ethical individual goes through the stages we previously set forth as separate stages. He is going to develop in his life the personal, the civic, the religious virtues, and his life advances through his continually translating himself from one stage to another. As soon as a person thinks that one of these stages is adequate and that he dares to concentrate on it one-sidedly, he has not chosen himself ethically but has failed to see the significance of either isolation or continuity and above all has not grasped that the truth lies in the identity of these two.

The person who has ethically chosen and found himself possesses himself defined in his entire concretion. He then possesses himself as an individual who has these capacities, these passions, these inclinations, these habits, who is subject to these external influences, who is influenced in one direction thus and in another thus. Here he then possesses himself as a task in such a way that it is chiefly to order, shape, temper, inflame, control—in short, to produce an evenness in the soul, a harmony, which is the fruit of the personal virtues. Here the objective for his activity is himself, but nevertheless not arbitrarily determined, for he possesses himself as a task that has been assigned him, even though it became his by his own choosing. But although he himself is his objective, this objective is nevertheless something else also, for the self that is the objective is not an abstract self that fits everywhere and therefore nowhere but is a concrete self in living interaction with these specific surroundings, these life conditions, this order of things.

The self that is the objective is not only a personal self but a social, a civic self. He then possesses himself as a task in an activity whereby he engages in the affairs of life as this specific personality. Here his task is not to form himself but to act, and yet he forms himself at the same time, because, as I noted above, the ethical individual lives in such a way that he is continually transferring himself from one stage to another. If the individual has not originally conceived of himself as a concrete personality in continuity, he will not gain this next continuity either. If he thinks that the art is to begin like a Robinson Crusoe, he remains an adventurer all his life. If, however, he realizes that if he does not begin concretely he will never make a beginning, and that if he never makes a beginning he will never finish, he will then be simultaneously in continuity with the past and the future. He transfers himself from personal life to civic life, from this to personal life. Personal life as such was an isolation and therefore imperfect, but when he turns back into his personality through the civic life, the personal life appears in a higher form. The personality appears as the absolute that has its teleology in itself. When living for the fulfillment of duty is made a person's task in life, what is often pointed out is the skepticism that duty itself is unstable, that laws can be changed. You easily see that this last remark concerns the fluctuations to which civic virtues are always exposed.

This skepticism, however, does not apply to the negative aspect of morality, for that continues unchanged. But there is another skepticism that applies to every duty; it is the skepticism that I cannot discharge the duty at all. The duty is the universal. What is required of me is the universal; what I am able to do is the particular. Yet this skepticism has great significance, inasmuch as it shows that the personality itself is the absolute. But this must be defined more closely. Curiously enough, language itself points up this skepticism. I never say of a man: He is doing duty or duties; but I say: He is doing *his* duty; I say: I am doing *my* duty, do *your* duty. This shows that the individual is simultaneously the universal and the particular. Duty is the universal; it is required of me. Consequently, if I am not the universal, I cannot discharge the duty either. On the other hand, my duty is the particular, something for me alone, and yet it is duty and consequently the universal. Here

II
236

personality appears in its highest validity. It is not lawless; neither does it itself establish its law, for the category of duty continues, but the personality takes the form of the unity of the
universal and the particular. That this is so is clear; it can be
made understandable to a child—for I can discharge the duty
and yet not do *my* duty, and I can do *my* duty and yet not discharge the duty.

   I am by no means of the opinion that the world would therefore sink into skepticism, because the difference between good
and evil always remains, responsibility and duty likewise,
even if it becomes impossible for someone else to say what *my*
duty is, whereas it will always be possible for him to say what
his duty is, which would not be the case if the unity of the universal and the particular were not posited. All skepticism may
seem to be removed if duty is made into something external,
fixed and specific, something of which it can be said: This is
duty. This, however, is a misunderstanding, for the doubt
does not reside in the external but in the internal, in my relation to the universal. As a particular individual, I am not the
universal, and to require it of me is unreasonable; consequently, if I am to be capable of performing the universal, I
must be the universal at the same time as I am the particular,
but then the dialectic of duty resides within me. As already
stated, this position does not pose any threat to the ethical; on
the contrary, it vindicates it. If this is not assumed, the personality becomes abstract, its relation to duty abstract, its immortality abstract. The difference between good and evil is not
canceled either, for I doubt that there has ever been anyone
who has claimed that it is a duty to do evil. That he did evil is
something else, but he also tried to delude himself and others
into thinking that it was good. That he would be able to persist
in this delusion is unthinkable, since he himself is the universal; thus his enemy is not something external but within himself. If, however, I assume that duty is something external,
then the difference between good and evil is canceled, for if I
myself am not the universal, I can form only an abstract relation to it; but the difference between good and evil is incom-
patible with an abstract relation.

The very moment it is perceived that the personality is the absolute, is its own objective, is the unity of the universal and the particular, that very moment every skepticism that makes the historical its point of departure will be vanquished. Too often freethinkers have tried to confuse the concepts by pointing out how at times a people has pronounced something to be sacred and lawful that in the eyes of another people was abominable and evil. [101]Here they have let themselves be blinded by the external, but with the ethical there is never a question of the external but of the internal. But however much the external is changed, the moral value of the action remains the same. Thus there has never been a nation that believed that children should hate their parents. In order to add fuel to doubt, however, it has been pointed out that whereas all civilized nations made it the children's duty to care for their parents, savages practiced the custom of putting their aged parents to death. This may very well be so, but still no headway is made thereby, because the question remains whether the savages intend to do something evil by this. The ethical always resides in this consciousness, whereas it is another question whether or not insufficient comprehension is responsible.

The atheist perceives very well that the way by which the ethical is most easily evaporated is to open the door to the historical infinity. And yet there is something legitimate in his behavior, for if, when all is said and done, the individual is not the absolute, then the empirical is the only road allotted to him, and the end of this road is just like the source of the Niger River—no one knows where it is. [102] If I am assigned to the finite, it is arbitrary to remain standing at any particular point. Therefore, along this road one never makes a beginning, for in order to start one must have come to the end, but this is an impossibility. When the personality is the absolute, then it is itself the Archimedean point from which one can lift the world. [103] It is easy to see that this consciousness cannot inveigle the individual to discard his actuality, for if he wants to be the absolute in that way, he is a nonentity, an abstraction. Only as the single individual is he the absolute, and this consciousness will save him from all revolutionary radicalism.

Here I shall cease my theorizing; I am well aware that I am not cut out for it, nor is that my ambition, but I shall be perfectly contented if I might be assumed to be a passable practitioner. Then, too, theorizing takes so much time; any act I can do in a moment or embark upon promptly involves a great deal of trouble and difficulty before it can be put into words or into writing. Now, it is not my intention to give you a lecture on a doctrine of duty or to speak according to custom about duties to God, oneself, and one's neighbor. Not that I would spurn this grouping or that what I would have to teach would be too profound to be joined to Balle's catechism[104] or would presuppose much more previous knowledge than this catechism presupposes—not at all for those reasons, but because I believe that with the ethical it is not a matter of the multiplicity of duty but of its intensity.

II
239
When a person has felt the intensity of duty with all his energy, then he is ethically matured, and then duty will break forth within him. The fundamental point, therefore, is not whether a person can count on his fingers how many duties he has, but that he has once and for all felt the intensity of duty in such a way that the consciousness of it is for him the assurance of the eternal validity of his being. That is why I by no means praise being a man of duty, no more than I recommend being a bookworm, and yet I am sure that the person for whom the meaning of duty has never become manifest in all its infinitude is just as second-rate a human being as someone is a scholar who *ad modum* [in the fashion of] "the Grenaa-men"[105] thinks he will find wisdom *mir nichts und dir nichts* [without further ado]. Let the casuist immerse himself in finding out the complexity of duty; the primary question, the only salutary thing, is always that a person with respect to his own life is not his uncle but his father.[106]

Let me illustrate what I mean by an example. To that end I select an impression I have preserved from my earliest childhood. When I was five years old, I was sent to school. That such an event always makes an impression on a child is natural, but the question is—what impression? Childish inquisitiveness is fascinated by all the bewildering ideas about what it may really mean. That this was also the case with me was to be expected; however, the main impression I received was entirely different. I arrived at school; I was presented to the teacher and was given my assignment for the next day—the first ten lines in Balle's catechism, which I was to learn by heart. Every other impression was now erased from my soul; only my task stood vividly before it. As a child I had a very good memory. Very soon I had done my homework. My sister had heard me several times and testified that I knew it. I went to bed, and before I fell asleep I recited it again to myself. I fell asleep with the firm intention of reading it over again the next morning. I awoke at five o'clock in the morning, dressed myself, took my catechism, and read it again. It is all as vivid to me this moment as if it happened yesterday. It seemed to me that heaven and earth would tumble down if I did not do my homework, and on the other hand it seemed to me that if heaven and earth did tumble down this upheaval would in no way excuse me from doing what had once been set before me—doing my homework. At that age I knew very little about my duties; I had not yet become acquainted with them in Balle's catechism. I had but one duty, to do my homework, and yet I can derive my whole ethical view of life from this impression.

II
240

I can smile at such a little fellow of five years who approaches a matter that passionately, and yet I assure you that I have no higher wish than that at any period of my life I may approach my work with the energy, with the ethical earnestness, I did then. It is true that later on in life one gets a better idea of what one's work is, but the energy is still the main thing. That this event made such an impression on me, I owe to my father's earnestness, and even if I owed him nothing else, this would be sufficient to place me in an eternal debt to him. What matters in upbringing is not that the child learns this or that but that the mind is matured, that energy is evoked. You speak often enough about the glory of being clever. Who will deny that it has importance? And yet I tend to believe that a person can make himself that if he so wills. Give a person energy, passion, and he is everything. Take a young girl; let her be silly, giddy, a really frivolous lass. Then imagine her deeply and fervently in love, and you will see that cleverness comes by itself; you will see how clever and cunning she becomes at ferreting out whether she is loved in return. Let her become happy, and you will see infatuation blossom on her lips; let her become unhappy, and you will hear the cold reflections of wittiness and common sense.

In that respect, I can say that my childhood was happy, because it enriched me with ethical impressions. Permit me to dwell on this for a moment. It reminds me of my father, and this is the fondest recollection I have and is by no means a meager and barren reminiscence. It can once again afford me an occasion to illustrate what I say—that the main thing is the total impression of duty, and not at all the multiplicity of duty. If the multiplicity is advanced, then the individual is diminished and destroyed. In that respect I was happy as a child, for I did not have many duties, ordinarily only one, but this was also of benefit. When I was two years older, I was sent to grammar school. Here a new life began, but again the main impression was the ethical, even though I enjoyed the greatest freedom. I mingled with other pupils, was surprised to hear them criticize their teachers, saw with amazement that a pupil was taken out of school because he could not get along with the teacher. If I had not been so deeply influenced earlier, such an event might have been harmful to me. Now this was not the case. I knew it was my task to go to school, to the school to which I had been sent; even if everything else had changed, this could not be changed. It was not only fear of my father's earnestness that gave me this idea, but it was the lofty impression of what constituted one's duty. Even if my father had died, even if I had been put in charge of someone else whom I could have prevailed upon to take me out of school, I would never have dared to do it or have really wanted it. It would have seemed to me as if my father's ghost would appear and follow me about in school, for here again I would have had an infinite impression of what constituted my duty, so that no amount of time would ever erase the recollection that I had offended against his will. Otherwise I enjoyed my freedom. I knew but one duty—to attend to my school, and in this respect I myself was entirely responsible.

When I was enrolled in the school and the required textbooks had been purchased, my father handed them to me and said: William, by the end of the month you are to be third in your class. I was spared all paternal prating. He never asked me about my homework, never heard me recite my lesson, never looked at my compositions, never reminded me that it was time to start studying or time to stop, never assisted the pupil's conscience as one often sees magnanimous fathers do when they pat their children on their cheeks and say: You know your lessons, I'm sure. If I wanted to go out, he first asked if I had time; I myself decided that, not he, and his question never entered into details. I am very sure, however, that he was very concerned about what I was doing, but in order that my soul could be matured by responsibility, he never allowed me to notice it. Here again it was the same—I did not have many duties, and how many children are warped by being overwhelmed by a whole ritual of duties. Thus I received a very profound impression that there was something called duty and that this had eternal validity.

In my day, we studied Latin grammar with a rigor that is unknown today. From this instruction I received an impression that in a different way affected my soul similarly. Insofar as I dare attribute to myself any capacity for taking a philosophic view of things, I owe it to this impression from childhood. The unconditioned respect with which I regarded the rule, the veneration I felt for it, the contempt with which I looked down on the miserable life the exception endured, the to my eyes righteous way in which it was pursued in my exercise book and always stigmatized—what else is this but the distinction that is the basis of all philosophic reflection? Under this influence, when I reflected on my father, he seemed to me to be the incarnation of the rule; what came from elsewhere was the exception insofar as it was not in harmony with his command. When I thought of that fellow pupil, I felt that he must be an exception who was not worth paying attention to, all the more so because all the fuss made over him adequately

II
242

showed that he was an exception. The childish rigorism with which I at that time distinguished between rule and exception, in life as well as in grammar, has certainly been mitigated, but I still have the distinction within me. I know how to call it up, especially when I see you and your kind, who seem to advance the doctrine that the exception is the more important—indeed, that the rule exists only so that the exception can show up to advantage.

The crux of the matter, then, is the energy by which I become ethically conscious, or, more correctly, I cannot become ethically conscious without energy. Therefore, I cannot become ethically conscious without becoming conscious of my eternal being. This is the true demonstration of the immortality of the soul. It is fully developed, of course, only when the task is congruent with the duty, but that to which I am duty-bound for an eternity is an eternal task. In a certain sense the circumstance of my being assigned ten lines in Balle's catechism as a task from which I could be ransomed by nothing in the world was the first demonstration given to me of the immortality of my soul. The deficiency was not in my energy but in the contingency of the task.

[107]It is not my intention to lead you into a consideration of the multiplicity of duty. If I wanted to express duty negatively, it would be easy to do; if I wanted to express it positively, it would be difficult and protracted—indeed, when I would come to a certain point, impossible. My intention, what I have tried to do to the best of my ability, was rather to throw some light on the absolute significance of duty, the eternal validity of duty-relationship for the personality. That is, as soon as the person in despair has found himself, has chosen himself absolutely, has repented of himself, he then has himself as his task under an eternal responsibility, and in this way duty is posited in its absoluteness. But since he has not created himself but has chosen himself, duty is the expression of his absolute dependence and his absolute freedom in their identity with each other.

He will teach himself the particular duty and will without avail seek enlightenment on it from anyone else, and yet here again he will be an autodidact just as he is a theodidact,[108] and vice versa. In no case does duty become abstract for him, partly because for him it is not something external, for in that case it is always abstract, partly because he himself is concrete, for when he chose himself ethically he chose himself in all his concretion and rejected the abstractness of arbitrariness.

What is left now is to show how life looks when it is regarded ethically. You and all the esthetes are very willing to make a division. You admit that the ethical has its significance; you say that it is respectable for a man to live for his duties, that it deserves every honor—indeed, you even drop a few equivocal comments about its being entirely appropriate that there are people who live for their duties, that it is good that the majority of people do it, and you sometimes meet persons with a strong sense of duty who are good-natured enough to find meaning in such talk, although, of course, like all skepticism, it is meaningless. But you yourselves do not wish to be involved with the ethical; to do so would take from life its significance and, above all, its beauty. The ethical is entirely different from the esthetic, and when it advances it completely annihilates the latter.

Now, if this were so, I still would have no doubt about what I would choose. In despair there is a moment when it seems to be so, and the person who has not felt this has experienced a fraudulent despair and has not chosen himself ethically. But it is not so, and that is why in the very next moment the despair proves to be not a break but a metamorphosis. Everything comes back again, but transfigured. Therefore, only when life is considered ethically does it take on beauty, truth, meaning, continuance; only when a person himself lives ethically does his life take on beauty, truth, meaning, security; only in the ethical life-view are autopathetic doubt and sympathetic doubt allayed. [109]In other words, autopathetic doubt and sympathetic doubt can be allayed only in one and the same thing, for essentially they are the same doubt. Autopathetic doubt is not a manifestation of egotism but a claim by the self-love that claims for its own self the same as it claims for everyone else's self. I think this is of great significance. Indeed, if an esthete were not an egotist, he would—presuming that every conceivable favor had fallen to his lot—have to despair over all his happiness, because he would have to say: What makes me happy is something that cannot be given in the same way to another person and that no one else can acquire. Indeed, he would have to be anxious lest someone ask him wherein he sought his happiness, for he had become happy so that all the others would feel that they could not become happy. If such a person had any sympathy, he would give himself no rest until he had found a higher point of departure for his life. When he had found it, he would not be afraid to talk about his happiness, because if he were to articulate it properly he would say something that absolutely reconciled him with every human being, with all humankind.

Let us pause, however, at the category the esthetic always claims for itself: beauty. Life loses its beauty, you say, as soon as the ethical is advanced. "Instead of the joy, happiness, carefreeness, and beauty that life has when we consider it esthetically, we have dutiful activity, praiseworthy effort, indefatigable and restless zeal." If you were here with me in person, I would ask you to give me a definition of beauty so that I could manage to make a beginning. Since that is not the case, I shall take the liberty of picking up the definition you usually give: The beautiful is that which has its teleology within itself. Using a young girl as an example, you say: She is beautiful, she is joyful, carefree, happy, a perfect harmony complete in herself, and it is a stupidity to ask why she exists, for she has her teleology within herself. I shall not badger you with the objection whether it really is to the young girl's advantage to have her teleology solely within herself in this way or whether you, if you were given a chance to present your opinion of the divineness of her existence, would not flatter yourself that she eventually would make the mistake of believing that she existed only to listen to your insinuations. You consider nature and find it just as beautiful and anathematize every finite view of it. Neither shall I vex you here with the comment about whether it does not belong essentially to nature to exist for something else. You consider the works of art and poetry and cry out with the poet: *Procul, O procul este profani* [Away, away, O unhallowed ones],[110] and by *profani* you understand those who want to debase poetry and art by giving them a teleology that is external to them.

As far as poetry and art are concerned, may I remind you of what I mentioned earlier, that they provide only an imperfect reconciliation with life, also that when you fix your eye upon poetry and art you are not looking at actuality, and that is what we really should be speaking about. So we come back to this again, and since you yourself presumably are aware that if you want to maintain the demands of art in all their stringency you probably will find very little beauty in life, you therefore give the beautiful another meaning. The beautiful you speak about is the individually beautiful. You regard each individual human being as a little element of the whole; you see him expressly in his distinctiveness and thus even the accidental, the insignificant, gains significance and life the stamp of beauty. Thus you view every individual human being as an element. But the beautiful was that which has its teleology within itself, but if a person is merely an element, then he does not have his teleology within himself but outside himself. Even if the whole is beautiful, the parts in themselves are not beautiful.

And now your own life. Does it have its teleology within itself? Whether a person is entitled to lead a merely spectating life, I shall not decide, but, *eh bien* [now then], let us suppose that the meaning of your life is that you exist in order to be a spectator observing others—then you would indeed have your teleology outside yourself. Only if every individual human being is an element and also the whole, only then do you consider him according to his beauty, but as soon as you consider him in this way, you consider him ethically. If you consider him ethically, you consider him according to his freedom. Let him have characteristics ever so distinctive; if these characteristics are a necessity, he is merely an element, and his life is not beautiful.

When you define the beautiful as that which has its teleology within itself and give as examples a girl, or nature, or a work of art, I can come to no other judgment than that all the talk

II
245

about all this having its teleology within itself is an illusion. If there is to be any question of teleology, there must be a movement, for as soon as I think of a goal, I think of a movement; even if I think of a person at his goal, I still am always thinking of a movement, since I am thinking that he arrived there by a movement. What you call beautiful obviously lacks movement, because the beauty in nature simply *is*, and if I behold a work of art and interpenetrate its thought with my own thought, it is really in me that movement takes place, not in the work of art. Thus you may well be correct in saying that the beautiful has its teleology within itself, but in the way you interpret and apply it, it still is really a negative expression that states that the beautiful does not have its teleology in something else. For this reason you will not be able to use an apparently synonymous expression, that the beautiful you speak of has an inner teleology or immanent teleology. As soon as you say that, you require movement, history, and you have thereby gone beyond the realms of nature and art and are in the realm of freedom, and thereby in the realm of ethics.

Now, when I say that the individual has his teleology within himself, this may not be misinterpreted to mean that the individual is central or that the individual in the abstract sense is supposed to be sufficient unto himself, because if it is taken abstractly I still have no movement. The individual has his teleology within himself, has inner teleology, is himself his teleology; his self is then the goal toward which he strives. But this self of his is not an abstraction but is absolutely concrete. In the movement toward himself, he cannot relate himself negatively to the world around him, for then his self is an abstraction and remains so. His self must open itself according to its total concretion, but part and parcel of this concretion are also the factors whose characteristic is to intervene actively in the world. In this way his movement becomes a movement from himself through the world to himself. Here is movement, and an actual movement, for this same movement is an act of freedom; but it is also an immanent teleology, and therefore only here can we speak of beauty. If this is the way things really are, then in a certain sense the individual comes to stand higher than every relationship, but from this it in no way follows that he is not in that relationship; nor does this mean that any despotism is implied here, since the same thing holds true for every individual. I am a married man, and you know that I have the most profound respect for this relationship, and I know that I humble myself in total love under it, but yet I know that in another sense I am higher than this relationship. But I also know that in entirely the same sense this is the case with my wife, and that is why I would not, as you know, love that young girl, because she would not have this point of view.

Therefore, it is not until I look at life ethically that I see it according to its beauty; not until I look at my own life ethically do I see it according to its beauty. If you say that this beauty is invisible, I shall reply: In one sense it is, in another, it is not; that is, it is visible in the footprints of the historical, visible in the sense in which one says: *Loquere, ut videam te* [Speak, in order that I may see you].[111] It is certainly true that I do not see the consummation but the struggle, but yet I also see the consummation at any moment I want to if I have the courage for it, and without courage I see nothing eternal at all, and consequently nothing beautiful either.

When I look at life ethically, I look at it according to its beauty. Life then becomes rich in beauty for me, not impoverished in beauty, as it actually is for you. I do not need to travel all over the country to find beauties or to rake about for them in the streets; I do not need to assess and sort out. Of course, I do not have as much time as you do either, for since I joyfully but also earnestly see my life in its beauty I always have plenty to do. If at times I have a free hour, I stand at my window and look at people, and I see each person according to his beauty. However insignificant he may be, however humble, I see him according to his beauty, for I see him as this individual human being who nevertheless is also the universal human being. I see him as one who has this concrete task for his life; even if he is the lowliest hired waiter, he does not exist for the sake of any other person. He has his teleology within himself, he actualizes this task, he is victorious—that I do see, for the courageous person does not see ghosts but sees conquering heroes

II
247

instead; the coward does not see heroes, but only ghosts. He is bound to be victorious, of that I am convinced; that is why his struggle is beautiful. Ordinarily I am very disinclined to struggle, at least with anyone other than myself; but you may be sure that for this faith in the victory of the beautiful I will struggle for dear life, and nothing in the world will wrench it from me. Even if somebody wanted to trick me out of this faith by entreaties, even if someone wanted to tear it from me by force, I will not let it be taken from me for anything in the world, and not for the whole world, because I would lose the whole world only when I lost this faith. With this faith, I see the beauty of life, and the beauty I see does not have the sadness and gloominess that are inseparable from the beauty of all nature and art, inseparable even from the eternal youth of the Greek gods. The beauty I see is joyous and triumphant and stronger than the whole world. And this beauty I see everywhere, also there where your eyes see nothing.

Just stand here at my window. A young girl is walking by; do you remember that we once met her on the street? She was not beautiful, you remarked, but when you had looked at her a bit more closely you recognized her and went on to say, "A few years ago she was exceedingly lovely and was very popular at parties; then she had a love affair, *et quidem* [that is], an unhappy one. The devil knows how she got into it, but she took the affair so to heart that her beauty faded with grief—in short, she was beautiful, now she is no longer beautiful, and that is the end of the story." You see, this is what could be called viewing life according to its beauty. In my eyes, however, she has lost nothing, and to me she seems more beautiful than ever. This is why to me your view of life's beauty seems very similar to the gaiety that prevailed in the age of the drinking songs, when men became jolly and elated by singing songs such as this:

II
248

> Were it not for the juice of the red, red grapes
> Who would here the longer tarry?
> For nothing the eye of wisdom escapes
> And all that it sees is misery.

Loud sounds the voice of the oppressed
The voice of the betrayed, from north to south.
Up brothers, let us drink instead
And forget this whole dismal earth.[112]

Let us now take up some life relationships in a little more detail, especially those where the esthetic and the ethical meet, in order to consider to what extent the ethical view deprives us of any beauty, or whether it does not rather give everything a higher beauty. I have in mind, then, a specific individual who in a certain sense is just like everyone else and in another sense is concrete in himself. Let us be utterly prosaic. This person must live, must clothe himself—in short, must be able to exist. Perhaps he turned to an esthete for advice on how he should order his life. He would not be short of information either. The esthete will perhaps say to him, "If one is single, one spends three thousand rix-dollars a year to live comfortably; if one has four thousand, one spends that too; if one wants to marry, then one needs at least six thousand. Money is and remains the *nervus rerum gerendarum* [moving force in accomplishing something], the true *conditio sine qua non* [necessary condition]. To be sure, it is beautiful to read about rustic contentment, about idyllic simplicity, and I like to read poetry of that sort; but one would soon become bored with that way of life, and the people who live that way do not enjoy that life half as much as the person who has money and then in all tranquillity and leisure reads the poets' songs. Money is and remains the absolute condition for living. As soon as a person has no money, he is and continues to be excluded from the class of patricians, he is and continues to be a plebian. Money is the condition, but this in no way means that everyone who has money knows how to use it. Those who know how to do this are in turn the true optimates[113] among the patricians."

But obviously this explanation would not help our hero; all the worldly wisdom of the other would leave him cold, and he must have felt just about as uncomfortable as a sparrow in a dance of cranes. If he said to the esthete, "That is all very fine, but I have neither three thousand nor six thousand a year. I have nothing at all either in capital or in interest; I own nothing at all, scarcely a hat," the esthete would shrug his shoulders and say, "Well, that's another matter; then there is nothing else to be done. Then you'll have to be satisfied with going to the workhouse." If the esthete is good-natured, he perhaps would motion to the poor wretch and say, "I don't want to bring you to despair before I have made a supreme effort; there are a couple of temporary expedients one ought not to leave unexplored before one says goodbye forever to joy and makes the pledge and puts on the straitjacket. Marry a rich girl, play the lottery, travel to the colonies, spend a few years scraping money together, insinuate yourself into the good graces of an old bachelor so that he will make you his heir. Just now our paths part; get some money, and you will always find in me a friend who can forget that there was a time when you did not have money."

But there is something terribly callous in such a view of life, to murder in cold blood all the joy in life for everyone who does not have money. This is indeed what the monied person does, for it is at least his view that without money there is no joy in life. If I were to lump you together with those esthetes, if I were to charge you with harboring or expressing such thoughts, I would be doing you a grave injustice. For one thing, your heart is too good to be the habitation of such disgusting meanness; for another, your soul is too sympathetic to express such thoughts, even if you had them. I do not say this as if I thought the person who does not have money needs such sympathetic solicitude, but because the least that one might ask of someone who fancied himself favored by fortune is that he should not be proud of it or have the urge to affront others who are not so favored. Good lord, let a person be proud; it would be better if he were not, but let him be proud; only do not let him be proud of money, for there is nothing that so debases a human being.

Now, you are accustomed to having money and know full well the implications of having it. You offend no one, therein you differ from those esthetes. You are willing to help where you can—indeed, when you point out the misery of not having money, you do it out of sympathy. Thus your scorn is not directed against people but against existence, where it happens that in the scheme of things not everybody has money. "Prometheus and Epimetheus," you say, "were undeniably very wise [*klog*],[114] but still it is inconceivable that whereas they otherwise equipped human beings so gloriously, it did not occur to them to give them money also." If you had been present on that occasion and had known what you know now, you would have come forward and said, "Gracious gods, thank you for everything, but—forgive me for speaking so frankly to you—you lack experience in worldly affairs; for a human being to be happy there is still one thing lacking—money. Of what use is it to him that he is created to rule over the world if he cannot spare the time for it because of financial worries? What is the idea—to turn a rational creature out into the world and then let him drudge and slave; is that a way to treat a human being?"

On this point you are inexhaustible. "Most men," you say, "live in order to make a living; when they have that, they live in order to make a good living; when they have that, they die. Therefore, I was genuinely moved some time ago when I read in the newspaper an announcement in which a wife reported her husband's death. Instead of copiously lamenting the pain of losing the best of husbands and the fondest of fathers, she was very brief: this death was so very grievous because just recently her husband had found such a good job. There is much more to this than the grieving widow or a casual newspaper reader sees in it.

"This comment can be developed into a demonstration of human immortality. This demonstration could be stated as follows: It is the destiny of every human being to make a good living. If he dies before he does that, he has not fulfilled his destiny, and it is left to anyone's guess whether he assumes he will fulfill his destiny on some other planet. But if he makes a good living, then he has achieved his destiny, but the destiny of making a good living cannot be that he is supposed to die but, on the contrary, that he is supposed to live well on his good living—*ergo*, man is immortal. This demonstration

could be called the popular demonstration or the making-a-
living demonstration. If this demonstration is added to the
previous demonstrations, then every reasonable doubt about
immortality must be regarded as conquered. This demonstration lends itself splendidly to being placed in conjunction with
the other demonstrations—indeed, it shows up here in its full
glory since as a conclusion it implies the others and substanti-
ates them. The other demonstrations presuppose that man is a
rational creature. Now insofar as anyone should doubt that,
the making-a-living demonstration steps up and demonstrates
this presupposition by means of the following syllogism: God
gives understanding to the person to whom he gives a living;
God gives a good understanding to the person to whom he
gives a good living—*ergo*. That grieving widow had an intimation of this; she felt the profound tragedy in life's contradiction."

Mockery and flippancy, then, are what you have to contribute to this matter. Presumably it does not dawn on you that
your comments would be beneficial or instructive to someone. Nor presumably does it dawn on you that this kind of talk
can do damage, for it is conceivable that a person who felt resentment enough over being forced to work might become
even more impatient, even more furious, through heeding the
not unwitty passionateness with which you reflect on his behalf and your sympathetic mockery. You might, however, be
circumspect on that score.

Taking that road, our hero will seek enlightenment in vain.
Listen now to what an ethicist would respond to him. His answer would be as follows: It is every person's duty to work for
a living. If he had no more to say, you would presumably answer, "There we have again that old stuff and nonsense about
duty and duty; it is duty everywhere. Is there anything more
boring than this straitlaced conformity that suppresses everything and clips its wings." Please recall that our hero had no
money, that the callous esthete had none to give him, and that
you, too, did not have so much to spare so that you could secure his future. Provided that he does not wish to sit down and
ponder what he would have done if he had had money, he will

have to think of another way out. Please also note that the ethicist addressed him very politely; he did not treat him as an exception, did not say to him: Good Lord, you are really in such bad shape that you will have to resign yourself to it. On the contrary, he made the esthete the exception, for he said: It is every person's duty to work for a living. Consequently, insofar as a person does not need to work, he is the exception, but to be an exception, as we agreed before, is not something great but inferior. If a person looks at the matter ethically he will look upon having money as a humiliation, for every preferential favor is a humiliation. If he looks at it this way, he will not become hypnotized by any preferential treatment. He will humble himself under it, and, having done that, he will be uplifted by the thought that the preferential treatment is a sign that a greater demand is made upon him.

II
252

If that ethicist from whom our hero gained enlightenment is himself familiar with what it means to work for a living, his words will have even more weight. Would that people had a little more courage in this respect. The reason we so often hear that strident, contemptible talk about money being everything is partly that those who must work lack the ethical vigor to acknowledge the meaning of working, lack the ethical conviction of its meaning. It is not the seducers who do harm to marriage, but cowardly married men. So also here. Contemptible talk such as that does no harm, but the ones who harm the good cause are those who, forced to work for a living, at one moment want to be recognized for the merit that is in it when they compare their lives with the loafers and the next moment complain and sigh and say: But still the most beautiful thing is to be independent. What respect, then, will a young person have for life if he hears the older people talk this way? Here again you have greatly harmed yourself by imaginatively constructing, for you have learned much that is not at all good and gratifying. You are very adept at tempting a person and wheedling a confession from him that in his innermost heart he would rather be exempt from working, and then you exult.

The question whether it is impossible to conceive of a world where it is unnecessary to work for a living is really a futile

question, since it does not have to do with the given actuality
but a fictitious one. At the same time it is still always an attempt to disparage the ethical view. If it really were indeed a
perfection in existence that one did not need to work, then the
person who did not need this would have the most perfect life.
Then one could say that it is a duty to work only in the sense
that those words are understood to mean a dismal necessity.

II
253

Then duty would not express the universally human but the
ordinary, and here duty would not be the expression for the
perfect. Therefore, I would also very correctly answer that it
must be regarded as an imperfection in existence that humankind would not need to work. The lower the level on which
human life stands, the less evident is the necessity to work; the
higher it stands, the more it stands out. The duty to work in
order to live expresses the universally human and in another
sense expresses the universal also, for it expresses freedom. It
is precisely by working that a person liberates himself; by
working, he becomes master over nature; by working, he
shows that he is higher than nature.

Or is life supposed to lose its beauty because a person must
work for a living? Here I am on the old point—it depends on
what is understood by beauty. It is beautiful to see the lilies of
the field, although they neither spin nor sew, so arrayed that
not even Solomon in all his splendor was so glorious; it is
beautiful to see the birds, free from care, find their food;[115] it is
beautiful to see Adam and Eve in a paradise where they can
have everything[116] to which they point, but it is nevertheless
even more beautiful to see a man acquiring through his work
that which he needs. It is beautiful to see a providence satisfy
all and take care of all, but it is even more beautiful to see a man
who is, so to speak, his own providence. A human being is
great, greater than any other creature, by being able to care for
himself. It is beautiful to see a man have an abundance that he
himself has acquired, but it is also beautiful to see a man perform a still greater feat—to change little into much. It is an
expression of man's perfection that he can work; it is a still
higher expression of it that he must work.[117]

If our hero will adopt this point of view, he will not feel

tempted to wish for a fortune that comes in his sleep, he will not be irritated by life's conditions, he will feel the beauty in working for a living, he will feel his human dignity in it, because it is not the greatness of the plant that it does not spin, but its imperfection that it cannot spin. He will not be inclined to form a friendship with that prosperous esthete. He will with steadiness of mind see what constitutes greatness and will not let himself be intimidated by rich men. Strangely enough, I have seen people who with gladness sensed the meaning of work, who were satisfied with their work, happy in their contentment with little, and yet did not seem to have the courage to admit it. If they talked about what they spent, they always made it seem that they spent much more than they actually did; they did not want to appear hard-working, although they actually were—just as if it were greater to spend much than to spend little, greater to be a loafer than to be hard-working. How rarely we meet a person who with calmness and cheerful dignity says: I do not do this or that, because it is beyond my means. It is as if he had a bad conscience, as if he feared for the answer the fox had.[118] In this way all true virtue is annihilated or changed into a phantom, for why should those who do not need to be contented with little be so? And those who need to be contented with little do indeed make a virtue of necessity. It is quite as if one could not be contented with little unless one had the possibility of abundance along with it, quite as if craving were not an equally great temptation to contentment with little.

Our hero presumably would decide to work, but nevertheless he would prefer to be free from cares about the necessities of life. I have never had cares about the necessities of life, for although up to a point I do have to work for a living, I nevertheless have always had my good income. Therefore I cannot speak from experience, but I have always kept my eyes open to the hardships involved, but have also kept my eyes open to the beauty in it, the educative and ennobling aspects of it, for I believe that there is no care that is as educative as this. I have known men whom I would never call craven or soft, men who in no way thought that life should be without struggle, who had the energy and courage and urge to go into battle where others would give up—I have also heard them say: Would that God would preserve me from cares about the necessities of life; there is nothing that smothers the higher life in a person as they do. On the occasion of such comments, it has often struck me that there is nothing as deceitful as the human heart, and my own life has also afforded me the occasion to experience the truth of this. We think we have the courage to venture out into the most perilous struggles, but we do not wish to struggle with cares about the necessities of life, and yet at the same time we want it to be greater to win that battle than this one. Now, that is easy enough; we choose an easier struggle, which nevertheless to most people seems much more dangerous. We fancy that this is the truth; we are victorious and so we are heroes, and heroes quite different from what we would be if we were victorious in that other wretched struggle unworthy of a human being. Indeed, when in addition to cares about the necessities of life we also have to fight a hidden enemy such as this within ourselves, it is no wonder that we wish to be free of that struggle. At least we still ought to be honest enough with ourselves to admit that the reason we shunned this battle was that it is much harder than all other trials; but if that is the case, then the victory is also much more beautiful. Insofar as we ourselves are not tested in this struggle, we owe it to every struggler to confess that his struggle is the most dangerous; we owe it to him to give him this recognition [*Æreserklæring*]. If a person regards cares about the necessities of life in this way, as a struggle for one's honor [*Ære*] in an even stricter sense than any other struggle, then he will already have gone somewhat further. Here as everywhere the point is to be rightly situated, not to waste time in wishing, but to take hold of one's task. If it seems to be a lowly and insignificant, petty and discouraging task, then one knows that it only makes the struggle more difficult and the victory more beautiful. There are men on whom a title bestows honor, and there are men who bestow honor on a title. Let a person apply this to himself, he who, although he feels the energy and the urge to venture into glorious battles,

II
255

must be content with the sorriest of all, struggling with the cares about the necessities of life.

A struggle with the cares about the necessities of life has the highly educative characteristic that the reward is so very little or, more correctly, nothing at all; the contender is struggling to provide the possibility of being able to keep on struggling. The greater the reward of the battle and the more extraneous it is to a person, the more the struggler dares to rely on all the equivocal passions that reside in every person. Ambition, vanity, pride—these are forces that have an enormous resiliency and can drive a person far. The person who struggles with the cares about the necessities of life soon perceives that these passions fail him, for how could he believe that such a struggle could interest others or excite their admiration? If he has no other forces, he is disarmed. The reward is very small, because when he has drudged and slaved he perhaps has acquired only what is needed—what is needed to keep on going so that he can in turn continue to drudge and slave.

As you can see, cares about the necessities of life are so ennobling and educative because they do not allow a person to delude himself about himself. If he does not see anything higher in this struggle, it is miserable, and he is right about its being misery to have to struggle to be able to eat his bread in the sweat of his brow.[119] But this struggle is so ennobling because it constrains him to see something else in it, constrains him—if he does not wish to throw himself away completely— to see it as a struggle for one's honor, and the reward is so small in order that the honor can be all the greater. To be sure, he struggles to gain a living, but what he nevertheless is struggling for is first and foremost to gain himself, and the rest of us, we who have not been tested but still have preserved a feeling for genuine greatness, will watch him if he lets us and will honor in him an honorary member of society. Thus he has a double struggle; he can lose in the one and at the same time win in the other. If I imagine the almost unthinkable, that all his efforts to gain a living failed, then he has certainly lost, and yet at the same time he may have won the most beautiful victory that can be won. Upon this he will fix his gaze, not upon the reward he failed to obtain, because it was too poor for that. The person who has a reward before his eyes forgets the other struggle; if he does not win the reward, he has lost everything; if he wins it, how he has won it is still always dubious.

And what struggle could be more educative than the struggle with the cares about the necessities of life! How much childlikeness it takes to be able almost to smile sometimes at the earthly toil and trouble an immortal spirit must have in order to live, how much humility to be content with the little that is gained with difficulty, how much faith to see the governance of a providence also in his life, for it is easy enough to say that God is greatest in the least, but to be able to see him there takes the strongest faith. How much love of people it takes to be happy with the fortunate, to be able to encourage those whose situation is equally distressing! What profound and penetrating consciousness of himself, that he does what lies within his power, what perseverance and alertness, for what enemy is more cunning than these cares? He does not get rid of them by a few bold moves; he does not scare them away with hubbub and noise. What grace and dignity it takes to turn away from them and yet not to run away from them! How often the weapons have to be changed—now it is a matter of working, then of waiting, then of holding one's own, then of praying! And with what joy and gladness and ease and agility the weapons have to be changed, for otherwise the enemy would win!

And during all this, time goes by; he is not granted the opportunity to see his beautiful plans actualized, the dreams of his youth fulfilled. He sees others who do succeed. They gather the crowd around them, harvest its applause; they revel in its enthusiasm, and he himself stands like a solitary artiste on the stage of life. He has no public; no one has time to look at him. No one has time, and, of course, this takes time, because his performance is not a half-hour juggling act; his tricks are more subtle and require more than a cultured public to be understood. But he does not crave that either. He perhaps says: When I was twenty years old, I, too, dreamed of combat; I imagined myself in the arena. I looked up at the balcony; I saw the clusters of girls, saw them alarmed for my sake, saw them wave their approval to me, and I forgot the difficulty of the struggle. Now I am older; my struggle has become a different one, but my soul is not less proud. I require another judge, an expert. I require eyes that see in secret,[120] that do not weary of watching, that see the struggle and see the danger. I require ears that hear the working of thoughts, that sense how my better nature extricates itself from the tortures of spiritual trials. I shall look up to this umpire; I shall covet his approval, even though I cannot deserve it. [121]And when the cup of suffering is handed to me, I shall not fix my gaze upon the cup but upon the one who hands it to me, and I shall not stare at the bottom of the cup to see whether I have quickly emptied it but steadfastly at the one who hands it to me. I shall gladly take the cup in my hand; I shall not empty it to somebody else's health as on a festive occasion when I myself delight in the delicious drink. No, I shall taste its bitterness, and while I am tasting it I shall cry out to myself "To *my* health," because I know and am convinced that with this drink I am acquiring by purchase an eternal health.

This, I believe, is the way a person must ethically regard the struggle that is carried on with the cares about the necessities of life. I shall not stand so solidly on my rights vis-à-vis you that I summon you to enlighten me as to the specific place in your esthetics where you deal with this subject, but I simply leave it up to your own deliberation whether life even in this struggle loses its beauty if one does not will it oneself, or whether it gains a higher beauty. To deny that such cares exist is, of course, madness; to forget that they exist because they go past one's own house is thoughtlessness; insofar as one claims to have a view of life, it is callousness or cowardliness.

That many people do not look upon the cares about the necessities of life this way is no objection; to wish that they might have enough loftiness of mind to look upon them in this way, enough aspiration not to make the mistake, as did those men who Scripture on another occasion says made the mistake of not looking toward heaven but at Susanna[122]—this certainly is a good and pious wish.

Thus the ethical view, that it is every person's duty to work for a living, has two advantages over the esthetic view. In the first place, it is in harmony with actuality, explains something universal in it, whereas the esthetic view puts forward something accidental and explains nothing. In the second place, it conceives of the human being according to his perfection, views him according to his true beauty. As far as this subject is concerned, this may be considered to be what is necessary and more than adequate. If you desire a few empirical comments, I give them to you as extras, not as if the ethical view needed any such support, but because you can perhaps benefit from them.

An elderly man whom I once knew always used to say that it was good for a person to learn to work for a living; it is true for adults as well as for children—they must be guided in sufficiently good time. Now, my idea is not that it would benefit a young man to be tied down right away to the cares of making a living. But just let him learn to work for a living. That highly praised independence is often a trap; every desire can be satisfied, every inclination pursued, every whim propagated—until they all conspire against the person himself. The one who has to work will be unfamiliar with the vain joy of being able to have everything; he will not learn to appeal self-confidently to his wealth, to remove every hindrance with money, and to buy every freedom for himself. But then his mind will not be embittered either; he will not be tempted to do what many a rich young man has done, to turn his back contemptuously on existence by saying with Jugurtha: Here is a city that is for sale if it finds a buyer.[123] He will not acquire in a short time a wisdom with which he does men an injustice and makes himself unhappy.

Therefore, when I hear people complain that they are compelled to work, compelled to be concerned about such matters, they whose souls' lofty flight should not be curtailed in this way, then I cannot deny that I sometimes become impatient, that I could wish that there were still among us a Harun-al-Raschid[124] who would administer a bastinado to everyone who complains out of season. You are not in the situation of needing to work for a living, and it is not at all my intention to advise you to throw away your fortune so that it can become a necessity for you to work; that is of no avail, and all imaginary constructing is futile folly that leads to nothing. But I believe that in another sense you are in a situation of having to acquire the conditions for living. In order that you will be able to live, you must see to mastering your innate depression. This circumstance leads me to apply that elderly man's words to you also, so that you have been guided in good time. This depression has been your misfortune, but you will see that a time will come when you yourself will admit that it has been your good fortune. Acquire, then, the condition that enables you to live. You are not one of those who would make me impatient with complaints, because I rather believe that you would do anything but complain, and you know very well how to swallow your sufferings. But watch yourself so that you do not fall into the opposite extreme, into a demented defiance that consumes the power to hide pain instead of utilizing it to bear and conquer it.

So our hero is willing to work, not because it is to him a *dura necessitas* [hard necessity],[125] but because he regards it as the most beautiful and the most perfect thing. (That he would be unable to see it this way because he is nevertheless obliged to put up with it is one of those partly foolish, partly malicious misconceptions that place a man's worth outside of himself, in the accidental.) But precisely because he is willing to work, his activity will, to be sure, become work, but not slave labor. So he requires a higher expression for his work, an expression that signifies the relation of his activity to his person and to that of others, an expression that can define it for him as pleasure and also uphold its meaning.

Here again deliberation will be necessary. He presumably finds it below his dignity to become involved with the wise man with the three thousand rix-dollars, but our hero is like most people. It is true that he was guided in good time, but he nevertheless has had a taste of living esthetically. Like most people, he is ungrateful. Therefore, although the ethicist was the one who helped him out of his previous predicament, he is not the first person to whom he turns. Perhaps he privately trusts that in the last resort the ethicist will help him out of it again, for our hero is not so despicable that he does not willingly admit that the ethicist actually did help him out of his predicament, even though he had no money to give him. So he turns to a somewhat more human esthete. He, too, perhaps knows how to recite something about the significance of working: without work life finally becomes boring. "One's work nevertheless ought not to be work in the strict sense but should be able to be continually defined as pleasure. A person discovers some aristocratic talent in himself that distinguishes him from the crowd. He does not develop this recklessly, because then he would soon be bored with it, but with all the esthetic earnestness possible. Life then has a new meaning for him, since he has his work, a work that nevertheless is really his pleasure. In his independence, he shelters it so that it can develop in all its luxuriance, undismayed by life. He does not, however, make this talent into a plank on which one manages to squeeze through life but into wings on which one soars over the world; he does not make it into a drudging hack but into a parade horse."

But our hero has no such aristocratic talent; he is like most people. The esthete knows no other way out for him than that "he has to resign himself to falling into the crowd's hackneyed category of a person who works. Do not lose heart; this, too, has its meaning, is decent and respectable; become a handy, industrious fellow, a useful member of society. I already look forward to seeing you, for the more varied life is, the more interesting for the observer. That is why I and all esthetes abhor a national costume, for it would be so tiresome to see everyone going around dressed alike. Let every individual take up his occupation in life that way; the more beautiful it will be for me and my kind, who make a profession of observing life." I hope that our hero will be somewhat impatient over such treatment and be indignant at the insolence of such a classification of people. Furthermore, independence played a role in this esthete's consideration also, and independent he certainly is not.

Perhaps he still cannot decide to turn to the ethicist; he

makes yet another effort. He meets a man who says: "One must work for a living—that's just the way life is." Here he seems to have found the person he was seeking, because this is just exactly what he thinks, too. So he will pay attention to these words. "One must work for a living in order to live— that's just the way life is—it's the shabby side of existence. We sleep seven hours out of the twenty-four; it is wasted time, but it has to be that way. We work five hours out of the twenty-four; it is wasted time, but it has to be that way. By working five hours, a person has his livelihood, and when he has that he begins to live. Now, a person's work should preferably be as boring and meaningless as possible, just so he has his livelihood from it. If he has a special talent, he should never commit the sin against it of making it his source of income. No, he coddles his talent; he possesses it for its own sake; he has even greater joy from it than a mother from her child. He cultivates it; he develops it for twelve hours of the day, sleeps for seven hours, is a nonhuman for five, and thus life becomes quite bearable, even quite beautiful, because working five hours is not so bad, inasmuch as, since a person's thoughts are never on the work, he hoards his energies for the pursuit that is his delight."

Our hero is making no headway. For one thing, he has no special talent with which to fill the twelve hours at home; for another, he has already gained a more beautiful view of working, a view he is unwilling to give up. So he probably will decide to seek help from the ethicist again. The latter is very brief. "It is every human being's duty to have a calling." More he cannot say, because the ethical as such is always abstract, and there is no abstract calling for all human beings. On the contrary, he presupposes that each person has a particular calling. Which calling our hero should choose, the ethicist cannot tell him, because for that a detailed knowledge of the esthetic aspects of his whole personality is required, and even if the ethicist did have this knowledge, he would still refrain from choosing for him, because in that case he would indeed deny his own life-view. What the ethicist can teach him is that there

II
261

is a calling for every human being and, when our hero has found his, that he is to choose it ethically.

What the esthete said about the aristocratic talents is confusing and skeptical talk about that which the ethical man clarifies. The esthete's view of life always involves the difference that some people have talent and others do not, and yet what separates people is a more or less quantitative determinant. Thus it is an arbitrariness on their part to stop at some particular point, and yet the nerve in their view of life lies precisely in this arbitrariness. Their life-view, therefore, establishes a division in all existence, which they do not see their way to eliminating; instead, they recklessly and callously try to arm themselves against it.

The ethicist, however, reconciles the person with life, for he says: Every human being has a calling. He does not annihilate the differences but declares: In all the differences there still remains the universal, that it is a calling. The most eminent talent is a calling, and the individual who possesses it cannot lose sight of actuality; he does not stand outside the universally human, because his talent is a calling. The most insignificant individual has a calling; he must not be expelled, must not be sent to live in a *confinium* [border territory] with animals. He does not stand outside the universally human; he has a calling.

The ethical thesis that every human being has a calling expresses, then, that there is a rational order of things, in which every human being, if he so wills, fills his place in such a way that he simultaneously expresses the universally human and the individual. Does this view make existence less beautiful? There is no aristocracy to rejoice over, the importance of which is based on accident, and accidentally based on that accident; no, there is a kingdom of gods.[126]

As soon as the talent is not regarded as a calling—and if it is regarded as a calling every human being has a calling—the talent is absolutely egotistic. [127]Therefore, everyone who bases his life on a talent establishes to the best of his ability a robber-existence. He has no higher expression for the talent than that it is a talent. Consequently, this talent wants to advance in all its difference. Therefore, every talent has a tendency to make itself central; every condition must be present to promote it, because only in this wild onrushing is there the genuinely esthetic enjoyment of the talent. If there is a concurrent talent going in another direction, they clash in a life-and-death struggle, since they have no concentricity, no higher shared expression.

So our hero has found what he was looking for, a work from which he can live; he has also found a more significant expression for the relation of this work to his personality: it is his calling—consequently, the carrying out of it is bound up with a satisfaction for his whole personality. He has also found a more significant expression for the relation of his work to other people; inasmuch as his work is his calling, he is thereby placed essentially on the same level as all other human beings. Hence through his work he is doing the same as everyone else—he is carrying out his calling. He insists on this acknowledgment; he does not insist on more, for this is the absolute. "If my calling is a humble one," he says, "I can nevertheless be faithful to my calling, and then according to what is essential I am just as great as the greatest, except that I would not for a moment be so foolish as to want to forget the differences. To do so would benefit me least of all, for if I forgot the differences, there would be an abstract calling for everyone, but an abstract calling is no calling, and then in turn I would have lost just as much as the greatest. If my calling is humble, I can nevertheless be unfaithful to it, and if I am, I am committing just as great a sin as the greatest. I shall not be so foolish as to want to forget the differences or to believe that my unfaithfulness would have just as corrupting consequences for the whole as the unfaithfulness of the greatest—to do so would be of no benefit to me; I myself would be the one who would lose the most."

The ethical view, then, that every human being has a calling, has two advantages over the esthetic theory of talent. First, it does not account for [*forklare*] anything accidental in existence but for the universal; second, it shows the universal in its true beauty. In other words, the talent is not beautiful until it is transfigured [*forklaret*] into a calling, and existence is not beautiful until every person has a calling. Since this is the case,

I ask you not to scorn a simple empirical observation, which in comparison with the main consideration you will be kind enough to regard as a superfluity. When a person has a calling, he generally has a norm outside himself, which, without making him a slave, nevertheless gives him some indication of what he has to do, maps out his time for him, often provides him with the occasion to begin. If at some time he fails in his task, he hopes to do it better the next time, and this next time is not so very far away. But the person who has no calling usually has to work much more *uno tenore* [incessantly], insofar as he wants to set himself a task. He has no intermission, except insofar as he himself wants to intermit. If he fails, then everything fails, and he has a very hard time managing to start again, because he lacks an occasion. Then, unless he wants to become an idler, he is tempted to become a pedant. It is quite common to put down as pedants those who have specific duties. Ordinarily such a person cannot become a pedant at all. But the person without specific duties is tempted to become that in order to exercise some restraining influence on the all too much freedom in which he can so easily go astray. Therefore, we are readily inclined to forgive him his pedantry, because it is a sign of something good; but on the other hand it must still be regarded as a punishment, since he has wanted to emancipate himself from the ordinary.

Our hero found a more meaningful expression for the relation of his work to the work of other men—that it was a calling. So he has been acknowledged, has received his credentials. But now when he carries out his calling—yes, then he finds his satisfaction in it, but he also insists on an expression of the relation of this activity to other people; he insists on *accomplishing* something. At this point he may again go astray. The esthete will explain to him that the satisfaction of the talent is the highest, and whether he accomplishes something or does not accomplish anything is entirely beside the point. He may encounter a practical narrow-mindedness that in its bungling zeal thinks it is accomplishing everything, or an esthetic snobbery that thinks that accomplishing something in the world falls to the lot of a chosen few, that there are a few very talented individuals who accomplish something, that the rest of the people are *numerus* [ciphers],[128] superfluities in life, extravagances of the creator. But none of these explanations helps our hero, because he is only like most people.

Let us turn once again to the ethicist. He says: What every human being accomplishes and can accomplish is that he can do *his* task in life. If it were true that there are some persons who accomplish something and others who do not and the reason for that lay in their accidentality, then skepticism would prevail again. Therefore, we must say: Essentially every person accomplishes equally much. I am by no means preaching laziness, but on the other hand one must be cautious in using the word "accomplish." It has always been the butt of your ridicule, and therefore you have, as you once put it, "studied integral calculus, differential calculus, and the calculus of the infinite in order to calculate how much a copy clerk in the admiralty, whom the whole office considers a good worker, did accomplish for the whole." Direct your ridicule only at all those who want to make themselves important in life, but never misuse it to confuse.

The phrase "to accomplish" signifies a relation between my action and something else that lies outside me. Now, it is easy to see that this relation does not lie in my power, and to that extent it is just as appropriate to say of the most talented person as of the humblest of men—that he accomplishes nothing. This implies no mistrust of life; on the contrary, it implies an acknowledgment of my own insignificance and a respect for the significance of every other person. The most talented person can complete his task, and so can the humblest of men. Neither of them can do more. Whether they accomplish something is not in their power; it is, however, indeed in their power to prevent themselves from doing so. So I surrender all that importance that often enough throws its weight around in life; I do my work and do not waste time calculating whether I am accomplishing anything. What I accomplish accompanies my work as my good fortune; I certainly dare to rejoice in it but do not dare attribute it entirely to myself. A beech tree grows, amasses its crown, and people take pleasure in sitting

in its shade. If it were to become impatient, if it would say,
"Scarcely any living creature ever comes to this place where I
am standing; what is the use, then, of my growing, of thrusting out my branches; what am I accomplishing by doing
that?" it would only retard its growth, and some day a traveler
might come along and say, "If this tree had been a full-leafed
beech instead of a stunted runt, I would have been able to rest
in its shade." Just imagine if the tree could hear!

Every human being, then, can accomplish something; he
can accomplish his task. The task can be very different, but
this is always to be maintained, that every human being has his
task, and thus all are reconciled in the expression that each of
them is doing his task. The relation of my task to anything else
or what I am supposed to accomplish (taking this word in its
common usage) does not lie in my power. Even the person
whose task in life is to develop himself, even he accomplishes
essentially just as much as anyone else. It might seem, therefore, as if that esthete were justified who thought that one
should not reflect at all upon what one accomplished but only
enjoy the satisfaction of expanding one's talent. The mistake,
however, was that he stopped with the selfish definition of the
talent. He counted himself among the chosen and was unwilling to accomplish the universal in his life and to regard his talent as his task. The person, however, of whom one might say
that his task in life is simply and solely to develop himself, is,
of course, one of the least gifted, humanly speaking. For example, a young girl. She certainly is one of those about whom
one is not tempted to say that they are able to accomplish
something. Let her also have an unhappy love affair to boot,
let her be robbed of the last prospect of accomplishing something—if she nevertheless does her task, if she develops herself, then she is accomplishing just as much, regarded essentially, as the greatest.

To accomplish, then, is identical with carrying out one's
task. Imagine a person who is deeply and sincerely motivated.
Whether or not he will accomplish something never crosses
his mind; only the idea wants to advance in him with all its
might. Let him be an orator, a pastor, or what you will. He

does not speak to the crowd in order to accomplish something, but the chimes inside him must ring—only then does he feel happy. Do you think he accomplishes less than the person who becomes self-important in his conception of what he will accomplish, who keeps himself at it by thinking about what he is going to accomplish? Think of an author. It never enters his head to consider whether he is going to have a reader or whether he is going to accomplish something with his book; he only wants to grasp the truth—that alone is the object of his pursuit. Do you suppose that such a writer accomplishes less than the one whose pen is under the supervision and direction of the thought that he is going to accomplish something?

Strangely enough, neither you nor I nor our hero himself nor that clever esthete has noticed it, and yet it is true—our hero possesses an exceptional talent. A person's mental capacities can be disappointing for a long time until their quiet growth has reached a certain point, and then they suddenly proclaim themselves in all their power. The esthete will presumably say: Well, it's too late now; he certainly has made a mess of it—too bad for the man. But the ethicist presumably will say: That was very fortunate, because now that he has perceived the truth his talent will certainly not become a snare for his feet; he will see that one needs neither independence nor five hours of slave labor in order to guard it, but that his talent is precisely his calling.

Our hero, then, works for a living; this work is also his delight; he carries out his calling, he accomplishes his task. To say everything in one phrase, a phrase that plunges you into anxiety—he has his bread-and-butter. Do not become impatient; let the poet say it so it sounds more beautiful: Instead of childhood's golden summer pears he has "his bread-and-butter with honor."[129] What next? You are smiling; you think I am up to some mischief. You are already shuddering at my prosiness, because "now it will end in no less than getting him married. Well, go ahead, publish the banns for him; I shall not have any objections against his or your pious resolve. It is unbelievable what rational consistency there is in existence: bread-and-butter and a wife. Yes, even that poet with his glockenspiel chimes in and hints unambiguously that the wife comes along with the bread-and-butter.[130] There is just one thing to which I must object—that you call your client a hero. I have been indulgent and yielding; I have been unwilling to denounce him. I have always had hope for him, but now you must really excuse me if I take another street and do not listen to you any more. A jobholder and a married man, I have all respect for him, but a hero—even he himself does not claim to be that."

It is your opinion, then, that for someone to be called a hero it is required that he do something out of the ordinary. In that case you have really brilliant prospects. Now suppose that it takes great courage to do the ordinary, and the person who shows great courage is indeed a hero. In order for a person to be called a hero, one must consider not so much what he does as how he does it. Someone can conquer kingdoms and countries without being a hero; someone else can prove himself a hero by controlling his temper.[131] Someone can display courage by doing the out-of-the-ordinary, another by doing the ordinary. The question is always—how does he do it? You will not deny, then, that in the foregoing our hero has manifested a tendency to want to do the out-of-the-ordinary; indeed, I still do not dare vouch for him entirely. Presumably from this arose your hope of his becoming a real hero; from this arose my fear of his becoming—a fool. Thus I have shown the same leniency toward him as you; I have had hope for him from the beginning, have called him "hero" although several times he made a move as if he were about to make himself unworthy of that title. Therefore, if I have him marry, I'll quietly manage to get him off my hands and happily hand him over to his wife. Through the recalcitrance displayed earlier, he has qualified himself to be placed under special surveillance. His wife will assume this task, and then everything will go well, for every time he is tempted to want to be an out-of-the-ordinary person, his wife will immediately straighten him out again; in this way he will quietly earn the name "hero," and his life will not be without achievements. Then I shall have nothing more to do with him, except insofar as he should feel drawn to me, just as I shall feel drawn to him if he continues his hero career. Then he will see me as a friend, and our relationship will not be without meaning. He will be able to reconcile himself to your breaking off acquaintance with him at that time, so much the more so because he could easily become a little suspicious if you should deign to take an interest in him. In this respect, I congratulate him and likewise congratulate every married man.

We are, however, still a long way from reaching that point. You can still go on hoping for a long time—namely, as long as I need to fear. In other words, our hero is like most people and has a certain predilection for the out-of-the-ordinary. He is also a little ungrateful and for that reason wants to try his luck with the esthetes again before he has recourse to the ethicist. He also knows how to gloss over his ingratitude, because, says he, the ethicist really did help me out of my confusion; the view of my occupation that I owe to him completely satisfies me, and its earnestness lifts me up. As far as love goes, however, I certainly would in this respect like to enjoy my freedom, to follow the prompting of my heart; love does not love this earnestness and demands the lightness and the loveliness of the esthetic.

You see, I can have difficulties enough dealing with him. It almost seems as if he has not completely understood the foregoing. He still persists in thinking that the ethical lies outside the esthetic, and this even though he himself must admit that life gains beauty through the ethical view. We shall see. Now just fan the flames a little; then I will get plenty of wrong conceptions.

Although you never answered a previous letter of mine either orally or in writing, presumably you nevertheless remember its contents and also how I tried to show that marriage, precisely by means of the ethical, is the esthetic expression for love. You will then probably make allowances for what was developed there in the conviction that if I managed to make it at all comprehensible to you, then I shall easily be able to explain it, if necessary, to our hero.

He has turned to the esthetes, and, not any wiser about what he should do but rather about what he should not do, he has left them. For a brief time he has witnessed the ingenuity of a seducer, has listened to his fawning talk, but he has learned to despise his art. He has learned to see through him: to see that he is a liar, a liar when he shams love, when he spruces up feelings that may once have been genuine, since in these feelings he himself belonged to another; to see that he doubly deceives, deceives the one he wants to fool into thinking that he has these feelings and the one to whom they legitimately belong; to see that he is a liar when he fools himself into believing there is something beautiful in his lust. He has learned to despise the clever ridicule that wants to make love into a childish trick at which one should only smile.

II
269

Our hero has seen your favorite play, *The First Love*.[132] He does not credit himself with enough culture to be able to evaluate the play esthetically, but he finds it unfair of the author to have Charles sink so low in the eight years. He readily admits that such a thing can happen in life, but he does not believe that this is what we ought to learn from a writer. He finds it to be a contradiction in the play that Emmeline is simultaneously an affected fool and a really lovable girl, which Rinville at first glance is sure she is, even though he is prejudiced against her. If that is the case, he again finds it unfair to have Charles become a ruin of a man in the eight years. It seems to him that the play ought to be a tragedy, not a comedy. He thinks it unfair of the writer to have Emmeline tolerate her mistake so thoughtlessly, thoughtlessly forgive Rinville for having deceived her, thoughtlessly forget Charles and thus thoughtlessly make a mockery of her own feelings, thoughtlessly build her future on her own thoughtlessness, on Rinville's thoughtlessness, on Charles's thoughtlessness. To be sure, he thinks the original Emmeline sentimental and high-strung, but to his eyes the improved Emmeline, the sagacious Emmeline, is nevertheless a creature much inferior to the former one in all her imperfection. He finds it unfair on the part of the author to portray love as a foolish prank one can enter into for eight years and turn topsy-turvy in half an hour without having this change leave any impression.

Our hero was pleased to note that the people who laughed at such plays were not exactly the ones he respected most. Momentarily the mockery chilled his blood, but he again felt the fountain of feelings flowing in his breast. He is sure that this artery is the life principle of the soul, and that one who severs it is dead and does not need to be buried. For a brief time he was lulled to sleep by a distrust of life that wants to teach him that everything is transitory, that time changes everything, that there is nothing upon which one dares to build, and therefore one should never plan for one's whole life. His indolence and cowardliness found this kind of talk very acceptable; it was a comfortable ensemble to wear and not unbecoming in the eyes of men. He has, however, taken a sharp look at this talk, has seen the hypocrite, has seen the self-indulgent who came in humble apparel, the predator who came in sheep's clothing,[133] and he has learned to despise this talk.

He has perceived that it was an insult and consequently ugly to want to love a person according to vague forces in his being but not according to a clear consciousness, to want to love in such a way that he could imagine it possible that this love could cease and he then would dare to say: I can do nothing about it; feelings are not within a person's power. He has perceived that it was an insult and consequently ugly to want to love with one part of the soul and not with the whole soul, to make his love into an element and yet take another's whole love, to want to be something of an enigma and a secret. He has perceived that it would be ugly if he had a hundred arms so that he could embrace many at a time; he has only one breast and wishes to embrace only one. He has perceived that it was an insult to want to be attached to another person in the way one is attached to finite and accidental things, conditionally, so that if there should prove to be problems later one could undo it. He does not believe it possible that the one he loves can change, except for the better, and if it should happen, he believes in the power of the relationship to make everything good again. He acknowledges that what love requires is, like a temple tax, a sacred tribute that is paid in its own coinage,[134] and that one does not accept all the wealth of the world as compensation for the most minor claim if the die-stamp is counterfeit.

You see, our hero is on a good path; he has lost faith in the callous common sense of the esthetes and in their superstitious belief in vague feelings that are supposed to be too delicate to be expressed as duty. He is content with the ethicist's explanation that it is every person's duty to marry; he has understood this correctly—namely, that the person who does not marry certainly does not sin, except insofar as he himself is responsible for it, because then he trespasses against the universally human, which is also assigned to him as a task to be fulfilled, but that the person who does marry fulfills the universal. The ethicist can lead him no further, because the ethical, as stated previously, is always abstract; it can only declare to him the universal. Thus, it can in no way tell him whom he should marry. A close acquaintance with all his esthetic qualities would be required for that, but the ethicist does not have that, and even if he did have it, he would still take care lest he annihilate his own theories by taking the choice upon himself on his behalf. When he himself has chosen, the ethical will then sanction the choice and elevate his love, and to a certain degree it will also help him in choosing, since it will save him from a superstitious belief in the accidental, for a purely esthetic choice is actually an endless choice. The ethical helps everyone unconsciously, but since it is unconscious, the assistance of the ethical takes on the appearance of being a depreciating of life, a consequence of the wretchedness of life, instead of being a heightening, a consequence of the divine character of life.

"A person with such remarkable principles," you say, "may be allowed to walk alone; great things may be expected of him." I agree, and I trust that his principles are so firm that they will not be affected by your ridicule. But there is still one more sharp turn we have to make before we are in the harbor. Our hero has heard a man (for whose judgment and opinion he has great respect) say that, since by marriage a person ties himself down to one individual for life he must be circumspect in choosing, it must be an uncommon girl who expressly by

II
271

her uncommonness would give one security for one's entire future. Would you not tend to hope for our hero a little while longer? I, at least, fear for him.

Let us radically examine this matter. You assume, of course, that in the solitary stillness of the forest there lives a nymph, a creature, a maiden. Now, then, this nymph, maiden, this creature leaves her solitude and appears in Copenhagen, or in Nuremberg like Kaspar Hauser[135]—after all, the place is unimportant; the important thing is that she puts in her appearance. There will be courting, believe me! I leave it to you to develop the details; indeed, you can write a novel titled "The Nymph, the Creature, the Maiden in the Seclusion of the Forest," *ad modum* [in the fashion of] the lending libraries' popular novel "The Urn in the Secluded Valley."[136] She has definitely appeared, and our hero has become the lucky man on whom she has bestowed her love. Do we agree on this? Being married myself, I have no objection to make. You, however, would perhaps feel insulted to have such an everyday person be preferred to you. But since you do have an interest in my client and this is the only way left for him to become a hero in your eyes, give your consent. Let us now see if his love, his marriage, becomes beautiful. The salient feature of his love and his marriage was that she was the only girl in the whole world. Consequently, the salient feature was her difference: the likes of such happiness could not be found in the whole world, and his happiness lay precisely in this. He is capable of not wanting to marry her at all, for would it not demean such a love to give it so common and vulgar an expression as marriage? Would it not be presumptuous to demand that two lovers like that enter the great company of matrimony so that in a certain sense no more could be said of them than of every married couple—that they are married? You perhaps would find this quite all right, and the only objection you would have to make would probably be that it is wrong that such a poor wretch as my hero runs off with a girl like that. If, however, he had been an out-of-the-ordinary man such as you, for example, or just as unusual a man as she was an unusual girl, then everything would be all right and their love affair the most perfect imaginable.

Our hero has put himself into a critical situation. Of the girl there is only one view: she is an unusual girl. I myself, a married man, say with Donna Clara: Here rumor has not overstated the case; she is a wonder child, the beautiful Preciosa.[137] It is very tempting to lose sight of the ordinary and to drift on the breezes of the fabulous. And yet he himself has indeed seen the beauty in marriage. What, then, does marriage do? Does it rob him of anything, does it deprive her of any beauty, does it cancel a single difference? Not at all. But it shows him all these things as accidentals when he is outside marriage, and not until he gives the differences the expression of the universal, and only then, is he in secure possession of them. The ethical teaches him that the relationship is the absolute. The relationship is, namely, the universal. It takes away from him the vain joy of being out–of–the–ordinary in order to give him the true joy of being the ordinary. It brings him into harmony with all existence, teaches him to rejoice in it, because as an exception, as an out–of–the–ordinary person he is in conflict, and since that which is the basis of the out–of–the–ordinary is here his good fortune, he must certainly become conscious of his existence as a torment to the universal, provided that there really was authenticity in his good fortune, and it truly must be a misfortune to be so fortunate that one's good fortune is essentially different from everybody else's. So he gains the accidental beauty and loses the true beauty. This he will realize, and he will turn back again to the ethicist's position that it is every human being's duty to marry, and he will perceive that it has not only truth but also beauty on its side. Then let him have that wonder child—he will not be hypnotized by the differences. He will fervently rejoice in her beauty, in her loveliness, in the richness of mind and warmth of feelings that she has; he will consider himself fortunate, but he will say: I am not essentially different from any other married man, because the relationship is the absolute. Let him have a less endowed girl, and he will be happy in his good fortune, because he will say: Even if she is far inferior to others, essentially she makes me just as happy, for the relationship is the absolute. He will not fail to appreciate the significance of the differences, for just as he perceived that there was no abstract calling but that every human had his own, so he will perceive that there is no abstract marriage. Ethics tells him only that he should marry, it does not say whom. Ethics explains [*forklare*] to him the universal in the differences, and he transfigures [*forklare*] the differences in the universal.

The ethical view of marriage, then, has several advantages over every esthetic concept of love. It elucidates the universal, not the accidental. It does not show how a pair of very specific people can become happy because of their extraordinariness but how every married couple can become happy. It sees the relationship as the absolute and does not take the differences as guarantees but understands them as tasks. It sees the relationship as the absolute and therefore looks upon love according to its true beauty—that is, according to its freedom; it understands its historical beauty.

Hence our hero lives by his work; his work is also his calling; therefore he works with a will. Since it is his calling, it places him in touch with other people, and in carrying out his task he accomplishes what he could wish to accomplish in the world. He is married, content in his home, and time runs smoothly for him. He cannot understand how time could be a burden for anyone, or be an enemy of his happiness; on the contrary, time seems to him to be a true blessing. On this point he admits that he owes his wife extraordinarily much.

It is true—I forgot to say this—I was mistaken about the nymph from the forest. He did not become the lucky one; he had to be satisfied with a girl like most girls in the same sense that he was like most people. Yet he was very happy—indeed, he once confided to me that he believed he was really fortunate not to win that wonder child. The task would have been too great for him; it is so easy to do harm when everything is so perfect before one begins. Now, however, he is full of courage and confidence and hope; he is very animated and enthusiastically says: The relationship is still the absolute. He is more positively sure than he is of anything else that the relationship will have the power to develop this ordinary girl into everything that is great and beautiful; his wife in all humility is of the

II
274

same mind. Yes, my young friend, surprising things do happen in the world. I simply did not believe that there was such a wonder child in the world as you speak of, and now I am almost ashamed of my unbelief, because this ordinary girl with her tremendous faith is a wonder child, and her faith is more precious than green forests and gold. In one respect I continue in my old unbelief that a wonder child like that is to be found in the seclusion of the forest.

My hero (or would you deny him the right to this designation—do you not think that a courage that dares to have faith in transforming an ordinary girl into a wonder child is a truly heroic courage?) is especially thankful to his wife because time has acquired such a beautiful meaning for him, and in turn he attributes this in part to marriage, and on this point he and I, we two married men, are in complete agreement. If he had won that forest nymph and had not married, he would have been afraid that their love would flame up in certain beautiful moments that would leave dull intervals. Then they perhaps would have wished to see each other only if the sight of each other would be really momentous; if this misfired a few times, he would have been afraid that the whole relationship would gradually dissolve into nothing. But the humble marriage that made it a duty for them to see each other daily, when they were rich and also when they were poor, had infused into the whole relationship an equality and steadiness that made it so very gratifying for him. In its humble incognito, the prosaic marriage had concealed a poet who not only transfigured life on special occasions but was always present and by his cadences gave a thrill even to the more impoverished hours.

My hero's view of marriage, as far as this aspect is concerned, I share entirely, and here it really shows its superiority not only over the single life but also over every solely erotic association. My new friend has just developed the latter point, and therefore I shall only briefly emphasize the former. One may be ever so intelligent, ever so industrious, ever so enthusiastic for an idea, but there nevertheless come moments when time drags. You often flout the opposite sex, and I have warned you often enough to desist. Look upon a young girl as an imperfect creature as much as you wish, but I would like to say to you: My wise fellow, go to the ant and become wise;[138] learn from a girl how to make time go by, for in that she is a natural virtuoso. She may not have the conception of rigorous and sustained work that a man has, but she is never idle, is always busy; time never drags for her. I am able to speak about this from experience.

It sometimes happens to me—to be sure, very rarely now, for I try to counteract it, since I consider it a husband's duty to be of about the same age as his wife—it sometimes happens that I sit and settle into myself. I have taken care of my work; I have no desire for any diversion, and something melancholy in my temperament gains the upper hand over me. I become many years older than I actually am, and I practically become a stranger to my home life. I can very well see that it is beautiful, but I look at it with different eyes than usual. It seems to me as if I myself were an old man, my wife my happily married younger sister in whose house I am sitting. In such hours, time almost begins to drag for me.

Now, if my wife were a man, the same thing would perhaps happen to her, and we might both come to a halt, but she is a woman and in harmony with time. Is it a perfection in a woman, this secret rapport she has with time; is it an imperfection? Is it because she is a more earthly creature than the man, or because she has more of eternity within her? Please do answer; after all, you have a philosophic mind.

When I am sitting this way, desolate and lost, and then I watch my wife moving lightly and youthfully around the room, always busy—she always has something to take care of—my eyes involuntarily follow her movements. I participate in everything she is doing, and in the end I find myself within time again, time has meaning for me again, and the moment hurries along again. What it is that she is taking care of—well, I could not tell you if I tried, not if my life depended on it; it remains a riddle to me. I know what it is to work far into the night, to be so tired that I can scarcely get up from my chair; I know what it is to think, what it is to be so completely empty of thoughts that it is impossible for me to get the slightest idea into my head; I also know what it is to loaf, but the way to be occupied in the way my wife is occupied is a riddle to me. She is never tired and yet never idle; it is as if what she is doing is a game, a dance, as if a game were her occupation. With what does she fill her time? You certainly can grasp that of course it is not acquired skills, not those dodges in which bachelors ordinarily excel. And since we are speaking of bachelors and in my mind's eye I see your youth coming to an end, it really is time for you to give some thought to being able to fill the idle moments. You should learn to play the flute or figure out some ingenious instrument for scraping out your pipe.

But I would rather not think about such things; I soon grow weary of thinking about them. I come back to my wife—I never grow weary of watching her. What she does I cannot explain, but she does it all with a charm and graciousness, with an indescribable lightness, does it without preliminaries and ceremony, like a bird singing its aria. Indeed, I do believe that her occupation can best be compared to a bird's work, and yet her arts seem to me to be genuine magic. In this respect, she is my absolute refuge. If when I am sitting in my study I grow weary and time is dragging for me, I slip into the living room, I sit down in a corner, I say not a word for fear of disturbing her in her task, for even though it looks like a game, it is done with a dignity and decorum that inspires respect, and she is far from being what you say Mrs. Hansen is, a top that hums and buzzes around and by its humming and buzzing makes matrimonial music in the living room.

Yes, my wise fellow, it is unbelievable what a natural virtuoso a woman is; she explains in the most interesting and beautiful manner the question that has cost many a philosopher his reason: time. A question about which one futilely seeks enlightenment from many philosophers in all their prolixity, she explains *ohne weiter* [without ado] at any time of the day. She explains this question, as she explains many others, in a manner that arouses the most profound amazement. Although I am not an old married man, I do believe that I could write a whole book about this. I shall not, however, do so, but

I do want to tell you a story that has always been very illustrative for me.

Somewhere in Holland there lived a scholar. He was an Orientalist and was married. One day he does not come to lunch, although he has been called. His wife waits expectantly at the table; she knows that he is home, and the longer she waits, the less she is able to explain his not coming. Finally she decides to go herself and persuade him to come. There he sits all alone in his study; there is no one with him. He is absorbed in his Oriental studies. I can picture it: she has leaned over him, put her arms around his neck, glanced down at his book, then looked at him and said, "Darling, why don't you come to eat?" Perhaps the scholar has scarcely had time to notice what was said, but when he sees his wife, he most likely answers, "My dear, lunch is out of the question. Here is a vowel marking I have never seen before; I have seen the passage quoted several times but never in this way, and yet my edition is an excellent Dutch edition. Do you see this dot here? It's enough to drive one mad." I can picture it: his wife looks at him, half smiling, half reproaching, that such a little dot should disturb the domestic routine, and the story says that she answers, "Is that anything to get upset about—blast it!" No sooner said than done; she blows, and look, the vowel point vanishes, for that remarkable dot was a grain of snuff. The scholar went happy to lunch, happy that the vowel marking had disappeared, even more happy over his wife.

Shall I draw the moral of this story for you? If that scholar had not been married, he probably would have gone mad; he perhaps would have taken several other Orientalists along with him, for I do not doubt that he would have raised a dreadful hue and cry in the literature. This is why I say one ought to live in harmony with the opposite sex, for, *unter uns gesagt* [between us], a young girl explains everything and tells the whole consistory to be blowed, and if a person is on good terms with her, he is happy for her elucidations, but otherwise she scoffs at him. But this story also teaches the way one should live in harmony with her. If that scholar had not been married, if he had been an esthete who had had all conditions under his control, perhaps he would have been the lucky man to whom that wonder child would have wanted to belong. He would not have married—their feelings were much above that. He would have built her a palace and spared no refinement to make her life rich in pleasure. He would have visited her in her chateau, because that is the way she wanted it; with erotic coquetry he himself would have come out to her on foot, while his valet followed in the carriage, bearing rich and costly gifts. In his Oriental studies, he would also have encountered that remarkable vowel marking. He would have stared at it without being able to explain it. Meanwhile, the time to visit the beloved would have come. He would have cast aside this concern, for how befitting is it to visit a beloved with thoughts of anything other than her loveliness and his own love? He would have invested himself in all possible charm; he would have been more endearing than ever before, would have delighted her inordinately, because there was the remote echo of many passions in his voice, because he had to wrestle cheerfulness out of his despondency. But when he had left her at dawn, had thrown his last kiss to her and now sat in the carriage, his face clouded. He arrived home. The shutters in his study were closed, the lamps lighted; he sat down fully dressed and stared at that marking he could not explain. To be sure, he had the girl he loved, yes, perhaps worshiped—the girl he visited only when his soul was rich and strong; but he did not have a wife who came and called him to lunch, he did not have a wife who could blow the marking away.

On the whole, woman has a native talent, an original gift, an absolute virtuosity for explaining the finite. When man was created, he stood there as nature's lord and prince, nature's magnificence and splendor; all the riches of finitude awaited only his nod, but he did not comprehend what he should do with it all. He looked at it, but everything seemed to vanish under this intellectual gaze; it seemed to him that if he moved he would be past it all in one single step. Thus he stood, an imposing figure, lost in thought and yet comic, because one had to smile at this rich man who did not know how to use his riches, but also tragic, because he could not use them. Then woman was created. She was in no quandary, knew at once how one should take hold of the situation; without any fuss, without any preparation, she was ready to start at once.

This was the first solace that was given to man [*Menneske*]. She approached the man [*Mand*], happy as a child, humble as a child, wistful as a child. She wished only to be a solace to him, to alleviate his need—a need she did not understand, but which she did not think she was filling either—she wished only to shorten the intervening time for him. And see, her humble solace became life's richest joy; her innocent diversion became life's beauty; her childlike playing became life's deepest meaning. A woman comprehends the finite; she understands it from the ground up. That is why she is exquisite, which every woman essentially is; that is why she is lovely, which no man is; that is why she is happy, happy as no man can or ought to be; that is why she is in harmony with existence as no man can or ought to be. Therefore, it can be said that her life is happier than the man's, because the finite can presumably make a person happy, the infinite *per se* never. She is more perfect than man, for surely the one who explains something is more perfect than the one who is hunting for an explanation. Woman explains the finite; man pursues the infinite. This is the way it must be, and everyone has his pain, for woman bears children in pain, but man conceives ideas in pain, and woman is not supposed to know the anxiety of doubt or the agony of despair. She is not supposed to stand outside the idea, but she has it at second hand. But because woman explains the finite in this way, she is man's deepest life, but a life that is supposed to be hidden and secret, as the life of the root always is.

That is why I hate all that detestable rhetoric about the emancipation of women.[139] God forbid that it may ever happen. I cannot tell you with what pain the thought can pierce my soul, nor what passionate indignation, what hate, I harbor toward anyone who dares to express such ideas. It is my consolation that those who propound such wisdom are not wise as serpents but ordinarily are like oafs whose blabbing can do no harm. Indeed, if the serpent could manage to delude her about this, could tempt her with this seemingly delightful

fruit,[140] if this infection were to spread, if it pushed its way
through even to her whom I love, my wife, my joy, my refuge, the root of my life, yes, then my courage would be
crushed, then freedom's passion in my soul would be exhausted. Then I know very well what I would do—I would sit
in the market place and weep, weep like that artist whose work
had been destroyed and even he could not remember what it
represented. But it will not happen, and it must not and cannot
happen; so let the evil spirits try it, let obtuse people try it,
people who have no concept of what it is to be a man, nor of
the greatness or the lowliness of it, no intimation of woman's
perfection in her imperfection! Could there really be one
woman simple and vain and pitiable enough to believe that
within the definition of man she would become more perfect
than man, not to perceive that her loss would be irreparable?
No black-hearted seducer could think up a more dangerous
theory for the woman than this, for once he has deluded her
into thinking this, she is completely in his power, abandoned
to his conditions; she can be nothing for the man except a prey
to his whims, whereas as woman she can be everything to
him. But the poor wretches do not know what they are doing;
they themselves are not much good at being men, and instead
of learning how to be men they want to corrupt the woman
and be united on the condition that they themselves remain
what they are, half-men, and the woman advances to the same
wretchedness.

II
280

I recall having read a not unwitty jibe at the emancipation of
women. The author dwelt particularly on clothing, which in
this case he thought ought to be identical for men and women.
Just imagine this atrocity. At the time, it seemed to me that the
author had not comprehended his task deeply enough, that the
contrasts he presented were not sufficiently relevant to the
idea. For a moment I shall venture to imagine something unbeautiful, for I know that the beauty will then manifest itself
in all its truth. What is more beautiful than a woman's luxuriant hair, than this exuberance of curls? And yet Scripture says
that this is a symbol of her imperfection and cites several reasons for it.[141] And is it not true! Watch her when she bows her

head toward the earth, when her luxuriant braids almost touch the earth, and they look as if they were the flower's tendrils by which she has grown fixed to the earth; does she not stand there a more imperfect creature than man, who gazes up toward heaven[142] and only touches the earth? And yet this hair is her beauty, yes, what is more, her strength, for it is with this, as the poet says, that she captivates man; it is with this that she captivates man and binds him to the earth. I would like to tell an oaf who preaches emancipation: Look! There she stands in all her imperfection, a more inferior creature than man; if you have courage, snip off those abundant curls, cut those heavy chains—and let her run like a crazy person, a criminal, to the terror of people.

Let man give up the claim to be nature's lord and prince; let him yield that place to woman. She is nature's mistress; her it understands, and she understands it; it is at her beck and call. The reason she is everything to man is that she presents him with the finite; without her he is an unstable spirit, an unhappy creature who cannot find rest, has no abode. It has frequently been my delight to see woman's meaning in this way; on the whole she is to me a symbol of the congregation, and the spirit is in great distress when it does not have a congregation in which to live, and when it lives in the congregation, it is the spirit of the congregation. This is why, as I already pointed out previously, Scripture does not say that a woman should leave father and mother and cling to her husband,[143] which one would expect, for, after all, woman is the weaker one who seeks protection from the man—no, it says that the man should leave father and mother and cling to his wife, because to the extent she bestows the finite on him, she is stronger than he. Thus nothing provides as beautiful an image of the congregation as a woman does. If one would look at it this way, I really believe many prospects for beautifying the church service would open up. How crude of our churches to have the congregation, provided it does not represent itself, be represented by a parish clerk or sexton. It should always be represented by a woman.

A really beneficial impression of the congregation I have al-

II
281

ways found to be lacking in our church service, and yet there
was a year in my life when every Sunday I came fairly close to
my idealized conception. It was in one of our churches here in
the city. The church itself appealed to me very much. The clergyman I heard every Sunday was a most worthy person, a
character in a class by himself, who knew how to draw the old
and the new[144] from the experiences of an eventful life; he was
entirely at home in the pulpit. As a pastor he satisfied the entire
ideal demand of my soul; he satisfied it as a figure, as an orator.
Every Sunday I was very happy when I thought of going to
hear him, but what contributed to enhancing my joy and made
the impression of the divine worship in this church complete
for me was another character, an elderly woman who likewise
appeared every Sunday. She was accustomed to coming a little
before the service began, and I likewise. To me her personality
was a symbol of the congregation, and seeing her I quite forgot the disturbing impression made by the parish clerk at the
church door. She was a woman along in years, looked to be
about sixty years old, but was still beautiful; her features were
noble, her expression full of a certain humble dignity, her
countenance an expression of her deep, pure, feminine de-
cency. She seemed to have experienced much, not just stormy
events, but as a mother who had carried the burdens of life and
yet preserved and won a joy over life. When I saw her enter far
down the aisle, when the sexton had met her at the door and
now, like a servant, respectfully escorted her to her pew, I
knew she would also pass the pew in which I was accustomed
to sit. As she walked by, I always arose and bowed to her, or,
as it says in the Old Testament, I did obeisance [*neiede*][145] to
her. For me this bow implied so very much; it was as if I
wanted to entreat her to include me in her intercessions. She
entered her pew; she nodded graciously to the sexton; she remained standing a moment, she bowed her head, briefly held
a handkerchief to her eyes for a prayer—it would take a powerful preacher to make as strong and beneficent an impression
as the solemnity of that venerable woman did.

At times it occurred to me: perhaps even you are included in
her prayer, for it is a woman's nature to pray for others. Imag-

ine her in whatever station of life you please, at any age whatsoever, imagine her praying, and as a rule you will find her
praying for others, for her parents, for her beloved, for her
husband, for her children, always for others. Man by nature
prays for himself. He has his specific task, his specific place.
Therefore, his resignation is different; even in prayer he is
struggling. He gives up on the fulfillment of his wish, and
what he prays for is the strength to be able to renounce it. Even
when he wishes for something, this idea is continually present.
Woman's prayer is much more substantial, her resignation different. She prays for the fulfillment of her wish; she gives up
on herself, that she would be able to make any difference. But
this, again, is why she is much better qualified to pray for
others than the man is, for if he wanted to pray for someone
else, he would essentially pray that the person might be
granted the strength to bear and happily to surmount the pain
caused by not having his wish fulfilled. But such an intercessory prayer is imperfect as intercessory prayer, although as a
prayer for oneself it is true and proper. In this respect man and
woman form, so to speak, two ranks. First comes woman
with her intercessory prayer; she moves, as it were, the deity
with her tears. Then comes man with his prayer; he halts the
first rank when in fear it wants to run away; he has another
kind of tactic that always brings victory. This, again, is because the man pursues the infinite. If woman loses the battle,
then from man she must learn to pray, and yet intercessory
prayer is so essentially her nature that even in that case her intercessory prayer for man will be different from his own
prayer. In a certain sense, then, woman has more faith than
man, because woman believes that for God all things are possible;[146] man believes that for God something is impossible.
Woman becomes more and more fervent in her humble peti-
tioning. Man gives up more and more, until he finds the im-
movable point from which he cannot be ousted. This is because it is in man's nature to have doubted, and all his wisdom
bears the mark of this.

My joy over the beautiful worship service in that church,
however, was short-lived. After a year, the pastor was trans-

ferred; the venerable matron—I could almost call her my devout mother—I saw no more. But I often thought of her. Later, when I was married, she often drifted into my thoughts. If the Church were aware of such things, our worship service would probably gain in beauty and solemnity. Imagine being at a baptism if a woman of such merit stood at the pastor's side and said Amen instead of having the sexton bray it as now. Imagine being at a wedding ceremony—would it not be beautiful, for who can give as sublime an impression of the beauty of an intercessory prayer as such a woman can!

But here I sit and preach and forget what I really should be speaking about, forget that it is you to whom I should be speaking. It is due to my having completely forgotten you because of my new friend. You see, I like to speak about such things with him; for one thing, he is no scoffer; for another, he is a married man, and only the person who has an eye for the beauty of marriage will also be able to see the truth in what I am saying.

So I turn back to our hero. This title he certainly deserves, but I shall not use it for him any more in the future but prefer another designation that is dearer to me; when I sincerely call him my friend, so do I with joy call myself his friend. You see, his life has supplied him with "that superfluous article that is called a friend."[147] You perhaps thought that in silence I would bypass friendship and its ethical validity or, more correctly, that it would be an impossibility for me to find an opportunity to speak of friendship since it has no ethical significance whatsoever but falls entirely within esthetic categories. It perhaps surprises you that I, provided I wanted to discuss it, first discuss it here, because friendship, after all, is youth's first dream; it is precisely in early youth that the soul is so tender and inspired that it seeks friendship. Therefore, it would have been more appropriate to speak of friendship before I had my friend enter the holy estate of marriage. I could answer that, curiously enough, in my friend's case it happened that before he was married he actually had not felt himself drawn to any person to such a degree that he dared designate their relation as friendship. I could add that I was glad of this, because I wanted to treat friendship last, since I do not consider that the ethical in it has validity in the same sense as in marriage, and precisely in this I see its imperfection. This answer might seem inadequate insofar as it is conceivable that it was an incidental abnormality in my friend; therefore, I am willing to dwell on this more meticulously.

You are indeed an observer, and therefore you will agree with me in the observation that a distinguishable individual difference is indicated if the period of one's friendship is in very early youth or not until a later age. The more superficial natures have no trouble feeling at home with themselves. At the very outset, their selves are current coinage, and now the transaction called friendship begins. It is not so easy for deeper natures to find themselves, and as long as they have not found their selves they cannot wish anyone to offer them a friendship that they cannot return. Such natures are partly absorbed in themselves, are partly observers, but an observer is no friend. This would have been the explanation if this had been the case with my friend. It would not be anything abnormal or a sign of his imperfection either. Indeed, he did marry.

Now the question is whether it was an abnormality that friendship did not appear until afterward, because previously we agreed only that it was proper that friendship commences at a later age, but we did not speak of its relation to marriage. Here let us once again use your power of observation and mine. We must also include the relation to the opposite sex in our deliberation. It often happens with those who seek friendship at a very early age that when erotic love [*Elskov*] begins to manifest itself, friendship dwindles entirely. They find that friendship was an imperfect form; they break the earlier relationships and concentrate all their soul exclusively on marriage. For others the reverse happens. Those who tasted the sweetness of erotic love too early, relished its joys in the intoxication of youth, may have a wrong view of the opposite sex. They perhaps became unjust to the opposite sex. Because of their light-mindedness they perhaps purchased costly experiences, perhaps believed in feelings within themselves that proved to have no constancy, or believed in feelings in others

II
285

that vanished like a dream. Then they abandoned love; it was both too much and too little for them, because they had come up against the dialectical in erotic love without being able to solve it. Now they chose friendship. Both these forms must be regarded as abnormal.

My friend is in neither of these situations. He had not made youthful attempts at friendship before he learned to know erotic love, but neither had he harmed himself by indulging in the immature fruit of erotic love too early. In his love [*Kjærlighed*] he found the deepest and fullest satisfaction, but precisely because he himself was so absolutely composed there emerged from him the possibility of other relationships, which in another way could acquire both deep and beautiful significance for him, because to him who has still more will be given[148] and he shall have in superabundance. In this connection, he is accustomed to recollect that there are trees on which the flower comes after the fruit and is also contemporary with it. He compares his life to such a tree.

But precisely because it was in and through his marriage that he learned to see the beauty in having a friend or friends, he has at no time been perplexed about how friendship ought to be regarded and how it loses its significance if it is not regarded ethically. The many experiences of his life had somewhat demolished his faith in the esthetes, but marriage had completely rooted out every trace of that in his soul. Thus he felt no need to be fascinated by esthetic juggling but had immediately acquiesced in the view of the ethicist.

If my friend had not been so disposed, I could have enjoyed referring him to you as a punishment, for your discourse on this topic is confused to such a degree that he probably would have become utterly bewildered by listening to you. You do the same with friendship as with everything else. Your soul so
lacks ethical focus that one can receive diametrically opposed explanations from you on the same subject, and your remarks eminently prove the correctness of the thesis that sentimentality and callousness are one and the same. Your attitude to friendship is best compared to a "magic" picture,[149] and the person who is willing to adopt it must go mad, just as the per-

son who propounds it must to some extent be presumed to be mad. If one listens to you—if you are so moved—holding forth on the divineness of loving young men, the beauty in the meeting of kindred souls, one can almost be tempted to fear that your sentimentality will cost you your young life. At other times, you talk in such a way one would almost believe you were an old hand at this game and had adequately experienced the emptiness and hollowness of the world. "A friend," you say, "is an enigma; like fog, he is seen only at a distance, for only when a person has become unhappy does he realize that he *has had* a friend." It is easy to see that the basis for such a judgment upon friendship is a claim on it different from the one you made before. You spoke before of intellectual friendship, of the beauty in the spiritual erotic, in a common passion for ideas; now you speak of a practical friendship in dealings, of mutual assistance in the inconveniences of earthly life. There is some truth in both claims, but if one cannot find a point of unity for them, it is surely best to concur with your principal conclusion, that friendship is nonsense, a conclusion you draw in part from each of your theses, in part from both of them in their struggle against each other.

The absolute condition for friendship is unity in a life-view. If a person has that, he will not be tempted to base his friendship on obscure feelings or on indefinable sympathies. As a consequence, he will not experience these ridiculous shifts, so that one day he has a friend and the next day he does not. He will not fail to appreciate the significance of the indefinable sympathies, because, strictly speaking, a person is certainly not a friend of everyone with whom he shares a life-view, but neither does he stop with only the mysteriousness of the sympathies. A true friendship always requires consciousness and is thereby freed from being infatuation [*Sværmeri*].

The life-view in which one is united must be a positive view. My friend and I, we share such a positive view. Therefore, when we look at each other, we do not begin to laugh as those augurs did;[150] on the contrary, we become earnest. It was quite appropriate for the augurs to laugh, because their shared life-view was a negative one. You understand that very well, because it is one of your extravagant wishes "to find a soul of like mind with whom you can laugh at it all, and the terrible thing about life, the almost alarming thing, is that scarcely anyone notices how wretched it is, and of these few it is only a very rare exception who knows how to keep in good humor and laugh at it all." If your longing is not alleviated, you know how to put up with it, "for it is pursuant to the idea that there is only one who laughs; such a one is the true pessimist; if there were many of that kind, it would indeed be a demonstration that the world is not utterly wretched." Now your thought is in full swing and knows no bounds. You believe, then, "that even laughing is itself only an imperfect expression for the real mockery of life. If it is to be perfect, one would actually have to be earnest. [151]It would be the consummate mockery of the world if the person who had propounded the most profound truth was not a visionary but a doubter. And that is not inconceivable, because no one can present the positive truth as superbly as a doubter, except that he does not believe it himself. If he were a hypocrite, the mockery would be at his own expense. If he were a doubter who himself perhaps wanted to believe what he was presenting, the mockery would be completely objective, existence would mock itself through him. He would present a doctrine that could explain everything; the whole human race could rest in it, but this doctrine could not explain its own founder. If a person were mad but so clever that he could hide his madness, he could make the whole world mad." See, if someone has a view of life like that, it is hard to find a friend who shares his life-view. Or have you perhaps found such a friend in the mystical society of Συμπαρανεκρώμενοι[152] of which you sometimes speak? Are you perhaps an association of friends who mutually regard each other as so very clever that you know how to hide your madness?!

[153]There was in Greece a wise man. He enjoys the singular honor of being counted among the seven wise men if it is assumed that the number of these was fourteen. If I am not mistaken his name is Myson. An ancient author states that he was a misanthrope. He is very brief: "It is said of Myson that he

was a misanthrope and that he laughed when he was alone. When someone asked him why he did so, he answered: Simply because I am alone."[154] You see, you have a predecessor; you will aspire in vain to be included among the number of the seven wise men, even if the number were set at twenty-one, for Myson stands in your way. But this is of minor importance; you yourself, however, will perceive that the person who laughs when he is alone cannot possibly have a friend, and for two reasons: partly because as long as the friend is present he cannot laugh, and partly because the friend is bound to fear that he is merely waiting for him to leave so that he can laugh at him. So, you see, the devil must be your friend. I could almost be tempted to ask you to take these words literally, for the devil is also said to laugh when he is alone. To me there is something very disconsolate in an isolation like that, and I cannot stop thinking how horrible it will be when a person who has lived in that way wakes up in another life on judgment day and again stands there all alone.

Consequently, friendship requires a positive life-view. But a positive view of life is unimaginable unless it has an ethical element in it. It is true that in our day we frequently enough meet people who have a system in which the ethical is not found at all. Let them have a system ten times over—a life-view they do not have. In our age, such a phenomenon can be explained very well, because, just as it is topsy-turvy in so many ways, it is here also in that one is initiated into the great mysteries before one is initiated into the lesser ones.[155] So the ethical element in the life-view becomes the essential point of departure for friendship, and not until friendship is looked at in this way does it gain meaning and beauty. If one stops with the sympathetic as the mysterious, friendship will find its fullest expression in the relation that prevails among gregarious birds whose concordance is so ardent that the death of one is the death of the other. In nature such a relation is beautiful, but in the world of spirit it is unbecoming. Unity in a life-view is the constituting element in friendship. If this is present, the friendship lasts even if the friend dies, inasmuch as the transfigured friend lives on in the other; if this ceases, the friendship is over even if the friend goes on living.

If friendship is looked at in this way, one is looking at it ethically and therefore according to its beauty. Then it gains beauty and meaning simultaneously. Must I cite an authority on my behalf and against you? So be it! How did Aristotle conceive of friendship? Did he not make it the point of departure for his entire ethical view of life, for with friendship, he says, the concepts of what is just are so expanded that they all amount to the same thing. So he bases the concept of justice on the idea of friendship.[156] In a certain sense, then, his category is superior to the modern one, which bases justice upon duty, the abstract-categorical;[157] he bases it upon the social. From this it is easy to see that for him the idea of the state becomes the highest,[158] but this, in turn, is the imperfection of his category.

I shall not, however, make so bold as to enter into such investigations as the relation between the Aristotelian and the Kantian views of the ethical. I mentioned Aristotle only to remind you that he, too, realized that friendship contributes to a person's ethical achieving of actuality.

The person who views friendship ethically sees it, then, as a duty. Therefore, I could say that it is every person's duty to have a friend. But I would rather use another expression that indicates the ethical in friendship and in everything that has been previously developed and at the same time sharply emphasizes the difference between the ethical and the esthetic: namely, [159]it is every human being's duty to become open. Scripture teaches that it is appointed to every human being to die and after that come to judgment, when everything will be disclosed.[160] Ethics says that it is the meaning of life and actuality that a person become open. If he does not, then the disclosure will prove to be a punishment. The esthete, however, does not want to give meaning to actuality; he continually remains hidden, because however often and however much he gives himself to the world, he never does it totally; there is always something he holds back. If he did it totally, he would do it ethically. But this wanting to play hide-and-seek always takes revenge, and usually in the form of one's becoming an enigma to oneself. That is why all mystics, inasmuch as they do not recognize actuality's demand that one must become open, encounter difficulties and spiritual trials that no one else knows anything about. It is as if they discovered an entirely different world, as if their nature were in itself double. Anyone who refuses to struggle with actualities acquires phantoms to struggle against.

With this I am through for now. It was never my purpose to present a doctrine of duty. What I wanted to do was to show how the ethical in the mixed territories is so far from depriving life of its beauty that it expressly gives it beauty. It gives life peace, safety, and security, because it continually calls out to us: *Quod petis, hic est* [What you are seeking is here].[161] It rescues from any fanaticism that would exhaust the soul and gives it health and strength. It teaches us not to overrate the accidental or to idolize good fortune. It teaches us to be happy over good fortune, and even this the esthete is not able to do, because good fortune as such is only an infinite relativity; it teaches us to be happy in misfortune.

II
290

Consider what I have written as a trifle; consider it as notes to Balle's catechism—it does not matter—yet it has an authority that I hope you will respect. Or does it perhaps seem to you that I have illegitimately arrogated such authority to myself, that I have improperly introduced my public position into this private dispute, have behaved like a judge and not as a litigant? I readily abandon every claim; I am not even a litigant in opposition to you, for although I willingly admit that esthetics would gladly give you power of attorney to represent it, I am far from daring to credit myself with enough significance to represent ethics with full power of attorney. If I am anything at all, I am nothing more than a witness, and it is only in this sense that I thought this letter had a certain authority, because the words of one who speaks about what he has experienced always have authority. I am only a witness, and you have my deposition *in optima forma* [in perfectly correct form].

I do my work as a judge in the court. I am happy in my calling; I believe it suits my capabilities and my whole personality;

I know that it demands all my capacities. I try to educate myself more and more for it, and in so doing I feel also that I am developing myself more and more. I love my wife, am happy in my home; I listen to my wife's lullaby, and to me it is more beautiful than any other song, but I do not therefore believe that she is a singer; I listen to the little one cry, and to my ears it is not discordant. I watch his older brother grow and make progress; I gaze happily and confidently into his future, not impatiently, for I have time enough to wait, and to me this waiting is in itself a joy. My work has meaning for me, and I believe that to a certain degree it also has meaning for others, even if I cannot define and measure it exactly. I rejoice that the personal lives of others have meaning for me and wish and hope that mine may also have meaning for those with whom I in my whole view of life am in sympathy. I love my native country, and I cannot imagine that I could really thrive in any other country. I love my mother tongue, which liberates my thoughts; I find that in it I can express extremely well what I may have to say in the world. In this way my life has meaning for me, so much that I feel happy and satisfied with it. Amidst all this, I also live a higher life, and when it happens at times that I inhale this higher life in the breathing of my earthly and domestic life, I count myself blessed, then art and grace fuse for me. So I love life because it is beautiful and hope for one even more beautiful.

Here you have my deposition. If I were to doubt whether it was right to submit it, it would be out of solicitude for you, because I am almost afraid that it will pain you to hear that life in its simplicity can be so beautiful. But accept my testimony anyway; let it cause you a little pain, but let it also have a gratifying effect on you. It has one quality that your life, I regret, does not have—faithfulness; you can safely build upon it.

Recently I have often spoken about you with my wife. She is really very fond of you, but no doubt I scarcely need to say this, because you have many capacities for being appealing if you so desire, but you have a still greater visual capacity for observing whether you succeeded. Her feeling for you has my full approval. I do not become jealous easily, and it would also

II
291

be indefensible on my part, not because I am too proud to be that, as you think one ought to be, proud enough "promptly to be able to give a receipt with thanks," but because my wife is too lovable for that. I have no fears.

In that respect, I think I may venture to say that Scribe himself would despair over our prosaic marriage, because I believe that even for him it would be impossible to make it poetic. That Scribe has capacities and talents, I do not deny, but that he, in my way of thinking, misuses his gifts, I do not deny either. Does he not do everything to teach young women that marriage's assured love is too little to make life poetic, that it would be unbearable if one could not count on little love affairs on the side?[162] Does he not show them that a woman continues to be charming even if she sullies herself and her marriage by a guilty love? Does he not darkly hint that, since a relationship such as this is discovered usually by accident, in real life a person might hope to hide her affair for a lifetime if she adds her own craftiness to what she has learned from the heroine in his play? Does he not try in every way to make husbands uneasy, does he not present the most respectable of women, of whom no one would dare to suspect anything, as sullied by a secret guilt? Does he not show again and again the vanity of what has hitherto been considered the best means to safeguard marital happiness, the vanity of a husband's placing unlimited trust in his wife, believing in her more than in anything else? Despite all this, it pleases Scribe that every married man is supposed to be a phlegmatic and sleepy sluggard, an imperfect creature who is himself to blame for his wife's delinquency. I wonder if Scribe is so modest as to assume that one learns nothing at all from his plays, for otherwise he would have to see that every husband would very soon have to discover that his position was by no means secure and peaceful, indeed, that no police informer could lead as jumpy and sleepless a life as he is compelled to lead, unless he tranquilizes himself with Scribe's consolations and himself seeks a diversion similar to his wife's and contends that marriage actually exists to remove every tiresome appearance of innocence from the liaison with others and to make it really interesting?

II
292

However, I let Scribe go; I am not in a position to combat him, but at times I think with a certain pride that by my marriage I, a lowly, insignificant man, make a liar of the great poet Scribe. Perhaps this pride is only a beggar's pride; perhaps I succeed only because I am an ordinary human being who stands outside poetry.

So my wife is fond of you, and I sympathize with her feelings on this matter, all the more so since I believe that the basis of her good will toward you involves in part her awareness of your weaknesses. She sees very well that you lack a certain degree of womanliness. You are too proud to be able to devote yourself. This pride tempts her in no way, because she considers it as true greatness to be able to devote oneself. You may not believe that, but I can assure you that I really do come to
your defense against her. She maintains that you in your pride reject everybody; I try to explain that perhaps the situation is not quite like that, that you reject people in the infinite sense, that the restlessness with which your soul seeks after the infinite makes you unjust to people. She will not comprehend that, and that I can understand very well, for when someone is as contented as she is—and how contented she is you can see, for example, in her feeling so indescribably happy over being united to me—it is difficult to avoid being critical of you. Thus my marriage also has conflict, and in a way it is your fault. We come out of it all right, and I only wish that you may never be the occasion for a conflict in someone else's marriage. You could, however, be somewhat instrumental in resolving the conflict between my wife and me. Do not think I want to force my way into your secrets, but I do have just one question to ask you, one that I believe you can answer without infringement on your rights. For once answer me very honestly and without beating about the bush: Do you really laugh when you are alone? You do understand what I mean; I do not mean whether it sometimes or even frequently happens that you laugh when you are alone, but whether you find your satisfaction in this solitary laughter. If you do not, then I have won, and then I shall certainly convince my wife.

Now, whether you, when you are alone, actually spend

your time laughing, I do not know, but that would be somewhat more than odd, it seems to me. Certainly the trend of your life is such that you must sometimes feel the urge to seek solitude, but not, as far as I can ascertain, in order to laugh. Just the most casual observation indicates that your life is patterned according to an unusual standard. You do not seem at all to find your satisfaction in following the public highways but prefer to take your own course. A young person can be forgiven a certain adventurousness; it is another matter when it so gains the upper hand that it wants to make itself the normal and the actual. We owe it to a person who is aberrant in this way to shout to him: *respice finem* [think of the end],[163] and explain that the word *finis* does not mean death, because even that is not a human being's most difficult task, but life, that there comes a moment when in reality the thing to do is to begin to live, and that it is dangerous then to have become so fragmented that to collect himself involves enormous difficulty—indeed, that he is compelled to do this in such haste that he cannot pull everything together and then ends up being a defective specimen of a human being instead of an extraordinary human being.

II
294

In the Middle Ages, the matter was approached in another way. One suddenly discontinued the course of one's life and entered the monastery. The mistake surely was not that one entered the monastery but the wrong ideas associated with this step. I for my part can very well reconcile myself to a person's deciding to do this—in fact, I can see it as really beautiful; but on the other hand I insist that he realize what it means. In the Middle Ages it was thought that in choosing the monastery one chose the extraordinary and became an extraordinary person oneself; from the altitude of the monastery one looked down proudly, almost pityingly, on the ordinary people. No wonder that people flocked into the monastery when they could become extraordinary persons at such a bargain! But the gods do not sell the extraordinary at a ridiculously low price.[164] If those who withdrew from life had been honest and frank with themselves and others, if they had loved being a human being above all else, if they had felt with some enthusiasm all the beauty there is in being human, if their hearts had not been unacquainted with genuine, deep human feelings, they perhaps would have also withdrawn into the solitude of the monastery, but they would not have foolishly deluded themselves into thinking that they had become extraordinary persons, except in the sense that they were more imperfect than others; they would not have looked down pityingly on the ordinary people but would have looked at them sympathetically, with a sad kind of joy that they succeeded in accomplishing the beautiful and the great that they themselves were unable to accomplish.

In our day the market value of the monastic life has fallen; we seldom see a person break altogether with existence, with the universally human. However, anyone with a more intimate knowledge of men will occasionally find in a single individual a heterodoxy that is vividly reminiscent of the monastic theory. For the sake of order, I shall here and now promptly state my idea of what an extraordinary person is. The genuinely extraordinary person is the genuinely ordinary person. The more of the universally human an individual can actualize in his life, the more extraordinary a human being he is. The less of the universal he can assimilate, the more imperfect he is. It is true that he may then be an extraordinary person, but not in the good sense.

If, then, a person, in his seeking to fulfill the task that is assigned to him as to everyone else—to express the universally human in his individual life—encounters difficulties, if it seems to become apparent that there is something of the universal he cannot incorporate in his life, what does he do then? If he is obsessed with the monastic theory, or with a quite analogous esthetic view, he is delighted; from the very outset he promptly feels himself in all his exclusiveness to be an exception, an extraordinary person, becomes conceited about it, just as childishly as if a nightingale that had a red feather in its wing were to be delighted that no other nightingale had anything like that. But if his soul is ennobled by love of the universal, if he loves man's life in this world, what does he do then? He ponders whether this is true. A person may himself be guilty of this imperfection; he may have it without guilt, but it may be true that he cannot actualize the universal. If people on the whole were more enterprising about becoming conscious of themselves, perhaps many more of them would arrive at this conclusion. He will also be aware that laziness and cowardliness can delude a person about such things and make the pain a triviality as he transforms the universal into the particular and in relation to the universal maintains an abstract possibility. In other words, the universal in itself is nowhere to be found, and it is up to me, to my enterprising consciousness, whether I will see the universal in the particular or see only the particular.

Perhaps this kind of deliberation will not seem adequate to him, and he will try an experiment. He will readily perceive that if the experiment brings him to the same conclusion, the truth will be all the more emphatically impressed upon him, and if he wants to coddle himself, he perhaps had better leave it alone, since he will smart with pain more than ever. He will realize that no particular is the universal. Then if he does not wish to deceive himself, he will transform the particular into the universal. He will see much more in the particular than what lies therein as such; for him it is the universal. He will come to the aid of the particular and give it meaning as the universal. If he then detects that the experiment is a failure, he will have arranged everything so that what wounds him is not the particular but the universal. He will keep watch on himself so that no mistake occurs, so that it is not the particular that wounds him, for its wound will be too light and he will love himself too earnestly to attach the greatest importance to receiving a light wound. He will love the universal too honestly to want to substitute the particular for it with the intention of escaping from it without a scratch. He will keep watch on himself lest he smile at the powerless reaction of the particular, will see to it that he does not ever regard the matter trivially, even if the particular as such tempts him to do so; he will not allow himself to be distracted by the curious misunderstanding that the particular has a greater friend in him than it has in itself. When he has done this, he will calmly go to meet the pain; even if his consciousness is shaken, it does not hesitate.

If it so happens that the universal he is unable to actualize is the very thing he desired, then in one sense he will, if he is high-minded, rejoice in this circumstance. He will then say: I have struggled under the most unfavorable conditions possible; I have struggled against the particular; I have transferred my desire to the side of the enemy; to make it compete, I have made the particular the universal. It is true that all this will make the defeat harder for me, but it will also strengthen my consciousness and give it energy and clarity.

At this point, then, he has emancipated himself from the universal. At no time will the meaning of such a step be unclear to him, because it was indeed actually he himself who made the defeat total and gave it meaning, for he knew where and how he was vulnerable, and he inflicted on himself the wound that the particular as such was unable to inflict. He will then be convinced that there is something of the universal that he cannot actualize. But he is not finished with this conviction, for it will generate a profound sorrow in his soul. He will rejoice over the others to whom it is granted to consummate it; perhaps he will perceive even better than they how beautiful it is, but he himself will grieve, not cravenly and dejectedly, but deeply and openly, for he will say: Nevertheless, I do love the universal. If it is the happy fate of others to testify to the universally human by actualizing it, well, then I testify to it by my grief, and the more deeply I grieve, the more significant is my testimony. And this grief is beautiful, is itself an expression of the universally human, an emotion of its heart within him, and will reconcile him with it.

With this conviction he has won he is not finished, because he will feel that he has placed an enormous responsibility upon himself. At this point, he says, I have placed myself outside the universal; I have deprived myself of all the guidance, the security, and the reassurance that the universal gives; I stand alone, without fellow-feeling, for I am an exception. But he will not become craven and disconsolate; he will confidently go his solitary way; indeed, he has demonstrated the correctness of what he did—he has his pain. He will not lack clarity about the step he has taken; he has an explanation that he can produce at any time. No tumult can confuse it for him, no absence of mind; if he woke up in the middle of the night, he would instantly be able to account for everything to himself. He will feel that the upbringing that has become his lot is hard, because the universal is a severe master when one has it outside oneself. It continually holds the sword of judgment over him and asks, "Why do you want to be an outsider?" And even if he says, "It is not my fault," it still blames him for it and demands itself of him. At times he will come back to the same point, go through the demonstration again and again, and then will go on dauntlessly. He rests in the conviction he has won and says, "What I depend on ultimately is that there is a just reasonableness, and I will put my trust in its mercy, that it is merciful enough to do justice, [165]for it certainly would not be dreadful if I should suffer the punishment that I deserved because I did wrong, but it would be dreadful if I should be able to do the wrong in such a way that no one punished it. And it certainly would not be dreadful if in the beguilement of my heart I were to wake up with anxiety and horror, but it would be dreadful if I could so beguile my heart that no one could awaken it."

This whole struggle, however, is a purgatory, the dreadfulness of which I can at least form an idea. People should not aspire to be extraordinary, because to be that means something different from a capricious satisfaction of one's arbitrary desire.

But the person who in pain has convinced himself that he was an extraordinary man, and who through his sorrow over it became reconciled again with the universal, will perhaps experience at some time the joy that what caused him pain and made him inferior in his own eyes proves to be an occasion for his being raised up again and in a nobler sense becoming an extraordinary human being. What he lost in extensiveness he may win in intensive inwardness. In other words, not everyone whose life is a mediocre expression of the universal is therefore an extraordinary person, for that would indeed be an idolization of triviality; for him to be called that legitimately, some questions must be asked about the intensive vitality with which he does this. That other one will now have this vitality at the points where he is able to actualize the universal. Then his grief will vanish again, will dissolve in harmony, because he will perceive that he has reached the limit of his individuality. He is well aware that every human being develops in freedom, but he is also aware that a person does not create himself out of nothing, that he has himself in its concretion as his task; he will once again be reconciled with existence in perceiving that in a certain sense every person is an exception, and that it is equally true that every human being is the universally human and also an exception.

Here you have my view of what it is to be an extraordinary person. I love life and being a human being too much to believe that the way to become an extraordinary person is easy or without spiritual trials. But even if a person is an extraordinary human being in the nobler sense, he nevertheless will continually admit that it would be even more perfect to incorporate the entire universal in himself.

So accept my greeting, take my friendship, for although, strictly speaking, I dare not describe our relationship this way, I nevertheless hope that my young friend may some day be so much older that I shall dare to use this word legitimately. Be assured of my fellow-feeling. Accept a greeting from her whom I love, whose thoughts are hidden in my thoughts; accept a greeting that is inseparable from mine, but accept also a special greeting from her, friendly and honest as always.

When you were here with us a few days ago, you perhaps had no idea that I once again had finished writing so voluminous a letter. I know that you do not take kindly to having anyone speak to you about your inner history; I have, therefore, chosen to write and will never speak to you of such matters. It will remain a secret that you are receiving a letter like this, and I would not want it to have any influence in changing your relationship with me and my family. I know that you have virtuosity enough to do that if you so desire, and this is why I ask it for your sake and for my own. I have never wanted to thrust myself upon you and am well able to love you at a distance, although we see each other frequently. You are too inclosed by nature for me to believe it would do any good to speak to you, but I do hope that my letters will not be without meaning. So when you work on yourself in the sealed-off machinery of your personality, I put in my contributions and am sure that they will be incorporated into the movement.

Since our relationship by letter remains a secret, I observe all the formalities, bid you farewell as if we lived a long way from each other, although I hope to see you at my house just as often as before.[166]

ULTIMATUM [A FINAL WORD]

Perhaps you have forgotten, just as I have, most of the contents of my previous letters. If so, I wish that you may be able, as I am, at any time and in any variable mood to give an account to yourself of the thought and the development. Like the flower that comes year after year, the expression, the presentation, the wrappings are the same and yet not the same, but the attitude, the development, the position are unchanged. If I were to write to you now, I perhaps would express myself differently. Perhaps at some point in my letters I even managed to be eloquent, something to which I certainly make no claim and which my position in life does not require of me either. If I were to write now, I might succeed at another point. I do not know, for expression is a gift, and "every age and every year has its own flowering springtime."[1] As far as the thought is concerned, however, it is and remains the same,[2] and I hope that in time the movements of thought will become easier and more natural for me, unchanged even if they are silent because the expression has faded.

I do not, however, pick up my pen for the purpose of writing a new letter to you but rather because the thought of you has been made so vivid to me by a letter I have received from an older friend who is a pastor in Jylland. As far as I know, you have never met him. My friendship with him began as early as my student days, and although there were five or six years between us, our relationship was nevertheless quite intimate. [3]He was a stocky little fellow, lively, cheerful, and unusually jovial. Although in the depths of his soul he was deeply earnest, in his outward life he seemed to follow the advice "Let things take their course." Scholarly studies enthralled him, but he was no good at taking the examinations. In his theological examination, he managed no more than a *haud illaudabilis* [not unpraiseworthy].[4] Five years ago, he was stuck out in a little parish on the heath in Jylland. He possessed, among his exter-

nal qualities, a stentorian voice; among his intellectual–spiritual qualities, he had an originality that always distinguished
him in the little circle in which I learned to know him. No
wonder, then, that in the beginning he was not entirely satisfied, that he thought his work was too insignificant for him.
But now he has regained his contentment, and it was really encouraging for me to read a letter I just received from him.
"The heath in Jylland," he says, "is a real playground for me,
a private study room beyond compare. I go out there on Sat-
urday and meditate on my sermons, and everything unfolds
for me. I forget every actual listener and gain an ideal one; I
achieve total absorption in myself. Therefore, when I step into
the pulpit, it is as if I were still standing out there on the heath,
where my eyes see no human being, where my voice rises to
its full power in order to drown out the storm."

It is not, however, to tell you this that I am writing, but to
send you a sermon by him that was enclosed in the letter. Not
wanting to instigate your criticism, I did not wish to show it
to you personally, but send it to you by letter so that it may
make its impression on you in quietness. He has not yet delivered the sermon but intends to deliver it next year and is confident that he will make every peasant understand it. Please do
not disdain it for that reason, because it is precisely the beauty
of the universal that all are able to understand it. In this sermon
he has grasped what I have said and what I would like to have
said to you; he has expressed it better than I am able to. Take
it, then; read it. I have nothing to add except that I have read it
and thought about myself, read it and thought about you.

[5]The Upbuilding That Lies in the Thought That in Relation to God We Are Always in the Wrong.[6]

PRAYER

Father in heaven! Teach us to pray rightly so that our hearts may open up to you in prayer and supplication and hide no furtive desire that we know is not acceptable to you, nor any secret fear that you will deny us anything that will truly be for our good, so that the laboring thoughts, the restless mind, the fearful heart may find rest in and through that alone in which and through which it can be found—by always joyfully thanking you as we gladly confess that in relation to you we are always in the wrong. Amen.

The Holy Gospel is written in the nineteenth chapter of the Gospel of St. Luke, from the forty-first verse to the end,[7] and reads as follows:

And when he drew near and saw the city, he wept over it, saying: Would that even today you knew the things that make for peace! But now they are hid from your eyes. For the days shall come upon you when your enemies will cast up a bank about you and surround you and hem you in on every side, and then will dash you to the ground and your children within you and will not leave one stone upon another in you, because you did not know the time of your visitation. And he entered the temple and began to drive out those who sold, saying to them: It is written, "My house is a house of prayer," but you have made it a den of robbers. And he taught daily in the temple. But the chief priests and the scribes and the principal men of the people sought to destroy him, but they did not find what they should do, for all the people clung to him and listened to him.

The event the Spirit had revealed in visions and dreams to the prophets, what they had proclaimed in a foreboding voice to one generation after the other—the repudiation of the Chosen People, the dreadful destruction of proud Jerusalem—was coming closer and closer. Christ goes up to Jerusalem. He is no prophet who prophesies the future; what he says does not arouse anxious unrest, for what is still hidden he sees before his eyes. He does not prophesy—there is no more time for that—he weeps over Jerusalem. And yet the city still stood in all its glory, and the temple still carried its head high as always, higher than any other building in the world, and Christ himself says: Would that even today you knew what was best for your good, but he also adds: Yet it is hidden from your eyes. In God's eternal counsel, its downfall is decided, and salvation is hidden from the eyes of its inhabitants.

Was, then, the generation living at that time more culpable than the previous one to which it owed its life; was the whole nation degenerate; was there no righteous person in Jerusalem, not a single one who could stay the wrath of God;[8] was there no pious person among all those from whose eyes salvation was hidden? And if there was such a person, was there no gate open for him in the time of anxiety and affliction; when the enemies laid siege to it all around and pressed it on every side, did no angel come down and rescue him before all the gates were closed; was no sign given on his behalf? Yet its downfall was fixed. In vain did the besieged city look in its anxiety for a way out. The hostile army squeezed it in its mighty embrace, and not one escaped, and heaven remained closed, and no angel was dispatched, except the angel of death, which waved its sword over the city.

For the offense this nation had committed, this generation had to pay the penalty; for the offense this generation had committed, each member of the generation had to pay the penalty. Must the righteous, then, suffer with the unrighteous? Is this the zealousness of God—to visit the sins of the fathers on the children to the third and fourth generation,[9] so that he does not punish the fathers but the children? What should we answer? Should we say: It will soon be two thousand years since those days; a nightmare such as that the world never saw before and will presumably never see again; we thank God that we live in peace and security, that the shriek of anxiety from those days sounds very faint to us. We will hope and trust that our days and our children's days may proceed in tranquillity, untouched by the storms of life! We do not feel strong enough to think about such things, but we will thank God that we are not tested in them.

II
309

Can anything more cowardly and dismal than this kind of talk be imagined? Does it explain the unexplainable to say that it has happened only once in the world? Or is this not the unexplainable—that it has happened? And does not this, that it has happened, have the power to make everything else unexplainable, even the explainable? If it happened once in the world that the human condition was essentially different from what it otherwise always is, what assurance is there that it cannot be repeated, what assurance that that was not the true and what ordinarily occurs is the untrue? Or is it a demonstration of the truth that it happens the most frequently? Do not the events that those ages witnessed actually repeat themselves more frequently? Is it not true, something we all have experienced in many ways, that the same thing that happens on a large scale is also experienced on a smaller scale? Do you think, Christ says, that those Galileans whose blood Pilate let be shed were worse sinners than all the other Galileans because they suffered this? Or the eighteen whom the tower in Siloam fell upon and killed, do you think that they were worse offenders than all the others who lived in Jerusalem? Consequently, some of those Galileans were not worse sinners than other people, those eighteen were not more guilty than everybody else who lived in Jerusalem[10]—and yet the innocent shared the same fate as the guilty. You may say that it was a dispensation of providence, not a punishment. But the destruction of Jerusalem was a punishment, and it fell on the innocent just as hard as on the guilty. Therefore you do not want to alarm yourself by deliberating upon such things, for you are able to understand that a person can have adversities and suffering, that such things fall like rain as much on the good as on the evil,[11] but that it is supposed to be a punishment . . . . . And yet this is how Scripture presents it.

Is then the lot of the righteous on a level with the lot of the unrighteous; does then godliness have no promise for this life that is; is then every uplifting thought that once made you so rich in courage and confidence only a fancy, a jugglery that a child believes in, a youth hopes for, but in which someone a little older finds no blessing but only mockery and offense? Yet this thought revolts you; it cannot and must not gain the power to beguile you, must not be able to dull your soul. Justice you will love; justice you will practice early and late. Even if it has no reward, you will practice it. You feel that it has an implicit demand that still must be fulfilled. You will not sink into lethargy and then at some time comprehend that justice did have promises but that you yourself had excluded yourself from them by not doing justice. You will not contend with men; you will contend with God and hold on to him; he is not going to get away from you without blessing you![12]

II
310

Yet Scripture says: You are not to argue with God.[13] Is not that what you are doing? Is not this once again a hopeless way of talking; is Holy Scripture, then, given to humankind only to humiliate it, to annihilate it? By no means! When it says that you are not to argue with God, it means that you must not insist on being in the right in relation to God; you may argue with him only in such a way that you learn that you are in the wrong. Indeed, that is what you yourself should want. To be forbidden to argue with God indicates your perfection and in no way says that you are an inferior being who has no significance for him. The sparrow falls to the ground—in a way it is in the right in relation to God; the lily fades—in a way it is in the right in relation to God. Only man is wrong; to him alone is reserved what is denied to everything else—to be in the wrong in relation to God.

If I should speak in a different way, I would remind you of a wisdom you certainly have frequently heard, a wisdom that knows how to explain everything easily enough without doing an injustice either to God or to human beings. A human being is a frail creature, it says; it would be unreasonable of

God to require the impossible of him. One does what one can, and if one is ever somewhat negligent, God will never forget that we are weak and imperfect creatures. Shall I admire more the sublime concepts of the nature of the Godhead that this ingenuity makes manifest or the profound insight into the human heart, the probing consciousness that scrutinizes itself and now comes to the easy, cozy conclusion: One does what one can? Was it such an easy matter for you, my listener, to determine how much that is: what one can? Were you never in such danger that you almost desperately exerted yourself and yet so infinitely wished to be able to do more, and perhaps someone else looked at you with a skeptical and imploring look, whether it was not possible that you could do more? Or were you never anxious about yourself, so anxious that it seemed to you as if there were no sin so black, no selfishness so loathsome, that it could not infiltrate you and like a foreign power gain control of you? Did you not sense this anxiety? For if you did not sense it, then do not open your mouth to answer, for then you cannot reply to what is being asked; but if you did sense it, then, my listener, I ask you: Did you find rest in those words, "One does what one can"?

Or were you never anxious about others? Did you not see them wavering in life, those you were accustomed to look up to in trust and confidence? And did you not then hear a soft voice whisper to you: If not even those people can accomplish the great things, what then is life but bad troubles, and faith but a snare that wrenches us out into the infinite, where we really are unable to live—far better, then, to forget, to abandon every requirement; did you not hear this voice? For if you did not hear it, then do not open your mouth to answer, for you cannot reply to what is being asked about; but if you did hear it, my listener, I ask you: Was it to your comfort that you said "One does what one can"? Was not the real reason for your unrest that you did not know for sure how much one can do, that it seems to you to be so infinitely much at one moment, and at the next moment so very little? Was not your anxiety so painful because you could not penetrate your consciousness, because the more earnestly, the more fervently you wished to act, the more dreadful became the duplexity in which you found yourself: that you might not have done what you could, or that you might actually have done what you could but no one came to your assistance?

So every more earnest doubt, every deeper care is not calmed by the words: One does what one can. If a person is sometimes in the right, sometimes in the wrong, to some degree in the right, to some degree in the wrong, who, then, is the one who makes that decision except the person himself, but in the decision may he not again be to some degree in the right and to some degree in the wrong? Or is he a different person when he judges his act than when he acts? Is doubt to rule, then, continually to discover new difficulties, and is care to accompany the anguished soul and drum past experiences into it? Or would we prefer continually to be in the right in the way irrational creatures are? Then we have only the choice between being nothing in relation to God or having to begin all over again every moment in eternal torment, yet without being able to begin, for if we are to be able to decide definitely whether we are in the right at the present moment, then this question must be decided definitely with regard to the previous moment, and so on further and further back.

Doubt is again set in motion, care again aroused; let us try to calm it by deliberating on:

THE *UPBUILDING* THAT LIES IN THE THOUGHT THAT IN RELATION TO GOD WE ARE ALWAYS IN THE WRONG.

To be in the wrong—can any more painful feeling than this be imagined? And do we not see that people would rather suffer everything than admit that they are in the wrong? To be sure, we do not sanction such stubbornness, either in ourselves or in others. We think the wiser and better way to act is to admit that we are in the wrong if we actually are in the wrong; we then say that the pain that accompanies the admission will be like a bitter medicine that will heal, but we do not conceal that it is a pain to be in the wrong, a pain to admit it. We suffer the pain because we know that it is to our good; we trust that

sometime we shall succeed in making a more energetic resistance and may reach the point of really being in the wrong only
in very rare instances. This point of view is very natural and
very obvious to everyone. Thus there is something upbuilding
in being in the wrong, provided that we, in admitting it, build
ourselves up by the prospect that it will more and more rarely
be the case. And yet we did not want to calm doubt by this
point of view but rather by reflecting on the upbuilding in the
thought that we are always in the wrong. But if that first point
of view, which provided the hope that in time one would
never be in the wrong, is upbuilding, how then can the opposite point of view also be upbuilding—the view that wants to
teach us that we always, in the future as well as in the past, are
in the wrong?

Your life brings you into a multiplicity of relationships with
other people. Some of them love justice and righteousness;
others do not seem to want to practice them—they do you a
wrong. Your soul is not hardened to the suffering they inflict
upon you in this way, but you search and examine yourself;
you convince yourself that you are in the right, and you rest
calm and strong in this conviction. However much they out-
rage me, you say, they still will not be able to deprive me of
this peace—that I know I am in the right and that I suffer
wrong. In this view there is a satisfaction, a joy, that presumably every one of us has tasted, and when you continue to suffer wrong, you are built up by the thought that you are in the
right. This point of view is so natural, so understandable, so
frequently tested in life, and yet it is not with this that we want
to calm doubt and to heal care but by deliberating upon the upbuilding that lies in the thought that we are always in the
wrong. Can the opposite point of view, then, have the same
effect?

Your life brings you into a multiplicity of relationships with
other people. To some you are drawn by a more fervent love
than to others. Now, if such a person who is the object of your
love were to do you a wrong, is it not true that it would pain
you, that you would scrupulously examine everything but
that you then would say: I know for sure that I am in the right;

this thought will calm me? Ah, if you loved him, then it would not calm you; you would investigate everything. You would be unable to perceive anything else except that he is in the wrong, and yet this certainty would trouble you. You would wish that you might be in the wrong; you would try to find something that could speak in his defense, and if you did not find it, you would find rest only in the thought that you were in the wrong. Or if you were assigned the responsibility for such a person's welfare, you would do everything that was in your power, and when the other person nevertheless paid no attention to it and only caused you trouble, is it not true that you would make an accounting and say: I know I have done right by him? —Oh, no! If you loved him, this thought would only alarm you; you would reach for every probability, and if you found none, you would tear up the accounting in order to help you forget it, and you would strive to build yourself up with the thought that you were in the wrong.

It is painful, then, to be in the wrong and all the more painful the more often one is in the wrong; it is upbuilding to be in the wrong, and all the more upbuilding the more often one is in the wrong. This is indeed a contradiction! How can this be explained except by saying that in the one case you are forced to acknowledge what in the second case you wish to acknowledge? But is not the acknowledgment nevertheless the same; does one's wishing or not wishing have any influence on it? How can this be explained except by saying that in the one case you loved, in the other you did not—in other words, in the one case you were in an infinite relationship with a person, in the other case in a finite relationship? Therefore, wishing to be in the wrong is an expression of an infinite relationship, and wanting to be in the right, or finding it painful to be in the wrong, is an expression of a finite relationship! Hence it is upbuilding always to be in the wrong—because only the infinite builds up; the finite does not!

Now, if it were a person whom you loved, even if your love managed piously to deceive your thinking and yourself, you would still be in a continual contradiction, because you would know you were right but you wished and wished to believe

that you were in the wrong. If, however, it was God you
loved, could there then be any question of such a contradiction, could you then be conscious of anything else than what
you wished to believe? Would not he who is in heaven be
greater than you who live on earth; would not his wealth be
more superabundant than your measure, his wisdom more
profound than your cleverness, his holiness greater than your
righteousness? Must you not of necessity acknowledge this—
but if you must acknowledge it, then there is no contradiction
between your knowledge and your wish.

And yet, if you must of necessity acknowledge it, then there
is indeed nothing upbuilding in the thought that you are always in the wrong, for it was stated that the reason it can be
painful in the one situation to be in the wrong, in the other
upbuilding, is that in the one case a person is forced to acknowledge what in the other case he wishes to acknowledge.
Thus it is true that in your relationship with God you would
be freed from the contradiction, but you would have lost the
upbuilding; and yet it was precisely upon this that we wanted
to deliberate: The upbuilding in our always being in the wrong
in relation to God.

Might it actually be this way? Why did you wish to be in the
wrong in relation to a person? Because you loved. Why did
you find it upbuilding? Because you loved. The more you
loved, the less time you had to deliberate upon whether or not
you were in the right; your love had only one desire, that you
might continually be in the wrong. So also in your relationship with God. You loved God, and therefore your soul could
find rest and joy only in this, that you might always be in the
wrong. You did not arrive at this acknowledgment out of
mental toil; you were not forced, for when you are in love you
are in freedom. When thought convinced you that this was
correct, that it could not be any other way than that you might
always be in the wrong or God might always be in the right,
then the acknowledgment followed. And you did not arrive at
the certainty that you were in the wrong from the acknowledgment that God was in the right, but from love's sole and
supreme wish, that you might always be in the wrong, you ar-

II
314

rived at the acknowledgment that God is always in the right. But this wish is love's wish and consequently a matter of freedom, and you were by no means forced to acknowledge that you were always in the wrong. Thus it was not through deliberation that you became certain that you were always in the wrong, but the certainty was due to your being built up by it.

It is, then, an upbuilding thought that in relation to God we are always in the wrong. If this were not the case, if this conviction did not have its source in your total being, that is, from the love within you, then your view would have had a different cast. You would have acknowledged that God is always in the right; this you would be forced to acknowledge as a result of being forced to acknowledge that you are always in the wrong. The latter is already more difficult to do, because you can indeed be forced to acknowledge that God is always in the right, but to apply that to yourself, to incorporate this acknowledgment in your whole being—this you cannot actually be forced to do. You acknowledge, then, that God is always in the right, and as a consequence of that you are always in the wrong, but this acknowledgment did not build you up. There is nothing upbuilding in acknowledging that God is always in the right, and consequently there is nothing upbuilding in any thought that necessarily follows from it. When you acknowledge that God is always in the right, you stand outside God, and likewise when, as a conclusion from that, you acknowledge that you are always in the wrong. But when you do not claim and are not convinced by virtue of any previous acknowledgment that you are always in the wrong, then you are hidden in God. This is your adoration, your devotion, your piety.

You loved a person, you wished that you might always be in the wrong in relation to him—but, alas, he was faithless to you, and however reluctant that it should be so, however much it pained you, you proved to be in the right in relation to him, and wrong in loving him so deeply. And yet your soul demanded you to love that way; only in that could you find rest and peace and happiness. Then your soul turned away from the finite to the infinite; there it found its object; there

II
315

your love became happy. I will love God, you said; he gives everything to the one who loves. He fulfills my highest, my only wish—that in relation to him I must always be in the wrong. Never will any alarming doubt ever tear me away from him; never will the thought terrify me that I could prove to be in the right in relation to him—in relation to God I am always in the wrong.

Or is it not so, was not this your only wish, your highest, and did not a terrible anxiety seize you when the thought could momentarily arise in your soul that you could be in the right, that God's governance was not wisdom but your plans were, that God's thoughts were not righteousness but your deeds were, that God's heart was not love but your feelings were? And was it not your bliss that you could never love as you were loved? Therefore this, that in relation to God you are always in the wrong, is not a truth you must acknowledge, not a consolation that alleviates your pain, not a compensation for something better, but it is a joy in which you win a victory over yourself and over the world, your delight, your song of praise, your adoration, a demonstration that your love is happy, as only that love can be with which one loves God.

Therefore this thought, that in relation to God we are always in the wrong, is an upbuilding thought; it is upbuilding that we are in the wrong, upbuilding that we are always in the wrong. It manifests its upbuilding power in a twofold way, partly by putting an end to doubt and calming the cares of doubt, partly by animating to action.

II
316

Do you still remember, my listener, a wisdom that was described earlier? It seemed so faithful and reliable. It explained everything so easily; it was willing to rescue every person throughout life, undismayed by the storms of doubt. "One does what one can," it shouted to the bewildered. And indeed it cannot be denied that it helps if only one does that. It had nothing more to say; it disappeared like a dream, or it became a monotonous repetition in the doubter's ear. Then when he wanted to use it, it turned out that he could not use it, that it entangled him in a snare of difficulties. He could not find time to deliberate upon what he could do, for at the same time he was supposed to be doing what he could do. Or if he found time to deliberate, then the examination gave him a more or a less, an approximation, but never anything exhaustive. How could a person ever gauge his relationship with God by a more or a less, or by a specification of approximation? Thus he ascertained that this wisdom was a treacherous friend who under the guise of helping him entangled him in doubt, worried him into an unremitting cycle of confusion. What had been obscure to him previously but had not troubled him did not become any clearer now, but his mind became anguished and careworn in doubt. Only in an infinite relationship with God could the doubt be calmed; only in an infinitely free relationship with God could his cares be turned to joy. He is in an infinite relationship with God when he acknowledges that God is always right; he is in an infinitely free relationship with God when he acknowledges that he is always wrong.

Then an end is put to doubt, for the movement of doubt consisted precisely in this: that at one moment he was supposed to be in the right, the next moment in the wrong, to a degree in the right, to a degree in the wrong, and this was supposed to mark his relationship with God; but such a relationship with God is no relationship, and this was the sustenance of doubt. In his relationship with another person, it certainly was possible that he could be partly in the wrong, partly in the right, to a degree in the wrong, to a degree in the right, because he himself and every human being is finite, and their relationship is a finite relationship that consists in a more or less. Therefore as long as doubt would make the infinite relationship finite, and as long as wisdom would fill up the infinite relationship with the finite—just so long he would remain in doubt. Thus every time doubt wants to trouble him about the particular, tell him that he is suffering too much or is being tested beyond his powers, he forgets the finite in the infinite, that he is always in the wrong. Every time the cares of doubt want to make him sad, he lifts himself above the finite into the infinite, because this thought, that he is always in the wrong, is the wings upon which he soars over the finite. This is the longing with which he seeks God; this is the love in which he finds God.

In relation to God we are always in the wrong. But is not this thought anesthetizing; however upbuilding it may be, is it not dangerous for a person? Does it not lull him into a sleep in which he dreams of a relationship with God that nevertheless is no actual relationship; does it not vitiate the power of the will and the strength of the intention? Not at all! Or the man who wished to be always in the wrong in relation to another man—was he apathetic and idle, did he not do all he could to be in the right and yet wished only to be in the wrong? And then should not the thought that in relation to God we are always in the wrong be inspiring, for what else does it express but that God's love is always greater than our love? Does not this thought make him happy to act, for when he doubts he has no energy to act; does it not make his spirit glow,[14] for when he reckons finitely, the fire of the spirit is extinguished? If your one and only wish was denied to you, my listener, you are still happy; you do not say: God is always in the right—for there is no joy in that; you say: In relation to God I am always in the wrong. If you yourself were the one who had to deny yourself your highest wish, you are still happy; you do not say: God is always in the right, for there is no rejoicing in that; you say: In relation to God I am always in the wrong. If your wish were what others and you yourself in a certain sense must call your duty, if you not only had to deny your wish but in a way betray your duty, if you lost not only your joy but even your honor, you are still happy—in relation to God, you say: I am always in the wrong. If you knocked but it was not opened,[15] if you searched but did not find, if you worked but received nothing, if you planted and watered but saw no blessing,[16] if heaven was shut and the testimony failed to come, you are still happy in your work; if the punishment that the iniquity of the fathers had called down came upon you, you are still happy— because in relation to God we are always in the wrong.

In relation to God we are always in the wrong—this thought puts an end to doubt and calms the cares; it animates and inspires to action.

Your thought has now followed the progress of this exposition, perhaps hurrying ahead when it took you on familiar paths, perhaps slowly, reluctantly, when the path was unfamiliar to you, but still you must admit this—that the situation was just as has been set forth and your thought had no objection to make. One more question before we part, my listener. [17]Would you wish, could you wish, that the situation were different? Could you wish that you might be in the right; could you wish that that beautiful law which for thousands of years has carried the generation through life and every member of the generation, that beautiful law, more glorious than the law which carries the stars on their paths across the arch of heaven, could you wish that that law would break, an even more terrible catastrophe than if the law of nature lost its power and everything disintegrated into dreadful chaos? Could you wish that? I have no words of wrath with which to terrify you; your wish must not be elicited by anxiety about the blasphemy in the thought of wanting to be in the right in relation to God. I merely ask you: Would you wish it to be different? Perhaps my voice does not have enough power and intensity; perhaps it cannot penetrate into your innermost thought—Oh, but ask yourself, ask yourself with the solemn uncertainty with which you would turn to someone who you knew could determine your life's happiness with a single word, ask yourself even more earnestly—because in very truth it is a matter of salvation. Do not interrupt the flight of your soul; do not distress what is best in you; do not enfeeble your spirit with half wishes and half thoughts. Ask yourself and keep on asking until you find the answer, for one may have known something many times, acknowledged it; one may have willed something many times, attempted it—and yet, only the deep inner motion, only the heart's indescribable emotion, only that will convince you that what you have acknowledged belongs to you, that no power can take it from you—for only the truth that builds up is truth for you. [18]

SUPPLEMENT

KEY TO REFERENCES

Marginal references alongside the text are to volume and page [I 100] in *Søren Kierkegaards Samlede Værker*, I-XIV, edited by A. B. Drachman, J. L. Heiberg, and H. O. Lange (1 ed., Copenhagen: Gyldendal, 1901-06). The same marginal references are used in Sören Kierkegaard, *Gesammelte Werke*, Abt. 1-36 (Düsseldorf: Diederichs Verlag, 1952-69).

References to Kierkegaard's works in English are to this edition, *Kierkegaard's Writings* [*KW*], I-XXV (Princeton: Princeton University Press, 1978-). Specific references to the *Writings* are given by English title and the standard Danish pagination referred to above [*Stages KW* XI (*SV* VI 100)].

References to the *Papirer* [*Pap*. I A 100; note the differentiating letter A, B, or C, used only in references to the *Papirer*] are to *Søren Kierkegaards Papirer*, I-XI³, edited by P. A. Heiberg, V. Kuhr, and E. Torsting (1 ed., Copenhagen: Gyldendal, 1909-48), and 2 ed., photo-offset with two supplemental volumes, I-XIII, edited by Niels Thulstrup (Copenhagen: Gyldendal, 1968-70), and with index, XIV-XVI (1975-78), edited by N. J. Cappelørn. References to the *Papirer* in English [*JP* II 1500] are to the volume and serial entry number in *Søren Kierkegaard's Journals and Papers*, I-VII, edited and translated by Howard V. Hong and Edna H. Hong, assisted by Gregor Malantschuk (Bloomington: Indiana University Press, 1967-78).

References to correspondence are to the serial numbers in *Breve og Aktstykker vedrørende Søren Kierkegaard*, I-II, edited by Niels Thulstrup (Copenhagen: Munksgaard, 1953-54), and to the corresponding serial numbers in *Kierkegaard: Letters and Documents*, translated by Henrik Rosenmeier, *Kierkegaard's Writings*, XXV [*Letters, KW* XXV, Letter 100].

References to books in Kierkegaard's own library [*ASKB* 100] are based on the serial numbering system of *Auktionsprotokol over Søren Kierkegaards Bogsamling* (Auction-catalog of

Søren Kierkegaard's Book-collection), edited by H. P. Rohde (Copenhagen: Royal Library, 1967).

In the Supplement, references to page and lines in the text are given as: 100:1-10.

In the notes, internal references to the present work are given as: p. 100.

Three periods indicate an omission by the editors; five periods indicate a hiatus or fragmentariness in the text.

Enten — Eller.

Et Livs-Fragment,

udgivet

af

Victor Eremita.

Anden Deel,

indeholdende B.'s Papirer,

Breve til A.

---

*Les grandes passions sont solitaires, et les transporter
au désert, c'est les rendre à leur empire.*
Chateaubriand.

Kjøbenhavn 1843.

Faaes hos Universitetsboghandler C. A. Reitzel.

Trykt i Bianco Luno's Bogtrykkeri.

Either-Or.

A Fragment of Life,

edited

by

Victor Eremita.

Part Two,

containing B's Papers,

Letters to A.

The great passions are hermits, and to transport them to the
desert is to hand over to them their proper domain.

Chateaubriand.

Copenhagen 1843.

Available at University Bookseller C. A. Reitzel's.
Printed by Bianco Luno Press.

SELECTED ENTRIES FROM
KIERKEGAARD'S JOURNALS AND PAPERS
PERTAINING TO
EITHER/OR, PARTS I-II

As I have tried to show in the preceding pages,[1] this is how things actually looked to me. But when I try to get clear about my life, everything looks different. Just as it takes a long time for a child to learn to distinguish itself from objects and thus for a long time disengages itself so little from its surroundings that it stresses the objective side and says, for example, "me hit the horse," so the same phenomenon is repeated in a higher spiritual sphere. I therefore believed that I would possibly achieve more tranquillity by taking another line of study, by directing my energies toward another goal. I might have succeeded for a time in banishing a certain restlessness, but it probably would have come back more intense, like a fever after drinking cold water.

What I really need is to get clear about *what I am to do,** not what I must know, except insofar as knowledge must precede every act. What matters is to find my purpose, to see what it really is that God wills that *I* shall do; the crucial thing is to find a truth that is truth *for me,***[2] to find *the idea for which I am willing to live and die.* Of what use would it be to me to discover a so-called objective truth, to work through the philosophical systems so that I could, if asked, make critical judgments about them, could point out the fallacies in each system; of

---

* How often, when a person believes that he has the best grip on himself, it turns out that he has embraced a cloud instead of Juno.

** Only then does one have an inner experience, but how many there are who experience life's different impressions the way the sea sketches figures in the sand and then promptly erases them without a trace.

I
A 75
54

what use would it be to me to be able to develop a theory of the state, getting details from various sources and combining them into a whole, and constructing a world I did not live in but merely held up for others to see; of what use would it be to me to be able to formulate the meaning of Christianity, to be able to explain many specific points—if it had no deeper meaning *for me and for my life*? And the better I was at it, the more I saw others appropriate the creations of my mind, the more tragic my situation would be, not unlike that of parents who in their poverty are forced to send their children out into the world and turn them over to the care of others. Of what use would it be to me for truth to stand before me, cold and naked, not caring whether or not I acknowledged it, making me uneasy rather than trustingly receptive. I certainly do not deny that I still accept an *imperative of knowledge* and that through it men may be influenced, but *then it must come alive in me*, and *this* is what I now recognize as the most important of all. This is what my soul thirsts for as the African deserts thirst for water. This is what is lacking, and this is why I am like a man who has collected furniture, rented an apartment, but as yet has not found the beloved to share life's ups and downs with him. But in order to find that idea—or, to put it more correctly—to find myself, it does no good to plunge still farther into the world. That was just what I did before. The reason I thought it would be good to throw myself into *law* was that I believed I could develop my keenness of mind in the many muddles and messes of life. Here, too, was offered a whole mass of details in which I could lose myself; here, perhaps, with the given facts, I could construct a totality, an organic view of criminal life, pursue it in all its dark aspects (here, too, a certain fraternity of spirit is very evident). I also wanted to become an *acteur* (actor) so that by putting myself in another's role I could, so to speak, find a substitute for my own life and by means of this external change find some diversion. This was what I needed to lead a *completely human life* and not merely one of *knowledge*,[3] so that I could base the development of my thought not on—yes, not on something called objective—something which in any case is not my own,

I
A 75
55

but upon something that is bound up with the deepest roots*
of my existence [*Existents*], through which I am, so to speak,
grafted into the divine, to which I cling fast even though the
whole world may collapse. *This is what I need, and this is what I
strive for.* I find joy and refreshment in contemplating the great
men who have found that precious stone for which they sell
all, even their lives,** whether I see them becoming vigorously
engaged in life, confidently proceeding on their chosen course
without vacillating, or discover them off the beaten path, absorbed in themselves and in working toward their high goal. I
even honor and respect the by-path which lies so close by. It is
this inward action of man, this God-side of man, that is decisive, not a mass of data, for the latter will no doubt follow and
will not then appear as accidental aggregates or as a succession
of details, one after the other, without a system, without a
focal point where all the radii come together. I, too, have certainly looked for this focal point. I have vainly sought an
anchor in the boundless sea of pleasure as well as in the depths
of knowledge. I have felt the almost irresistible power with
which one pleasure reaches a hand to the next; I have felt the
counterfeit enthusiasm it is capable of producing. I have also
felt the boredom, the shattering, which follows on its heels. I
have tasted the fruits of the tree of knowledge and time and
again have delighted in their savoriness. But this joy was only
in the moment of cognition and did not leave a deeper mark
on me. It seems to me that I have not drunk from the cup of
wisdom but have fallen into it. I have sought to find the principle for my life through resignation [*Resignation*], by suppos-
ing that since everything proceeds according to inscrutable

I
A 75
56

---

* How close does man, despite all his knowledge, usually live to madness?
What is truth but to live for an idea? When all is said and done, everything is
based on a postulate; but not until it no longer stands outside him, not until he
lives in it, does it cease to be a postulate for him. (Dialectic—Dispute)

** Thus it will be easy for us once we receive that ball of yarn from Ariadne
(love) and then go through all the mazes of the labyrinth (life) and kill the
monster. But how many are there who plunge into life (the labyrinth) without
taking that precaution (the *young* girls and the little boys who are sacrificed
every year to Minotaurus)—?

laws it could not be otherwise, by blunting my ambitions and the antennae of my vanity. Because I could not get everything to suit me, I abdicated with a consciousness of my own competence, somewhat the way decrepit clergymen resign with pension. What did I find? Not my self [*Jeg*], which is what I did seek to find in that way (I imagined my soul, if I may say so, as shut up in a box with a spring lock, which external surroundings would release by pressing the spring). —Consequently the seeking and finding of the Kingdom of Heaven was the first thing to be resolved. But it is just as useless for a man to want first of all to decide the externals and after that the fundamentals as it is for a cosmic body, thinking to form itself, first of all to decide the nature of its surface, to what bodies it should turn its light, to which its dark side, without first letting the harmony of centrifugal and centripetal forces realize [*realisere*] its existence [*Existents*] and letting the rest come of itself. One must first learn to know oneself before knowing anything else (γνῶθι σεαυτόν). Not until a man has inwardly understood *himself* and then sees the course he is to take does his life gain peace and meaning; only then is he free of that irksome, sinister traveling companion—that irony of life*⁴ that manifests itself in the sphere of knowledge and invites true knowing to begin with a not-knowing (Socrates⁷),** just as God created the world from nothing. But in the waters of morality it is especially at home to those who still have not entered the tradewinds of virtue. Here it tumbles a person about in a horrible way, for a time lets him feel happy and content in his resolve to go ahead along the right path, then hurls him into the abyss of despair. Often it lulls a man to sleep with the

---

* It may very well in a certain sense remain, but he is able to bear the squalls of this life, for the more a man lives for an idea, the more easily he comes to sit on the "wonder stool"⁵ before the whole world. —Frequently, when a person is most convinced that he has understood himself, he is assaulted by the uneasy feeling that he has really only learned someone else's life by rote.⁶

** There is also a proverb that says: "One hears the truth from children and the insane." Here it is certainly not a question of having truth according to premises and conclusions, but how often have not the words of a child or an insane person thundered at the man with whom penetrating discernment could accomplish nothing—?

thought, "After all, things cannot be otherwise," only to awaken him suddenly to a rigorous interrogation. Frequently it seems to let a veil of forgetfulness fall over the past, only to make every single trifle appear in a strong light again. When he struggles along the right path, rejoicing in having overcome temptation's power, there may come at almost the same time, right on the heels of perfect victory, an apparently insignificant external circumstance[8] that pushes him down, like Sisyphus, from the height of the crag. Often when a person has concentrated on something, a minor external circumstance arises that destroys everything. (As in the case of a man who, weary of life, is about to throw himself into the Thames and at the crucial moment is halted by the sting of a mosquito.) Frequently a person feels his very best[9] when the illness is the worst, as in tuberculosis. In vain he tries to resist it but he has not sufficient strength, and it is no help to him that he has gone through the same thing many times; the kind of practice acquired in this way does not apply here. Just as no one who has been taught a great deal about swimming is able to keep afloat in a storm, but only the man who is intensely convinced and has experienced that he is actually lighter than water, so a person who lacks this inward point of poise is unable to keep afloat in life's storms. —Only when a man has understood himself in this way is he able to maintain an independent existence and thus avoid surrendering his own *I*. How often we see (in a period when we extol that Greek historian because he knows how to appropriate an unfamiliar style so delusively like the original author's, instead of censuring him, since the first praise always goes to an author for having his own style— that is, a mode of expression and presentation qualified by his own individuality)—how often we see people who either out of mental-spiritual laziness live on the crumbs that fall from another's table or for more egotistical reasons seek to identify themselves with others, until eventually they believe it all, just like the liar through frequent repetition of his stories. Although I am still far from this kind of interior understanding of myself, with profound respect for its significance I have sought to preserve my individuality—worshiped the un-

I
A 75
58

known God. With a premature anxiety I have tried to avoid coming in close contact with the phenomena whose force of attraction might be too powerful for me. I have sought to appropriate much from them, studied their distinctive characteristics and meaning in human life, but at the same time guarded against coming, like the moth, too close to the flame. I have had little to win or to lose in association with the ordinary run of men, partly because what they do—so-called practical life*—does not interest me much, partly because their coldness and indifference to the spiritual and deeper currents in man alienate me even more from them. With few exceptions my companions have had no special influence upon me. A life that has not arrived at clarity about itself must necessarily exhibit an uneven side-surface; confronted by certain facts [*facta*] and their apparent disharmony, they simply halted there, for they did not have sufficient interest in me to seek a resolution in a higher harmony or to recognize the necessity of it. Their opinion of me was always one-sided, and I have vacillated between putting too much or too little weight on what they said. I have now withdrawn from their influence and the potential variations of my life's compass resulting from it. Thus I am again standing at the point where I must begin again in another way. I shall now calmly attempt to look at myself and begin to initiate inner action; for only thus will I be able, like a child calling itself "I" in its first consciously undertaken act, be able to call myself "I" in a profounder sense.

I
A 75
59

But that takes stamina, and it is not possible to harvest immediately what one has sown. I will remember that philosopher's method of having his disciples keep silent for three years;[10] then I dare say it will come. Just as one does not begin a feast at sunrise but at sundown, just so in the spiritual world one must first work forward for some time before the sun really shines for us and rises in all its glory; for although it is

---

* This life, which is fairly prevalent in the whole era, is manifest also in big things; whereas the past ages built works before which the observer must stand in silence, now they build a tunnel under the Thames (utility and advantage). Yes, almost before a child gets time to admire the beauty of a plant or some animal, it asks: Of what use is it?

true as it says that God lets his sun shine upon the good and the
evil and lets the rain fall on the just and the unjust,[11] it is not so
in the spiritual world. So let the die be cast—I am crossing the
Rubicon! No doubt this road takes me *into battle*, but I will not
renounce it. I will not lament the past—why lament? I will
work energetically and not waste time in regrets, like the person stuck in a bog and first calculating how far he has sunk
without recognizing that during the time he spends on that he
is sinking still deeper. I will hurry along the path I have found
and shout to everyone I meet: Do not look back as Lot's wife
did, but remember that we are struggling up a hill.—*JP* V 5100
(*Pap.* I A 75) August 1, 1835

I
A 75
60

In margin of Pap. I A 75; *see 362: 36*:

This explains a not uncommon phenomenon, a certain av-
arice* concerning ideas. Precisely because life is not healthy
but knowledge is too dominant, ideas are not regarded as the
natural flowers on the tree of life, are not adhered to as such
and as having significance only if they are that—but are regarded as separate flashes of illumination, as if life became
richer because of a crowd, so to speak, of such external ideas
(if I may use this expression [*sit venia verbo*]—aphoristically).
They forget that the same thing happens to ideas as to Thor's
hammer—it returns to the point from which it was thrown,
although in a modified form.—*JP* V 5100 (*Pap.* I A 76) *n.d.*

Addition to Pap. I A 76:

*A similar phenomenon is the erroneous view of knowledge
and its results in regarding the objective results and forgetting
that the genuine philosopher is to the highest degree sub-ob-
jective. I need only mention Fichte.[12] Wit is treated the same
way; it is not regarded as Minerva, necessarily springing from
the author's whole individuality and environment, therefore
in a sense something lyrical,* but as flowers one can pick and
keep for one's own use. (The forget-me-not has its place in the

field, hidden and humble, but looks drab in a park.)—*JP* V 5102 (*Pap*. I A 77) *n.d.*

Addition to Pap. I A 77:

*And this also accounts for the blushing that usually accompanies a certain type of witticism, suggesting that it came forth naturally, newborn.—*JP* V 5103 (*Pap*. I A 78) September 20, 1836

Addition to Pap. I A 75:

*A curious kind of irony is also to be found in an Arabian tale "Morad the Hunchback" (in *Moden Zeitung*, "*Bilder Magazin*," no. 40, 1835). A man comes into possession of a ring that provides everything he wishes but always with a "but" attached—for example, when he wishes for security he finds himself in prison etc. (this story is found in *Riises Bibliothek for Ungdommen*, II, 6, 1836, p. 453). I have also heard or read someplace about a man who, standing outside a theater, heard a soprano voice so beautiful and enchanting that he promptly fell in love with the voice; he hurries into the theater and meets a thick, fat man who, upon being asked who it was who sang so beautifully, answered: "It was I"—he was a castrato.—*JP* V 5104 (*Pap*. I A 79) *n.d.*

Addition to Pap. I A 75:

"Es ist, wie mit den anmuthigen Morgenträumen, aus deren einschläferndem Wirbel man nur mit Gewalt sich herausziehen kann, wenn man nicht in immer drückender Müdigkeit gerathen, und so in krankhafter Erschöpfung nachher den ganzen Tag hinschleppen will [It is, as with pleasant morning dreams, from whose drowsy confusion one can extricate oneself only by force, if one does not wish to go about in increasingly oppressive weariness and later drag through the day in sickly exhaustion]." Novalis, *Schriften*. Berlin: 1826. I, p. 107.[13]—*JP* V 5105 (*Pap*. I A 80) *n.d.*, 1835

From draft:

[1.] Do you recollect when you at once scoffed at a remark, surely a well-intentioned and by no means unfelicitous remark oratorically, by a clergyman that when one really was in need and stretched his beseeching arms toward heaven, then the clouds would part and not only God's finger would become visible in the governance of our fate, but his arm would stretch out to grasp the beseeching one's hand,[14] and you made the comment that you had never noticed a hand or arm like that in the cloud, except once where you were contentedly riding alone, not wishing for any assistance, and then noticed a dark shape in the cloud that looked just like an arm and was a waterspout [*Vandhose*] that in a highly precarious manner reached out of the cloud and lifted you off the horse, a mode of treatment you found neither gentle nor seemly toward rational beings. You went on to say that for that reason you found it absolutely right for you to be such a great disdainer of nature, since it was an empty fancy about all the dominion and rule mankind was legitimately supposed to have over nature, inasmuch as it considered rational creatures to be nothing at all, which it demonstrated on many occasions.

[2.] Like all demonic natures, you often betray in a singularly unfree manner your innermost condition. For example, you once said of yourself that you were like a team of horses you had on a long ride into the country. The hackney driver did not have others at home and did not want to let you have them because they were so bad. For example, they could not stand still, but they turned out to be the very best runners, and you claimed that never in your life had you ridden so fast; you added that it is indeed unimportant whether a team of horses can stand still or not if only they can run. As usual, your remark evoked laughter and yet it hid more than those present noticed, even more perhaps than you yourself were thinking, although that seldom happens with you. It is said that man's walking is a continuous falling.[15] This is even more the case with his running; he is continually prevented from falling by a new fall. So it is with you; you lack the firm posture of a point

III
B 181:1
216

III
B 181:1
217

of view, and therefore you cannot stand but you certainly can run.

[*3.*] —If there was a young girl who had become unhappy in love, you would talk with her and tell her the contents of her life in the form of fairy tales.

[*4.*] Love does not merely make one blind; it also makes one sighted, and I have often wondered at the not merely poetically true but in the deepest sense poetically true secret that in the *Marriage of Figaro* Susanne and Figaro immediately recognize each other in the fourth act,[16] whereas the count continually remains deceived. Thus innocent love is always sighted.—

[*5.*] To be a complete human being does indeed remain the highest.[17] You are of that opinion as well, even if at times you can be shameless enough to sneer at it, just as you once insisted that to be a complete human being also involved having corns.

III
B 181:5
218

[*6.*] You with your exaggerated ideals, you who behave so oddly in life, you totally lack a criterion, just like a tower watchman when he leaves his lofty guard station and wanders around the streets like a stranger!

[*7.*] But wanting to construct imaginatively is futile.[18] You know how Rübezahl was fooled by the young girl who sent him to count turnips;[19] he never finished, you see—but he is the very picture of you, who like him in a certain sense are very smart, in another extremely obtuse. —You become fooled out of life.

[*8.*] There is a religiousness that seems very devoted to God and yet is a kind of despair. For example, when someone in defending the reality [*Realitet*][20] of prayer points out that one does not need to pray about the immediate fulfillment of the prayer but pray that God will give one strength to bear it if it is not fulfilled. This may conceal a pride and a mistrust of God. One makes God into two beings, so to speak; the one wants evil for us, as it were, and the other wants to help us bear it. Why not instead directly pray to God about fulfilling our desire? If it is not fulfilled, then there can always be time enough to pray for strength to bear the loss.

[*9.*] Generally it is regarded as the true wisdom of life to live as if one were about to die. I knew a man who became very unhappy precisely because he continually believed that he would die—this robbed him of all patience to live.

[*10.*] It is fine that you cannot allow yourself to be satisfied with such a life, that your ravenous hunger for pleasure is not satisfied by it—but is it more satisfied by the satiety that comes almost in the very moment of pleasure, the satiety you experience in the same instant you experience the pleasure?

III
B 181:10
219

[*11.*] You speak so much about the ludicrous perspective of the finite categories in which you involuntarily come to view every human being, and you find it incomprehensible that people are able to endure it; but is it any better, then, the perspective in which you see every joy vanish? When you see a young girl, you immediately become very anxious because it seems to you as if this were her happy moment that will never come again.—*Pap.* III B 181:1-11 *n.d.*, 1841-42

On front flyleaf of copy of Either/Or, II; *repeated on division page, p. 3:*

When asked why he did not wish to be a father, Thales is supposed to have answered: Out of love for children. When his mother pressured him to get married, he said: By Zeus, it is not the time for that yet. After he came of age and she again kept on with this, he said: Now it is no longer the time for that.

See Diogenes Laertius, I, para. 26.
Kleobulos gave the maxim: Daughters should be married when they are maidens in age and women in understanding.

See Diogenes L., I, para. 91.[21]
—*JP* III 2592 (*Pap.* IV A 237) *n.d.*, 1843

In top margin of draft; see 6:5-13:

Either/Or

In the preface it might, of course, be recalled that I had also found this piece ["*The Esthetic Validity of Marriage*"] among

other documents from B to A. All sorts of conclusions might
be drawn from it with respect to A's possible situation—about
having been engaged, married etc. etc. But here again the pe-
culiar characteristic of A's life is recalled—that one did not
know whether it was experience or mood. Goethe truthfully,
yet with deep meaning, called his life *Dichtung und Wahrheit*
[*Poetry and Truth*], for if a man has really experienced something, it will be impossible for him to abstain totally from reproduction.—*Pap*. III B 182 *n.d.*, 1841–42

From draft; see 3:

An Attempt to Save Marriage Esthetically
—*Pap*. III B 41:1 *n.d.*, 1841

From draft; see 7:9:

. . . . . and as you once very wittily observed, when the
idea of society really ascends, communication will become so
intense that even to the experienced eye the human race will
become an ocean where it will be impossible to distinguish the
hordes of infusoria who previously formed isolated exist-
ences.—*JP* IV 4101 (*Pap*. III B 41:2) *n.d.*, 1841

From draft; see 7:17:

. . . . . like the Page in *Figaro*, but an adult.
—*Pap*. III B 41:3 *n.d.*, 1841

From draft; see 13:7:

. . . . . to say at this moment with Brause[22] that I would not
be fate for ten rix-dollars.[23]
—*Pap*. III B 41:4 *n.d.*, 1841

From draft; see 22:31:

. . . . . , as the Duke of Richelieu says,[24] . . . . .
—*Pap*. III B 41:5 *n.d.*, 1841

From draft; see 34:13:

. . . . . or, to use a favorite expression of Magister Kierkegaard's, that marriage is a Chladni figure.

—*Pap.* III B 41:6 *n.d.*, 1841

In margin of draft; see 38:2-8:

You very likely know the story about the sorcerer Vergilius,[25] who wanted to rejuvenate himself; bear the story in mind. (N.B. In order to mystify the reader, this story must not be developed further. On the whole, no more must be done in this respect.)—*Pap.* III B 41:7 *n.d.*, 1841

From draft; see 45:10:

. . . . . that could almost become dangerous for the leading people concerned . . . . .

In margin: halb Kinderspiel, halb Gott im Herzen [half child's play, half God at heart].[26]

—*Pap.* III B 41:8 *n.d.*, 1841

In margin of draft; see 49:6-13:

See Rosenkrantz, pp. 308-309.[27]

—*Pap.* III B 41:9 *n.d.*, 1841

From draft; see 59:1:

. . . . . it is a tone deeper; it is a bass tone that cuts in under the lighter . . . . .

—*Pap.* III B 41:10 *n.d.*, 1841

From draft; see 67:28:

. . . . . to come with live coals, but please note, charcoal, in his chafing dish, ...

—*Pap.* III B 41:12 *n.d.*, 1841

In copy of Either/Or, *II; see 68:35-69:4:*

> *Underlined:* Or a person marries—*to have children*
> *In lower margin:* Zeno says: The wise man marries and makes having children the purpose of marriage. See Tennemann, *Ges. d. Ph.,* IV, p. 145.[28]—*Pap.* IV A 240 *n.d.,* 1843

From draft; see 71:9:

> . . . . . I received from Pastor Olufsen, who, just between us, does not seem very familiar with the N.T., for he promptly had to go to a concordance, the most important passages . . . . .
> —*Pap.* III B 41:13 *n.d.,* 1841

From draft; see 71:10:

> . . . . . this passage is, I believe, in Ephesians or in I Timothy.
> —*Pap.* III B 41:14 *n.d.,* 1841

In margin of draft; see 79:29:

> If I were to use an adequate expression for the comic impression you make on me, I would say that you are like a spider, one of those with long thin fine legs, shrewd eyes, and that is how you run over existence. —From another side I would say that you are like an ethereal figure, like an elf man—handsome but hollow, seductive but corrupting.—*Pap.* III B 41:16 *n.d.,* 1841

From draft; see 86:20:

> Imagine a king who ruled over a happy nation, a kingdom where peace and prosperity really seemed to have taken up residence, imagine him saying to himself in one of his solitary moments: I have the allegiance of my people, they praise and bless my regime, and yet what have I done and what am I

doing. If, then—in order to do something—he did not resort
to something that destroyed his people but calmly told himself: I have the responsibility, my crown does not weigh heavily upon me, but yet the responsibility does rest upon me—if
he said and felt this, then he would also be justified in enjoying
all the approval a grateful people could shower upon him.—*JP*
IV 4102 (*Pap.* III B 41:18) *n.d.*, 1841

From draft; see 92:4:

But just as this has something uplifting in it, there is something depressing in the thought that sin is supposed to be the
basis for it. To that I must reply: In the wedding ceremony the
Church proclaims sin only as the universally human lot; thus
it actually is only for reflection that the contradiction asserts itself, but first love does not have reflection, and consequently I
cannot reflect upon this.—*Pap.* III B 41:19 *n.d.*, 1841

From draft; see 92:37-93:2:

This is clear in Holy Scripture, and therefore it was much
more important to emphasize the latter; but there is also a presentation of the woman as the one who forms the home[29] precisely through her passive sustaining character. The man shall
forsake father and mother (this is his first home) and keep to
his wife (this is the second home that she forms). This is also
beautifully expressed in the word "wife" [*Hustru*], i.e., faithfulness in the house, a house where faithfulness dwells, or a
faithfulness in which love finds its home. Such an expression,
so simple and plain and yet so rich in blessing, romantic love
does not have.—*JP* II 1157 (*Pap.* III B 41:20) *n.d.*, 1841

From draft; see 93:18:

Christianity does not want to annihilate the flesh; it does not
want mortification of the flesh or the extreme thereof, de-
baucheries; it wants humility, and this can exist very well with
love.—*Pap.* III B 41:21 *n.d.*, 1841

From draft; see 95:15:

The latter is presumably what the coryphaei of philosophy have really wanted to praise, and I can remember that you once read to me a passage from Hegel[30] that in my opinion clearly showed that he recommended only scientific reflection upon systematic truth and the intellectual reflection contained therein.—*Pap.* III B 41:22 *n.d.*, 1841

From draft; see 95:19:

. . . . . or calling to doubt (for there is a certain doubt on the part of genius that has its authorization in itself; where that is not a case, as a rule the doubt is simply egotistical and selfish, in quite ordinary terms, mutiny against God) . . . . .—*Pap.* III B 41:23 *n.d.*, 1841

From draft; see 101:13:

. . . . . before "the whole world," an expression that cannot possibly disturb even the most polemical nature, since it asserts a publicity, but so unlimited that its alarming boundary is not perceived, and asserts it with a boldness, with a lyrical excessiveness, as if it wanted to make nature itself witness to this festival.—*Pap.* III B 41:24 *n.d.*, 1841

In margin of draft; see 104:3:

When God gave Adam company by giving him Eve, this by no means entails extensive marital sociability, for Eve did not bring along a swarm of women friends.—*JP* II 2589 (*Pap.* III B 41:25) *n.d.*, 1841

From sketch; see 104:36-105:13:

But marriage is impossible without confidence.—*JP* II 2588 (*Pap.* III B 39) *n.d.*, 1841

From draft; see 117:29-30:

But this is by no means the case, and such a person will easily be tempted, even if not to marry, yet to tempt the opposite sex by his contacts. He will also easily be able to make an impression. If someone were to ask me who is the more dangerous seducer, a Don Juan or a Faust, I would answer Faust. In Faust, a world has been destroyed, but for this reason he has at his disposal the most seductive tones, the double tones that quiver in two worlds at once, compared with which Don Juan's most baneful tenderness and sweetness are childish babbling.* If someone were to ask me which victim is more to be lamented, a girl who is seduced by a Don Juan or by a Faust, [I would answer that] there is no comparison—the one who is seduced by a Faust is utterly lost. Thus it is very profound that the legend puts 1,003 on Don Juan's list; Faust has only one, but she is also crushed on an entirely different scale. A girl who is seduced by a Don Juan has the world of spirit before her; a girl who is seduced by a Faust, for her even that is poisoned.

III
B 41:26
132
III
B 41:26
133

In margin: *In Faust, a world is destroyed, but the inconstant light that falls upon this ruin alarms and tempts.—*Pap.* III B 41:26 *n.d.,* 1841

From draft; see 118:16:

. . . . . klip klap, and then everything was supposed to be finished, and if one wanted to be perfect, one could present one's wife with some book containing a collection of substantial aphorisms about marriage. I know that you have a talent for being amused by human foolishness, and I shall now give you an occasion to do so, which may also confirm the correctness of the old saying: Is there anything a German will not do for money? It is a book I chanced upon. Its title is: *Orakel der Liebe, Ehe und Freundschaft, eine alphabetisch geordnete Samlung gehaltreicher Gedanken über das Wesen, die Erfordernisse und den Zweck der Liebe, Ehe und Freundschaft.* Magdeburg: 1841, by Gustav Friedrich Koch.

III
B 41:27
133

The preface reads as follows: "Der Zusammenstellung dieses Werkchens hat die Absicht zum Grunde gelegen: Erklärungen, Regeln und Anhaltepunkte zum Nachdenken über das Wesen, die Erfordernisse und den Zweck der Liebe, Ehe und Freundschaft, sowie überhaupt einen Umgangs- und Lebensleitfaden für Liebende, Eheleute und Freunde in Hinsicht ihres Verkehrs mit einander und mit dritten Personen darzureichen. Um das Ganze zum Gebrauche geeigneter zu machen, Diesem oder Jenem einen entsprechende Gedanken, ein Motto, einen Stammbuchvers u. dergl. schnell an die Hand zu geben, und zugleich dem bisher fühlbar gewordenen Mangel an einem Wörterbuche der Liebe zum Theil abzuhelfen, habe ich die einzelnen Stellen unter bestimten Rubriken gebracht und solche alphabetisch geordnet [The underlying aim for writing this small book is to provide some explanatory comments, rules, and clues for reflecting upon the nature, requirements, and purpose of love, marriage, and friendship and generally to offer lovers, spouses, and friends a guide for socializing and living in commerce with each other and with a third person. In order to make this whole enterprise more accessible for use—quickly making available a suitable thought, motto, album verse, or the like for this or that person—and also partly in order to remedy the continued lack of a dictionary on love, so sorely felt until now, I have placed particular passages under definite rubrics and organized them alphabetically]." For the future, then, we must be prepared for a new kind of love, the encyclopedic, the degree and intensity of which one will be able to determine by the letter of the alphabet to which it has arrived.— —*Pap.* III B 41:27 *n.d.*, 1841

III
B 41:27
134

In margin of draft; see 137:

. . . . . thus it reverts to epic again, has the scope of the epic but not the lyrical impatience of drama, but it is not the immediate externality that is at one with the external, and therefore it is a higher kind of epic. Here everyone becomes his own troubador and can await the explanation, the transfiguration an eternity will give. This is not understood in a fantastic way, as was the case, I recall, with a religious fanatic who thought that judgment day would last several thousand years in order to have time to see to everything properly.—*Pap.* III B 41:28 *n.d.*, 1841

From reading notes; see 153:20-31:

Erzählungen und Märchen, herausgegeben v. Friedrich Heinrich v. der Hagen. *1ster Band.* Prenzlau: 1825.
In volume II of this collection (Prenzlau: 1826), pp. 325ff., *there is a Serbian tale with the title "Bärensohn."* . . . . . There is a very striking similarity between this story and what is told here in the north about Thor and his adventures. . . . . . Now he comes to a farmer and once again he wants to enter an eating match, but the farmer recommends that before touching the food he should cross himself and say "In the name of the Father and of the Son and of the Holy Spirit"; when he had done that, he was surfeited before he had eaten half the food placed before him. . . . .
A very singular, naive, childish tone runs through the whole story,* which is characterized by numerous contradictions in the determination of the size of the persons appearing in the poem. In other respects, as mentioned, there is a striking similarity to the Scandinavian, which can be reserved perhaps for a convenient time.
In margin: *See Mag. Hammerich on Ragnarok, p. 93 note.—*JP* V 5127 (*Pap.* I C 82) *n.d.*, 1836

From draft under last line; see 154:20:

Your sincerely devoted
B.
—*Pap.* III B 41:29 *n.d.*, 1841

In copy of Either/Or, II; *see 155:3:*

Ariston of Chios says that one should not allow oneself to be disturbed by the diversity of external circumstances: the

wise person ought to be a good actor who can play an Agamemnon or a Thersites[31] equally well[32] (see Tennemann, *Ges.
d. Phil.*, IV, p. 218, note 23).—*Pap*. IV A 245 *n.d.*, 1845

In copy of Either/Or, *II; see 155:3:*

"To choose oneself" is no eudaimonism, as one will readily
perceive. It is quite remarkable that even Chrysippus sought to
elevate eudaimonia as the highest aim by showing that the
basic drive in everything is to preserve and maintain itself in
the original condition, and pleasure and happiness appear insofar as it succeeds.[33]

See Tennemann, *Ges. d. Ph.*, IV, pp. 318-19.

—*JP* V 5636 (*Pap*. IV A 246) *n.d.*, 1843

From sketch; see 166:28:

Either/Or

*so reit' ich hin in alle Ferne
Über meiner Mütze nur die Sterne*[34]

a fragment.

"As I have said to you again and again, so I also write to
you—either/or—and one *aut* [or] is not enough, for the one
view does not allow itself to be attached to the other as a coordinate, but it is the excluding *aut/aut* [either/or]. Therefore,
whether you now become angry and break with me as you
have broken with so many others—or whether you take it in a
friendly way—in any case, I continue: Either/Or—"— —*Pap*.
III B 31 *n.d.*, 1841

From final draft; see 167:25-27:

Therefore even if a person chose the wrong (by this I do indeed ask you to bear in mind that it is not a question of the contrast between good and evil, for in this choice the actual will
most likely choose the right most of the time) . . . . . . —
Pap. III B 42:1 *n.d.*, 1841

From draft; see 171:23-24:

. . . . . mediate Christianity and philosophy . . . . .
                    —*Pap.* III B 42:2 *n.d.*, 1841

See 185:30:

What in a certain sense is called "spleen" and what the mystics know by the designation "the arid moments," the Middle Ages knew as *acedia* (αχηδια, aridity). Gregory, *Moralia in Job,* XIII, p. 435: *Virum solitarium ubique comitatur acedia* . . . . . . *est animi remisso, mentis enervatio, neglectus religiosae exercitationis, odium professionis, laudatrix rerum secularium* [Wherever aridity encompasses a solitary man . . . . . . there is a lowering of the spirit, a weakening of the mind, a neglect of religious practice, a hatred of professing, a praise of secular things].*

That Gregory should emphasize *virum solitarium* points to experience, since it is a sickness to which the isolated person [is exposed] at his highest pinnacle (the humorous), and the sickness is most accurately described and rightly emphasized as *odium professionis,* and if we consider this symptom in a somewhat ordinary sense (not in the sense of churchly confession of sins, by which we would have to include the indifferent church member as *solitarius*) of a self-expression, experience will not leave us in the lurch if examples are required.

                                        July 20, 1839
The ancient moralists show a deep insight into human nature in regarding *tristitia* [sloth, dejection, moroseness] among the *septem vitia principalia* [seven deadly sins]. Thus Isidorus Hisp. See de Wette, translated by Scharling, p. 139, note q, top; see Gregor and Maximus Confessor in the same note.[35]—
JP I 739 (*Pap.* II A 484) July 20, 1839

In margin of Pap. II A 484:

*This is what my father called: *a quiet despair.*[36]
                    —*JP* I 740 (*Pap.* II A 485) *n.d.*, 1839

See 99:26; 187:35-36:

Caligula's idea of wanting all heads on one neck is nothing else than premeditated, cowardly suicide. It is the counterpart of suicide. Both are equally desperate world views.—*JP* I 738 (*Pap.* II A 409) May 4, 1839

In copy of Either/Or, *II; see 200:18-20:*

Underlined: I believe that there is indeed meaning in the world if only I *could find it.*

In margin: Carneades expressed his skepticism by saying that there is something true but it cannot be known.

See Tennemann, *Ges. d. Ph.*, IV, p. 342.
—*Pap.* IV A 249 *n.d.*, 1843

In margin of draft; see 207:19-22:

Must be used in the introduction to the whole work, for here the married man has let himself be carried away, because according to this calculation no one at all is lost.—*Pap.* III B 42:3 *n.d.*, 1841

See 265:8-19:

The main point is still that one should not be diverted by the external. When, in order to subvert the position that there is an absolute in morality, an appeal is made to variations in custom and use and such shocking examples as savages putting their parents to death, attention is centered merely upon the external. That is to say, if it could be proved that savages maintain that a person ought to hate his parents, it would be quite another matter; but this is not their thought; they believe that one should love them, and the error is only in the way of expressing it. But it is indeed clear that the savages do not intend to harm their parents but to do good to them.—*JP* I 889 (*Pap.* III A 202) *n.d.*, 1842

In copy of Either/Or, *II; see 270:20-23:*

Underlined: It is not my intention to lead you into a consideration of the *multiplicity of duty.*

In bottom margin: Ariston of Chios was also of the opinion that one ought not to teach any specific doctrine of duty (see Tennemann, *Ges. d. Ph.,* IV, p. 212[37]).—*Pap.* IV A 252 *n.d.,* 1843

On front fly-leaf of copy of Either/Or, *II; see 271:33-38:*

Autopathetic and sympathetic doubt are identical.
                                        —*JP* V 5635 (*Pap.* IV A 236) *n.d.,* 1843

See 287:10-20:

. . . . . and if the bitter cup of suffering is handed to me, I shall ask that, if possible, it be taken away, and if it is not possible, I shall take it cheerfully, and I shall not fix my gaze upon the cup but upon the one who hands it to me, and I shall not turn my eyes toward the bottom of the cup to see if it is soon empty, but I shall look at him who hands it to me, and while I trustingly raise the goblet I shall not say to any other man: Here's to your health, as I myself am savoring it, but I shall say: Here's to my health, and empty its bitterness, to my health, for I know and am convinced that it is to my health that I empty it, to my health, as I leave not one drop behind.—*JP* V 5562 (*Pap.* III A 228) *n.d.,* 1842

See 292:34-293:5:

. . . . . and everyone who bases his life upon something accidental leads a robber-existence [*Røverexistents*], be it upon beauty, wealth, background, science, art—in short, upon anything that cannot be every man's fate. And even if you are successful in carrying this out—and if then a young person turns to you with all the confidence and prerogative of youth, and you cannot deny youth the prerogative of asking you how you have grounded your life—would you not be ashamed, for you would not be able to divulge to him all your cunning and craft, would you?—*JP* I 885 (*Pap*. III A 135) *n.d.*, 1841

On front fly-leaf of copy of Either/Or, *II; see 320:14-16; 322:28; 354:7-18:*

IV
A 234
91

P. 336 [*SV* II 289], "every human being ought to become open" actually says the opposite of what the whole first part says, as the lines just quoted do in fact say. The esthetic is always hidden: if it expresses itself at all, it is coquettish. Therefore it would have been wrong to have A express his interior nature directly or, indeed, even in B's papers. In A's papers there are intimations of his interior being; in B's papers we see the exterior with which he is accustomed to deceive people— that is why A can come up with the statement about what would be the ultimate mockery of existence (p. 334 [*SV* II 287]).

The aim of the sermon is not to lull, not to win a metaphysical position, but to motivate to action. That I can in fact do at every moment.

IV
A 234
92

Healing and reconciliation take place essentially by means of compassion. It is a blessing for a man that there is something that he cannot, despite his freedom, will. He cannot will to destroy all existence.[38] Arid morality would merely teach man that he is incapable, would mock his impotence; the upbuilding lies in seeing that one cannot will it.

The second part begins with marriage, because it is the most profound form of the revelation of life. It is ingenious to have Jupiter and Juno called *adultus* and *adulta*, τέλειος, τελεία, in connection with tracing marriage back to them.—*JP* V 5634 (*Pap*. IV A 234) *n.d.*, 1843

In margin of draft; see 320:34:

N.B. Preface

—*Pap*. III B 42:4 *n.d.*, 1841

See 331:16-19:

The words that are found someplace in the second part of *Either/Or* could be a good theme for a sermon.

It is not dreadful that I have to suffer punishment when I have acted badly; it would be dreadful if I could act badly—and there were no punishment.—*JP* III 3638 (*Pap.* X² A 115) *n.d.*, 1849

From final copy under last line; see 332:12:

> Your friend.
> —*Pap.* III B 191:15 *n.d.*, 1841

In copy of Either/Or, II; *see 337:15:*

Asterisk added: the same and yet not the same*
In bottom margin: *It is as Heraclitus says: One cannot walk through the same river twice.[39] (See Tennemann, *Gesch. d. Phil.*, I, p. 220.)—*Pap.* IV A 255 *n.d.*, 1843

From sketch; see 337:26-338:15:

. . . . . a stocky little man with a head bigger than an ox's. Jovial from his youth, he had only received a bare pass in his theological examination. His oratory would have appalled the capital city—now he had become a pastor out on the heath in Jylland. Yet this satisfied him—the heath was a playground—as to a swamp bittern—he had given this talk on the occasion of a crop failure, maintains that every peasant can understand it; he writes that he has given it word for word in pure Jylland dialect. —"Every man is by nature a philosopher," every peasant lad learns, and also the words, "What does it profit a man etc. and not damage his own soul"—he who has understood this has essentially understood all philosophy.

At a pastoral conference in one of the provinces.—*JP* III 3287 (*Pap.* III B 183) *n.d.*, 1842

From seminary notebook; see 340:1-2:

The Upbuilding That Lies in the Thought That
in Relation to God We Are **Always in the Wrong**

Otherwise we might be tempted to despair of providence.

For if there were one man, one single man, no matter if he were the most powerful who ever lived in the world or the most humble, a man who on judgment day could justifiably say: I was not provided for, in the great household I was forgotten, or even if he put much of the blame at his own door yet could justifiably say: I acknowledge that I went astray in the world, I departed from the way of truth, but I did repent of my sin, I honestly intended and strove to the uttermost for the good, I lifted up my voice and shouted to heaven for help, but no one answered, there was no constructive solution, not even the remotest relief . . . . . if there were such a man, then everything would be foolishness, where then would the limit be.

—Anyone who has ever yielded to temptation must confess, however, that there was a possibility that in the next moment help was already at hand, and this is an observation, not a sophism, as it might seem to a despairing mind inclined to say: One can always say that.—*JP* V 5486 (*Pap*. III C 5) *n.d.*, 1840-41

See 306:

All infinite knowledge is negative ("always to be in the wrong" is also an infinite relation), and yet the negative is higher than the positive.* Thus Pythagoras also taught that the even number is imperfect, the uneven number perfect.[40]

*The Pythagoreans also regarded the finite as higher and more perfect than the infinite.

See Tennemann, I, p. 115.

In margin: As a rule the Pythagoreans did not regard as perfect that from which something arises, but that which arises from something.

See Tennemann, I, p. 119.—*JP* V 5616 (*Pap*. IV A 56) *n.d.*, 1843

In copy of Either/Or, *II; see 306:*

Sura twelve in the *Koran* deals with Joseph. He comes forward, his innocence with respect to Potiphar's wife is completely proved, and yet he says: *Doch will ich mein Herz nicht ganz frei sprechen von Schuld* [Yet I will not say that my heart is entirely free of guilt].
See Ulmann's translation of the *Koran*, p. 194.[41]
If a person is completely in the right, in relation to God he always ought to have a higher expression: That he is in the wrong, for no person can absolutely penetrate his consciousness.—*Pap*. IV A 256 *n.d.*, 1843

See 354:34-35:

When I had *Either/Or* end with the clause: "Only the truth that builds up is truth for you," only a few, I regret, perceived the outlook involved. There was considerable argument among Greek philosophers about the criterion of truth[42] (see, for example, Tennemann, *Geschichte d. Philos.*, V, p. 301); it would be very interesting to pursue this matter further. I doubt very much, however, that a more concrete expression will be found. Probably people think that these words stand there in *Either/Or* as a phrase, that another expression could also be used. Indeed, the words are not even italicized. Good Lord, then they probably are not very significant.—*JP* IV 4847 (*Pap*. IV A 42) *n.d.*, 1843

See 354:34-35:

Wonderful! The category "for you" (subjectivity, inwardness) with which *Either/Or* concludes (only the truth that builds up [*opbygge*] is truth for you) is Luther's own. I have never really read anything by Luther. But now I open up his sermons[43] —and right there in the Gospel for the First Sunday in Advent he says "for you," on this everything depends (see second leaf, first column, and first leaf, fourth column).—*JP* II 2463 (*Pap.* VIII¹ A 465) *n.d.*, 1847

Letter for possible publication in the Berlingske Tidende*:*

IV
B 19
185

Summons

That a police adjutant must be on the spot whenever the watchman whistles, that the fire chief must get up whenever the alarm goes off, that the censor has no quiet day or night as soon as it pleases an author to set him in motion by his mental activity—I, too, find to be quite in order that these men receive therefore an appropriate wage, enjoy glory and honor in society, are loved and respected by the entire community. But that I, an unemployed man, who in my life unite what is rarely seen united, have neither business affairs nor wages, that I without any compensation whatever, must be disturbed in my quiet inactivity every time it pleases a joker to attribute to me the authorship of things of which no one wants to be the author— this I do not find to be in order, no more than if someone for a joke were to hang on my door the sign of the police or of the fire chief or to persuade people to think that I am the censor in order to create for me the inconvenience of opening the door at every moment in the day in order to explain that I am neither the one nor the other.

What the majority of readers probably never knew and the others have long since forgotten, what I myself would have forgotten in a short time if the aftereffects did not still pain me, is at this moment still all too much alive in my memory: that

IV
B 19
186

six months ago, driven to extremities by the informing voices that announced me as the author of various articles, I disclaimed in a solemn declaration[44] all association with these pieces, that in order to secure for myself a carefree and undisturbed future, I "begged every reader never to regard me as author of anything that does not bear my name,"*[45] that as a result of this step I have for a long time now met with caustic

*See *Fædrelandet.*

glances, derisive looks, mocking faces, which to me were inexplicable until spoken and written expressions made it clear
beyond all doubt that people had seen through me, had seen
that it was vanity that had led me to bring myself to attention
in an unseemly way, that there was actually only one person
who regarded me as capable of being the author of those remarkable articles. The mistake was unpleasant for me; the
mortification that followed, I have sought to overcome, and I
perhaps would have succeeded if the same story had not
started all over again. During the past fortnight I have heard
that an article in *Ny Portefeuille*[46] has been fathered upon me,
two letters in the *Berlingske Tidende*[47] (or just one), a letter in
Fædrelandet,[48] and the big work *Either-Or*.[49] My situation is
just as painful as formerly, is even more painful, since it is a
repetition. It is just as difficult as before, is even more difficult
since by experience I have learned the distressing consequences
that warn me against every step, although a step nevertheless
seems necessary, a step that would be just as dangerous for me
as it would be for the man Jean Paul tells about, if he, as he
stood on one leg and read a sign saying, "A fox-trap is set
here,"[50] put his other foot on the ground. If I declare that I have
no part either in those articles or in that work, I run the risk of
seeing later that people only wanted to get the best of me, that
they will again mock me because I am so vain as to believe that
anybody could seriously suppose that I, in one way or another,
was capable of writing those articles, a book of exactly 864
pages, or of writing half of it, if one assumes that there are two
authors. If I remain silent, then the daily scene repeats itself,
then in some way I must do the honors of an author, receive
courtesies and lying-in visits appropriate to an author, endure
an ironic smile that gives me a presentiment of what I can expect if I am so imprudent as to disclaim the authorship. In order to avoid, if possible, this difficult situation, I have decided
to do what I hereby do: to call upon Victor Eremita to abandon
his pseudonymity so that I can live in peace and at ease, to call
upon him to do this as soon as possible, so that it will not be
said later that I have pretended to be an author, although I my-

self know that in this respect I am as innocent as a child born yesterday.

As far as the newspaper articles are concerned, I would wish that the writers would do the same, but since the matter seems almost forgotten because of *Either/Or*, I will not ask them to do what I, if they did it, would always regard as a proof of the noble rectitude that has sympathy for the calamities of others.

Copenhagen, February 22, 1843

S. KIERKEGAARD
Magister Artium

Postscript. I have placed my summons in this paper so that Victor Eremita, if he does not live here in the city, will receive it as quickly as possible, and in conclusion I request that he not delay longer than is absolutely necessary.—*Pap.* IV B 19 February 22, 1843

Letter for possible publication in Fædrelandet:

IV
B 20
188

A Letter to Herr Magister Kierkegaard

Dear Sir:

If I had fallen down from the clouds,[51] I could not hasten more speedily to your aid in your distress. As you will please note from the Preface,[52] before I published *Either/Or* I had already taken care of the irregularity that authors unknown to me would come forward. It never occurred to me that what has now happened could happen. My honest admission presumably does not help you, but on the other hand it may nevertheless comfort you to know that if I had thought of it I would not have known what I should do to prevent it.

That your position must be unpleasant and regrettable, I am well aware, but if you, Herr Magister, will allow me to say so, it seems to me that your vehemence makes the whole matter worse. Your request is written in such a passionate tone that one does not know whether to laugh or to cry about it. With all due respect to your words, I cannot quite believe that you have earlier met "caustic glances" on every side. Are you per-

fectly sure that you have not been deceived by your state of
mind, a kind of hypochondria frequently found among schol-
ars? The more emotionally someone reacts, the more fun people have in teasing him. For someone, in the event that things
become outrageous, abruptly to wish everything interrupted
and destroyed is in turn vehemence. It is wrong for someone,
simply to pursue his private battle, to go so far that he forgets
what can be in another's interest.

You request that I give up my pseudonymity. You give no
other reason than that you are involved in a disagreement with
those around you. I cannot conceal that it has almost insulted
me that you so uncontrollably think that everyone should be
at your beck and call. In an equally unjustified manner, you
lump *Either/Or* together with some newspaper articles merely
because they have in common that you have been construed to
be the author. Even if you had added several reasons, even if
you had spoken in the name of several people, even if you had
tried to tempt me in some other way—it would still be ludicrous if I, provided I otherwise had sufficient reason to be
pseudonymous, for that reason would give it up; it would be
foolish of me, provided I otherwise had reason to give up my
pseudonymity, if I gave the impression that it was your request that motivated me.

IV
B 20
189

You perhaps have already yourself perceived the rashness of
your step. In that case, you can always be assured that I shall
do what you in fairness can request of me. In my heart, I shall
have sympathy for your sufferings; every time I think of you,
I shall soberly think of the quiet resignation that is not re-
warded in this world but has its own intrinsic reward. Even if,
like you, Herr Magister!, one is so fortunate as to have no duties, the practical jokes of fate are also adversities, and he who
bears them also bears his cross. No one considers such a person
to be great; as far as you are concerned, I take pride in daring
to admire you—on my own behalf, I beg you to be assured of
that.

In conclusion, I shall allow myself to suggest to you that
your position has been very much on my mind also in another
way. What amazed me in your request was that it is diametri-

cally opposed to the old rule that a *Magister Artium* dares least of all to be ignorant of or to ignore in his conduct: *Quod fieri potest per pauca, non debet fieri per plura* [That which can be effected by means of a few things ought not to be effected by means of many]. Instead of asking me to give up my pseudonymity, it would, after all, be far simpler to request of me the explanation that you are not the author. It has been incomprehensible to me that this did not occur to you, but I also thank the gods that in this respect they have struck you with blindness. However reasonable your asking would have been, it still would have been an impossibility for me to fulfill it. Since I myself do not know who the honored authors are, I cannot positively know that you are not one of them, although, to be honest, I do not find it probable, since your passion as manifested does not exactly tempt one to credit you with the necessary patience. If I can in this respect be of service to you with any declaration, it will always be a pleasure for me to show in deed "as swiftly as possible" what I in any case continue to be in my heart,

Herr Magister's obedient servant,
Victor Eremita
—*Pap.* IV B 20 *n.d.*, 1843

Underlined in "The Episode of 'The Seducer's Diary' " in a copy of Den Frisindede, *23, February 23, 1843:*

One could be tempted to call upon the moral supervisors of the Society for the Freedom of the Press to excommunicate the author and ask the police morals squad to confiscate the work and burn the unknown author in effigy; *but at the next moment one will admit that in any case those who read this book can scarcely be harmed by it.*—*Pap.* IV B 21 *n.d.*, 1843

Draft of letter for possible publication:

A Warning to Den Frisindede

Den Frisindede has, as far as I know, led a quiet and innocent life for a long time. Politically speaking, it now seems to have served its time and now is amusing itself by writing riddles, charades, anagrams, mathematical puzzles, and puns that *Den Frisindede* itself or some other seedy character solves in the next number. It is rather well known that on occasion, when it sees its chance, it tries to jump on the bandwagon every time a phenomenon in literature makes it possible, and thus the editor of *Either/Or* must be prepared to have that newspaper intrude upon this work also and if possible hold fast to it for a moment. This has already happened on Thursday, February 23, in its issue no. 23.

On the strength of *Den Frisindede*'s words "that one must admit that those who read this book (*Either/Or*) can scarcely be harmed by it"—in view of the fact that on the other hand those who do not read it cannot possibly be deemed to be harmed by it, except the negative harm that they do not read it, which in turn can be remedied by their reading it, since in that case, of course, they are sure of not being harmed by it—on the strength thereof and in view thereof, every lover of mankind can be assured, which was the publisher's conviction also, that this book will do no harm.

IV
B 22
191

That *Den Frisindede* can reason so circumspectly at a time when all the rest of what it does manifests inexplicable haste is remarkable—if only it will not "at a time more leisurely for it" reason all the more uncircumspectly. Therefore, we want to warn *Den Frisindede* against publishing extracts or making copies, because in that case it would undoubtedly be possible that harm would be done.* We especially wish to warn it** against surrendering to the quiet lunacy† "of fearlessly and uncompromisingly expressing, at a time more leisurely for it, its honest opinion of this amazing work."

*indeed, we wish that *Den Frisindede*, which, when it has not had time to read the work, nevertheless has found time to review it, may never find time to read it, in order to remove the only conceivable possibility that anyone at all would be harmed by reading it.

**if *Den Frisindede* fears that harm may be done
†that it would be called to the task

—*Pap.* IV B 22 *n.d.*, 1843

Addition to Pap. IV B 22:

So rarely does *Den Frisindede* make a good and in the profounder sense true observation that we urgently request the publisher to reread what he himself says: One must admit that those who read this book etc.—*Pap.* IV B 23 *n.d.*, 1843

Addition to Pap. IV B 22:

—A work consisting of several parts can be so constituted that the reader has the option of reading it consecutively or each part separately; it can be so constituted that not to read it consecutively betrays tactlessness; it can be so constituted that it makes it an obligation and necessity for the reader to read it consecutively and to read all of it if he wants to read it at all. In this respect, I consider it to be an impossibility to come up with a more cogent title than *Either/Or*. If a man begins his discourse with *Either*—and in addition does not leave the listener unaware that the preliminary part will be very long—then one owes it to him either to request him not to begin or to hear his *Or* along with it. One cannot call for silence in this way with a printed work titled *Either/Or*, but the issue remains the same: one must either read it in its entirety or not read it at all.

If in a printed work titled *Either/Or* there is an article called "The Seducer's Diary," a person does not read it first, does not read it exclusively, and if he does read it exclusively he does not allow himself to have any opinion about the work, or if he does have a quasi-opinion he does not express it, or if he finally must express it he does it quite privately in his room or, if he has to confide his opinion to others, he does it orally—but above all he does not write a review of it, does not print any of it, because he prostitutes himself both by admitting that this is the only part he has read and by wanting to justify a judgment of the whole work after having read a single article—in short, one makes a fool of oneself and, N.B., by a rush job that without a doubt is completely unwarranted.

Admittedly, it must be assumed to be in order that in a story titled "The Seducer's Diary" there are seductive and salacious things, unless it is assumed that a conflict between the esthetic and the ethical would compel an author to be [like the man] who by way of precaution advertised his lost umbrella as a cotton umbrella lest someone keep it if he found out that it was a silk umbrella. That such a story must be read cautiously is clear enough; that one can require of the editor that he do all that he can to prevent harmful effects is clear enough. That this is the case is, I believe, quite obvious; that no one can blamelessly be misled is, I believe, evident. If anyone wants to make a test, he can easily convince himself of this. Take a lightminded, even a very corrupt, person (and to the editor a person like that is certainly the most disadvantageous exception), hand him a bound copy of *Either/Or* and say to him: Here is a book in which among other things there is a story called "The Seducer's Diary." The title will perhaps tempt him, but if he still has any respect for the productions of others he will say: Why is it not published separately? Why does it stand here as an episode? Why is the book called *Either/Or*? He will take the book and go home with the good intention of reading it in its entirety. If inclination prevails over intention, so that he reads the diary first and only this, he will be ashamed of himself, but he will keep quiet about this shame and least of all will he shove any guilt onto the editor.

IV
B 24
193

But what such a person would *not* do, even if he wanted to express himself, we learn from *Den Frisindede*. He would *not* write a review with the title: "The Episode of 'The Seducer's Diary' " and in a note give one to understand that the diary is an episode in *Either/Or*; he would title his article *Either/Or*. He would *not* rip an episode out of it and thus in a double sense rip it out of its coherence with the whole. Whether he would write a note that contradicts itself in every other line, I shall not decide—I regard that of minor importance. In view of the fact, however, that his paper is read by the simple class, he would *not* choose an episode that might especially disturb them. Finally, he would *not* with hypocritical zeal do what the editor of *Either/Or* has never done: he would *not* contribute to publicizing what he regards as corrupting and precisely by this publicizing make it what it was not previously. He would *not* quite *en passant* declare in a note that alongside the hilarity in this work "the most profound earnestness immediately intervenes"—without even citing an example of it.

When someone does as *Den Frisindede* has done, the person who is the natural guardian of that work owes it to himself, to the unknown authors, and to the reading public not to let it go unchallenged; he owes it to the work to reprimand *Den Frisindede*. Since, however, this paper sees itself able to appeal to sound common sense only by seeming to fear that "Hegel, Greek, and Latin would take exception to its conduct," there is nothing else to do in this respect than to let it continue in the voluntary exile it has itself necessarily chosen. All I want to do is warn against *Den Frisindede*'s sound common sense, warn every reader against reading *Either/Or* in the pirated version of *Den Frisindede*.

I have imagined what even a very corrupt person would do; I have explained what *Den Frisindede* has done; in order once again to throw light upon its conduct, I shall show what it could have done. First and foremost, it could have given itself time, for there surely is no one who is particularly desirous of its opinion—if it believes this, then it could have been quick about reading the whole book. Then if it wanted to tell its readers something about this work, it would say, in view of the fact that its readers belong to the simple class, "A work has been published that the average reader of this paper will no doubt scarcely understand. But in the second part of the book there is a profound earnestness, a sincerely sympathetic love for and interest in every human being. An attempt is made here to show how all the many differences in life nevertheless vanish before this good fortune: to be a human being; it is shown that this is the only thing of which one dares to be proud; the circumstances of those to whom abundance has not been given are described with unaffected emotion; every honorable endeavor in life is praised." This *Den Frisindede* would do out of love for its readers; if it believed itself able to do it better than that author, it would have added a few friendly and admonishing words. Then it would have done a good deed. Then it would have earned the gratitude of the author of that work; then it would have laid claim to the gratitude of its readers. Then no one would be more willing to appreciate its endeavor than the natural guardian of that work. No one would be more willing to thank it, provided it was able to do it better than that guardian has done it, who surely would say, if one could request of him his explanation, that it gave him as much pleasure as if he had done it himself.

Victor Eremita
—*Pap*. IV B 24 *n.d.*, 1843

My Opinion of *Either/Or*

There was a young man as favorably endowed as an Alcibiades. He lost his way in the world. In his need he looked about for a Socrates but found none among his contemporaries. Then he requested the gods to change him into one. But now—he who had been so proud of being an Alcibiades was so humiliated and humbled by the gods' favor that, just when he received what he could be proud of, he felt inferior to all.

—*JP* V 5613 (*Pap*. IV A 43) *n.d.*, 1843

Even if I proved nothing else by writing *Either/Or*, I proved that in Danish literature one can write a book, that one can work, without needing the warm jacket of sympathy,[53] without needing the incentives of anticipation, that one can work even though the stream is against one, that one can work hard without seeming to, that one can privately concentrate while practically every bungling student dares look upon one as a loafer.[54] Even if the book itself were devoid of meaning, the making of it would still be the pithiest epigram I have written over the maundering philosophic age in which I live.—*JP* V 5614 (*Pap*. IV A 45) *n.d.*, 1843

In *Intelligensblade*,[55] I see that Professor Heiberg thinks that it is indelicate of me to publish such a story. That he is in a way right about that I have no doubt, for otherwise how else could he say it? What a pity that prior to the publication it did not occur to me to think about what Herr Professor Heiberg would say—what a pity!—*Pap.* IV B 27 *n.d.*, 1843

Professor Heiberg thinks that it is necessary to be rude toward me. Alas, alas, alas, that I have come to that—for if Professor Heiberg says it, I have no doubt that it actually is so. Yet it comforts me to know that Professor Heiberg wants to be rude, because he is concerned for my temporal and eternal welfare. Oh, that Prof. H. might succeed in being sufficiently rude! Yet I do not doubt it, since it is Prof. H. I doubt it even less, since it is the year 1843. Over the years, a wonderful change has taken place in H.*; he has become less jocular, more earnest, less facetious, more severe, less witty, more rude.[**] What was difficult for him thirteen years ago, what was impossible for him fifteen years ago, will no doubt, with the aid of all good jinn, succeed for him now.

In margin: *another person
[**]*In margin:* less entertaining, more boring.
—*Pap.* IV B 28 *n.d.*, 1843

Wholesaler Nathanson is of the same opinion.[56] If there was a proud thought in my soul that dared at any moment to rise in protest against Professor Heiberg's authority—it is now squelched, for Wholesaler Nathanson is of the same opinion. In vain do I look for an escape; if rudeness cannot do it, then wittiness can; if Heiberg cannot do it, then N. can.—*Pap.* IV B 29 *n.d.*, 1843

Prof. Heiberg believes that I am allowing myself to make fun of him. —That would be an appalling thought. I would rather have expected the professor to have gone along with the judge's train of thought in *The Marriage of Figaro:*[57] Would anyone dare to make fun of me—I make fun of my benefactor!—*Pap.* IV B 30 *n.d.*, 1843

From D. I understand that some students declare that no one laughs at what I write. This does not surprise me, since it has never been my intention that anyone should laugh at it. My soul is somewhat doubtful; if it had been my intention to arouse laughter, I presumably would have taken the precaution of adding "laugh" at particular points just as *plaudite* [applaud] was inserted in the old comedies; for it is not granted to everyone to be as certain of laughter as my most honored *comilitones* [comrades-in-arms] could be.—*Pap.* IV B 31 *n.d.*, 1843

Prof. Heiberg must not think that I say this because I envy him the dignity of being the authority.[58] Indeed, I find it highly desirable that there is an authority, provided only that I myself may be exempted from it, for it always makes for complications. If Professor Heiberg will make up his mind to take upon himself this honorable calling, I do not need to come out with my proposal to the Assembly that an authority must be established,[59] a post that will rotate among all the authors of twenty-four printing sheets for the term of one year, as with the consulship in Rome, and of such a nature that what the ruling authority says during the year when he is the authority is and shall be regarded as the truth by the king of all the Danish lands and provinces, and those who do not share this view must wait until they themselves or one of their friends become the authority.—*Pap.* IV B 32 *n.d.*, 1843

That there are a few printer's errors, I do not deny; that it would be better if they were not there is readily admitted— that Professor Heiberg dwells on them does not surprise me. The concept of classical prose he has seen fit to establish seems to be a suitable model in a school—soon things will go with the professor so that we shall sing about the professor what the professor himself has taught us to sing:

> He pays attention to every noise
> to every basement doorway
> to every weather vane,
> and in plain sight scrupulously scrutinizes the
> prescribed bell pull[60]

that is: the requisite question and exclamation marks.
I have a little nephew who goes to grammar school. I have

IV B 33 197

IV B 33 198

had him go through the book, and he has pointed out exactly the same thing as the professor. Two such authorities are enough.—*Pap.* IV B 33 *n.d.*, 1843

I am being asked to declare that the work is not by me. What does this mean? This is indeed something totally unheard of in Denmark! I have always been a great enemy of lawsuits and depositions and thus have been a good friend of the police and the criminal court judge—but this is indeed a terror-tribunal. —Although I could very easily answer and thereby put an end to the matter, I perceive both that it will not amount to much and that the whole thing ought to be regarded as a matter of principle. Yet perhaps my poor insignificant life will acquire significance for the whole thing. In the name of all authors, I protest against such conduct.

But do stop vexing my peaceful life in this way (just as when one person looks like another); it is a matter of principle.

—*Pap.* IV B 34 *n.d.*, 1843

IV
B 35
198

A Painful Situation (Distress Signal).[61]

It is now about four months since I, in the newspaper *Fædrelandet*, with all respect permitted myself to divert any suspicion from me in connection with the authorship of several things—yet readers may have forgotten this, and I also, but not the consequences of it. For several days, I encountered on all sides caustic glances, the meaning of which I did not at first understand, but I soon learned to interpret them. A letter from a friend explained everything. That is, the friend had seen through me, had perceived that it was vanity, as if I wanted to make people believe that anyone had talked about such things. Now everything became clear to me; various covert statements became more clear to me, those glances easily explained. They felt sorry for me and my vanity, that it could occur to me that it could occur to anyone that I was the author; they pitied me for wanting to join in. —And yet I dare to maintain that it was on account of certain charges that I de-

IV
B 35
199

cided on that step, decided to beg my contemporaries not to regard me as author of anything that did not bear my name. —Now I am right where I started—an article in *Ny Portefeuille*, a letter in the *Berlingske* (opinions differ; some think that the letter including the point is by me, others that it is the letter in which it was omitted[62]), a similar letter in *Fædrelandet*, and finally the big work *Either/Or*. If I had not been so unfortunate as to have made an admission once, I would do it now; but since it failed once, what are my prospects now—will I not expose myself once again to letters and caustic glances; will anyone believe my declaration? In civic life we encounter people who are promptly willing when it is a matter of being a guarantor, but no innkeeper wants them; so also with my explanation—no one will believe it—*Pap.* IV B 35 *n.d.*, 1843

> Prof. Heiberg is an ingenious man.
> Fa-la-la-da-da
> [*Vitte-vit-vit-bom-bom*].
> —*Pap.* IV B 36 *n.d.*, 1843

You, Herr Professor Heiberg, are a man of letters, and I am anything but. Please allow me for a moment to draw my words from the world of horses. A horse trainer can train even a less spirited horse to be a parade horse, and it is quite enjoyable to see its measured step. When one has no other place to ride than on the embankment, where accidents can so easily happen, or even in a very restricted area, it can be quite all right, and the ladies out for a stroll and concerned about their finery enjoy both paraders—the horse and the rider—and parents have nothing against letting their children, even the small, walk up and watch them. —A young wild horse, however, does not have such beautiful and measured movements; at times its fiery mettle is almost ridiculous, its friskiness a bit uncouth, but beneath all this it nevertheless has one thing no horse trainer can give, and that is the snort in its nostrils, its fiery breathing. Anyone who knows anything about this will also have the courage to watch it, to delight in it.

IV
B 37
199

IV
B 37
200

You simply have not plumbed the human heart, its passions, etc.; whether you nevertheless are completely finished with your life-view I do not know; the passions developed in *Either/Or* are already too high for you, and if I had the honor of speaking with you I would whisper in your ear something whereby you would see that more is needed in order to explain life.—*Pap.* IV B 37 *n.d.*, 1843

An author who prefers to be a supplementary clerk[63] in literature, as one sees from the preface, and by no means craves any appointment in Professor Heiberg's office.—*Pap.* IV B 38 *n.d.*, 1843

Professor Heiberg is very welcome to go further; he is welcome to throw both volumes at the head of the unknown authors—he has my word for that, and he needs it, because otherwise he might perhaps have scruples about it, he in particular, since he seems so unusually disturbed by the thought of the size of the book.[64] The effect will be dreadful if he hits them.—*Pap.* IV B 39 *n.d.*, 1843

I do not wish to be an authority; it must be embarrassing. For instance, if I could receive an honorable and lucrative appointment as a model of virtue, I would decline it, since it must be a burden to be a model of virtue day in and day out.
—*Pap.* IV B 40 *n.d.*, 1843

Prof. Heiberg is also in the habit of "holding judgment day in literature." Have you forgotten what happened to Xerxes? He had even taken scribes along to describe his victory over little Greece.[65] —*Pap.* IV B 41 *n.d.*, 1843

He is not alone, has muses and graces—and for safety's sake he has acquired a new co-worker: "one",[66] an energetic co-worker who demands no fee and accepts any treatment.—*Pap.* IV B 42 *n.d.*, 1843

It says in the hymnbook that all the princes of the world are unable to create a straw—while any miserable prattler can create a "one".[67] —*Pap.* IV B 43 *n.d.*, 1843

On the birthday of *Intelligensblade*,[68] congratulations to Professor Heiberg from my wife and myself and several friends who read the copy of the paper to which I subscribe.

> Respectfully,
> MADSEN
> retired mailman
> —*Pap.* IV B 44 *n.d.*, 1843

We have now given an account of how "one",[69] according to our knowledge, has treated this work. —Prof. Heiberg is too important a figure to be classified in any way under the rubric "one". Let us now see how he has treated it. It has (1) surprised Prof. Heiberg that the book is so big[70] —indeed, so big that one could be paid for exhibiting it (one would almost believe that the professor was describing what he himself had done); (2) provokes . . . . . —*Pap.* IV B 45 *n.d.*, 1843

How Does "One" Treat *Either/Or?*

IV
B 46
202

Everyone will find it quite in order that it frequently occurs to the one who is the natural guardian of this work to ponder its future fate. Even before he published it, he had thought about this, of which one will readily be convinced by merely reading the preface, without sniffing through *Either* and paging through *Or*. I have briefly pronounced judgment there on both parts since A. says: Read it or do not read it, you will regret it either way, whereas B. wishes the book to pass by the critic unnoticed and rather to visit a single individual so that the book might encounter a reader in a kindly disposed hour. I, of course, did not dare expect it to turn out quite this way, for how often does one have one's wish fulfilled in this manner? After the work appeared, I again occasionally paid heed to the verdict of the public. This at times can be difficult enough, and for that reason I am really pleased that Professor Heiberg with unusual courtesy has had the kindness to enlighten, in a prophetic vision, the book-reading public and thereby me, too, with regard to how "one" treats and will treat *Either/Or*. As far as I know, Prof. H. certainly has not so far tried his hand at prophecy, but one does grow older, and Prof. H. is very perfectible.[*] It will soon be two years since Herr Professor changed from being the witty, jesting, hilarious vaudeville playwright who yet at times seemed* somewhat astray in the faith, the victorious polemicist, the measured esthetician, and became Denmark's Dante,[71] the musing genius who in his apocalyptic poem peered into the secrets of eternal life, became the Church's dutiful son from whom the esteemed clergy of the diocese expected everything for the good of the "parish."[72] If it had not happened, who would believe that it could happen, but after it has happened, who then is not bound to believe Prof. H. capable of everything?

But to the matter at hand. In no. 24 of *Intelligensblade* there is a little article by Prof. Heiberg titled "*Litterær Vintersæd.*"[73] In this little article the professor has managed to discuss incredibly much. The first part is brilliant; the second is complimentary to various Danish authors; the third is prophetic; the fourth doubtful; the fifth is a single reader's opinion of *Or*; the sixth opens the prospect that someday[**] there may come a reader who will read both parts, both *Either* and *Or*.[74]

The first part, the brilliant part, does not concern me, and therefore I shall not discuss it further, however pained I am not to be able to dwell on the beautiful, moving thought advanced by the professor, the edifying thought that *Intelligensblade* is now beginning a new annual series, for the thought could actually make a stone cry, so moving it is. It is comforting and encouraging for all of us, like the immortality of Kildevalle the poet.[75]

[*]*Penciled in margin:* new directions
In margin: *to nourish straying views of faith
[**]*In margin:* in the fullness of time.

IV
B 46
203

The complimentary part does not concern me either, and the only thing that almost pains me is that the reader will forget it when he comes to the next part, which deals with how "one" treats *Either/Or*.[76]

This part, then, does concern me, and the readers of this paper will then forgive the absence in this number of that which they usually look for or of that which can engage them, and it is my wish that the single solitary reader who actually reads *Either/Or* may come upon these lines and have enough patience to read them also.—*Pap*. IV B 46 *n.d.*, 1843

IV
B 46
204

That H. P. Holst[77] does not know what style is, to say nothing of the meaning of the old thesis *stil c'est l'homme* [the style is the man], can be taken quite for granted, without therefore denying his qualification as a useful teacher of poetic fine writing. He confuses style and fine writing.[78] —We would have nothing against his continuing a means of making a living. —He actually does not prattle, that is saying too much—he rattles on. —We do not doubt that now; in consequence of this short reply, he will once again spin out the thin and finical and brittle thread of his chatter, which he moistens with esthetic dishwater, and he especially wants it to become a whole fabric if he should manage to give the appearance that he in any way ventures to attach himself to Heiberg and that his web could in any way be regarded as a fringe on Heiberg's *Intelligensblade*, for it really does not seem that the muses and graces inspire him as does the good fortune of being included in a footnote in Heiberg.[79] When it is a matter of placing the period in the right place etc. etc., he is right there, but when it is a matter of ideas, thoughts, of untamed passions, of the fervent emotions of the heart, where one hears the squealing of laughter and the deep sighing of the heart, there Holst is always *outside* even though he gives the appearance of being *at home*.[80] I do not intend to answer him, unless, contrary to expectation, the devil should slip into him and make him malevolent, because then the fun begins. But I do not believe him capable even of this; his whole existence is a languishing aftertaste of a poetic taste; his esthetic

IV
B 48
204

IV
B 48
205

competence is an unlovely voluptuousness.—*Pap.* IV B 48 *n.d.*, 1843

. . . . . the esthetic writing teacher—the literary telegraph operator—a tax collector who counts votes[81]—and although he tries in every way to save the *Intelligensblade* from becoming half-hour reading by having it come out in double issues, it does not help—if three issues came out at once, it would still be only half-hour reading.—*Pap.* IV B 51 *n.d.*, 1843

For several years now Prof. Heiberg has been sitting at the window of literature all prinked up and waving to the passersby, especially if it was a smart looking man and he heard a little applause from the adjoining street.—*Pap.* IV B 49 *n.d.*, 1843

Underlined in copy of Intelligensblade, *26-27, April 15, 1843* ASKB U 56), *p. 50:*

Consequently, it is a mistake if one believes that genuine romanticism is confined to Catholicism, if one believes, as does the author of *Either/Or*, that in our day it should be annulled—first in the esthetic, then in the ethical . . . . . —*JP* III 3823 (*Pap.* IV B 50:4) *n.d.*, 1843

Heiberg, who previously was a denominator in literature—indeed almost a common denominator—has now become a numerator [*Tæller*]—a teller [*Tæller*] in the literary bank.
—*Pap.* IV B 52 *n.d.*, 1843

. . . . . it is a pleasure to see how Herr Professor Heiberg's recent astronomical, astrological, chiromantic, necromantic, chronologic, topographic, statistical, horoscopic, metascopic studies[82] are beneficial not only to his most gracious majesty the king[83] but also to the neighbor.—*Pap.* IV B 53 *n.d.*, 1843

Heiberg ought to know that for some time now he has become an uncle. Indeed, it is beautiful when an uncle knows how to make himself loved by his young relatives, but he must not be grumpy,[84] for then it is a disastrous position. —Perhaps Uncle Heiberg is striving for this.—*Pap*. IV B 54 *n.d.*, 1843

Prof. Heiberg has "the measure in his mouth," just like the sergeant who demanded an aquavit from a barmaid. Then in the very same moment there was a bugle call to arms, and in the rush she could not find the measure, but the sergeant snatched the bottle, saying: I have the measure in my mouth— which was no help at all to the poor barmaid, who probably was a poor woman and herself had her aquavit measured out by the distiller. —Thus, I am not helped either; I am a poor man.—*Pap*. IV B 55 *n.d.*, 1843

God bless your incoming, Herr Prof. Heiberg! As for your outgoing, I shall take care of that adequately.—*Pap*. IV B 56 *n.d.*, 1843

Everyone has his hobbyhorse, and if one leads it out to him well saddled, he mounts, and then it is: "Gee up" at a gallop.
—*Pap*. IV B 57 *n.d.*, 1843

Heiberg remarked in his outcry over *Either/Or* that it was really hard to tell whether some of the observations in it were profound or not.[85] Professor Heiberg and his consorts have the great advantage that what they say is known in advance to be profound. This is partly due to the fact that not a single prim- itive thought is to be found in them, or at least rarely. What they know they borrow from Hegel, and Hegel is indeed pro- found—ergo, what Professor Heiberg says is also profound. In this way every theological student who limits his sermon to nothing but quotations from the Bible becomes the most pro- found of all, for the Bible certainly is the most profound book of all.—*JP* V 5697 (*Pap*. IV A 162) *n.d.*, 1843

When I am not *reus voti* [one bound by a vow], nothing hap- pens for me. Because of it I got my theological certificate; because of it I wrote my dissertation,[86] because of it I was all through with *Either/Or* in eleven months.[87] If anyone were to find out the actual incentive . . . . . Good Lord, they no doubt are thinking, such a big book as that must certainly have a very profound incentive . . . . . and yet it is exclusively concerned with my private life—and the purpose—well, if this were discovered, I would be declared stark raving mad. I perhaps would be excused for personally regarding it as an interesting piece of work, but for me to look upon it as a good deed, that for me this is the most appealing aspect of the whole thing . . . . . . —*JP* V 5626 (*Pap.* IV A 70) *n.d.*, 1843

Theodorus Atheos said: He gave his teaching with the right hand, but his listeners received it with the left.[88]
See Tennemann, *Ges. d. Phil.*, II, p. 124, note 39.—*Pap.* IV A 75 *n.d.*, 1843

I must get at my Antigone[89] again. The task will be a psychological development and motivation of the presentiment of guilt. —With that in mind I have been thinking of Solomon and David,[90] of the relation of Solomon's youth to David, for no doubt both Solomon's intellect (dominant in the relationship) and his sensuousness are the results of David's greatness. He had earlier intimations of David's deep agitation without realizing what guilt might rest upon him, and yet he had seen this profoundly God-fearing man give such an ethical expression to his repentance, for it would have been a quite different matter if David had been a mystic. These ideas, these presentiments, smother energies (except in the form of imagination), arouse the intellect, and this combination of imagination and intellect, where the factor of the will is lacking, is sensuousness proper.—*JP* V 5669 (*Pap.* IV A 114) *n.d.*, 1843

I have half a mind to write a counter-piece to "The Seducer's Diary." It would be a feminine figure: "The Courtesan's Diary." It would be worth the trouble to depict such a character.—*JP* V 5676 (*Pap.* IV A 128) *n.d.*, 1843

The sequel to "The Seducer's Diary" must be in a piquant vein, his relation to a young married woman.—*JP* V 5677 (*Pap*. IV A 129) *n.d.*, 1843

The Seducer's Diary
No. 2
A Venture in the Demonic
by
Johannes Mephistopheles

IV
A 181
66

N.B. It is what the age wants, to become dizzy over the abominable and then fancy itself to be superior. They will not get that from me.

IV
A 181
67

Foreword

I am indebted for the idea to what Victor Eremita has published, and I can only lament that this author has not pursued the excellent ideas at his disposal but instead has become an upbuilding writer.

The scene is in the house of Cordelia, who is married to Edward—in her house there is a young girl who is the object; the fact that it is in Cordelia's house is a subtle refinement.

He heightens his pleasure by constantly clinging to the thought that this will be his last adventure and by parceling it out, as it were, into enjoyment. Moreover, he heightens the enjoyment by reproducing, from everything erotic in the particular situation, a compendious memory of the girl who then goes to ruin on this side of the idea of femininity; he heightens the enjoyment by reproducing all of his own life, and in this way the psychological presuppositions of his soul come to light.

He gets to know a courtesan and establishes a psychological union with her to explore the relation between the seduction that originates with a man and that which originates with a woman—eventually he decides to ruin her, too.

He collides with a Don Juan over the same girl. This throws light on the method, but he knows how to put Don Juan to good use as a serviceable element in his plan.—*JP* V 5705 (*Pap.* IV A 181) *n.d.*, 1844

On front fly-leaf of copy of Either/Or, *I:*

The first part contains depression (egotistic–sympathetic) and despair (in understanding and passion). The second part therefore teaches despair and choosing oneself. Even the essay on Don Juan has depression, an enthusiasm that robs him of understanding, a dreaming, almost deranged, reveling in fantasy. The first part is therefore essentially paradoxical—that is, it does not contain this or that paradoxical thought, but it is sheer passion, and this is always paradoxical and must not be destroyed; for paradox is the passion of thought. The motto also suggests that it is sheer passion in its arbitrariness.

The first part is continually stranded on time. This is why the second part strongly affirms it, since it is shown in the first discussion that the esthetic is broken upon time, and in the second discussion it is shown that the meaning of finitude and temporality is to be able to become history, to gain a history.

Fantasy like this always creates depression; therefore the first part is depressed.—*JP* I 907 (*Pap.* IV A 213) *n.d.*, 1843

On front fly-leaf of copy of Either/Or, *I:*

Probably no one suspects that *Either/Or* has a plan from the first word to the last, since the preface makes a joke of it[91] and does not say a word about the speculative.—*JP* V 5627 (*Pap.* IV A 214) *n.d.*, 1843

On front fly-leaf of copy of Either/Or, *I:*

Some think that *Either/Or* is a collection of loose papers I had lying in my desk. Bravo! —As a matter of fact, it was the reverse. The only thing this work lacks is a narrative, which I did begin but omitted, just as Aladdin left a window incomplete. It was to be called "Unhappy Love." It was to form a contrast to the Seducer. The hero in the story acted in exactly the same way as the Seducer, but behind it was depression. He was not unhappy because he could not get the girl he loved. Such heroes are beneath me. He had capacities comparable to the Seducer's; he was certain of capturing her. He won her. As long as the struggle went on, he detected nothing; then she surrendered, he was loved with all the enthusiasm a young girl has—then he became unhappy, went into a depression, pulled back; he could struggle with the whole world but not with himself. His love made him indescribably happy at the moment; as soon as he thought of time, he despaired.—*JP* V 5628 (*Pap.* IV A 215) *n.d.*, 1843

On front fly-leaf (continued on title page of Diapsalmata) of copy of Either/Or, *I:*

The first Διάψαλμα is really the task of the entire work, which is not resolved until the last words of the sermon.[92] An enormous dissonance is assumed, and then it says: Explain it. A total break with actuality is assumed, which does not have its base in vanity but in depression and its predominance over actuality.

The last διάψ. tells us how a life such as this has found its satisfactory expression in laughter. He pays his debt to actuality by means of laughter, and now everything takes place within this contradiction. His enthusiasm is too intense, his sympathy too deep, his love too burning, his heart too warm to be able to express himself in any other way than by contradiction. Thus A himself would never have come to a decision to publish his papers.—*JP* V 5629 (*Pap.* IV A 216) *n.d.*, 1843

In copy of Either/Or, *I, after Diapsalmata:*

If I had not decided when publishing *Either/Or* not to use any old material,[93] I would have found in going through my papers some aphorisms that could have been used very well. Today I found a little scrap of paper with the following written on it: "I am so tired that I feel that I need an eternity to rest, so troubled that I feel that I need an eternity to forget my sorrow; I wish that I could sleep so long that I would wake up an old man and could then lie down again to sleep the eternal sleep."—*JP* V 5631 (*Pap.* IV A 221) March 15, 1843

I reject all reviews, for to me a reviewer is just as loathsome as a street barber's assistant who comes running with his shaving water, which is used for all customers, and fumbles about my face with his clammy fingers.[94]—*JP* V 5698 (*Pap.* IV A 167) *n.d.*, 1843-44

IV
B 58
208

A Deplorable, an Amusing, an Innocent Madness.

Whoever finds someone
raving or mad must tie him up.
Danish law, 1,19,7.

On account of an article in Prof. Heiberg's *Intelligensblade* ("Ecclesiastical Polemics"[95] by Kts[96]), a man has gone mad in *Kjøbenhavnsposten.*[97] This is deplorable. The amusing thing about it, however, is that his madness and fixed idea consist of deluding himself and others that he is a pastor. This is the best interpretation of the article's signature: A Pastor. In any other case, one would inevitably hazard the just as insulting as difficult and highly unlikely explanation that a pastor could so forget himself and his senses that after having written an article like that he did not at least abstain from signing it: A Pastor.

The article's very reverend author* must be from this city, for it is chiefly something Kts said about the considerable church attendance in the capital that has become the object of his attack, and certainly one cannot assume that a rural pastor could find time to travel so frequently to Copenhagen, especially on Sunday. He thinks that Kts untruthfully represents (he is so pure that he is unwilling to use the word "lie") the attendance in the capital's churches as high. To that end, he ap-

---

*Note. Everyone knows how gratifying it is to a man who has a fixed idea for someone to enter into it and speak to him on the basis of it.

peals to his own experience, which indeed also ought to be worthy of credence, for presumably he ordinarily** goes to only a few churches; but occasionally, when he happens to be passing by, he also goes into other churches for a moment in order to see how many people there are. It is incredible how much this self-appointed pastor on his own responsibility manages to accomplish every Sunday. Ordinarily he attends a few churches (it is difficult to manage more if one is going to remain through the whole service, except for several festival days, when there is also divine service at noon); occasionally he visits several other churches in order to count. What time does this good parson save for preaching? A real pastor would hardly have written as thoughtlessly as this.

In another respect also, to the credit of the author, I believe that he ought to be assumed to be mad. That is, if he is not mad and as such is an absolutely isolated case, even if he represents a new tendency in the sphere of church attendance, then Kts's church attendance record under discussion gains a new increase. It surely has not occurred to Kts to suggest this type of churchgoer, churchgoers who come in order to count those in attendance. But regardless of what brings a person to church, if there is only the question of frequency entirely *in abstracto*, then everyone counts, even someone who comes only in order to count.

Now if only one dares hope that the mad pastor in *Kjøbenhavnsposten* will limit himself to counting, even if he does not give up his fixed idea that he is a pastor, his madness will be completely innocent, and his endeavor may even be of benefit to him in the future.* He certainly cannot be assumed to have

IV
B 58
209

IV
B 58
210

**Note. "Ordinarily"—this word must not be misinterpreted as if he went properly to church in the few churches to which he ordinarily goes. His meaning is perceived from the contrast that he occasionally goes in for a moment in order to count the number of those in attendance. That is, taking a census such as that, if it is to be of any use, is not a matter of a moment, and therefore he does it properly in the few churches he ordinarily visits. In other words, if he remained properly for the whole service in the few churches he ordinarily visits, it stands to reason that he would have to come to the churches he occasionally visits at a time when they were empty—in order to count how many there are.

qualified his competence by this article in *Kbhp.*, but if in the course of the next few well-spent years he appears in public and publishes a tabulated and statistical survey of church attendance in this city, a work he rightfully may dare call the fruit of his church attendance, he certainly will be suitably placed. Without a doubt, the municipality, when the time comes to appoint a new tax collector, will give him preference,** or a bank director will consider him in the selection of a teller.

A Grocer

*without his daring therefore to count absolutely on becoming a real pastor.
**over any other theological candidate

—*Pap.* IV B 58 *n.d.*, 1844

IV
B 59
210

Post-Scriptum
to
Either/Or
by
Victor Eremita[*]

Everything has an end; "even Jesper Morten's sermon at the recent vespers came to an end."[98] This is a rather bleak view, especially for Jesper Morten, to whom it is no benefit, even though for everyone else it is cheering. [*Deleted:* Neither does he dare count it to his credit if the congregation were to become so independent that it did not listen to his closing prayer, but itself, motivated by his Reverence, sent up its own fervent prayer of thanksgiving to heaven for its visible assistance by which the sermon came to an end.] But one must not lightly make fun of Jesper Morten or egotistically reassure oneself that one does not belong to those who begin something. For one thing, that would be a poor eulogy on oneself, and for another, it is still always true that every human being begins something, and then for the whole human race that statement becomes a dismal truth. That of which the philosophers in so

IV
B 59
211

[*]*In margin: to the typesetter:* to be printed like the title page

many ways in word and deed show the difficulty—namely, to begin—appears to my more simple and popular view, which sees everything from the opposite end or, to say it more briefly, from the end, to be bound up with enormous difficulties. That is, if what one begins has an end, how then should one decide to begin it? And if what one begins does not have an end, who would have any desire to begin something? This deliberation, if it cannot be stopped, will end in the quandary that ordinary language rightly describes in saying that one knows neither how one shall begin nor end; the person who actually knows how he shall begin knows *eo ipso* [precisely thereby] how he shall end, and the person who knows how to end knows in that knowledge also how he shall begin. Therefore, it has often amazed me that in our time one so one-sidedly perfects oneself in the art of beginning while practically no word is ever heard about the art of ending. Would it not be timely to commence this art that has the most beautiful promises, for if the end is good, then everything is good. But the beginning is difficult, and yet one cannot begin properly before one knows how to end.

Inasmuch as the bleak view that everything has an end and the equally bleak view that it never has an end could discourage one from beginning, the point is to overcome the doubt that arises, especially when one follows the old advice: *respice finem* [attend to the end]. The point is that freedom gives existence elasticity and that the corruptible is changed into the incorruptible. The thesis "Everything of humankind has an end" signifies the human suffering in existence. Freedom expresses it by saying: Everything must have an end—by which it signifies that the free individual comes to the aid of existence, or steals a march on existence, and by magnanimously putting an end to the affair itself saves itself from the dying-in-bed of finitude or its parodying metamorphoses. The thesis "Nothing has an end" is the expression for the toughness of finitude and for the individual's negative absorption in existence. Here freedom once again comes to the aid of existence by heroically giving the affair an end. The twin expressions of doubt and suffering—that everything has an end and that nothing has an end—are transfigured in freedom by giving everything an end. How many a happy moment has not been destroyed because the end came upon it like a thief in the night and so terribly that with retroactive power it embittered even the past? How many a vigorous, sonorous, profoundly modulated mood ended in toothless twaddle because one was unwilling to understand that everything must have an end? How many a fortunate constellation that by a momentary interplay of the most varied powers enchanted everyone ended in mutual disgust because one did not know how to end? How many a sweet, blissful morning dream that promised the moon and stars ended in a state of fatigue because one did not know how to break off? How many an erotic thrill that rightly used would have been invigorating for a long time ended in a paralytic yawn because one was unwilling to understand that everything must have an end?

In order, then, to carry out, if possible, what is set forth here, I, by retiring, take the liberty of putting an end to what I once began and, if you will, make so bold as to dismiss the reader, something I already had contemplated in the beginning.

For five years I kept the manuscript that in *Either/Or* I ventured to submit to the reading public; one year has now passed since its publication, and the moment seems appropriate for me to break off. Someone may say that five years was too short a time to wait, one year too long a time. Perhaps so, perhaps the work appeared too early, and my *Postscriptum* perhaps comes *post festum* [after the festivity, too late]. If so, I console myself with *in magnis voluisse* [in important things the will is already enough],[99] although I would still like to point out that the end can also come prematurely like a rash caprice, and that in the external circumstances there can sometimes be a situation that requires attention and that bears the immediate blame for one's postponing the time. This is very much the case here, because this *Postscriptum* would already have come out seven months ago if a courteous regard for a careless prophecy,[100] which, if it had been fulfilled, perhaps would have made additional and more detailed communications necessary, had not drawn out the time from month to month.

There is a queer master in life that no one can make out, an ex-potentate who because of eccentricity is often subject to very different judgments: namely, fate. When great human enterprises are undertaken with all conceivable energy and accompanied by the greatest expectations, when a man-of-war puts out to sea, fate does not feel like blowing, seems to have blown away and is nowhere to be found. Meanwhile it may find its pleasure in delighting a child who puts his little boat in a puddle of water. For him it ripples the water; for him it indulges every wish, takes his boat with a favorable wind to the other side, shifts the wind and takes the boat back again to him; for his sake it has the waves pile up, subjects the boat's crew to distress at sea and rescues them again—in short, the child can have his own way with it. One would think that no windmill could go when there was a dead calm, and yet we learn from the fairy tale that there was one windmill that did go. The hero in the tale cannot explain this phenomenon, but then many miles from the mill in question he meets a corpulent man who quite phlegmatically places his finger on one nostril and blows through the other but blows only upon that one windmill[101]—it was fate, which is not without a sense of humor or without a certain kindness either.

Several have no doubt been surprised, as I have been, that a book like *Either/Or* created a certain more general, sympathetic sensation, that it was read—indeed, that it was purchased. I confess that it amazed me, and I for my part attribute it all to fate, without therefore being so ungrateful as to repay with this remark the thanks I owe to the kindness of the reading public, for not even fate was capable of bringing about the reading of the book but rather the purchasing of it. I attribute it all to fate and for that reason am circumspect enough not to draw any conclusions from that, because fate is a very touchy character and one must be extremely cautious in association with it. I have, therefore, always tried to place myself on a firm footing in relation to it. If it meets me on my way, if it takes care of me, well, then I thank it, even though I would rather thank a human being. But I do not go a step out of my way in order to meet it on the next street; I do not cling to it when it leaves me. If I had known that not one single person would care about that work, not one single person would read it, not one single person would buy it—it would still have been published. I had another hope for it: that perhaps after a time there would be a single young person who would really delight me by reading the book for its own sake. Yes, even if I had thought I ought to give up this hope, the book would still have been published.

That the book was read, I thank fate only insofar as its clever head has hit upon various ways of occasioning this. For the reading itself, I would much rather thank the reader, since I am convinced that this was the unknown authors' wish. Therefore, I have no doubt that the reader has become aware of an irregularity in the book: namely, that a movement is undertaken that cannot be made or at least not made in this way. The judge has unquestionably perceived this himself, I cannot believe otherwise. Since his task was only to circumscribe an ethical view, an irregularity of that sort was unavoidable, and I rather believe that on behalf of his view he has tried to hide it. Yet I need not say this to the reader, who knows how to check upon an author insofar as he imitates his movements, a method by which one immediately discovers whether a middle term has been left out. That such an irregularity should escape the armed eyes of reviewers is inconceivable; therefore, I explain their complete silence with regard to this point as leniency, for which I am obliged to thank them on behalf of those concerned. The reviewers I am thinking of are the anonymous reviewer in *Forposten*;[102] Mr. Hagen, M.A., in *Fædrelandet*;[103] and the esteemed unknown reviewer in the *Fyenske Tidsskrift*.[104] And I thank them collectively and individually for their kindness. To have even one well-disposed reviewer is a rarity, but such a trinity among reviewers, at least well-disposed toward the whole if not in judgment of the parts, is a rarity that surely will please the book's unknown authors. I dare not call Professor Heiberg a reviewer; [105]his advertisement or, more accurately, his mixed notice in *Intelli-*

gensblade, was probably intended only "to orient,"[106] and I can only thank him for the courtesy and service shown.*

Deleted marginal note: *His outcry did not make reading the book exactly superfluous but rather necessary in order to understand the advertisement; he did more for the book than all the reviewers, for would there not be many who enthusiastically undertook the labor of reading through two thick volumes simply in order to understand a few pages in *Intelligensblade*? No wonder, then, that I hastened at the time to vent my feelings in a discriminating expression of gratitude?[107] Half constrained [*Das half gewaltig*], since the book would have to be read—for the sake of the advertisement. [*Two lines crossed out and completely illegible.*]

When at the time I had made a copy of the manuscript, had given the book a title, and by doing so had been so bold as to influence the interpretation, since I had written the preface—in short, when I had finished all my domestic tasks, there was still one thing left to be done: to think a little about my attire and harmonize it with the bill of fare. A name in literature is what clothes are in life. Just as on festive occasions in families the domestic servant also receives a new suit of clothes so that everything harmonizes, so I thought that I, too, had to consider a suitable name. Yes, it is both good and bad that fate plays a manuscript like that into one's hands! What complications simply in having to give oneself a name! How fortunate that one is baptized as an infant, that one's parents see to it that one as early as possible acquires a name to go about with!* How wise and paternal of the government that in later years one cannot change one's name! Even if one has been given an unfortunate name, even if through the ignorance of the parish clerk one has been given a meaningless name, it is still always better to keep it than to become depressed, as one uncondi-

IV
B 59
216

Lines added and crossed out: *From the point of view of the public good and the friend of the masses, are not the efforts of the Anabaptists [*Gjendøber,* rebaptizers] just as corrupt as from the point of view of dogmatics—![108]

tionally becomes by having to choose one's own name. Someone may sink so deeply into depression that something may happen to him that as a rule never happens to any human being—that he would die without leaving a name because he never finished choosing one.

In the choice of a literary name, one is more limited—that is, if one has what I had, a specific work in relation to which it is to be chosen, for if someone who does not have one line finished were to devote himself entirely to deliberating upon what name he should use as author, he very likely would never finish. An editor has less trouble, because an author might be tempted to change his work simply for the sake of the name, and then again change his name for the sake of the work, until both come to nothing. This cannot possibly happen to an editor. For him the work is a completed entity that dare not be altered during all the name changes, which do not easily become numerous either, since an editor, in view of his subordinate position, is especially obliged to apply himself to modesty. What he must do is to immerse himself in the work itself and by this descent allow the work to baptize itself, so to speak.

IV
B 59
217

I called the work *Either/Or* and in the preface attempted to explain what I meant by this title. After having familiarized myself with all the details, I had let the whole thing come together before me in one moment of contemplation; my recommendation was that the reader do the same. For him, too, the whole thing would become like one sentence disjunctively separated. The reader would hereby enter into a self-active relation to the book, which was my aim and which I had tried to foster by totally refraining from any comment on the plan of the work, since in addition I could not, after all, know more definitely than any other reader if there was such a thing. The plan was a task of self-activity and to want to force my conception on the reader seemed to me to be an insulting and impertinent intrusion. Everyone experiences an "either/or" in his life (as does Charles in *The First Love* when he says: Either one has an uncle or one does not have an uncle[109]). This is the essential thing; the accidental is the length of the sentences and

the multiplicity of the clauses, but the individual will understand the plan differently according to his own development.
The book had no author, because the esteemed unknowns are
and were to me and presumably likewise to the reader—unknown; then it should have no title either. Its title, therefore,
does not look outward but inward into the book itself. The
person who says "The book *is called Either/Or*" actually says
nothing, but the person who says "The work *is* an either/or"
creates the title himself. Every individual reader can, of
course, do this just as well as the editor. This is also the reason
the preface has left it up to the reader to give the work this title,
something it would hardly ever occur to an editor to suggest.

The editor should now have a name. It goes without saying
that this name must be chosen in consequence of and in harmony with the rest. I decided to choose one that would not so
much designate the editor as a factual individual but would instead describe an abstract relation to the work as a whole. This
relation could then become an actual relation and the name an
actual name, since the single individual would lend his name
in the Danish sense by *nomen huic operi dare* [giving a name to
this work] in the Latin sense. Thus, the editor's name would
again look inward [*indadskue*] into the work itself. The book
had no author and no title; it should have no editor either but
should round itself off in its own soaring and as a book not
stand in any finite relation to an individual. Thus the editor
saw his position as quite ordinary, even if there were only one
person beside himself who would assume it; he regarded himself as the book's first reader—no more and no less. He called
himself "Victor Eremita," a name that in his opinion would
not be a *proprium* [proper name] for the editor but an *apellati-
vum* [descriptive name] for *the reader*, even if he were the only
one. If the reader in his self-activity came up with the title
Either/Or, there would come a moment when he perhaps
would prefer to designate himself as *Eremita* [eremite, hermit],
because more earnest contemplation always creates solitude.
Perhaps there would come a next moment when he would call
himself *Victor*, no matter how he would more explicitly understand this victory.

IV
B 59
218

An editor's relation to a book can be such that his actual name is of extreme importance. If a well-known author publishes a work by someone else, then that famous name is the absolute. If a work contains communications and information that fall under the rubric of factual truth, a *nomen proprium* is very important. Neither of these applies to me or to my situation. My name is not at all well known; nor have the unknown authors exactly persuaded me to publish these papers, which in turn are rather indifferent with respect to the category of factual documents. In view of the work's special character, an editor may wish to be pseudonymous, but then again in his pseudonymity he may prefer to designate and preserve his special relation as editor so that he can continue his pseudonymity in the publication of other books. This was not my wish, nor did my situation, as far as I could perceive, bear any visible sign of being pregnant with a continuation. The coincidence that placed this manuscript in my hands was so strange that any conjecture about a repetition would have to be regarded as foolish, whether I myself were to put everything into buying old writing desks from secondhand dealers or form a corporation in order to speculate in antique furniture on an even greater scale. The manuscript itself was so tricky, the editor's relation so questionable, that he was obliged to contemplate vanishing as soon as possible and making way for the book that had no author, no title, no editor, but did have an altogether solitary reader who himself published the book under the name "Victor Eremita."

What is set forth here I have sufficiently pondered beforehand. I intended sooner or later, if necessary, to make such an explanation, although to a certain degree I regarded it as superfluous, since the individual reader upon whom I had placed my hope would read it precisely in this way.

The actuality, however, turned out to be quite different. The book did not go its way unnoticed; on the contrary, it created a certain sensation; the firm "Victor Eremita" climbed several points a few mail-days in succession. What temptations to a poor vain heart! What bright prospects for someone so fortunate as to bear that name! He could confirm the pub-

IV
B 59
219

lic's misunderstanding—for which he certainly was not to blame—that he is the author; he could let the beautiful sunshine, the mild weather, the hospitable reception, and the obliging curiosity divest him of his cloak of pseudonymity and reveal himself to the gaze of his contemporaries as shy as a reclusive secret. We have seen something like this before. There has been many a traveler who honestly walked the narrow path of anonymity and renounced the world's favor—as long as it was dubious. Then he allowed himself to be discovered, and *der verschämte* [the abashed] author blushed as deeply as an Anadyomene[110] who seeks a hiding place in vain. —He could continue in his incognito but quickly see to scribbling a little book that could be by "Victor Eremita, editor of *Either/Or*." He could have a friend announce in the newspaper, "At New Year we may anticipate a new work by V. E., the editor of *Either/Or*." In the old days, the announcement came to the one giving birth; in our day this is less common, but it is all the more usual for it to come to the sponsors. Or he could . . . . . . if he himself could not hit upon something, he could appeal to . . . . . .

Honesty, however, is the best policy, and therefore I did not succumb to the temptation but on the contrary am attempting with these lines to bid farewell as Victor Eremita forever. By this I hope to do what I owe both to myself and to the reading public, which even in relation to the author, to say nothing of the editor, certainly would be best served if every author were pseudonymous and if with every work began from the beginning in everything pertaining to the external person. To my mind, the surprise of occasionally encountering a good book where one had expected nothing is in all ways preferable to being freshly reminded of a talented piece of work by seeing the same talent in degenerated form. Even if one has not been pseudonymous before, as soon as one notices retrogression, one either ought to stop writing, which is the more praiseworthy, or one ought to hasten to be pseudonymous. And this nudge to stop, this termination point, an author ought to discover a little before it becomes obvious to the reader.

How desirable it would be if an author actually loved the

IV
B 59
220

erotic contacts with the reading public, had the power to keep
the idea of it living, the faith in it burning, the responsibility
to it chastening in his soul, unmoved by actuality's dreary
protests! Then he would not totally regard his existence as a
livelihood, or desire a seniority system to be instituted, or entertain himself like a Don Ranudo by rattling off the list of his
works every time he added a new one,[111] but be matured and
ennobled in the pain and joy of existing in uncertainty in this
way, without having any past to appeal to, without having
any future to anticipate, without demanding a pension or advance payment. How desirable it would be if every author had
in himself his severest critic whom he loved and feared more
than a woman fears her mirror! He would then have a witness
who would testify with him that he was faithful to the idea as
long as it loved and visited him; he would then have a friend
who would not lack the courage to knock him down if at any
moment he, disabled and decrepit, should pretend that the idea
still visited him, if he himself should permit the obscenity that
the young muse lived in an erotic intimacy with the decrepit
one. Then he would experience a beautiful old age. Yes, even
if the muse, who loved him because he had been faithful to her,
wanted to tempt him to try his hand once again, he would
speak admonishingly to her: My dear child! Could you have
joy out of humiliating me or being humiliated by me, do you
love me as of old? Then jest with me a little the way a child
cheers up the oldster. This the muse would indeed do for him
and love him even more and say: A human being is still the
wonder of creation. When he was young and strong, he
bowed in admiration and adoration to me; now that he is
weak, he is unwilling to accept my favor—his freedom humbles me.

IV
B 59
221

Yet this comment pertains mostly to the authors, and to that
extent it may be unfair that a reader makes it since he cannot
possibly know the difficulty of self-denial, how hard it is to
give up the sure prospects while youth still offers the human
probability, how hard it is to have ceased to govern. If the
temptation is greater than the person who has not been tested
and tried in it can visualize, then it is still certain that in any

case freedom will make the victory easier and the joy more indescribable. But it is even more certain than this that such conduct will be a great joy and blessing to the reader. Then he will not be kept in any misplaced expectancy, even less be cast into despondency over the loss of the superior, the downfall of the great, but undisturbed will bring forth the particular works, without pity will reject what cannot satisfy, since he would not know whose work it is that he rejects. Without any enclitic prejudice he will with originality devote himself in the hour of surprise to the particular work, which did not wish to influence by anything except itself.

This the reader can perceive, and an editor who is neither more nor less than the first reader can also understand it and easily act in accordance with what he actually has understood. Even if I were author of that work, I would nevertheless hasten to dissolve the firm "Victor Eremita," because through fate, many accidental circumstances, and the kindness of the reading public, it has become something different from what it originally could be for the author himself, and in this change it would contain a standard for the author and with respect to a subsequent performance develop in the reader a demand that could be of no service to either party. If in the course of time it should occur to a reader to say, "I wonder if we will not soon be hearing something from Victor Eremita," such an expectancy would be a source of anxiety even for an author. If this comment pertained to an editor, for him it would undoubtedly take on the proportions of profound derision. He would perhaps think, "Good lord, what should anyone hear from me! It is no wonder at all that no one hears anything, since I have never had anything to say. An editor does not have much to do; at most he can sit at home all day like a girl and wait to see if fate will not propose to him with a new manuscript. And even this method is very exhausting and also uncertain."

In view of this, I deem it best to dissolve a firm that has never actually existed. In the meantime, I nevertheless trust that with this explanation I will do what I owe to that work and to my position, do what I can to keep the reader from any misunderstanding with respect to his own expectation and my

IV
B 59
222

person by asking him to be assured that if he should ever encounter the name "Victor Eremita" in any other connection or relation than it has as *Either/Or*'s natural guardian,[112] then the person who writes it is *not* the one who here in all likelihood is signing his name this way for the last time, the person who here in the moment of farewell does not place his trust in his own power but trusts only in the consistency with which a "kindly disposed reader" will sometimes kindly recollect a discharged editor.

IV
B 59
223

That I as editor have left no stone unturned in trying on my own to find the unknown authors, that in precisely this respect I have been happy to see the book arouse a certain attention, since it is good, after all, to fish in troubled waters, I certainly need not say; it was, however, in vain. Yet for a period I believed, with the help of Mr. Hagen, M.A., that I had come upon a clue. In *Fædrelandet* (col. 9854 fn.), he reproaches me for having said of A.[113] that there was nothing to be found in the work to enlighten us about his personal existence in society. (I have not, however, actually said this. I have only said that A. did not have any name in the way, as was well known, that the judge was called William, and that because of this lack of analogy I had preferred to call the esteemed authors A. and B. instead of inventing a name for A. myself.) Mr. Hagen is of the opinion that I have made a mistake here and emphasizes one aspect in particular—namely, that A. is supposed to have lived alongside a pharmacist[114] here in the city. When I read this I was at first humbled to think that I who for five years had intimately lived together with the manuscript had not discovered what a critic's clever pate had speedily discovered; next, I was amazed that Mr. Hagen dropped the comment so casually. It seemed to me that this clue could lead to something. With this piece of information one could perhaps jog the secondhand furniture dealer's memory. Perhaps one could pick up some evidence from the pharmacists and especially from their neighbors etc. Before taking any step in this direction, I decided to examine A.'s papers very carefully. The passage alluded to is unquestionably found in one of the diapsalmata, where A., according to his own words, from his gloomy apartment hears the minuet from *Don Giovanni* being played in the neighboring courtyard, which must be the courtyard of a pharmacist, since the pharmacist accompanies the beckoning tones by pounding in his mortar. I stake my honor in *omnem lapidem movisse* [turning every stone] in order to find the unknown authors; so please forgive me if I am somewhat prolix. I honestly confess that Mr. Hagen's whole review has not occupied me as much as this little passage, for the rest of it has to do with the authors, but this touches me in the most tender spot. According to what Mr. Hagen himself points out, A. has been an adjunct and later was engaged by a traveling theater group; he has, as I myself recollect, also traveled abroad (see the article about *The First Love*[115]). The diapsalma referred to has no date and no other stipulation of place than the one cited. Since the matter is of extreme importance to me, I would be reluctant to come with unfounded assertions. I have gone to all imaginable trouble to find an authority who could in the most satisfactory way vouch for what I am now going to say. I have not succeeded; geography books as well as other statistical works leave me in the lurch. I trust myself, however, to vouch for the truth and ask Mr. Hagen to take my word for it. "There are pharmacies in most Danish towns; in the great cities of foreign countries there are numerous pharmacies; pharmacies do not lie in remote spots, and in all likelihood next to every pharmacy there is a neighboring courtyard. Pharmacists in Danish towns, no less than foreign pharmacists, pound in their mortars just as much as those in the capital." If one believes this on the strength of my honesty or on other more persuasive grounds, one perceives how this clue vanishes without a trace, since the only established fact that remains is that once a man well-traveled in Denmark and in foreign lands lived alongside a pharmacist at precisely the moment when it so curiously happened that the pharmacist was pounding in his mortar. Then Mr. Hagen's clue was a mistake and all my trouble wasted. Yet I readily forgive him, for on this point I am so

IV
B 59
224

sensitive that I do not hesitate to submit to everything. But what I cannot forgive Mr. Hagen is that he, without exactly wanting to encourage people in an injustice of this sort, nevertheless indirectly, by mentioning it and thereby publicizing it and thus perhaps making it tempting, although this was contrary to his intention, has contributed to disparaging the properties lying alongside a pharmacy. In other words, he says that "men have shed tears of joy on behalf of their wives and daughters for not having lived in the neighborhood of any pharmacist."[116] One would think that if anyone had occasion to shed tears of joy it ought to be those who had lived in the vicinity of a pharmacist *without* having their wives and daughters harmed by it. But to go so far as to have even those who have not lived in the vicinity of a pharmacist shed tears of joy shows what enormous hostility and what insuperable idiosyncrasies many people must have about living near a pharmacist. To publicize this and thereby contribute to spreading this attitude harms all who have property in the vicinity of a pharmacist; it is the ruination of those whose property is situated alongside a pharmacy. —This I am unable to forgive Mr. Hagen; in my opinion, this is frivolous and injudicious of him.

IV
B 59
225

This, like so much else, can be a matter of complete indifference to me, for if these noble men and fathers, whose tears of joy Mr. Hagen makes public to all, should wish to know who I am, then there is nothing on my side to prevent it:

> Ich bin die lebendige Definition eines pragmatischen Geschichtschreibers, habe kein Vaterland, keinen Freund, weder Weib noch Kind, ziehe keinen Sold, erkenne keinen Herrn, binde mich an kein Gesetz und bekenne mich zu keiner Kirche; die Welt ist für mich eine Insel Juan Fernandez [I am the living definition of a history writer, have no fatherland, no friends, neither wife nor child, draw no pay, acknowledge no master, bind myself to no law and belong to no church; for me the world is a Juan Fernandez island].[117]

My moral principle, to be of service; my highest ethical maxim is to regard all existence as an old novel or chronicle, where in the progress of the story it is inestimably amusing and utterly amazing to be reading continually about oneself.

VICTOR EREMITA

March 1844

—*Pap*. IV B 59 March 1844

Note on Post-Scriptum *to* Either/Or:

For p. 217 [*SV* VII 246].

VII¹
B 83
276

A note that was not printed because it was prepared later, although it was rough-drafted, and for certain reasons I did not want to change or add the least thing in the manuscript as it was delivered lock, stock, and barrel to Luno[118] the last days of December, 1845.

Note. This imaginary construction [*Experiment*] (" 'Guilty?' /'Not Guilty?' ")[119] is the first attempt in all the pseudonymous writings at an existential dialectic in double-reflection. It is not the communication that is in the form of double-reflection (for all pseudonyms are that), but the existing person himself exists in this. Thus he does not give up immediacy, but he keeps it and yet gives it up, keeps erotic love's desire and yet gives it up. Viewed categorically, the imaginary construction relates to "The Seducer's Diary" in such a way that it begins right there where the seducer ends, with the task he himself suggests: "to poetize himself out of a girl." (See *Either/Or*, I, p. 470 [*SV* I 412].) The seducer is egotism; in *Repetition* feeling and irony are kept separate, each in its representative: the Young Man and Constantin. These two elements are put together in the one person, Quidam of the imaginary construction, and he is sympathy. To seduce a girl expresses masculine superiority; to poetize oneself out of a girl is also a superiority but must become a *suffering* superiority if one considers the relationship between masculinity and femininity and not a particular silly girl. Masculinity's victory is supposed to reside in succeeding; but the reality [*Realitet*] of femininity is supposed to reside in its becoming a story of suffering for the

VII¹
B 83
277

man. Just as it is morally impossible for Quidam of the imaginary construction to seduce a girl, so it is metaphysically-esthetically impossible for a seducer to poetize himself out of a girl when it is a matter of the relationship between masculinity and femininity, each in its strength, and not of a particular girl. The seducer's egotism culminates in the lines to himself: "She is mine, I do not confide this to the stars . . . . . . not even to Cordelia, but say it very softly to myself." (See *Either/Or*, I, p. 446 [*SV* I 409].) Quidam culminates passionately in the outburst: "The whole thing looks like a tale of seduction."[120] What is a triumph to one is an ethical horror to the other.—*JP* V 5865 (*Pap.* VII¹ B 83) *n.d.*, 1846

Addition to Pap. VII¹ B 83:

The imaginary construction, however, is precisely what is lacking in *Either/Or* (see note in my own copy);[121] but before it could be categorically correct, an enormous detour had to be made.

The imaginary construction is the only thing for which there existed considerable preliminary work[122] before it was written. Even while I was writing *Either/Or* I had it in mind and frequently dashed off a lyrical suggestion. When I was ready to work it out, I took the precaution of not looking at what I had jotted down in order not to be disturbed. But not a word escaped me, although it came again in a superior rendering. I have now gone through what I had jotted down, and nothing was missing, but if I had read it first, I could not have written it. The imaginary construction is the most exuberant of all I have written, but it is difficult to understand because natural egotism is against adhering so strongly to sympathy.—*JP* V 5866 (*Pap.* VII¹ B 84) *n.d.*, 1846

It could be a very funny plot for a vaudeville play to have a Swedish family, having read in the papers[123] about the matchless Danish hospitality (that barbers give shaves gratis, that prostitutes operate gratis [see *Either/Or*[124]] etc.), take off for

Copenhagen—a fortnight later in the firm conviction that this is the way it always is in Copenhagen—and then develop it in situations. To compensate for the misunderstanding, the play could end with a happy love affair, germinating from sympathy with the situation of misunderstanding.—*JP* V 5830 (*Pap.* VI A 87) *n.d.*, 1845

The Relation between *Either/Or* and the *Stages*[125]

VI
A 41
16

In *Either/Or* the esthetic component was something present battling with the ethical, and the ethical was the choice by which one emerged from it. For this reason there were only two components, and the Judge was unconditionally the winner, even though the book ended with a sermon and with the observation that only the truth that builds up is the truth for me (inwardness—the point of departure for my upbuilding discourses).

In the *Stages* there are three components and the situation is different.

1. The esthetic-sensuous is thrust into the background as something past[126] (therefore "a recollection"), for after all it cannot become utterly nothing).

The Young Man (thought-depression); Constantin Constantius (hardening through the understanding). Victor Eremita, who can no longer be the editor (sympathetic irony); the Fashion Designer (demonic despair); Johannes the Seducer (damnation, a "marked" individual).[127] He concludes by saying that woman is merely a moment. At the very point the Judge begins: Woman's beauty increases with the years; her reality [*Realitet*] is precisely in time.[128]

VI
A 41
17

2. The ethical component is polemical: the Judge is not giving a friendly lecture but is grappling in existence, because he cannot end here, even though with pathos he can triumph again over every esthetic stage but not measure up to the esthetes in wittiness.[129]

3. The religious comes into existence in a demonic approx-

imation (Quidam of the imaginary construction) with humor as its presupposition and its incognito (Frater Taciturnus).[130]

—*JP* V 5804 (*Pap.* VI A 41) *n.d.*, 1845

From sketch of Postscript:

A story of *suffering*; suffering is precisely the religious category.

In *Stages* the esthete is no longer a clever fellow frequenting B's living room—a hopeful man, etc., because he still is only a possibility; no, he is existing [*existere*].

"It is exactly the same as *Either/Or.*"

Constantin Constantius and the Young Man placed together in Quidam of the imaginary construction (advanced humor) as a point of departure for the beginning of the religious.— just as the tragic hero was used to bring out faith.

Three Stages and yet an Either/Or.

—*JP* V 5805 (*Pap.* VI B 41:10) *n.d.*, 1845

[VI B 192 1845]

A Request to *The Corsair*[131]

Sing sang resches Tubalcain—which translated means: Cruel and bloodthirsty *Corsair*, high and mighty Sultan, you who hold the lives of men like a plaything in your right hand and as a whim in the fury of your invective, let me move you to compassion, curtail these sufferings—slay me, but do not make me immortal! High and mighty Sultan, in your quick wisdom consider what it would not take long for the paltriest of all those you have slain to see, consider what it means to become immortal, and particularly to become that through the testimonial of *The Corsair*. What cruel grace and mercy to be forever pointed to as an inhuman monster because *The Corsair* inhumanly had spared him! But above all not this—that I shall never die! Uh, such a death penalty is unheard of.* I get weary of life just to read it. What a cruel honor and distinction to have no one be moved by my womanly wailing: This will kill me, this will be the death of me—but everybody laughs and says:

He cannot die. Let me move you to compassion; stop your lofty, cruel mercy; slay me like all the others.

Victor Eremita

(Here perhaps could be added the words at the end of the postscript to *Either/Or*,[132] which is in the tall cupboard closest to the window.)

In margin: *Slay me so I may live with all the others you have slain, but do not slay me by making me immortal.—*JP* V 5853 (*Pap.* VI B 192) *n.d.*, 1845

My contemporaries cannot grasp the design of my writing. *Either/Or* divided into four parts or six parts and published separately over six years would have been all right. But that each essay in *Either/Or* is only part of a whole, and then the whole of *Either/Or* a part of a whole: that, after all, think my bourgeois contemporaries, is enough to drive one daft.—*JP* V 5905 (*Pap.* VII¹ A 118) *n.d.*, 1846

No doubt part of what contributed to making *Either/Or* a success has been that it was a first book and therefore one could take it to be the work of many years—and thus conclude that the style was good and well developed. It was written lock, stock, and barrel in eleven months. At most there was only a page (of "Diapsalmata") prior to that time. As far as that goes, I have spent more time on all the later works. Most of *Either/ Or* was written only twice (besides, of course, what I thought through while walking, but that is always the case); nowadays I usually write three times.[133]—*JP* V 5931 (*Pap.* VII¹ A 92) *n.d.*, 1846

People do not really understand the dialectical, least of all the dialectic of inversion. People have the same experience with this kind of dialectic as dogs have with learning to walk on two legs: they succeed for a moment but then promptly go back to walking on all fours.[134] They understand the dialectic of inversion at the time it is being presented to them, but as soon as the presentation is over they understand it again in terms of the dialectic of immediacy.— For example, to have but one reader or very few is easily understood in terms of the dialectic of immediacy: that it is too bad for the author etc., but that it is very nice of him to make the best of it etc. —But in the dialectic of inversion the author himself voluntarily works to bring this about, desires only one or a few readers—this, you see, will never be popular. —Yesterday Molbech[135] wrote to me (in a note dated April 29, 1847) that the sell-out of *Either/ Or* is "a phenomenon in the literary history of our day that may need to be studied." And why? The Councilor of State does not know that it has been sold out for a long time; he does not know that a year ago Johannes Climacus in *Concluding Unscientific Postscript* expressed his opinion in the matter,[136] that already two years ago Reitzel[137] talked about the new edition, that I am the obstacle; he has no idea of how I work against myself in the service of the dialectic of inversion and, if possible, in a somewhat cleansing service of truth. Whether right now at this time it would be possible to sell out a book of mine, I do not know, but before I began to set teeth on edge somewhat I really did manage to do it. A few flattering words to this one and that, no more than a half or a tenth of what an author usually does to get his books sold—and they would have been sold out. And even now, when I have set people's teeth on edge so much, even now it would all begin again if I simply let up a bit, become less productive (for what actually antagonizes them the most is the extent of my productivity), write a little book or a smaller book and only one (*Upbuilding Discourses in Various Spirits*)—then it would all begin again. That I was playing a cunning game, that I had a very large book[138] finished and ready, that in order to have a witness to refer to, I showed it to Giødwad[139] the same day we began proofreading the *Discourses*, that I had counted on trapping P. L. Møller[140] or some other bandit to write a eulogy on the *Upbuilding Discourses* and say, "It is obvious that Magister Kierkegaard, if he is willing to take the time, can produce something great etc.; much greater pains than usual have been taken with this book and for that reason it has taken him longer etc." A pack of lies, which, however, would be be-

VIII[1]
A 84
42

lieved and would be regarded as very sensible, also that I did a botchy job with the large books. Oh, what a fate to be something out of the ordinary in a market town! Then I would have rushed ahead with the large book, with Giødwad's testimony that it was finished at the same time, etc. And then what? Then the provincials with whom I live would have become angry once again, and why? Because they cannot bear the scale. They cannot understand working on that scale and doing it as assiduously as I do: ergo, the author is doing a botchy job.

No wonder I am nauseated time and again by the rabble one must live with, no wonder that I can keep on working only by shutting my eyes. For when I shut my eyes I am before God, and then everything is all right, then I personally am not of any importance, which, humanly and comparatively speaking, I am, insofar as it is my lot to live in a small town and with nonentities.—*JP* V 5997 (*Pap.* VIII¹ A 84) *n.d.*, 1847

. . . my thought was to become a pastor. When I began writing *Either/Or*, then through an unhappy relationship to another person my life's deep-rooted hurt and torment were again ripped up and intensified, and as a consequence I understood that my existence, humanly speaking, was grounded for my lifetime. This is how I became an author.—*Pap.* VIII¹ A 422 *n.d.*, 1847

If one aims to elevate a whole period, one must really know it. That is why the proclaimers of Christianity who begin right off with orthodoxy actually do not have much influence and only on a few. For Christendom is very far behind. One has to begin with paganism. So I begin with *Either/Or*. In that way I have managed to get the age to go along with me without ever dreaming where it is going or where we now are. But men have become aware of the issues. They cannot get rid of me just because they went along with *Either/Or* so happily. Now they may want to abandon me; they could put me to death, but it is of no use—they have me for good. If one begins immediately with Christianity, they say: This is nothing for us—and put themselves immediately on guard.

But as it says in my last discourses, my whole huge literary work has just one idea, and that is: to wound from behind.[141]

Praise be to God in heaven—I say no more; anything else a man adds is rubbish.—*JP* V 6107 (*Pap*. VIII[1] A 548) *n.d.*, 1848

I concede that I began my work as an author with an advantage: being regarded as something of a villain but extremely brilliant—that is, a salon hero, a real favorite of the times. There was a bit of untruth in it—but otherwise I would not have gotten people along with me. As they gradually became aware that this was not quite the case, they fell away and continue to fall away. If it gets to be known that I am working out my salvation in fear and trembling,[142] then it is goodbye to the world's favors.

But here lurked the secret agent. —And they did not look out for that. For someone to be first of all a dissipated sensualist, a party-lion, and then many years later, as they say, to become a saint, this does not capture men. But they are not at all accustomed to having a penitent, a preacher of repentance, begin in the costume of a party-lion as a kind of cautionary measure.

This has also served to provide me with an almost prodigious knowledge of men.—*JP* VI 6198 (*Pap*. IX A 155) *n.d.*, 1848

IX
A 166
79

IX
A 166
80

As early as the article "Public Confession"[143] there was a signal shot (I was at the time finished with the manuscript of *Either/Or*, and immediately after that *Either/Or* followed; the article was also a mystification: after having disavowed the authorship of the many newspaper articles, which, to be sure, no one had attributed to me, I ended by asking people never to regard anything as mine that was not signed by me, and that was just the time I planned to begin using a pseudonym) suggesting that Professor Heiberg was the literary figure I wanted to protect; he and Mynster both were mentioned there and as unmistakably as possible. But then Heiberg himself came along with his impertinent and foppish review of *Either/Or*, also with a careless promise that he never kept. Then the opposition of his clique, his attempt at the silent treatment, fakery in such a small literature—all this gave the occasion for rabble barbarism to emerge so strongly. I was the one who could and should strike but could not because I constantly had to keep the way clear for a possible polemic against Heiberg. Finally I struck at the barbarism—and Heiberg left me in the lurch. Prior to that time it had often been whispered about that I approved or indulged that revolt. Now one got an insight into the affair—but Heiberg thought: Now if Kierkegaard could get shafted, it would be a good thing. Pfui!—*JP* VI 6201 (*Pap.* IX A 166) *n.d.*, 1848

I have been thinking these days of having the little article "The Crisis in the Life of an Actress"[144] printed in *Fædrelandet*. The reasons *for* doing it are the following. There are some minor reasons, but they have persuasive power, and therefore I must first subject them to a critique. I believe I owe it to Mrs. Heiberg,[145] partly also because of the piece about Mrs. Nielsen[146] at one time. I would like to poke Heiberg a little again. This way certain things can be said that I otherwise could not say so lightly and conversationally. It would make me happy to humor Giødwad,[147] who has asked for it. And then the main reason that argues for it: I have been occupied now for such a long time exclusively with the religious, and yet people will perhaps try to make out that I have changed, have become earnest (which I was not previously), that the literary attack has made me sanctimonious; in short, they will make my religiousness out to be the sort of thing people turn to in old age. This is a heresy I consider extremely essential to counteract. The nerve in all my work as an author actually is here, that I was essentially religious when I wrote *Either/Or*. Therefore, I have thought that it could be useful in order once again to show the possibility. I regard this as precisely my task, always to be capable of what the vanity and secular-mindedness of the world hanker after as supreme, and from which point of view they patronizingly look down on the religious as something for run-down subjects—always to be capable but not essentially to will it. The world, after all, is so

IX
A 175
84

IX
A 175
85

insipid that when it believes that one who proclaims the religious is someone who cannot produce the esthetic it pays no attention to the religious. . . . —*JP* VI 6209 (*Pap*. IX A 175) *n.d*., 1848

IX
A 213
110

I cannot repeat often enough what I so frequently have said: I am a poet, but a very special kind, for I am by nature dialectical, and as a rule dialectic is precisely what is alien to the poet. Assigned from childhood to a life of torment that perhaps few can even conceive of, plunged into the deepest despondency, and from this despondency again into despair, I came to understand myself by writing. It was the ethical that inspired me—alas, me, who was painfully prevented from realizing it fully because I was unhappily set outside the universally human. If I had been able to achieve it, I no doubt would have become terribly proud. Thus in turn I related to Christianity. It was my plan as soon as *Either/Or* was published to seek a call to a rural parish and sorrow over my sins. I could not suppress my creativity, I followed it—naturally it moved into the religious. Then I understood that my task was to do penance by serving the truth in such a way that it virtually became burdensome, humanly speaking, a thankless labor of sacrificing everything. That is how I serve Christianity—in all my wretchedness happy in the thought of the indescribable good God has done for me, far beyond my expectations.

IX
A 213
111

The situation calls for Christianity to be presented once again without scaling down and accommodation, and since the situation is in Christendom: indirectly. I must be kept out of it: the awakening will be all the greater. Men love direct communication because it makes for comfortableness, and communicators love it because it makes life less strenuous, since they always get a few to join them and thus escape the strain of solitariness.

Thus do I live, convinced that God will place the stamp of Governance on my efforts—as soon as I am dead, not before— this is all connected with penitence and the magnitude of the plan. I live in this faith and hope to God to die in it. If he wants it otherwise, he will surely take care of that himself; I do not dare do otherwise.—*JP* VI 6227 (*Pap*. IX A 213) *n.d.*, 1848

Yes, it had to be this way. I have not become a religious author; I was that: simultaneously with *Either/Or* appeared two upbuilding discourses—now after two years of writing only religious books there appears a little article about an actress.[148]

Now there is a moment, a point of rest; by this step I have learned to know myself and very concretely. . . . —*JP* VI 6229 (*Pap*. IX A 216) *n.d.*, 1848

N.B.   N.B.

Yes, it was a good thing to publish that little article. I began with *Either/Or* and two upbuilding discourses; now it ends, after the whole upbuilding series—with a little esthetic essay.[149] It expresses: that it was the upbuilding—the religious —that should advance, and that now the esthetic has been traversed; they are inversely related, or it is something of an inverse confrontation, to show that the writer was not an esthetic author who in the course of time grew older and for that reason became religious.

But it is not really to my credit; it is Governance who has held me in rein with the help of an extreme depression and a troubled conscience.

But there still would have been something lacking if the little article had not come out; the illusion would have been established that it was I who essentially had changed over the years, and then a very important point in the whole productivity would have been lost.

It is true I have been educated by this writing, have developed more and more religiously—but in a decisive way I had experienced the pressures that turned me away from the world before I began writing *Either/Or*. Even then my only wish was to do, as decisively as possible, something good to compensate, if possible in another way, for what I personally had committed. That I have developed more and more religiously is seen in my now saying goodbye to the esthetic, because I do

IX
A 227
124

IX
A 227
125

not know where I would find the time that I could, would, would dare fill up with work on esthetic writings. . . . —*JP* VI 6238 (*Pap*. IX A 227) *n.d.*, 1848

Now add the thought of death to the publication of that little article![150] If I were dead without that: indeed, anyone could publish my posthumous papers, and in any case R. Nielsen[151] would be there. But that illusion that I did not become religious until I was older and perhaps by reason of accidental circumstances would still have been possible. But now the dialectical breaks are so clear: *Either/Or* and *Two Upbuilding Discourses, Concluding Postscript*, the upbuilding writings of two years, and then a little esthetic treatise.—*Pap*. IX A 228 *n.d.*, 1848

The relationship to R. Nielsen[152] in this matter has made me very uneasy in fear and trembling. I had given R. N. a more direct communication. But on the other hand, to what extent R. N. had really understood me, to what extent he was capable of venturing something for the truth, is not at all clear to me. Here was the opportunity to make a test, and I felt that I owed it to the cause, to him, and to myself. Fortunately he was staying in the country. He has maintained constantly that he had understood the esthetic to have been used as an enticement and an incognito. He has also maintained that he understood that it always depends entirely upon involvement. But whether that is entirely true, he never did really put to the test. He scarcely understood the significance of *Either/Or* and of the two upbuilding discourses. . . . —*JP* VI 6239 (*Pap*. IX A 229) *n.d.*, 1848

N.B.   N.B.

Strange, strange about that little article[153]—that I had so nearly gone and forgotten myself. When one is overstrained as I was, it is easy to forget momentarily the dialectical outline of a colossal structure such as my authorship. That is why Governance helps me.

Right now the totality is so dialectically right. *Either/Or* and the two upbuilding discourses*—*Concluding Postscript*—for two years only upbuilding discourses and then a little article about an actress. The illusion that I happened to get older and for that reason became a decisively religious author has been made impossible. If I had died beforehand, then the writing I did those two years would have been made ambiguous and the totality unsteady.

In a certain sense, of course, my concern is superfluous when I consider the world of actuality in which I live—for as a matter of fact I have not found many dialecticians.

In margin: *Note. And these two discourses quite properly did not appear at the same time as *Either/Or* but a few months later—just as this little article now.—*JP* VI 6242 (*Pap.* IX A 241) *n.d.*, 1848

IX
A 241
136

From final draft of "Appendix," Point of View:

. . . That it was an age of disintegration, an esthetic, enervating disintegration, and therefore, before there could be any question of even introducing the religious, the ethically strengthening, *Either/Or* had to precede, so that *maieutically* a beginning might be made with esthetic writings (the pseudonyms) in order if possible to get hold of men, which after all comes first before there can be any thought of moving them over into the religious, and in this way it was also assured that in the sense of reflection the religious would be employed with dialectical care. . . . —*JP* VI 6255 (*Pap.* IX B 63:7) *n.d.*, 1848

IX
B 63:7
362

IX
B 63:7
363

From final draft of "Appendix," Point of View:

. . . The first form of rulers in the world was "the tyrants"; the last will be "the martyrs." In the development of the world this is the movement [*in margin:* toward a growing secular mentality, for secularism is greatest, must have achieved a frightful upper hand, when only the martyrs are able to be rulers. When one person is the tyrant, the mass is not completely secularized, but when "the mass" wants to be tyrant, then the

IX
B 63:13
373

secular mentality is completely universal, and then only the
martyr can be the ruler]. No doubt there is an infinite difference between a tyrant and a martyr; yet they have one thing in
common: the power to constrain. The tyrant, with a craving
for power, constrains by force; the martyr, personally unconditionally obedient to God, constrains by his own sufferings.
Then the tyrant dies, and his rule is over; the martyr dies, and
his rule begins. The tyrant was the egotistic individual who inhumanly ruled over the masses, made the others into a mass
and ruled over the mass. The martyr is the suffering single individual who in his love of mankind educates others in Christianity, converting the mass into single individuals—and there
is joy in heaven for every single individual he thus rescues
from the mass, from what the apostle himself calls the "ani-
mal-category." —Whole volumes could be written about this
alone, even by me, a kind of poet and philosopher, to say
nothing of the one who is coming, the philosopher-poet or the
poet-philosopher, who, in addition, will have seen close at
hand the object of my presentiments at a distance, will have
seen accomplished what I only dimly imagine will be carried
out sometime in a distant future.

IX
B 63:13
374

There are *really* only two sides to choose between—Either/
Or. Well, of course, there are many parties in the practical
world [*in margin:* Not really but only *figuratively* is there any
question of "choosing," since what is chosen makes no difference—one is just as wrong as the other. In the practical world
there are many parties]—there are the liberals and the conservatives etc.—and all the strangest combinations, such as the
rational liberals and rational conservatives. Once there were
four parties in England, a large country; this was supposedly
also the case in smaller Odense. But in the profoundest sense
there really are only two parties to choose between—and here
lies the category "the single individual": *either* in obedience to
God, fearing and loving him, to take the side of God against
men so that one loves men in God—*or* to take the side of men
against God, so that by distortion one humanizes God and
does not "sense what is God's and what is man's" (Matthew
16:23). There is a struggle going on between man and God, a

struggle unto life and death—was not the God-Man put to death! —About these things alone: about what constitutes earnestness and about "the single individual," about what constitutes the demonic, whether the demonic is the evil or the good, about silence as a factor contributing to evil and silence as a factor contributing to good, about "deceiving into the truth," about indirect communication, to what extent this is treason against what it is to be human, an impertinence toward God, about what one learns concerning the demonic by considering the God-Man—about these things alone whole volumes could be written, even by me, a kind of philosopher, to say nothing of him who is coming, "the philosopher" who will have seen "the missionary to Christendom" and at first hand will know about all this of which I have only gradually learned to understand at least a little.—*JP* III 2649 (*Pap.* IX B 63:13) *n.d.*, 1848

. . . [*In margin:* The King then showed the Queen the copy of the new book, which led me to say: Your Majesty embarrasses me for not having brought along a copy for the Queen. He answered: Ah, but we two can be satisfied with one.]

X¹
A 42
33

The Queen said that she recognized me, for she once had seen me on the embankment (where I ran off and left Tryde high and dry), that she had read a part of "your *Either and Or* but could not understand it." I replied: Your Majesty realizes that it is too bad for me. But there was something more unusual in the situation. Christian VIII promptly heard the mistake, *Either **and** Or*, and I certainly did hear it, too. It amazed me to hear the Queen say precisely what seamstresses etc. say. The King looked at me; I avoided his glance. . . . —*JP* VI 6310 (*Pap.* X¹ A 42) *n.d.*, 1849

X¹
A 42
34

"The Seducer's Diary" had to come first in order to shed light on the "Imaginary Psychological Construction."[154] The latter lies in the confinium between the interesting and the religious. If "The Seducer's Diary" had not come out first, the result would have been that the reading world would have found it interesting. "The Seducer's Diary" was a help, and now it was found to be boring—quite rightly so, for it is the religious. Frater Taciturnus himself also explains this.—*JP* VI 6330 (*Pap.* X^1 A 88) *n.d.*, 1849

If I wanted to tell about it, a whole book could be written on how ingeniously I have fooled people about my pattern of life.

During the time I was reading proofs of *Either/Or* and writing the upbuilding discourses I had almost no time to walk the streets. I then used another method. Every evening when I left home exhausted and had eaten at Mini's, I stopped at the theater for ten minutes—not one minute more. Familiar as I was, I counted on there being several gossips at the theater who would now say: Every single night he goes to the theater; he does not do another thing. O you darling gossips, thank you—without you I could never have achieved what I wanted.

I did it also for the sake of my former betrothed. It was my melancholy wish to be scorned if possible, merely to serve her, merely to help her offer me proper resistance. Thus there was within me unanimous agreement from all sides with respect to wanting to impair my public image.—*JP* VI 6332 (*Pap.* X^5 A 153) *n.d.*, 1849

X^1
A 116
86

N.B.   N.B.

N.B.

"A Cycle of Minor Ethical-Religious Essays,"[155] if that which deals with Adler[156] is omitted (and it definitely must be omitted, for to come in contact with him is completely senseless, and furthermore it perhaps is also unfair to treat a contemporary merely psychologically this way), has the defect that what as parts in a total study does not draw attention to itself (and originally this was the case) will draw far too much attention to itself now and thereby to me. Although originally an independent work, the same applies to no. 3, a more recent work.

X^1
A 116
87

But if no. 2 and no. 3,[157] which are about Adler, are also to be omitted, then "A Cycle" cannot be published at all.

Besides, there should be some stress on a second edition of

Either/Or. Therefore either—as I previously thought—a quarto with all the most recent writing or only a small fragment of it, but, please note, a proper contrast to *Either/Or.* The "Three Notes"[158] on my work as an author are as if intended for that, and this has a strong appeal to me.

If I do nothing at all directly to assure a full understanding of my whole authorship (by publishing "The Point of View for My Work as an Author") or do not even give an indirect telegraphic sign (by publishing "A Cycle" etc.)—then what? Then there will be no judgment at all on my authorship in its totality, for no one has sufficient faith in it or time or competence to look for a comprehensive plan [*Total-Anlæg*] in the entire production. Consequently the verdict will be that I have changed somehow over the years.

So it will be. This distresses me. I am deeply convinced that there is another integral coherence, that there is a comprehensiveness in the whole production (with the special assistance of Governance), and that there certainly is something else to be said about it than this meager comment that the author has changed.

I keep this hidden deep within, where there is also something in contrast: the sense in which I was more guilty than other men.

These proportions strongly appeal to me. I am averse to being regarded with any kind of sympathy or to representing myself as the extraordinary.

This suits me completely. So the best incognito I can choose is quite simply to take an appointment.

X¹
A 116
88

The enticing aspect of the total productivity (that it is esthetic—but also religious) will be very faintly intimated by the "Three Notes." For that matter, if something is to function enticingly, it is wrong to explain it. A fisherman would not tell the fish about his bait, saying "This is bait." And finally, if everything else pointed to the appropriateness of communicating something about the integral comprehensiveness, I cannot emphasize enough that Governance actually is the directing power and that in so many ways I do not understand until afterward.

This is written on Shrove-Monday. A year ago today, I decided to publish *Christian Discourses*;[159] this year I am inclined to the very opposite.

For a moment I would like to bring a bit of mildness and friendliness into the whole thing. This can best be achieved by a second edition of *Either/Or*[160] and then the "Three Notes." In fact, it would be odd right now when I am thinking of stopping writing to commence a polemic in which I do not wish to engage by replying (a polemic that is unavoidable because of no. 1 and no. 2 in "A Cycle").

Let there be moderation on my part: if someone wants a fight, then behind this I certainly am well armed.[161]—*JP* VI 6346 (*Pap.* X¹ A 116) February 19, 1849

. . . At first I planned to stop immediately after *Either/Or*. That was actually the original idea. But productivity took hold of me. Then I planned to stop with the *Concluding Postscript*. But what happens, I get involved in all that rabble persecution, and that was the very thing that made me remain on the spot. Now, I said to myself, now it can no longer be a matter of abandoning splendid conditions; no, now it is a situation for a penitent. Then I was going to end with *Christian Discourses* and travel, but I did not get to travel—and 1848 was the year of my richest productivity.[162] Thus Governance himself has kept me in the harness. . . . —*JP* VI 6356 (*Pap.* X¹ A 138) *n.d.*, 1849

X¹
A 147
109

N.B.   N.B.
N.B.

X¹
A 147
110

It will never do to let the second edition of *Either/Or* be published without something accompanying it.[163] Somehow the accent must be that I have made up my mind about being a religious author.

To be sure, my seeking an ecclesiastical post[164] also stresses this, but it can be interpreted as something that came later.

Therefore, do I have the right (partly out of concern lest I say too much about myself, partly because of a disinclination to expose myself to possible annoyances) to allow what I have written to be vague, lie in abeyance as something indefinite and thus as being much less than it is, although it no doubt will embitter various people to have to realize that there is such ingeniousness in the whole [authorship]. It is, in fact, comfortable to regard me as a kind of half-mad genius—it is a strain to have to become aware of the more extraordinary.

And all this concern about an appointment and livelihood is both melancholy and exaggerated. And a second question arises: Will I be able to endure living if I must confess to myself that I have *acted prudently* and avoided the danger that the truth could require me to confront?

Furthermore, the other books ("The Sickness unto Death," "Come to Me," "Blessed Is He Who is Not Offended")[165] are extremely valuable.[166] In one of them in particular it was granted to me to illuminate Christianity on a scale greater than I had ever dreamed possible; crucial categories are directly disclosed there. Consequently it must be published. But if I publish nothing at present, I will again have the last card.

"The Point of View" cannot be published.

I must travel.

But the second edition of *Either/Or* is a critical point (as I did in fact regard it originally and wrote "The Point of View" to be published simultaneously with it and otherwise would scarcely have been in earnest about publishing the second edition)—it will never come again. If this opportunity is not utilized, everything I have written, viewed as a totality, will be dragged down mainly into the esthetic.—*JP* VI 6361 (*Pap.* X¹ A 147) *n.d.*, 1849

X¹
A 147
111

. . . Although "the pseudonyms expected to get only a few readers," it can still be quite all right that the esthetic productivity "was used maieutically to get hold of men." For one thing, the human crowd is inquisitive about esthetic productions; another matter is the concept of "readers" that the pseudonyms must advance. How many readers *Either/Or* has had—and yet how few readers it has truly had, or how little it has come to be "read"!—*JP* VI 6363 (*Pap.* X¹ A 152) *n.d.*, 1849

What if I wrote at the back of the second edition of *Either/Or*:[167]

Postscript

I hereby retract this book. It was a necessary deception in order, if possible, to deceive men into the religious, which has continually been my task all along. Maieutically it certainly has had its influence. Yet I do not need to retract it, for I have never claimed to be its author.—*JP* VI 6374 (*Pap*. X[1] 192) *n.d.*, 1849

X[1]
A 266
177

. . . It is true, for example, that when I began as an author I was "religiously resolved," but this must be understood in another way. *Either/Or*, especially "The Seducer's Diary," was written for her sake, in order to clear her out of the relationship.[168] On the whole, the very mark of my genius is that Governance broadens and radicalizes whatever concerns me personally. I remember what a pseudonymous writer said about Socrates: "His whole life was personal preoccupation with himself, and then Governance comes and adds world-historical significance to it."[169] To take another example—I am polemical by nature, and I understood the concept of "that single individual" [*hiin Enkelte*] early. However, when I wrote it for the first time (in *Two Upbuilding Discourses*),[170] I was thinking particularly of *my* reader, for this book contained a little hint to her, and until later it was for me very true personally that I sought only one single reader. Gradually this thought was taken over. But here again Governance's part is so infinite.

The rest of the things written can very well be published. But not one word about myself.

So I must take a journey.—*JP* VI 6388 (*Pap*. X[1] A 266) *n.d.*, 1849

X[5]
B 191
376

From draft of "Supplement," On My Work as an Author:

. . . When I began writing *Either/Or*, I was just as profoundly moved by the religious as I am now at the end, except that the work has been for me a second upbringing and I have become more mature. . . . The directly religious was present from the beginning; for *Two Upbuilding Discourses* of 1843 are, after all, concurrent with *Either/Or.—Pap.* X⁵ B 191, May [*changed to:* April; *changed to:* March] 5, 1849

X⁵
B 191
377

. . . Humanly speaking, there really is no pleasure or joy in having to be the extraordinary in such cramped quarters as Denmark; it gets to be a martyrdom. But now, now, after God has inundated me with kindness, granted me so indescribably much more than I expected, now when he (both by means of the abundance he has showered on me during the year past—and its sufferings) has led me to understand my destiny (true enough, it is different from what I originally supposed, but things had already worked out earlier in such a way that all my religious writings, yes, everything I wrote after *Either/Or*, are not as I originally planned and presumably I could not have understood everything right away), should I now fail, I would shrewdly take it all back because of apprehensions about making ends meet and become a poet—that is, religiously understood, a deceiver. No, no, from the very beginning I had no such ideas: either an author in character—or a country pastor, and then not a word more from me ever, but not a poet, not an author on the side.

X¹
A 309
205

X¹
A 309
205

The future looks dark, and yet I am so at peace.

This day, my birthday, will be an unforgettable day for me!—*JP* VI 6394 (*Pap.* X¹ A 309) *n.d.* [May 5], 1849

From draft of On My Work as an Author*:*

X⁵
B 201
382

. . . The whole authorship, regarded in its entirety, is planned with this wish in mind [to become a rural pastor]. The movement it describes is: from "the poet"—from the esthetic, from the philosopher—from the speculative to the intimation of the most inward interpretation of the essentially Christian: **from** the pseudonymous *Either/Or*, which, nevertheless, was immediately accompanied by *Two Upbuilding Discourses* with *my name* as author, **through** *Concluding Postscript*, with my name as editor, **to** *Discourses at the Communion on Fridays* [*here a double dagger in red crayon, in margin a double dagger and:* see the enclosed], the last work I have written, and "of which two have been delivered in Frue Kirke." . . . —*Pap.* X⁵ B 201 *n.d.*, 1849

X¹
A 351
228

The Total Production with the Addition of the Two Essays by H. H.

X¹
A 351
229

The authorship conceived as a whole (as found in "One Note Concerning My Work as an Author," "Three Notes Concerning My Work as an Author," and "The Point of View for My Work as an Author") points definitively to "Discourses at the Communion on Fridays."

The same applies to the whole structure. "Three Godly Discourses" comes later and is supposed to accompany the second edition of *Either/Or* and mark the distinction between what is offered with the left and what is offered with the right. . . .

—*JP* VI 6407 (*Pap.* X¹ A 351) *n.d.*, 1849

Each of the writers here at home received a copy of *Either/Or*. I felt it was my duty, and I could do it at this time, for now there can be no apparent notion of trying in this way to create a coterie for the book—for the book, after all, is old, its peak is passed. Of course, they received the copy from Victor Eremita. As far as Oehlenschläger and Winther are concerned, it pleased me very much to send them a copy, for I admire them. I was happy to send one to Hertz[171] as well, for he has significance and there is something charming about the man.—*JP* VI 6413 (*Pap.* X¹ A 402) *n.d.*, 1849

In margin: the significance of the pseudonyms.]
The Significance of the Pseudonyms

All communication of truth has become abstract; the public has become the authority; the newspapers call themselves the editorial staff; the professor calls himself speculation; the pastor is meditation—no man, none, dares to say *I*.

But since without qualification the first prerequisite for the communication of truth is personality, since "truth" cannot possibly be served by ventriloquism, personality had to come to the fore again.

But in these circumstances, since the world was so corrupted by never hearing an *I*, it was impossible to begin at once with one's own *I*. So it became my task to create author-personalities and let them enter into the actuality of life in order to get men a bit more accustomed to hearing discourse in the first person.

Thus my task is no doubt only that of a forerunner until he comes who in the strictest sense says: *I*.

But to make a turn away from this inhuman abstraction to personality—that is my task.—*JP* VI 6440 (*Pap.* X¹ A 531) *n.d.*, 1849

X¹
A 541
344

. . . When I began as the author of *Either/Or*, I no doubt had a far more profound impression of the *terror* of Christianity than any clergyman in the country. I had a fear and trembling such as perhaps no one else had. Not that I therefore wanted to relinquish Christianity. No, I had another interpretation of it. For one thing I had in fact learned very early that there are men who seem to be selected for suffering, and, for another thing, I was conscious of having sinned much and therefore supposed that Christianity had to appear to me in the form of this terror. But how cruel and false of you, I thought, if you use it to terrify others, perhaps upset ever so many happy, loving lives that may very well be truly Christian. It was as alien as it could possibly be to my nature to want to terrify others that I both sadly and perhaps also a bit proudly found my joy in comforting others and in being gentleness itself to them—hiding the terror in my own interior being.

X¹
A 541
345

So my idea was to give my contemporaries (whether or not they themselves would want to understand) a hint in humorous form (in order to achieve a lighter tone) that a much greater pressure was needed—but then no more; I aimed to keep my heavy burden to myself, as my cross. I have often taken exception to anyone who was a sinner in the strictest sense and then promptly got busy terrifying others. Here is where *Concluding Postscript* comes in. . . . —*JP* VI 6444 (*Pap.* X¹ A 541) *n.d.*, 1849

X²
A 560
402

Reduplication

Every striving that does not apply one-fourth, one-third, two-thirds, etc. of its power *working against* itself systematically is essentially secular striving, in any case unconditionally not a *reforming* effort.

Reduplication means to work also against oneself while working; it is like the pressure on the plow-handles, which determines the depth of the furrow—whereas a striving that while working does not work also against itself is merely a superficial smoothing over.

What does it mean to work against oneself? It is quite simple. If the established, the traditional, etc., in the context of which a beginning is to be made, is sound, thoroughly sound—well, then apply *directly* what is to be applied; in any case there can be no talk or thought of reforming, for if the established is sound, then there is nothing, after all, to reform.

To the same degree, however, that the established, consequently *there* where one's striving begins, is corrupt, to the same degree the dialectical begins: to work against oneself becomes more and more necessary, so that the new, by being applied directly, is not itself corrupted, does not at once succeed etc., and thus is not maintained in its heterogeneity.

X²
A 560
403

Again the difference is between the direct and the inverted, which is the dialectical. Working or striving directly is to work and strive. The inverted method is this: while working also to work against oneself.

But who dreams that such a standard exists, and that I use it on such a large scale! Understood I will never be. People think I am involved in a direct striving—and now they believe that I have achieved a kind of breakthrough! Oh, such ignorance! The publication of *Either/Or* was a huge success; I had it in my power to continue. After all, what is the origin of all the problems in my striving; I wonder if it is not in myself? It is public knowledge that not one single person has really dared to oppose me. But I have done that myself. What a wrong turn on my part, if my striving was to be direct, to publish *Two Upbuilding Discourses* after *Either/Or*, which could only have a disturbing effect, instead of letting *Either/Or* stand with its glittering success, continuing in the direction that the age demanded, only in slightly reduced portions. What a counter effort against myself that I, the public's darling, introduce the single individual, and finally that I plunge myself into all the dangers of insults!

But such things can be understood only by someone who himself has risked something essentially similar. Someone else cannot conceive it or believe it.

R. Nielsen[172] is actually confused about this, for he interprets my striving in direct striving.—*JP* VI 6593 (*Pap.* X² A 560) *n.d.*, 1850

From final draft of For Self-Examination:

Preface

X⁶
B 4:3
14

What I have understood as the task of the authorship has been done.

It is one idea, this continuity from *Either/Or* to Anti-Climacus, the idea of religiousness in reflection.

X⁶
B 4:3
15

The task has occupied me totally, for it has occupied me religiously; I have understood the completion of this authorship as my duty, as a responsibility resting upon me. Whether anyone has wanted to buy or to read has concerned me very little.

At times I have considered laying down my pen and, if anything should be done, to use my voice.

However, I came by way of further reflection to the realization that it perhaps is more appropriate for me to make at least an attempt once again to use my pen but in a different way, as I would use my voice, consequently in direct address to my contemporaries, winning men, if possible.

The first condition for winning men is that the communication reaches them. Therefore I must naturally want this little book to come to the knowledge of as many as possible.

If anyone out of interest for the cause—I repeat, out of interest for the cause—wants to work for its dissemination, this is fine with me. It would be still better if he would contribute to its well-comprehended dissemination.*

A request, an urgent request to the reader: I beg you to read aloud, if possible; I will thank everyone who does so; and I will thank again and again everyone who in addition to doing it himself influences others to do it.

Just one thing more. *I hardly need say that by wanting to win men it is not my intention to form a party, to create secular, sensate togetherness; no, my wish is only to win men, if possible all men (each individual), for Christianity.

June 1851   S. K.

—*JP* VI 6770 (*Pap.* X⁶ B 4:3)

X⁶
B 145
202

. . . As is well known, my authorship has two parts: one pseudonymous and the other signed. The pseudonymous writers are poetized personalities, poetically maintained so that everything they say is in character with their poetized individualities; sometimes I have carefully explained in a signed preface my own interpretation of what the pseudonym said. Anyone with just a fragment of common sense will perceive that it would be ludicrously confusing to attribute to me everything the poetized characters say. Nevertheless, to be on the safe side, I have expressly urged once and for all that anyone who quotes something from the pseudonyms will not attribute the quotation to me (see my postscript to *Concluding Postscript*). It is easy to see that anyone wanting to have a literary lark merely needs to take some quotations higgledy-piggledy from "The Seducer," then from Johannes Climacus, then from me, etc., print them together as if they were all my words, show how they contradict each other, and create a very chaotic impression, as if the author were a kind of lunatic. Hurrah! That can be done. In my opinion anyone who exploits the poetic in me by quoting the writings in a confusing way is

X⁶
B 145
203

more or less a charlatan or a literary toper. . . . —*JP* VI 6786
(*Pap.* X⁶ B 145) *n.d.*, 1851

Either/Or

Every cause that is not served as an Either/Or (but as a both-
and, also, etc.) is *eo ipso* not God's cause; yet it does not therefore follow that every cause served as an either/or is therefore
God's cause.

Either/Or, that is, that the cause is served as an Either/Or,
is an endorsement similar to "in the royal service."

The symbol for the merely human, for mediocrity, the secular mentality, dearth of spirit, is: both-and, also.

And this is the way Mynster[173] actually has proclaimed
Christianity, that is, if consideration is given to his own personal life.—*JP* VI 6841 (*Pap.* X⁵ A 119) *n.d.*, 1853

. . . When I left "her"[174] I begged God for one thing, that I
might succeed in writing and finishing *Either/Or* (this was also
for her sake, because *The Seducer's Diary* was, in fact, intended
to repel, or as it says in *Fear and Trembling*, "When the child is
to be weaned, the mother blackens her breast.")[175] —and then
out to a rural parish—to me that would be a way of expressing
renunciation of the world.

I succeeded with *Either/Or*. But things did not go as I expected and intended—that I would be hated, loathed, etc.—
Oh, no, I scored a big success.

So my wish, my desire, to finish *Either/Or* was fulfilled. . . .
—*JP* VI 6843 (*Pap.* X⁵ A 146) *n.d.*, 1853

X⁵
A 146
151

The Honesty of Ideality
or
Either/Or

XI¹
A 476
369

An orientation toward quality, always an eye to quality, is required for the honesty of ideality (which is purity of spirit or is
spirit)—and then Either/Or.

Mediocrity, on the other hand, sordidness, niggardliness, shabbiness, etc. are immersed in: "also," that is, wanting to be along quantitatively, approximately, etc., instead of honestly manifesting quality and giving it its due.

Example. If there is someone who really handles an instrument with some competence and if he has the honesty of ideality referred to, then confronted by a virtuoso he will immediately manifest that quality: He is a virtuoso, and I, no, I am not a virtuoso. He will abhor misusing the competence he has by claiming to be a virtuoso *also*, or by claiming fellowship with the virtuoso, or by diminishing him in any way. On the contrary, he will use his comparatively greater insight based on his competence in order to make others aware of the virtuoso and of his virtuosity. This is the honesty of ideality; yet the common thing—niggardliness, sordidness, shabbiness—is to say "also," if not quite as good, still "also"—"we lords."

If this honesty of ideality were more common in the world, how different everything would appear! Excellence needs a middle instance with enough insight to point out excellence. The tragedy in the world is precisely that the middle instance is generally dishonesty, which, instead of decently letting either/or, that master of ceremonies of ideality, show it to its place and gladly accepting it, wants to pretend to be excellence also, if not quite as excellent, nevertheless "also."

So it goes in all relationships. Take the most important one—the relationship to Christianity. If pastors had this kind of honesty of ideality, things would be entirely different with Christianity. But they do not have this kind of honesty at all. It is disgusting how they have spoiled everything just because they "also" claim to have experienced, to have suffered—well, not quite as God's great instruments have, but nevertheless "also." They themselves have suffered the ordinary sufferings just as everyone may have, and now they take the apostle's life and talk as if they had suffered not quite as the apostle had, perhaps, but nevertheless "also."

I am most deeply opposed to this kind of behavior. No, even though compared with men generally I can be said to have suffered unusually, I am far from making the most of

XI[1]
A 476
370

this in order to fraternize with the apostle or weaken his impression with my wretched "also." On the contrary, I have immediately pointed out the quality and actually used my acquaintance with suffering to point him out—"for I am only a poet."

With the aid of mediocrity's cheap dishonesty, Christendom has managed to lose the prototypes [*Forbilleder*] completely. We need to reintroduce the prototypes, make them recognizable, something that can be done only by: Either/Or. Either you have quality in common, or you are on another qualitative level—but not this "also—well, not quite, but nevertheless—also."

But with respect to what is a qualitative level different from oneself, even though one is, if you please, the closest approximation, the essential thing is that one has the honesty of ideality not to accept approximations but to uphold only qualities, so one finds one's sole joy in pointing out what is a quality higher.

This is the theme in *Fear and Trembling* in the presentation of the relation between the poet and the hero.[176] —*JP* II 1812 (*Pap.* XI¹ A 476) *n.d.*, 1854

XI¹
A 476
371

My Program.
Either/Or.[177]
By
S. Kierkegaard.

—*JP* VI 6944 (*Pap.* XI³ B 54) *n.d.*, 1854

Addition to Pap. XI³ B 54:

It is laughter that must be used—therefore the line in the last diapsalm in *Either/Or*.

But laughter must first of all be divinely consecrated and devoutly dedicated. This was done on the greatest possible scale.

An example. From a Christian point of view, Mynster[178] was comical—like someone about to run a race who then puts on three coats—intending to proclaim him who was mocked and spit upon, to proclaim renunciation and self-denial, and then pompously appearing in silk and velvet and in possession of all earthly advantages and goods. But on the other hand, the comic of this sort is Christianly something to weep over, for it is something to weep over that this has been regarded as Christian earnestness and wisdom.

And this is how the comic must be used. The laughter must not prevail; it must not end with laughter either—no, it is merely a power that is to throw some light on the trumpery and the illusions so that I might succeed, if possible, "to influence by means of the ideals."—*JP* VI 6945 (*Pap.* XI³ B 55) *n.d.*, 1854

Addition to Pap. XI³ B 54:

Either/Or! We must examine the implications of the Christian requirement, that whole side of Christianity which is suppressed these days.

We must examine this, and then we must—Either/Or— *either* our lives must express the requirement and we are then justified in calling ourselves Christian, *or*, if our lives express something quite different, we must give up being called Christian, we must be satisfied with being an approximation of what it is to be a Christian, etc.

The latter is my aim (at least for the time being). But there must be truth in this whole affair—this shirking and suppressing and concealing and blurring must go—divine worship must not be: making a fool of God.—*JP* VI 6946 (*Pap.* XI³ B 56) *n.d.*, 1854

XI³
B 57
105

XI³
B 57
106

. . . I am without authority, only a poet—but oddly enough around here, even on the street, I go by the name "Either/Or."

The illuminating light is "Either/Or." Under this illuminating light there must be an examination of the doctrine of the imitation of Christ, the doctrine of grace (whether it can give indulgence for the future, scale down the requirement for the future, or only forgive the past), the doctrine of the Church, whether a relaxed Christianity, established Christianity, is not Judaism.

[*In penciled parentheses:* O Luther, you had ninety-five theses; in our present situation there is only one thesis: Christianity does not exist at all.] . . . —*JP* VI 6947 (*Pap.* XI³ B 57) *n.d.*, 1854

EDITORIAL APPENDIX

ACKNOWLEDGMENTS

Preparation of manuscripts for *Kierkegaard's Writings* is supported by a genuinely enabling grant from the National Endowment for the Humanities. The grant includes gifts from the Dronning Margrethe og Prins Henriks Fond, the Danish Ministry of Cultural Affairs, the Augustinus Fond, the Carlsberg Fond, the Konsul George Jorck og Hustru Emma Jorcks Fond, and the A. P. Møller og Hustru Chastine Mc-Kinney Møllers Fond.

The translators–editors are indebted to Grethe Kjær and Julia Watkin for their knowledgeable observations on crucial concepts and terminology.

John Elrod, Per Lønning, and Sophia Scopetéa, members of the International Advisory Board for *Kierkegaard's Writings*, have given valuable criticism of the manuscript on the whole and in detail. Julia Watkin, Jack Schwandt, and Pamela Schwandt have helpfully scrutinized all or parts of the manuscript. The index was prepared by Francesca Rasmus. The entire work has been facilitated by George Coulter and Lavier Murray.

Acknowledgment is made to Gyldendals Forlag for permission to absorb notes to *Søren Kierkegaards Samlede Værker*.

Inclusion in the Supplement of entries from *Søren Kierkegaard's Journals and Papers* is by arrangement with Indiana University Press.

The book collection and the microfilm collection of the Kierkegaard Library, St. Olaf College, have been used in preparation of the text, Supplement, and Editorial Appendix.

The manuscript, typed by Dorothy Bolton and Kennedy Lemke, has been guided through the press by Cathie Brettschneider.

COLLATION OF *EITHER/OR*, PART II,
IN THE DANISH EDITIONS OF
KIERKEGAARD'S COLLECTED WORKS

Vol. II Ed. 1 Pg.	Vol. II Ed. 2 Pg.	Vol. 3 Ed. 3 Pg.	Vol. II Ed. 1 Pg.	Vol. II Ed. 2 Pg.	Vol. 3 Ed. 3 Pg.
5	7	11	39	47	44
6	8	11	40	48	45
7	9	12	41	49	46
8	10	13	42	50	47
9	11	14	43	52	48
10	12	15	44	53	49
11	14	16	45	54	50
12	15	17	46	55	51
13	16	18	47	56	52
14	17	19	48	58	53
15	18	20	49	59	54
16	19	21	50	60	55
17	21	22	51	61	56
18	22	23	52	63	57
19	23	24	53	64	58
20	24	25	54	65	59
21	25	26	55	66	60
22	27	27	56	68	61
23	28	28	57	69	62
24	29	29	58	70	63
25	30	30	59	71	64
26	31	31	60	72	65
27	32	32	61	73	66
28	34	33	62	75	67
29	35	34	63	76	68
30	36	35	64	77	69
31	37	36	65	78	70
32	38	37	66	79	71
33	40	38	67	81	72
34	41	39	68	82	73
35	42	40	69	83	74
36	43	41	70	84	75
37	44	42	71	85	76
38	46	43	72	87	77

Vol. II Ed. 1 Pg.	Vol. II Ed. 2 Pg.	Vol. 3 Ed. 3 Pg.	Vol. II Ed. 1 Pg.	Vol. II Ed. 2 Pg.	Vol. 3 Ed. 3 Pg.
73	88	78	116	139	121
74	89	79	117	140	122
75	90	80	118	141	123
76	91	81	119	142	124
77	92	82	120	144	125
78	94	83	121	145	126
79	95	84	122	146	127
80	96	85	123	147	128
81	97	86	124	148	129
82	98	87	125	150	130
83	99	88	126	151	131
84	101	89	127	152	132
85	102	90	128	153	133
86	103	91	129	154	134
87	104	92	130	155	135
88	106	93	131	157	136
89	107	94	132	158	137
90	108	95	133	159	138
91	109	96	134	160	139
92	110	97	135	161	140
93	111	98	136	163	141
94	112	99	137	164	142
95	114	100	138	165	143
96	115	101	139	166	144
97	116	102	140	167	145
98	117	103	143	171	149
99	118	104	144	172	149
100	120	105	145	173	150
101	121	106	146	174	151
102	122	107	147	175	152
103	123	108	148	177	154
104	125	109	149	178	154
105	126	110	150	179	156
106	127	111	151	180	157
107	128	112	152	181	158
108	129	113	153	182	159
109	131	114	154	184	159
110	132	115	155	185	160
111	133	116	156	186	161
112	134	117	157	187	162
113	135	118	158	188	163
114	137	119	159	190	164
115	138	120	160	191	165

Vol. II Ed. 1 Pg.	Vol. II Ed. 2 Pg.	Vol. 3 Ed. 3 Pg.	Vol. II Ed. 1 Pg.	Vol. II Ed. 2 Pg.	Vol. 3 Ed. 3 Pg.
161	192	167	204	245	211
162	193	168	205	247	212
163	194	169	206	248	213
164	196	170	207	249	214
165	197	171	208	250	215
166	198	172	209	251	216
167	199	173	210	253	217
168	201	174	211	254	218
169	202	175	212	255	219
170	203	176	213	256	220
171	204	177	214	257	221
172	205	178	215	258	222
173	207	179	216	260	223
174	208	180	217	261	224
175	209	181	218	262	225
176	211	182	219	263	226
177	212	183	220	264	227
178	213	184	221	266	228
179	214	185	222	267	228
180	216	186	223	268	229
181	217	187	224	269	230
182	218	188	225	270	231
183	219	189	226	272	232
184	220	190	227	273	233
185	222	191	228	274	234
186	223	192	229	275	235
187	224	193	230	276	236
188	225	194	231	278	237
189	227	195	232	279	238
190	228	196	233	280	239
191	229	197	234	281	240
192	230	198	235	282	241
193	232	199	236	284	242
194	233	201	237	285	244
195	234	202	238	286	245
196	236	203	239	287	246
197	237	204	240	289	247
198	238	205	241	290	248
199	239	206	242	291	249
200	240	207	243	292	250
201	242	208	244	294	251
202	243	209	245	295	252
203	244	210	246	296	253

Vol. II Ed. 1 Pg.	Vol. II Ed. 2 Pg.	Vol. 3 Ed. 3 Pg.	Vol. II Ed. 1 Pg.	Vol. II Ed. 2 Pg.	Vol. 3 Ed. 3 Pg.
247	297	254	281	337	288
248	298	255	282	339	289
249	299	256	283	340	289
250	301	257	284	341	290
251	302	258	285	342	292
252	303	259	286	343	293
253	304	260	287	345	294
254	306	261	288	346	295
255	307	262	289	347	295
256	308	263	290	348	296
257	309	264	291	349	297
258	310	265	292	350	298
259	311	266	293	352	299
260	313	267	294	353	300
261	314	268	295	354	301
262	315	269	296	355	302
263	316	270	297	356	303
264	317	271	298	358	304
265	318	272	299	359	305
266	320	273	303	363	309
267	321	274	304	364	309
268	322	274	307	367	313
269	323	276	308	368	313
270	324	277	309	369	314
271	325	277	310	370	315
272	326	278	311	371	316
273	328	279	312	373	318
274	329	280	313	374	319
275	330	281	314	375	320
276	331	282	315	376	321
277	333	284	316	378	322
278	334	284	317	379	323
279	335	286	318	380	324
280	336	287			

NOTES

TITLE PAGE

François René de Chateaubriand, *Atala ou Les Amours de deux sauvages dans le désert* (Paris: 1801), p. 83. Cf. epigraph, *Either/Or*, I, title page, *KW* III (*SV* I).

THE ESTHETIC VALIDITY OF MARRIAGE

1. See Supplement, p. 371 (*Pap*. IV A 237).
2. See II Samuel 12:1-7. Cf. *For Self-Examination, KW* XXI (*SV* XII 325-27).
3. See Supplement, pp. 371-72 (*Pap*. III B 182). For section heading in draft, see Supplement, p. 372 (*Pap*. III B 41:1).
4. For continuation of the sentence, see Supplement, p. 372 (*Pap*. III B 41:2).
5. See *Either/Or*, I, pp. 75-78, *KW* III (*SV* I 57-60); Supplement, p. 372 (*Pap*. III B 41:3).
6. German in the text with the Danish ø instead of ö.
7. At one time, Algiers, Tunis, and Tripoli were known as pirate cities, and protection against their pirate ships could be obtained for a fee.
8. Cicero, *De natura deorum*, III, 40; *M. Tullii Ciceronis opera omnia*, I-IV and index, ed. Johann August Ernesti (Halle: 1757; *ASKB* 1224-29), IV, p. 604; *Cicero De natura deorum, Academica*, tr. H. Rackham (Loeb, New York: Putnam, 1933), pp. 380-81.
9. Adelbert v. Chamisso, *Peter Schlemihl's wundersame Geschichte* (Nuremberg: 1835; *ASKB* 1630), pp. 19-20; *Peter Schlemihl's forunderlige Historie*, tr. Frederik Schaldemose (Copenhagen: 1841), p. 11; *The Wonderful History of Peter Schlemihl*, tr. Ilsa Barea (Emmaus, Penn.: Story Classics, n.d.), p. 10.
10. See *Either/Or*, I, pp. 29-30, *KW* III (*SV* I 4).
11. See Homer, *Odyssey*, X, 237-40; *Homers Odyssee*, tr. Christian Wilster (Copenhagen: 1837), p. 137; *Homer The Odyssey*, I-II, tr. A. T. Murray (Loeb, New York: Putnam, 1927-29), I, p. 363.
12. At the time, the rix-dollar was worth about $5.00 (1973 value).
13. Kierkegaard rarely uses the term *Realitet* (reality) and very frequently uses *Virkelighed* (actuality). The dominant meaning of "reality" is genuineness, validity; "actuality" stresses being and becoming in time and space. See *JP* III 3651-55 and pp. 900-03, especially pp. 902-03.
14. For continuation of the sentence, see Supplement, p. 372 (*Pap*. III B 41:4).
15. See Job 2:9.
16. See *Kierkegaard: Letters and Documents*, Letter 217, *KW* XXV.
17. See Philippians 4:7.

18. See Philippians 2:6.

19. See *Either/Or*, I, pp. 233-79, *KW* III (*SV* I 205-51).

20. Eugène Scribe, *For evig, eller Medicin mod en Elskovsruus*, tr. Theodor Overskou, *Kongelige Theaters Repertoire* (1833), 51. See *Letters*, Letter 211, p. 294, *KW* XXV.

21. See Gottfried Wilhelm Leibniz, *Monadology*, 78; *Guil. Leibnitii opera philosophica*, I-II, ed. Johann Eduard Erdmann (Hanover, Leipzig: 1763; *ASKB* 619), II, p. 711; *Leibniz: The Monadology and Other Philosophical Writings*, tr. Robert Latta (London: Oxford University Press, 1965), pp. 262-63: "These principles have given me a way of explaining naturally the union or rather the mutual agreement [*conformité*] of the soul and the organic body. The soul follows its own laws, and the body likewise follows its own laws; and they agree with each other in virtue of the pre-established harmony between all substances, since they are all representations of one and the same universe." See *JP* III 2360; V 5667 (*Pap.* IV A 11, 111).

22. See Johann Wolfgang v. Goethe, *Wahlverwandtschaften, Goethe's Werke*, I-LX (Stuttgart, Tübingen: 1828-33; *ASKB* 1641-68 [I-LV]), XVII, pp. 47-57; *Elective Affinities*, tr. Elizabeth Mayer and Louise Bogan (Chicago: Regnery, 1963), pp. 36-44.

23. See *Either/Or*, I, p. 56, and note 13, *KW* III (*SV* I 40).

24. Here "moral" corresponds to Hegel's interpretation of *Sittlichkeit* (custom, law, "ethical life," or social morality) in contrast to *Moralität*, which Hegel associates with Socrates' ethical consciousness. Except in *Irony*, Kierkegaard does not follow Hegel's usage but instead associates Socrates with the ethical, the ethical consciousness, in contrast to *Sædelighed*, social morality. See, for example, *Philosophie des Rechts*, para. 33, *Georg Wilhelm Friedrich Hegel's Werke*, I-XVIII, ed. Philipp Marheineke et al. (Berlin: 1832-45; *ASKB* 549-65), VIII, pp. 68-69; *Jubiläumsausgabe* [*J.A.*], I-XXVI, ed. Hermann Glockner (Stuttgart: 1927-40), VII, pp. 84-85; *Philosophy of Right* (tr. of *P.R.*, 1 ed., 1821, with reference to later editions; Kierkegaard had 2 ed., 1833), tr. T. M. Knox (Oxford: Oxford University Press, 1967), pp. 35-36:

Division of the Subject

In correspondence with the stages in the development of the Idea of the absolutely free will, the will is

A. immediate; its concept therefore is abstract, namely personality, and its embodiment is an immediate external thing—the sphere of *Abstract* or *Formal Right*;

B. reflected from its external embodiment into itself—it is then characterized as subjective individuality in opposition to the universal. The universal here is characterized as something inward, the good, and also as something outward, a world presented to the will; both these sides of the Idea are here mediated only by each other. This is the Idea in its division or in its existence as particular; and here we have the right of the subjective will in relation to the right of the world and the right of the idea, though only the Idea implicit—the sphere of *Morality*;

C. the unity and truth of both these abstract moments—the Idea of the good not only apprehended in thought but so realized both in the will reflected into itself and in the external world that freedom exists as substance, as actuality and necessity, no less than as subjective will; this is the Idea in its absolutely universal existence—*Ethical Life.*

But on the same principle the ethical substance is

(*a*) natural mind, the *Family*;

(*b*) in its division and appearance, *Civil Society*;

c) the *State* as freedom, freedom universal and objective even in the free self-subsistence of the particular will. This actual and organic mind (α) of a single nation (6) reveals and actualizes itself through the inter-relation of the particular national minds until (γ) in the process of world-history it reveals and actualizes itself as the universal world-mind whose right is supreme.

See also the note on this theme by the translators of *Hegel's Lectures on the History of Philosophy*, I-III, tr. E. S. Haldane and Frances H. Simson (New York: Humanities Press, 1955), I, pp. 387-88:

> The distinction between these two words is a very important one. Schwegler, in explaining Hegel's position in his "History of Philosophy," states that Hegel asserts that Socrates set *Moralität*, the subjective morality of individual conscience, in the place of *Sittlichkeit*, "the spontaneous, natural, half-unconscious (almost instinctive) virtue that rests in obedience to established custom (use and wont, natural objective law, that is at bottom, according to Hegel, rational, though not yet subjectively cleared, perhaps, into its rational principles)." As Dr. Stirling says in his Annotations to the same work (p. 394), "There is a period in the history of the State when people live in tradition; that is a period of unreflected *Sittlichkeit*, or natural observance. Then there comes a time when the observances are questioned, and when the right or truth they involve is reflected into the subject. This is a period of *Aufklärung*, and for *Sittlichkeit* there is substituted *Moralität*, subjective morality: the subject will approve nought but what he finds inwardly true to himself, to his conscience."

25. See George Gordon Byron, "To Eliza," *Hours of Idleness; Lord Byron's sämmtliche Werke . . . neu übersetzt von Mehreren*, I-X (Stuttgart: 1839; *ASKB* 1868-70), I, p. 83; *The Poetical Works of Lord Byron* (London: Oxford University Press, 1945), p. 29: " 'Though women are angels, yet wedlock's the devil.' "

26. For continuation of the sentence, see Supplement, p. 372 (*Pap.* III B 41:5).

27. See note 13 above.

28. The Strasbourg geese were stuffed with food in order that their livers would become enlarged for the production of pâté de foie gras.

29. Horace, *Epistles*, I, 4, 6; Q. *Horatii Flacci opera* (Leipzig: 1828; *ASKB* 1248), p. 230 ("*Di tibi formam, di tibi divitias dederunt, artemque fruendi*"); *Horace Satires, Epistles and Ars Poetica*, tr. H. Rushton Fairclough (Loeb, New York: Putnam, 1929), pp. 276-77.

30. Cf. *Repetition*, pp. 135-36, *KW* VI (*SV* III 177-78).

31. See *Either/Or*, I, pp. 133-39, *KW* III (*SV* I 112).

32. According to some writers, the truce concluded September 1, 1192, between Richard the Lionhearted and Saladin, Moslem sultan of Egypt, lasted for three years, three months, three days, and three hours.

33. See Matthew 6:34.

34. See, for example, Hegel, *Encyclopädie der philosophischen Wissenschaften*, I, *Die Logik*, para. 94 and *Zusatz, Werke*, VI, pp. 184-85; *J.A.* (*System der Philosophie*), VIII, pp. 222-23; *Hegel's Logic* (tr. of *L.*, 3 ed., 1830; Kierkegaard had 3 ed.), tr. William Wallace (Oxford: Oxford University Press, 1975), pp. 137-38:

This **Infinity** is the wrong or negative infinity: it is only a negation of a finite: but the finite rises again the same as ever, and is never got rid of and absorbed. In other words, this infinite only expresses the *ought-to-be* elimination of the finite. The progression to infinity never gets further than a statement of the contradiction involved in the finite, viz. that it is somewhat as well as somewhat else. It sets up with endless iteration the alternation between these two terms, each of which calls up the other.

If we let somewhat and another, the elements of determinate Being, fall asunder, the result is that some becomes other, and this other is itself a somewhat, which then as such changes likewise, and so on *ad infinitum*. This result seems to superficial reflection something very grand, the grandest possible. But such a progression to infinity is not the real infinite. That consists in being at home with itself in its other, or, if enunciated as a process, in coming to itself in its other. Much depends on rightly apprehending the notion of infinity, and not stopping short at the wrong infinity of endless progression. When time and space, for example, are spoken of as infinite, it is in the first place the infinite progression on which our thoughts fasten. We say, Now, This time, and then we keep continually going forwards and backwards beyond this limit. The case is the same with space, the infinity of which has formed the theme of barren declamation to astronomers with a talent for edification. In the attempt to contemplate such an infinite, our thought, we are commonly informed, must sink exhausted. It is true indeed that we must abandon the unending contemplation, not however because the occupation is too sublime, but because it is too tedious. It is tedious to expatiate in the contemplation of this infinite progression, because the same thing is constantly recurring. We lay down a limit: then we pass it: next we have a limit once more, and so on for ever. All this is but superficial alternation, which never leaves the region of the finite behind. To suppose that by stepping out and away into that infinity we release ourselves from the finite, is in truth but to seek the release which comes by flight. But the man who flees is not yet free: in fleeing he is still conditioned by that from which he flees. If it be also said that the infinite is unattainable, the statement is true, but only because to the idea of infinity has been attached the circumstance of being simply and solely negative. With such empty and otherworld stuff philosophy has nothing to do.

35. Cf. *Either/Or*, I, p. 54, *KW* III (*SV* I 37-38).

36. The quotation has not been located.

37. Johann August Musäus, "*Liebestreue*," *Volksmärchen der Deutschen*, I-V (Vienna: 1815; *ASKB* 1434-38), III, p. 133.

38. See Luke 1:37.

39. *Elskov* is immediate, romantic, dreaming love, as between a man and a woman. *Kjærlighed* is love in a more inclusive and also higher sense. *Elskov* and *Kjærlighed* correspond to "eros" and "agape."

40. A sound picture produced by the nodal lines in sand on a vibrating plate. Named after the German physicist Ernst Florens Friedrich Chladni (1756-1827). See Supplement, p. 373 (*Pap.* III B 41:6); *Either/Or*, I, p. 418, *KW* III (*SV* I 385).

41. See note 13 above.

42. See *Fear and Trembling*, pp. 36, 119, *KW* VI (*SV* III 87, 164).

43. A character in *Figaros Givtermaal eller den gale Dag. Syngestykke i fire Akter oversat til Musik af Mozart efter den italiensk Omarbeidelse af Beaumarchais' franske Original*, tr. Niels Thoroup Bruun (Copenhagen: 1817); *Le Nozze di Figaro* (*The Marriage of Figaro*), tr. Ruth and Thomas Martin (New York: G. Schirmer, 1951).

44. Cf. Matthew 16:26.

45. In Greek mythology, Zeus (L. Jupiter) came to Danae, daughter of Acrisius and mother of Perseus, in a shower of gold. See Paul Friedrich A. Nitsch, *neues mythologisches Wörterbuch*, I-II, rev. Friedrich Gotthilf Klopfer (Leipzig, Sorau: 1824; *ASKB* 1944-45), I, p. 592.

46. With reference to the following two sentences, see Supplement, p. 373 (*Pap.* III B 41:7).

47. See Matthew 2:16.

48. Christian Wilster, "*Studentervise*," *Digtninger* (Copenhagen: 1827), p. 38.

49. See, for example, *The Concept of Anxiety*, p. 52, *KW* VIII (*SV* IV 323).

50. See Hebrews 6:4-6.

51. Byron, "The First Kiss of Love," *Hours of Idleness*; *Werke*, I, p. 22; *Works*, p. 8.

52. See *Either/Or*, I, pp. 75-78, *KW* III (*SV* I 57-60).

53. See Genesis 24.

54. See, for example, Hegel, *Philosophie der Religion, Werke*, XII, pp. 81-82; *J.A.*, XVI, pp. 81-82; *Lectures on the Philosophy of Religion*, I-III (tr. of *P.R.*, 2 ed., 1840; Kierkegaard had this ed.), tr. E. B. Spiers and J. Burdon Sanderson (New York: Humanities Press, 1974), II, pp. 209-10:

The Jewish God exists only for Thought, and that stands in contrast with the idea of the limitation of God to the nation. . . . According to the dominant fundamental idea, the Jewish people are the chosen people, and the universality is thus reduced to particularity. . . .

This harmonises, too, with the history of the people. The Jewish God is the God of Abraham, of Isaac, and of Jacob, the God who brought the Jews out of Egypt, and there is not the slightest trace of the thought that God may have done other things as well, and that He has acted in an affirmative way amongst other people too.

55. For addition, see Supplement, p. 373 (*Pap.* III B 41:8).

56. *"Jeg beder jer hellige Konger tre,"* Just Matthias Thiele, *Danske Folkesange,* I-IV (Copenhagen: 1819-23; *ASKB* 1591-92), III, p. 96.

57. For a consideration of "reflexion" and "reflection," see *Two Ages,* p. ix, *KW* XIV.

58. With reference to the following sentence, see Supplement, p. 373 (*Pap.* III B 41:9).

59. Cf. Genesis 3:15.

60. See Genesis 3:12, 17.

61. See, for example, Genesis 3:16.

62. Cf. Genesis 1:22.

63. Virgil, *Æneid,* VI, 258; *Virgils Aeneide,* tr. Johan Henrik Schønheyder (Copenhagen: 1812), p. 263; *Virgil,* I-II, tr. H. Rushton Fairclough (Loeb, New York: Putnam, 1920), I, pp. 524-25.

64. See Luke 7:36-47.

65. In Norse mythology, Freya secured the promise from all of nature not to harm Balder, god of light, son of Odin and Frigga, but she had omitted the mistletoe, which later became, through Loki, the personification of evil, the instrument of Balder's death.

66. See, for example, Hegel, *Vorlesungen über die Aesthetik, Werke,* X¹, pp. 137-38, 145, 150; *J.A.,* XII, pp. 153-54, 161, 166; *The Philosophy of Fine Art,* I-IV (tr. of *V.A.,* 1 ed., 1835-38; Kierkegaard had this ed.), tr. F.P.B. Osmaston (London: Bell, 1920), I, pp. 147, 154, 159:

> We have defined beauty to be the Idea of the beautiful. By this definition is implied that we have to conceive the beautiful as Idea, and, moreover, as Idea in a determinate shape, as *Ideal.* Idea, as thus posited, is just this, the conceptive notion, the realization of the same, and the unity of both. The understanding remains rooted in the finite, the incomplete and untrue abstraction. The beautiful is on the contrary itself essentially *infinite* and free.

> The understanding remains rooted in the finite, the incomplete and untrue abstraction. The beautiful is on the contrary itself essentially *infinite* and free.

> In virtue of the freedom and infinitude above analysed, which is inherent in the notion of beauty, whether we view it in its objective presence as a

thing of beauty, or under its aesthetic contemplation, we disengage the province of the beautiful from the relations of finite condition, to exalt it into that of the idea and its truth.

67. For continuation of the sentence, see Supplement, p. 373 (*Pap.* III B 41:10).

68. See *Either/Or*, I, pp. 254, *KW* III (*SV* I 227).

69. See Mozart, *Figaro*, I, 7; Bruun, pp. 25–31; Martin, pp. 83–99.

70. In "The Boasting Traveler," Aesop tells of a character who claims to have made an extraordinary leap on the island of Rhodes. A bystander replies, "*Hic Rhodos; hic salta* [Here is Rhodes; leap here]." *The Fables of Aesop*, ed. Thomas Bewick (New York: Paddington Press, 1975), p. 59. In citing Aesop, Hegel sometimes uses "dance." See, for example, *Philosophie des Rechts, Werke*, VIII, p. 19; *J.A.*, VII, p. 35; *Philosophy of Right*, p. 11:

The instruction which it may contain cannot consist in teaching the state what it ought to be; it can only show how the state, the ethical universe, is to be understood.

Ἰδοὺ Ῥόδος ἰδοὺ καὶ τὸ πήδημα.
Hic Rhodus, *hic* saltus.

To comprehend what is, this is the task of philosophy, because what is, is reason. Whatever happens, every individual is a child of his time; so philosophy too is its own time apprehended in thoughts. It is just as absurd to fancy that a philosophy can transcend its contemporary world as it is to fancy that an individual can overleap his own age, jump over Rhodes. If his theory really goes beyond the world as it is and builds an ideal one as it ought to be, that world exists indeed, but only in his opinions, an unsubstantial element where anything you please may, in fancy, be built.

With hardly an alteration, the proverb just quoted would run:
Here is the rose, dance thou here.

71. Johan Ludvig Heiberg, *Alferne*, 4; *Skuespil*, I-VII (Copenhagen: 1833–41; *ASKB* 1553-59), VI, p. 66.

72. See Diogenes Laertius, *Lives of Eminent Philosophers*, II, 36–37; *Diogenis Laertii de vitis philosophorum*, I-II (Leipzig: 1833; *ASKB* 1109), I, pp. 77–78; *Diogen Laërtses filosofiske Historie*, I-II, tr. Børge Riisbrigh (Copenhagen: 1812; *ASKB* 1110-11), I, pp. 72–73; *Lives of Eminent Philosophers*, I-II, tr. R. D. Hicks (Loeb, New York: Putnam, 1925), p. 167:

When Xanthippe first scolded him and then drenched him with water, his rejoinder was, "Did I not say that Xanthippe's thunder would end in rain?" When Alcibiades declared that the scolding of Xanthippe was intolerable, "Nay, I have got used to it," said he, "as to the continued rattle of a windlass. And you do not mind the cackle of geese." "No," replied Alcibiades, "but they furnish me with eggs and goslings." "And Xanthippe," said Socrates, "is the mother of my children." When she tore his coat off his back in the market-place and his acquaintances advised him to hit back, "Yes, by Zeus," said he, "in order that while we are sparring each of you may join in with 'Go it, Socrates!' 'Well done, Xanthippe!' " He said he lived with a shrew, as horsemen are fond of spirited horses, "but just as, when they have mastered these, they can easily cope with the rest, so I in the society of Xanthippe shall learn to adapt myself to the rest of the world."

73. For continuation of the sentence, see Supplement, p. 373 (*Pap.* III B 41:12).

74. See I Corinthians 13:4-7.

75. See Matthew 6:34.

76. With reference to the following sentence, see Supplement, p. 374 (*Pap.* IV A 249).

77. Genesis 1:28.

78. See Genesis 2:18.

79. See Genesis 1:22.

80. Cf. I Timothy 2:11-15.

81. This saying has not been located in Seneca's writings. See *Letters*, Letter 176, *KW* XXV.

82. For continuation of the sentence, see Supplement, p. 374 (*Pap.* III 41:13).

83. For continuation of the sentence, see Supplement, p. 374 (*Pap.* III B 41:14).

84. Troels in Ludvig Holberg, *Barselstuen*, I, 1; *Den Danske Skue-Plads*, I-VII (Copenhagen: 1788; *ASKB* 1566-67), II, no pagination (ed. tr.): "I would obligate myself to produce a half hundred such children a year; there is no greater miracle."

85. See Romans 8:20.

86. Frederiksberg, a castle and gardens on the west edge of Copenhagen. See *Either/Or*, I, pp. 339, 412, *KW* III (*SV* I 310, 379).

87. See Homer, *Iliad*, I, 528-30; *Homers Iliade*, tr. Christian Wilster (Copenhagen: 1836), p. 15; *Homer The Iliad*, I-II, tr. A. T. Murray (Loeb, Cambridge: Harvard University Press, 1924-25), I, p. 43: "The son of Cronos spake, and bowed his dark brow in assent, and the ambrosial locks waved from the king's immortal head; and he made great Olympus to quake."

88. See Luke 16:25.

89. See M.E.G. Théaulon de Lambert (music by F. A. Boildieu), *Den lille Rødhætte*, tr. Niels Thoroup Bruun (Copenhagen: 1819), I, 10 (ed. tr.):

> Tell me, Jeannette,
> Why we have missed you so long in our meadows
> Where you used to come with us
> And with the flute went swinging?
> Now you flee the joys of youth
> And seek the solitary places.
> Tell me, why.

90. See *Either/Or*, I, p. 43, *KW* III (*SV* I 27).

91. For addition, see Supplement, p. 374 (*Pap.* III B 41:16).

92. Sirach 36:24-26.
93. See Genesis 21:10; Galatians 4:30.
94. See Nehemiah 4:16-18, 23.
95. See, for example, J. G. Fichte, *Grundlage des Naturrechts, Johann Gottlieb Fichte's sämmtliche Werke*, I-XI (Berlin: 1834-46; *ASKB* 489-99), III, pp. 313-15, 327-28.
96. See Ephesians 2:19; Hebrews 11:13.
97. See *Letters*, Letter 54, 103, *KW* XXV; *JP* V 5403 (*Pap.* II A 250).
98. For addition, see Supplement, pp. 374-75 (*Pap.* III B 41:18).
99. Jens Immanuel Baggesen, "*Scheerenschleifer-Epopee*," *Poetische Werke in deutscher Sprache*, I-V (Leipzig: 1836), II, p. 228.
100. See Revelation 14:13.
101. See I Peter 3:15.
102. Heinrich Heine, "*Ein Jüngling liebt ein Mädchen*," *Lyrisches Intermezzo*, 39, *Buch der Lieder, Sämmtliche Werke*, I-XII (Leipzig: 1839), I, p. 39. See *JP* II 1626 (*Pap.* I A 208).
103. See, for example, *Irony, KW* II (*SV* XIII 359 fn.).
104. For continuation of the paragraph, see Supplement, p. 375 (*Pap.* III B 41:19).
105. See I Timothy 2:14.
106. See Genesis 2:18.
107. See Genesis 2:24.
108. For continuation of the paragraph, see Supplement, p. 375 (*Pap.* III B 41:20).
109. The Danish *Hvedebrøds-Dage* (literally "days of wheat bread") refers to the celebratory honeymoon days when the newlyweds would eat the more expensive white wheat bread rather than the ordinary dark rye bread.
110. For continuation of the paragraph, see Supplement, p. 375 (*Pap.* III B 41:21).
111. See, for example, Hegel, *Vorlesungen über die Aesthetik*, II, *Werke*, X², pp. 137-41; *J.A.*, XIII, pp. 137-41; *Philosophy of Fine Art*, II, pp. 297-301:

> Inasmuch as romantic art, in the representation of the consciousness of absolute subjectivity, understanding this as the comprehension of all truth, the coalescence of mind with its essence—receives its substantive content in the satisfaction of soul-life, in other words the reconciliation of God with the world and therein with Himself, it follows that at this stage the Ideal for the first time is completely at home. For it was blessedness and self-subsistency, contentment, repose, and freedom which we declared as most fundamentally defining the Ideal. Of course, we cannot therefore on this account deduce the Ideal simply from the notion and reality of romantic art; but relatively to the classical Ideal the form it receives is entirely altered. This relation, already in general terms indicated, we must now before everything else establish in its fully concrete significance, in order to elucidate the fundamental type of the romantic mode of presentation. In the classical Ideal the Divine is in one aspect of it restricted to pure individuality; in another aspect the soul and spiritual blessedness of particular gods find their

exclusive discharge through the physical medium; and as a third characteristic, for the reason that the inseparable unity of each individual both essentially and in its exterior form supplies the principle of the same, the negativ-
ity of the dismemberment implied in human life, that is the pain of both
body and soul, sacrifice, and resignation are unable to appear as essentially
pertinent to these godlike figures.

112. See, for example, *Johannes Climacus, or De omnibus dubitandum est*, pp.
130-32, *KW* VII (*Pap.* IV B 1, pp. 114-16).

113. For continuation of the paragraph, see Supplement, p. 376 (*Pap.* III B
41:22).

114. For continuation of the sentence, see Supplement, p. 376 (*Pap.* III B
41:23).

115. The political motto of the French king Louis XI (1423-83); attributed
to Philip (382-336 B.C.) of Macedonia.

116. The text has *det Romantiske*. The draft has *det Historiske, det Romantiske*
(meaning *det Historiske*, according to the editors of *SV* 1 ed.). *SV* 2 and 3 ed.
have *det Historiske*. In the context, "the historical" seems appropriate here.

117. See Matthew 17:20, 21:21; Mark 11:23; I Corinthians 13:2.

118. See "To Gain One's Soul in Patience," *Eighteen Upbuilding Discourses*
KW V (*SV* IV 54-68).

119. Cf. p. 138 and note 160.

120. See I Timothy 4:4.

121. Probably an echo of Jean Paul's use of the Latin logical locution *Posito*
and a repetition in translation. See, for example, "*Vierte Ruhestunde*," *Das*
heimliche Klaglied der ietzigen Männer, Jean Paul's sämmtliche Werke, I-LX (Berlin: 1826-28; *ASKB* 1777-99), XXXIX, p. 35. See also *Prefaces, KW* IX (*SV*
V 43).

122. See Adam Gottlob Oehlenschläger, "*Skattegraveren*," *Digte* (Copenhagen: 1803), p. 29; *JP* V 5547 (*Pap.* II A 780).

123. See Suetonius, "Gaius C. Caligula," 30, *Lives of the Caesars; Caji Sue-*
tonii Tranquilli Tolv første Romerske Keiseres Levnetsbeskrivelse, I-II, tr. Jacob
Baden (Copenhagen: 1802-03; *ASKB* 1281), I, p. 312; *Suetonius*, I-II, tr. J. C.
Rolfe (Loeb, New York: Macmillan, 1914), I, p. 453: "Angered at the rabble
for applauding a faction which he opposed, he cried: 'I wish the Roman people
had but a single neck . . . .' " See also Supplement, p. 382 (*Pap.* II A 409).

124. Presumably the reference is to Emperor Domitian. See Suetonius,
Domitian, III, 1; Baden, II, p. 231; Loeb, II, p. 345: "At the beginning of his
reign he used to spend hours in seclusion every day, doing nothing but catch
flies and stab them with a keenly-sharpened stylus. Consequently when someone once asked whether anyone was in there with Caesar, Vibius Crispus
made the witty reply: 'Not even a fly.' " See *Repetition*, p. 179, *KW* VI (*SV* III
214).

125. With reference to the remainder of the sentence, see Supplement, p.
376 (*Pap.* III B 41:24).

126. The quotation has not been located.

127. See Matthew 10:32; Mark 8:38.

128. See Supplement, p. 376 (*Pap*. B 41:25).

129. With reference to the following paragraph, see Supplement, p. 376 (*Pap*. III B 39).

130. Danish: *Experiment*. See *Repetition*, pp. xxi-xxviii, 357-62, *KW* VI.

131. A play on the Danish, which literally means "go out from" and figuratively means "presuppose," "assume," "take as a point of departure," "proceed from the assumption."

132. See, for example, *The Concept of Irony*, *KW* II (*SV* XIII 364), for a token of the more than incidental association of Mr. A and Schlegel's *Lucinde*.

133. See Matthew 6:27.

134. Cf. Matthew 10:39, 16:25; Mark 8:35; Luke 9:24; John 12:25.

135. The source of this passage has not been located.

136. In Norse mythology, Valhalla was Odin's hall for slain heroes, the palace of immortality, to which the slain heroes were carried by the Valkyries.

137. Prince Alexandrovitsch Potemkin (1739-1791), the prime minister of Catherine II of Russia. To conceal his mismanagement, he contrived the impression of colonization and prosperity in areas that she visited. See Karl F. Becker, *Verdenshistorie*, I-XII, tr. Jacob Riise (Copenhagen: 1822-29; *ASKB* 1972-83), XI, pp. 207-08; *Postscript*, *KW* XII (*SV* VII 237).

138. See Job 38:11.

139. With reference to the following sentence, see Supplement, p. 377 (*Pap*. III B 41:26).

140. See Supplement, p. 377 (*Pap*. III B 41:27); *Either/Or*, I, p. 235, *KW* III (*SV* I 209).

141. See Genesis 3:19.

142. *Werke*, XVII, pp. 78-319; *Elective Affinities*, pp. 59-305.

143. King of Denmark from 1086 to 1095, during which time there was a great famine.

144. Cf. II Timothy 4:7.

145. See Horace, *Ars poetica*, 323; *Opera*, p. 693 ("*ore rotundo*"); Loeb, pp. 476-77 ("well-rounded phrase").

146. See p. 105 and note 130.

147. Cf. *Either/Or*, I, p. 39, *KW* III (*SV* I 23).

148. See "Sermon on the Seventh Sunday after Trinity (Mark 8:1-9)," *En christelig Postille sammendragen af Dr. Marten Luthers Kirke- og Huuspostiller*, I-II, tr. Jørgen Thisted (Copenhagen: 1828; *ASKB* 283), I, p. 441; cf. *Luther's Church Postil Gospels First to Twelfth Sunday after Trinity*, tr. John Nicholas Lenker (Minneapolis: Lutherans in All Lands Co., 1904), p. 222.

149. Cf. Hesiod, *Works and Days*, 289-90; *Hesiod The Homeric Hymns and Homerica*, tr. Hugh G. Evelyn-White (Loeb, New York: Macmillan, 1914), p. 25: "But between us and Goodness the gods have placed the sweat of our brows . . . ." See p. 327.

150. Judge William is quoting Mr. A's version of Leibniz. See Leibniz, *Nouveaux essais*, II, 27, 1-3; *Opera*, I, pp. 277-78; *New Essays on Human Understand-*

ing, tr. Peter Remnant and Jonathan Bennett (Cambridge: Cambridge University Press, 1981), pp. 229-31.

151. See Matthew 11:25.

152. See, for example, Leibniz, *Discourse on Metaphysics*, XXII; *Opera*, II, p. 826; *Leibniz Discourse on Metaphysics Correspondence with Arnauld and Monadology*, tr. George R. Montgomery (Chicago: Open Court, 1931), p. 39: "For since the rays while in the same media always maintain the same proportion of sines, which in turn corresponds to the resistance of the media, it appears that they follow the easiest way, or at least that way which is the most determinate for passing from a given point in one medium to a given point in another medium."

153. See, for example, Jens Baggesen, *"Kallundborgs Krønike," Jens Baggesens danske Værker*, I-XII (Copenhagen: 1827-32; *ASKB* 1509-20), I, 245 (ed. tr.):

> One still does not know with certainty
> (for the way of the law is very long)
> To which corner it will turn.

154. See p. 12 and note 13.

155. See Leviticus 24:9; Mark 2:26.

156. See Friedrich Wilhelm Joseph v. Schelling, *"Ueber das Verhältnis der bildenden Künste zu der Natur"* (1807), *Philosophische Schriften*, I [all published] (Landshut: 1809; *ASKB* 763), pp. 364-65.

157. See Supplement, pp. 378-79 (*Pap*. III B 41:28).

158. See Schelling, *System des transzendentalen Idealismus* (Tübingen: 1800), pp. 436-37; *System of Transcendental Idealism*, tr. Peter Lauclan Heath (Charlottesville: University Press of Virginia, 1978), p. 210:

> If we think of history as a play in which everyone involved performs his part quite freely and as he pleases, a rational development of this muddled drama is conceivable only if there be a single spirit who speaks in everyone, and if the playwright, whose mere fragments (*disjecta membra poetae*) are the individual actors, has already so harmonized beforehand the objective outcome of the whole with the free play of every participant, that something rational must indeed emerge at the end of it. But now if the playwright *were to exist* independently of his drama, we should be merely the actors who speak the lines he has written. If he *does* not exist independently of us, but reveals and discloses himself successively only, through the very play of our own freedom, so that without this freedom even he himself *would not be*, then we are collaborators of the whole and have ourselves invented the particular roles we play.

159. See *Eighteen Discourses*, *KW* V (*SV* IV 54-68).

160. See *Fragments*, p. 76, *KW* VII (*SV* IV 240).

161. See *Irony*, *KW* II (*SV* XIII 357-76), a discussion of Friedrich v. Schlegel's version of "living poetically" in *Lucinde* (Berlin: 1799); *Friedrich Schle-*

gel's Lucinde *and the Fragments*, tr. Peter Firchow (Minneapolis: University of Minnesota Press, 1971).

162. See *JP* I 831 (*Pap.* I C 80).

163. Julius in Schlegel's *Lucinde*. See note 161 above.

164. See Oehlenschläger, "*Valravnen*," *Digte*, pp. 88-89; Thiele, *Danske Folkesagn*, III, p. 150.

165. See I Peter 3:4.

166. Don Quixote. Kierkegaard had M. de Cervantes Saavedra, *Don Quixote af Manchas Levnet og Bedrifter*, I-IV, tr. Charlotte Dorothea Biehl (Copenhagen 1776-77; *ASKB* 1937-40); *Don Quixote von La Mancha*, I-II, tr. Heinrich Heine (Stuttgart: 1837; *ASKB* 1935-36).

167. Cf. *Letters*, Letter 15, *KW* XXV.

168. See Horace, *Ars poetica*, 365; *Opera*, p. 696 (*decies repetita placebit*); Loeb, pp. 480-81.

169. See *Either/Or*, I, pp. 222-26, *KW* III (*SV* I 196-200); *Repetition*, pp. 131-33, *KW* VI (*SV* III 173-75).

170. Cf. Hesiod, *Works and Days*, 109-79; Loeb, 11-17.

171. Oehlenschläger, "*Freiers Sang ved Kilden*," *Nordens Guder* (Copenhagen: 1837; *ASKB* 1600), pp. 272-73; *The Gods of the North*, tr. William Edmund Frye (London, Paris: 1845), p. 243. See *Two Ages*, p. 44, *KW* XIV (*SV* VIII 41).

172. A decorated birch branch, also called Master Erik, with which children awaken their parents on Shrove Monday.

173. See I John 4:18.

174. See *Either/Or*, I, pp. 38-39, *KW* III (*SV* I 22-23).

175. See Matthew 22:37; Mark 12:30.

176. See note 115 above.

177. Title of a play by the Roman dramatist Terence (195-159 B.C.). See *Stages*, *KW* XI (*SV* VI 433).

178. Cf. Ezekiel 3:19, 21.

179. See *Fear and Trembling*, p. 27 and note 2, *KW* VI (*SV* III 79).

180. With reference to the remainder of the paragraph, see Supplement, p. 379 (*Pap.* I C 82).

181. *Serbische Erzählungen und Mährchen*, ed. F. H. v. d. Hagen (Prenzlau: 1826).

182. See Supplement, p. 379 (*Pap.* III B 41:29).

THE BALANCE BETWEEN THE ESTHETIC AND THE ETHICAL IN THE DEVELOPMENT OF THE PERSONALITY

1. See Supplement, pp. 379-80 (*Pap.* IV A 245, 246).

2. See Mark 5:9; Luke 8:30.

3. On this theme, see, for example, *Anxiety*, pp. 123-30, *KW* VIII (*SV* IV 391-97).

4. See Joshua 6:3-20.

5. In the Danish game *Gnavspil*, if the player who has the counter with the picture of a house does not want to make an exchange, he says, "Go to the next house." See *Fear and Trembling*, p. 100, *KW* VI (*SV* III 147); *Fragments*, p. 22, *KW* VII (*SV* IV 191).

6. See Plato, *Parmenides*, 156; *Platonis quae exstant opera*, I-XI, ed. Friedrich Ast (Leipzig: 1819-32; *ASKB* 1144-54), III, pp. 76-79; *The Collected Dialogues of Plato*, ed. Edith Hamilton and Huntington Cairns (Princeton: Princeton University Press, 1963), pp. 947-48. See also *Anxiety*, pp. 82-84, *KW* VIII (*SV* IV 351-54).

7. See *JP* IV 3996 (*Pap*. II A 65).

8. On the root meaning of "expectorate," see *Fear and Trembling*, p. 27 and note 2, *KW* VI (*SV* III 79).

9. Cf. I Corinthians 1:23.

10. The iron maiden, a medieval torture device.

11. See Ecclesiastes 1:2.

12. Johann Wolfgang v. Goethe, *"Vanitas! vanitatum vanitas!"* *Gesellige Lieder, Goethe's Werke. Vollständige Ausgabe letzter Hand*, I-LX (Stuttgart, Tübingen: 1828-42; *ASKB* 1641-68 [I-LV]), I, p. 145; *The Poems of Goethe*, tr. Edgar Alfred Bowring (New York: Hurst, 1897), p. 98:

> My trust in nothing now is placed,
> Hurrah!
> So in the world true joy I taste,
> Hurrah!

See also *JP* IV 4386 (*Pap*. I A 121).

13. Quoted with some variation from Goethe, *"Freisinn," West-östlicher Divan, Werke*, V, p. 7 (ed. tr.). See Supplement, p. 380 (*Pap*. III B 31).

14. With reference to the following sentence, see Supplement, p. 167 (*Pap*. III B 42:1).

15. The term for the marking in Greek that indicates smooth breathing or lack of *h*-sound.

16. The elder Cato (234-149 B.C.) repeatedly concluded his speeches in the senate with *"Ceterum* [or *Praeterea*] *censeo Carthaginem esse delendam"* (Furthermore, I am of the opinion that Carthage must be destroyed). See *Either/Or*, I, p. 65, *KW* III (*SV* I 47).

17. See Matthew 16:26.

18. A reference to the permanent character of baptism and the ordination vow in Roman Catholicism.

19. See, for example, G.W.F. Hegel, *Wissenschaft der Logik, Georg Wilhelm Friedrich Hegel's Werke. Vollständige Ausgabe*, I-XVIII, ed. Philipp Marheineke et al. (Berlin: 1832-45; *ASKB* 549-65), IV, pp. 57-63; *Jubiläumsausgabe* [*J.A.*], I-XXVI, ed. Hermann Glockner (Stuttgart: 1927-40), IV, pp. 535-51; *Hegel's Science of Logic* (tr. of *W.L.*, Lasson ed., 1923; Kierkegaard had 2 ed., 1833-34), tr. A. V. Miller (New York: Humanities Press, 1969), pp. 431-43, especially p. 433:

Contradiction resolves itself. In the self-excluding reflection we have just considered, positive and negative, each in its self-subsistence, sublates itself; each is simply the transition or rather the self-transposition of itself into its opposite. This ceaseless vanishing of the opposites into themselves is the *first unity* resulting from contradiction; it is the null.

See also Hegel, *Encyclopädie der philosophischen Wissenschaften, Erster Theil, Die Logik, Werke,* VI, p. 242; *J.A.,* VIII, p. 280; *Hegel's Logic* (tr. of *L.,* 3 ed., 1830; Kierkegaard's ed., 1840, had the same text, plus *Zusätze*), tr. William Wallace (Oxford: Oxford University Press, 1975), p. 174:

> Contradiction is the very moving principle of the world: and it is ridiculous to say that contradiction is unthinkable. The only thing correct in that statement is that contradiction is not the end of the matter, but cancels itself. But contradiction, when cancelled, does not leave abstract identity; for that is itself only one side of the contrariety. The proximate result of opposition (when realized as contradiction) is the Ground, which contains identity as well as difference superseded and deposited to elements in the completer notion.

See also *Fragments,* pp. 108-09, *KW* VII (*SV* IV 270); *Postscript, KW* XII (*SV* VII 261, 264, 271, 284, 301, 365-66, 497).

20. "Mediation" is the Danish (and English) version of the German *Vermittlung.* See, for example, Hegel, *Wissenschaft der Logik, Werke,* III, pp. 100, 105, 110; IV, p. 75; *J.A.,* IV, pp. 110, 115, 120, 553; *Science of Logic,* pp. 99, 103, 107, 445; *Encyclopädie, Die Logik, Werke,* VI, pp. 133-34, 138; *J.A.,* VIII, pp. 171-72, 176; *Hegel's Logic,* pp. 101, 105; *Repetition,* pp. 148-49, *KW* VI (*SV* III 189); *Anxiety,* pp. 81-93, *KW* VIII (*SV* IV 350-63). See also *JP* II 1578; III 3072, 3294 (*Pap.* II A 454; III A 108; IV A 54).

21. The allusion has not been identified.

22. With reference to the following phrase, see Supplement, p. 380 (*Pap.* III B 42:2).

23. The Danish term here is *Moment,* not *Øieblik,* which is usually translated "moment" and usually has a special meaning in Kierkegaard's writings (see *JP* III 2739-44 and p. 821; VII, p. 62). Here "moment" is used as it is found in Hegel's works: a vanishing element, factor, or particular in a whole, a constituent or a part of a unity. See, for example, *Wissenschaft der Logik, Werke,* III, pp. 108, 111, 121; *J.A.,* pp. 118, 121, 131; *Science of Logic,* pp. 105, 107, 116:

> *Becoming* is the unseparatedness of being and nothing, not the unity which abstracts from being and nothing; but as the unity of *being* and *nothing* it is this *determinate* unity in which there *is* both being and nothing. But in so far as being and nothing, each unseparated from its other, *is,* each *is not.* They *are* therefore in this unity but only as vanishing, sublated moments. They sink from their initially imagined *self-subsistence* to the status of *moments,* which are still *distinct* but at the same time are sublated.

Grasped as thus distinguished, each moment is in this *distinguishedness* as a unity with the *other*. Becoming therefore contains being and nothing as *two* such unities, *each* of which is itself a unity of being and nothing; the one is being as immediate and as relation to nothing, and the other is nothing as immediate and as relation to being; the determinations are of unequal values in these unities. Something is sublated only in so far as it has entered into unity with its opposite; in this more particular signification as something reflected, it may fittingly be called a *moment*.

This mediation with itself which something is *in itself*, taken only as negation of the negation, has no concrete determinations for its sides; it thus collapses into the simple oneness which is *being*. Something *is*, and *is*, then, also a determinate being; further, it is *in itself* also *becoming*, which, however, no longer has only being and nothing for its moments. One of these, being, is now determinate being, and, further, *a* determinate being. The second is equally a *determinate* being, but determined as a negative of the something— an *other*. Something as a *becoming* is a transition, the moments of which are themselves somethings, so that the transition is *alteration*—a becoming which has already become *concrete*. But to begin with, something alters only in its Notion; it is not yet *posited* as mediating and mediated, but at first only as simply maintaining itself in its self-relation, and its negative is posited as equally qualitative, as only an *other* in general.

24. See note 23 above.
25. An element or factor in the historical process. Here Judge William applies Hegelian historical dialectic to the Hegelian system. See, for example, *Encyclopädie*, I, *Die Logik, Werke*, VI, pp. 146–47, 151–52; *J.A.*, VIII, pp. 184–85, 189–90; *Hegel's Logic*, pp. 113, 115–16:

In point of form Logical doctrine has three sides: (α) the Abstract side, or that of understanding; (ϐ) the Dialectical, or that of negative reason; (γ) the Speculative, or that of positive reason.

These three sides do not make three *parts* of logic, but are stages or "moments" in every logical entity, that is, of every notion and truth whatever. They may all be put under the first stage, that of understanding, and so kept isolated from each other; but this would give an inadequate conception of them. The statement of the dividing lines and the characteristic aspects of logic is at this point no more than historical and anticipatory.

In the Dialectical stage these finite characterizations or formulae supersede themselves, and pass into their opposites. . . .

It is of the highest importance to ascertain and understand rightly the nature of Dialectic. Wherever there is movement, wherever there is life, wherever anything is carried into effect in the actual world, there Dialectic is at work. It is also the soul of all knowledge which is truly scientific. In the popular way of looking at things, the refusal to be bound by the abstract deliverances of understanding appears as fairness, which, according to the proverb Live and let live, demands that each should have its turn; we admit the one, but we admit the other also. But when we look more closely, we find that the limitations of the finite do not merely come from without; that its own nature is the cause of its abrogation and that by its own act it passes into its counterpart.

26. The Danish here is *Modsætning* (contrast, opposition) rather than *Modsigelse* (contradiction), which seems more appropriate in the context. The explanation may be the use of the two terms synonymously by one of Kierkegaard's philosophy professors. In his *Logik som Tankelære* (Copenhagen: 1835; *ASKB* 777), p. 302, Frederik Christian Sibbern uses *Modsætning* in his discussion of the principle of contradiction. Cf. *Johannes Climacus*, p. 168 and note 20, *KW* VII (*Pap.* IV B 11, p. 146).

27. See *Anxiety*, pp. 49, 112, *KW* VIII (*SV* IV 320, 381).

28. See, for example, Immanuel Kant, *Religion innerhalb der Grenzen der blossen Vernunft* (Königsberg: 1793), pp. 3-58; *Religion within the Limits of Reason Alone*, tr. Theodore M. Greene and Hoyt H. Hudson (Chicago: Open Court, 1934), pp. 15-39; *Irony*, *KW* II (*SV* XIII 195).

29. See, for example, Hegel, *Vorlesungen über die Aesthetik*, III, *Werke*, X³, p. 182; *J.A.*, XIV, p. 182; *The Philosophy of Fine Art*, I-IV (tr. of *V.A.*, 1 ed., 1835-38; Kierkegaard had this ed.), tr. F.P.B. Osmaston (London: Bell, 1920), III, p. 395; *Vorlesungen über die Philosophie der Geschichte*, *Werke*, IX, p. 49; *J.A.*, XI, p. 71; *The Philosophy of History* (tr. of *P.G.*, 1 ed., 1837; Kierkegaard had this edition), tr. J. Sibree (New York: Dover, 1956), p. 39:

> Genuine liberty is not opposed to the principle of necessity as a foreign and therefore oppressive and suppressive power; rather it possesses in the substantive character of the same what is a constituent of and identical with the core of its being; in following the demands of it it therefore is only conforming to its own laws, acting in accordance with its own nature.

> In the history of the World, only those peoples can come under our notice which form a state. For it must be understood that this latter is the realization of freedom, *i.e.* of the absolute final aim, and that it exists for its own sake. It must further be understood that all the worth which the human being possesses—all spiritual reality, he possesses only through the State. For his spiritual reality consists in this, that his own essence—Reason—is objectively present to him, that it possesses objective immediate existence for him. Thus only is he fully conscious; thus only is he a partaker of morality—of a just and moral social and political life. For Truth is the Unity of the universal and subjective Will; and the Universal is to be found in the State, in its laws, its universal and rational arrangements. The State is the Divine Idea as it exists on Earth. We have in it, therefore, the object of History in a more definite shape than before; that in which Freedom obtains objectivity, and lives in the enjoyment of this objectivity. For Law is the objectivity of Spirit; volition in its true form. Only that will which obeys law, is free; for it obeys itself—it is independent and so free. When the State or

our country constitutes a community of existence; when the subjective will of man submits to laws—the contradiction between Liberty and Necessity vanishes.

30. See, for example, Hegel, *Philosophie der Geschichte, Werke*, IX, pp. 59-60; *J.A.*, XI, pp. 38-39; *Philosophy of History*, pp. 29-30:

It is quite otherwise with the comprehensive relations that History has to do with. In this sphere are presented those momentous collisions between existing, acknowledged duties, laws, and rights, and those contingencies which are adverse to this fixed system; which assail and even destroy its foundations and existence; whose tenor may nevertheless seem good—on the large scale advantageous—yes, even indispensable and necessary. These contingencies realize themselves in History: they involve a general principle of a different order from that on which depends the *permanence* of a people or a State. This principle is an essential phase in the development of the *creating* Idea, of Truth striving and urging towards [consciousness of] itself. Historical men—*World-Historical Individuals*—are those in whose aims such a general principle lies. . . . They are men, therefore, who appear to draw the impulse of their life from themselves; and whose deeds have produced a condition of things and a complex of historical relations which appear to be only *their* interest, and *their* work.

Such individuals had no consciousness of the general Idea they were unfolding, while prosecuting those aims of theirs; on the contrary, they were practical, political men. But at the same time they were thinking men, who had an insight into the requirements of the time—*what was ripe for development.* This was the very Truth for their age, for their world; the species next in order, so to speak, and which was already formed in the womb of time. It was theirs to know this nascent principle; the necessary, directly sequent step in progress, which their world was to take; to make this their aim, and to expend their energy in promoting it. World-historical men—the Heroes of an epoch—must, therefore, be recognized as its clear-sighted ones; *their* deeds, *their* words are the best of that time. Great men have formed purposes to satisfy themselves, not others. Whatever prudent designs and counsels they might have learned from others, would be the more limited and inconsistent features in their career; for it was they who best understood affairs; from whom *others* learned, and approved, or at least acquiesced in—their policy.

31. See Revelation 14:13.
32. See, for example, Hegel, *Encyclopädie, Zweiter Theil, Die Naturphilosophie, Werke*, VII[1], pp. 501-02; *J.A.*, IX, pp. 527-28; *Hegel's Philosophy of Nature*, I-III (tr. of 4 ed., 1842, in *Werke*, 1 and 2 ed., the text Kierkegaard had in 1 ed. of *Werke*), tr. Michael John Petry (New York: Humanities Press, 1970), III, p. 67.
33. See Matthew 16:26.
34. See Hebrews 1:4.

35. See *Either/Or*, I, p. 25, *KW* III (*SV* I 9).

36. See p. 12 and note 13.

37. See I Corinthians 2:9.

38. See Galatians 4:1-2.

39. An important term used in a number of Kierkegaard's writings. See, for example, *Sickness unto Death*, pp. 14, 30, 42, 46, 49, 82, 101, 124, 131, *KW* XIX (*SV* XI 129, 144, 154, 158, 161, 194, 211, 233, 241).

40. With reference to the following paragraph, see Supplement, pp. 383-84 (*Pap*. III A 135).

41. See *Either/Or*, I, p. 292, *KW* III (*SV* I 263).

42. See Supplement, p. 381 (*Pap*. II A 484-85).

43. See p. 99 and note 123.

44. See Luke 18:11.

45. See, for example, Diogenes Laertius, "Antisthenes," *Lives of Eminent Philosophers*, VI, 2, 3, 11, 13, 15; *Diogenis Laertii de vitis philosophorum*, I-II (Leipzig: 1833; *ASKB* 1109), I, pp. 251, 254, 254-55, 255; *Diogen Laërtses filosofiske Historie*, I-II, tr. Børge Riisbrigh (Copenhagen: 1812; *ASKB* 1110-11), I, pp. 231, 234, 235, 236; *Lives of Eminent Philosophers*, I-II, tr. R. D. Hicks (Loeb, New York: Putnam, 1925), II, pp. 5, 13, 15:

> From Socrates he learned his hardihood, emulating his disregard of feeling, and thus he inaugurated the Cynic way of life. He demonstrated that pain is a good thing by instancing the great Heracles and Cyrus, drawing the one example from the Greek world and the other from the barbarians. . . . He used repeatedly to say, "I'd rather be mad than feel pleasure" . . . .

> And he held virtue to be sufficient in itself to ensure happiness, since it needed nothing else except the strength of a Socrates. And he maintained that virtue is an affair of deeds and does not need a store of words or learning; that the wise man is self-sufficing . . . .

> And he was the first, Diocles tells us, to double his cloak and be content with that one garment and to take up a staff and a wallet. . . .
> Antisthenes gave the impulse to the indifference of Diogenes, the continence of Crates, and the hardihood of Zeno, himself laying the foundations of their state.

46. Cf. Matthew 16:26; Luke 9:25.

47. See Matthew 20:3.

48. See I Corinthians 15:31.

49. With reference to the following sentence, see Supplement, p. 382 (*Pap*. IV A 249).

50. See *Stages*, *KW* XI (*SV* VI 13-93).

51. Johann August Musäus, "*Rolands Knappen*," *Volksmärchen der Deutschen*, I-V (Vienna: 1815; *ASKB* 1434-38), I, p. 129; "*Rolands Vaabendragere*," *Musæus' Folkeæventyr*, I-III, tr. Frederik Schaldemose (Copenhagen: 1840), I, pp. 144-45.

52. Horace, *Epistles*, I, 1, 46; Q. *Horatii Flacci opera* (Leipzig: 1828; *ASKB* 1248), p. 541. *Horace Satires, Epistles and Ars Poetica*, tr. H. Rushton Fairclough (Loeb, New York: Putnam, 1929), pp. 255-56.

53. Cf. Galatians 6:7.

54. Cf. Hegel, *Wissenschaft der Logik*, I, *Werke*, IV, pp. 67-70; *J.A.*, IV, pp. 545-48; *Science of Logic*, pp. 439-41:

> *Remark 3: The Law of Contradiction* . . . The ancient dialecticians must be granted the contradictions that they pointed out in motion; but it does not follow that therefore there is no motion, but on the contrary, that motion is *existent* contradiction itself.
>
> Similarly, internal self-movement proper, *instinctive urge* in general (the appetite or *nisus* of the monad, the entelechy of absolutely simple essence), is nothing else but the fact that something is, in one and the same respect, *self-contained and* deficient, *the negative of itself.* Abstract self-identity is not as yet a livingness, but the positive, being in its own self a negativity, goes outside itself and undergoes alteration. Something is therefore alive only in so far as it contains contradiction within it, and moreover is this power to hold and endure the contradiction within it. But if an existent in its positive determination is at the same time incapable of reaching beyond its negative determination and holding the one firmly in the other, is incapable of containing contradiction within it, then it is not the living unity itself, not ground, but in the contradiction falls to the ground [*zugrunde geht*]. *Speculative thinking* consists solely in the fact that thought holds fast contradiction, and in it, its own self, but does not allow itself to be dominated by it as in ordinary thinking, where its determinations are resolved by contradiction only into other determinations or into nothing.

See *Irony, KW* II (*SV* XIII 332, 346); *Fragments*, p. 86, *KW* VII (*SV* IV 250).

55. See, for example, *Irony, KW* II (*SV* XIII 368).

56. With reference to the remainder of the sentence, see Supplement, p. 382 (*Pap.* III B 42:3).

57. See I John 5:4.

58. The Sibylline Books of prophecy. See Dionysius, *Roman Antiquities*, IV, 62, 1-6; *The Roman Antiquities of Dionysius of Halicarnassus*, I-VII, tr. Earnest Cary (Loeb, Cambridge: Harvard University Press, 1937-50), II, pp. 465-69.

59. See I Corinthians 7:2-31.

60. See *Either/Or*, I, pp. 19, 36, *KW* III (*SV* I 20).

61. See Plato, *Symposium*, 216 c-217 a; *Opera*, III, pp. 530-33; *Udualgte Dialoger af Platon*, I-VIII, tr. Carl Johan Heise (Copenhagen: 1830–59; *ASKB* 1164–67, 1169 [I-VII]), II, pp. 90-91; *Dialogues*, p. 568 (Alcibiades speaking about Socrates):

> Take my word for it, there's not one of you that really knows him. But now I've started on him, I'll show him up. Notice, for instance, how Socrates is attracted by good-looking people, and how he hangs around them, positively gaping with admiration. Then again, he loves to appear utterly uninformed and ignorant—isn't that like Silenus? Of course it is. Don't you see that it's just his outer casing, like those little figures I was telling you

about? But believe me, friends and fellow drunks, you've only got to open him up and you'll find him so full of temperance and sobriety that you'll hardly believe your eyes. Because, you know, he doesn't really care a row of pins about good looks—on the contrary, you can't think how much he looks down on them—or money, or any of the honors that most people care about. He doesn't care a curse for anything of that kind, or for any of us either—yes, I'm telling you—and he spends his whole life playing his little game of irony, and laughing up his sleeve at all the world.

I don't know whether anybody else has ever opened him up when he's been being [sic] serious, and seen the little images inside, but I saw them once, and they looked so godlike, so golden, so beautiful, and so utterly amazing that there was nothing for it but to do exactly what he told me.

62. See, for example, *Irony, KW* II (*SV* XIII 368, 392).

63. See *Johannes Climacus*, pp. 133-59, *KW* VII (*Pap.* IV B 1, pp. 116-41).

64. See I John 4:19.

65. Cf. Matthew 16:26; Luke 9:25.

66. See Matthew 12:26.

67. See, for example, Hegel, *Vorlesungen über die Philosophie der Religion*, I, *Werke*, XI, p. 216; *J.A.*, XV, p. 216; *Lectures on the Philosophy of Religion*, I-III (tr. of *P.R.*, 2 ed., 1840; Kierkegaard had this edition), tr. E. B. Speirs and J. Burdon Sanderson (New York: Humanities Press, 1974), I, p. 206:

The finiteness of consciousness comes in here, since Spirit by its own movement differentiates itself; but this finite consciousness is a movement of Spirit itself, it itself is self-differentiation, self-determination; that is to say, positing of itself as finite consciousness. By means of this, however, it is only mediated through consciousness or finite spirit in such wise that it has to render itself finite in order to become knowledge of itself through this rendering of itself finite. Thus religion is the Divine Spirit's knowledge of itself through the mediation of finite spirit. Accordingly, in the Idea in its highest form, religion is not a transaction of man, but is essentially the highest determination of the absolute Idea itself.

68. Presumably a reference to Friedrich v. Schiller, *Die Räuber, Schillers sämmtliche Werke*, I-XII (Stuttgart, Tübingen: 1838; *ASKB* 1816-25), II, pp. 1-176; *The Robbers Wallenstein*, tr. F. J. Lamport (New York: Penguin, 1979), pp. 21-160.

69. On the first part of the sentence, see *JP* V 5988. The Danish of the second part is literally "Before God we are all Jutlanders." See J. H. Wessel, "Cavalieren," 3-4, *Johan Herman Wessels samtlige Skrivter*, I-II (Copenhagen: 1787), II, p. 61.

70. Presumably a reference to Ludvig Thostrup, *Østergade og Vestergade, Kongelige Theaters Repertoire* (1828), 12.

71. See *Irony, KW* II (*SV* XIII 355).

72. See, for example, J. G. Fichte, *Die Bestimmung des Menschen* (Berlin: 1838; *ASKB* 500), pp. 117-18; *Johann Gottlieb Fichte's sämmtliche Werke*, I-XI

(Berlin, Bonn: 1834–46; *ASKB* 489–90), II, pp. 249–50; *The Popular Works of Johann Gottlieb Fichte*, I–II, tr. William Smith (London: Trübner, 1889), I, pp. 406–07:

> There is within me an impulse to absolute, independent self-activity. Nothing is more insupportable to me than to be merely by another, for another, and through another; I must be something for myself and by myself alone. This impulse I feel along with the perception of my own existence, it is inseparably united to my consciousness of myself.
>
> I explain this feeling to myself by reflection; and, as it were, endow this blind impulse with the gift of insight by the power of thought. According to this impulse I must act as an absolutely independent being:—thus I understand and translate the impulse. I must be independent. Who am I? Subject and object in one,—the conscious being and that of which I am conscious, gifted with intuitive knowledge and myself revealed in that intuition, the thinking mind and myself the object of the thought—inseparable and ever present to each other. As both, must I be what I am, absolutely by myself alone;—by myself originate conceptions,—by myself produce a condition of things lying beyond these conceptions.

73. See Ovid, *Metamorphoses*, III, 402–37; *P. Ovidii Nasonis opera*, I–VI, ed. Antonius Richter (Leipzig: 1828; *ASKB* 1265), II, pp. 65–66; *Metamorphoses*, I–II, tr. Frank Justus Miller (Loeb, New York: Putnam, 1916), I, pp. 153–55:

> Thus had Narcissus mocked her, thus had he mocked other nymphs of the waves or mountains; thus had he mocked the companies of men. At last one of these scorned youth, lifting up his hands to heaven, prayed: "So may he himself love, and not gain the thing he loves!" The goddess, Nemesis, heard his righteous prayer. There was a clear pool with silvery bright water, to which no shepherds ever came, or she-goats feeding on the mountainside, or any other cattle; whose smooth surface neither bird nor beast nor falling bough ever ruffled. Grass grew all around its edge, fed by the water near, and a coppice that would never suffer the sun to warm the spot. Here the youth, worn by the chase and the heat, lies down, attracted thither by the appearance of the place and by the spring. While he seeks to slake his thirst another thirst springs up, and while he drinks he is smitten by the sight of the beautiful form he sees. He loves an unsubstantial hope and thinks that substance which is only shadow. He looks in speechless wonder at himself and hangs there motionless in the same expression, like a statue carved from Parian marble. Prone on the ground, he gazes at his eyes, twin stars, and his locks, worthy of Bacchus, worthy of Apollo; on his smooth cheeks, his ivory neck, the glorious beauty of his face, the blush mingled with snowy white; all things, in short, he admires for which he is himself admired. Unwittingly he desires himself; he praises, and is himself what he praises; and while he seeks, is sought; equally he kindles love and burns with love. How often did he offer vain kisses on the elusive pool? How often did he plunge his arms into the water seeking to clasp the neck he sees there, but

did not clasp himself in them! What he sees he knows not; but that which he sees he burns for, and the same delusion mocks and allures his eyes. O fondly foolish boy, why vainly seek to clasp a fleeting image? What you seek is nowhere; but turn yourself away, and the object of your love will be no more. That which you behold is but the shadow of a reflected form and has no substance of its own. With you it comes, with you it stays, and it will go with you—if you can go.

74. See Exodus 3:2.

75. See *Either/Or*, I, pp. 228-30, *KW* III (*SV* I 202-03).

76. See *JP* VI 6186 (*Pap*. IX A 131).

77. Rasmus Frankenau, "*Paa en Reise man finder,*" *Samlede Digte* (Copenhagen: 1815), p. 283.

78. Cf. Wolfgang Amadeus Mozart, *Don Juan*, I, 18, tr. Laurids Kruse (Copenhagen: 1807), pp. 56, 59; *Don Giovanni*, tr. Ellen H. Bleiler (New York: Dover, 1964), pp. 128, 131.

79. Possibly a play on the Jutland saying, "Gilding passes away, but pig leather lasts."

80. See *Either/Or*, I, pp. 148-49, *KW* III (*SV* I 125-26).

81. See, for example, Augustin Eugène Scribe, *De Utrøstelige, Repertoire* (1842), 145.

82. In Greek mythology, Kronos, the father of six gods, devoured five of the children born to Rhea; only Zeus escaped. Later Κρόνος became confused with Χρονος (time), which became the devourer of children. See Paul Friedrich A. Nitsch, *neues mythologisches Wörterbuch*, I-II (Leipzig, Sorau: 1824; *ASKB* 1944-45), II, pp. 524-27 (Saturnus).

83. See I Thessalonians 4:13.

84. See pp. 341-46; Luke 19:41-42.

85. The reference is presumably to Socrates in particular and in general to the Cynics and in part to the Stoics. See, for example, *Irony, KW* II (*SV* XIII 307).

86. See I Samuel 15:22.

87. See Romans 8:16.

88. See Matthew 10:35-37.

89. See p. 63 and note 70.

90. See Shakespeare, *Hamlet*, III, 1, 56; *William Shakspeare's Tragiske Værker*, I-IX, tr. Peter Foersom and Peter Frederik Wulff (Copenhagen: 1807-25; *ASKB* 1889-96), I, p. 97 (ed. tr., "to be, or not"); *Shakspeare's dramatische Werke*, I-XII, tr. August Wilhelm v. Schlegel and Ludwig Tieck (Berlin: 1839-41; *ASKB* 1883-88), VI, p. 63 (ed. tr., "to be or not to be"); *The Complete Works of Shakespeare*, ed. George Lyman Kittredge (Boston: Ginn, 1936), p. 1167 ("to be, or not to be").

91. See Eugène Scribe, *Aurelia*, I, 2; II, 7, *Repertoire* (1834), 65, pp. 2, 18-19.

92. Danish: *Pligt*; the verb, *pligte*, to bind, is related to the English verb "plight." The text proceeds to give another etymology with the same emphasis upon inner orientation and commitment.

93. See II Timothy 4:7.

94. See Matthew 23:24.

95. Danish: *Hexebrev*, literally "witch's letter," which is a "magic" set of picture segments of people and animals that recombine when unfolded and turned. See *Anxiety*, p. 159, *KW* VIII (*SV* IV 425); *Stages, KW* XI (*SV* VI 232).

96. The inscription on the temple of the Delphic oracle. See *Irony*, *KW* II (*SV* XIII 259-60); *Fear and Trembling*, p. 100, *KW* VI (*SV* III 148); *Anxiety*, p. 79, *KW* VII (*SV* IV 347).

97. See Genesis 4:1.

98. The Latin phrase was used by Kierkegaard in 1848 as a pseudonym for the author of *The Crisis and a Crisis in the Life of an Actress, KW* XVII (*SV* X 319-44).

99. See Exodus 3:2.

100. The Adamites, such as an Anabaptist sect in Holland in mid-sixteenth century and an Austrian sect in mid-nineteenth century. See *JP* II 1234 (*Pap*. II A 280).

101. With reference to the following five sentences, see Supplement, p. 382 (*Pap*. III A 202).

102. The source of the Niger River was not discovered until 1879 by M. Moustier and J. Zweifel.

103. See *Either/Or*, I, p. 295, *KW* III (*SV* I 266).

104. Nicolai Edinger Balle, *Lærebog i den Evangelisk-christelige Religion indrettet til Brug i de danske Skoler* (Copenhagen: 1824; *ASKB* 183). First published in 1791, the religious instruction book for use in the schools was frequently reprinted for over fifty years.

105. A reference to the Molboer (inhabitants of the island of Mols, near the town of Grenaa in northeast Jylland), the butt of stories similar to those about the Wise Men of Gotham. See, for example, *Either/Or*, I, p. 10, *KW* III (*SV* I xi).

106. See *Fear and Trembling*, p. 27, *KW* VI (*SV* III 80).

107. With reference to the following sentence, see Supplement, p. 383 (*Pap*. IV A 252).

108. See I Thessalonians 4:9.

109. With reference to the following two sentences, see Supplement, p. 383 (*Pap*. IV A 236).

110. See p. 53 and note 63.

111. According to Erasmus, Socrates was supposed to have said this to a boy. See *Apophthegmata*, III, 70, *Opera*, I-VIII (Basle: 1540), IV, p. 148 (ed. tr.):

> Quum diues quidam filium adolescentulum ad Socratem misisset, ut indolem illius insiceret, ac paedagogus diceret, Pater ad te, O Socrates, misit filium, ut eum videres: tum Socrates ad puerum, Loquere igitur, inquit, adolescens, ut te videam: significans, ingenium hominis non tam in vultu relucere, quam in oratione, quod hoc sit certissimum [When a certain wealthy man had sent his very young son to Socrates to observe his genius,

and his slave said, "His father sent his son to you that you might see him, Socrates"; thereupon Socrates said to the boy, "Speak, lad, in order that I may see you," thus signifying that the character of a man comes to light not so much in his countenance as in his manner of speaking, in that this is most certain].

See also Johann Georg Hamann, *Aesthetica in Nuce, Hamann's Schriften*, I-VIII[1-2], ed. Friedrich Roth and G. A. Wiener (Berlin, Leipzig: 1821-43; *ASKB* 536-44), II, pp. 261-62: "*Rede, dasz ich Dich sehe! . . . Reden ist übersetzen* [Speak, so that I may see you! . . . Speaking is translating]." See *Irony, KW* II (*SV* XIII 110, 450); *Stages, KW* XI (*SV* VI 371), 450; *Letters*, Letter 8, *KW* XXV; *JP* II 2115 (*Pap.* VI B 53:16).

112. Jens Baggesen, "*Jordens Lethe. Drikkevise*," *Jens Baggesens danske Værker*, I-XII (Copenhagen: 1827-32; *ASKB* 1509-20), II, p. 378 (ed. tr.).

113. See *Either/Or*, I, p. 48, *KW* III (*SV* I 32).

114. In Greek mythology, Prometheus (fore + learner, knower; Danish: *Forklog*) and his brother Epimetheus (after + learner, knower; Danish: *Bagklog*) created and equipped mankind. See Nitsch, II, pp. 492-96.

115. See Matthew 6:6-29; "What We Learn from the Lilies of the Field and the Birds of the Air," *Upbuilding Discourses in Various Spirits, KW* XV (*SV* VIII 245-96); *The Lily of the Field and the Bird of the Air, KW* XVIII (*SV* XI 3-46); *Judge for Yourself! KW* XXI (*SV* XII 449-55).

116. See Genesis 2:16.

117. See Genesis 3:17,19; II Thessalonians 3:10.

118. Presumably a reference to the fable of the fox and the grapes. See *Phaedri Augusti Liberti: fabularum Aesopiarum*, I-V, ed. C. H. Weise (Leipzig: 1828), IV, 3, p. 39; *The Fables of Aesop*, ed. Thomas Bewick (New York: Paddington Press, 1975), pp. 167-68.

119. See Genesis 3:19.

120. See Matthew 6:4,6,18.

121. With reference to the remainder of the paragraph, see Supplement, p. 383 (*Pap.* III A 228).

122. See Susanna 8-12.

123. The comment of the exiled Jugurtha as he leaves Rome. See Sallust, "Jugurtha," 35; *C. Sallusti Crispi opera*, I-II, ed. Friedrich Kritzius (Leipzig: 1828; *ASKB* 1269-70), III, pp. 210-11; *Sallusts Jugurthinske Krig*, tr. Rasmus Møller (Copenhagen: 1812), p. 48; *Sallust*, tr. J. C. Rolfe (Loeb, New York: Putnam, 1921), p. 213:

> Jugurtha, however, although he was clearly responsible for so flagrant a crime, did not cease to resist the evidence, until he realized that the indignation at the deed was too strong even for his influence and his money. Therefore, although in the first stage of the trial he had given fifty of his friends as sureties, yet having an eye rather to his throne than to the sureties, he sent Bomilcar secretly to Numidia, fearing that if he paid the penalty, the rest of his subjects would fear to obey his orders. A few days later he himself

returned home, being ordered by the senate to leave Italy. After going out of the gates, it is said that he often looked back at Rome in silence and finally said, "A city for sale and doomed to speedy destruction if it finds a purchaser!"

124. Harun-al-Raschid, Caliph of Bagdad (786-809), celebrated in tradition and especially in *Arabian Nights*. See *Tausend und eine Nacht*, I-IV, tr. Gustav Weil (Stuttgart, Pforzheim: 1838-41; *ASKB* 1414-17); *The Arabian Nights' Entertainments*, tr. Richard F. Burton, ed. Bennett A. Cerf (New York: Random House, 1959).

125. Cf. Horace, *Odes*, III, 24, 6; *Opera*, p. 218; *Horace The Odes and Epodes*, tr. C. E. Bennett (Loeb, New York: Putnam, 1930), pp. 252-53 (*dira necessitas*, dire necessity).

126. Cf. *Either/Or*, I, p. 49, *KW* III (*SV* I 33).

127. With reference to the remainder of the paragraph, see Supplement, pp. 383-84 (*Pap*. III A 135).

128. See Horace, *Epistles*, I, 2, 27; *Opera*, p. 549; Loeb, pp. 264-65: "We are but ciphers, born to consume earth's fruits, Penelope's good-for-naught suitors . . . ."

129. A free conflation of lines from Jens Baggesen, "*Tilegnelse*," *Værker*, VI, pp. 44, 47.

130. Ibid., p. 48.

131. See Proverbs 16:32.

132. See *Either/Or*, I, pp. 231-79, *KW* III (*SV* I 205-52).

133. See Matthew 7:15.

134. See Exodus 30:13 and Matthew 21:1, Mark 11:15, and John 2:14-15, in which the money changers exchange temple coins for Roman coins. See also *Either/Or*, I, p. 117, *KW* III (*SV* I 97).

135. A mysterious German youth who appeared in Nuremberg in 1828 without any knowledge of his past or awareness of his identity. See *Kjøbenhavns flyvende Post*, 65, 66, 70, 71, 73, August 15, 18, 29, September 5, 12, 1828; *Dansk Ugeskrift*, II, 1833, pp. 309-12; Anselm v. Feuerbach, *Kaspar Hauser* (Ansbach: 1832). See also *Stages, KW* XI (*SV* VI 202).

136. L. F. Freiherr v. Bilderbeck, *Die Urne in einsame Thale* (Leipzig: 1799); *Urnen i den eensomme Dal*, I-IV, tr. Otto Horrebow and Jacob Carl Frederik Primon (Copenhagen: 1804-06).

137. See Pius Alexander Wolff, *Preciosa*, tr. Claudius Julius Boye (Copenhagen, 1822), IV, p. 67. The piece (with music by Carl Maria v. Weber) was performed at the Royal Theater on January 5, 1843.

138. See Proverbs 6:6.

139. Cf. "Another Defense of Woman's Great Ability," *Early Polemical Writings, KW* I (*SV* XIII 5-8).

140. See Matthew 10:16; Genesis 3:6.

141. See I Corinthians 11:5-15.

142. A reference to the etymology, common at the time, of the Greek *anthropos* (man): one who looks up.

143. See Genesis 2:24.

144. See Matthew 14:52.

145. See, for example, Genesis 23:7, 24:26; Exodus 18:7. The Danish translation of the Bible in Kierkegaard's time has *neiede* (did obeisance). The King James and the Revised Standard Version translations have "bowed" in Genesis and "did obeisance" in Exodus.

146. See Luke 1:37.

147. See *Either/Or*, I, p. 295, *KW* III (*SV* I 267).

148. See Matthew 13:12; Mark 4:24-25; Luke 8:18, 19:26.

149. See p. 258 and note 95.

150. See *Either/Or*, I, p. 142 and note 9, *KW* III (*SV* I 119).

151. With reference to the following sentence, see Supplement, p. 384 (*Pap.* IV A 234).

152. See *Either/Or*, I, p. 137, *KW* III (*SV* I 115).

153. See Supplement, p. 385 (*Pap.* III B 42:4).

154. The Danish text of the quotation differs from the Danish translation available in Kierkegaard's time. Cf. Diogenes Laertius, I, 107-08; *Vitis*, I, pp. 52-53; Riisbrigh, I, p. 49; Loeb, I, p. 113:

Myson is mentioned by Hipponax, the words being:

> And Myson, whom Apollo's self proclaimed
> Wisest of all men.

Aristoxenus in his *Historical Gleanings* says he was not unlike Timon and Apemantus, for he was a misanthrope. At any rate he was seen in Lacedaemon laughing to himself in a lonely spot; and when some one suddenly appeared and asked him why he laughed when no one was near, he replied, "That is just the reason." And Aristoxenus says that the reason why he remained obscure was that he belonged to no city but to a village and that an unimportant one. Hence because he was unknown, some writers, but not Plato the philosopher, attributed to Pisistratus the tyrant what properly belonged to Myson. For Plato mentions him in the *Protagoras*, reckoning him as one of the Seven instead of Periander.

155. See Plato, *Gorgias* 497 c; *Opera*, I, pp. 390-91; Heise, III, p. 128; *Dialogues*, p. 279.

156. See Aristotle, *Nicomachean Ethics*, 1159 b, 1161 a; *Aristoteles graece*, I-II, ed. Immanuel Bekker (Berlin: 1831; *ASKB* 1074-75), II, pp. 1159, 1161; *The Works of Aristotle*, I-XII, ed. J. A. Smith and W. D. Ross (Oxford: Oxford University Press, 1908-52), IX: "Friendship and justice seem, as we have said at the outset of our discussion, to be concerned with the same objects and exhibited between the same persons."

"Each of the constitutions may be seen to involve friendship just in so far as it involves justice."

157. See, for example, Immanuel Kant, *Grundlegung zur Metaphysik der Sitten* (Riga: 1786), pp. 43, 111-13; *The Moral Law or Kant's Groundwork of the*

Metaphysic of Morals, ed. and tr. H. J. Paton (London: Hutchinson, 1951), pp. 83-84, 122-23:

> Finally, there is an imperative which, without being based on, and conditioned by, any further purpose to be attained by a certain line of conduct, enjoins this conduct immediately. This imperative is *categorical*. It is concerned, not with the matter of the action and its presumed results, but with its form and with the principle from which it follows; and what is essentially good in the action consists in the mental disposition, let the consequences be what they may. This imperative may be called the imperative of *morality*.
>
> And in this way categorical imperatives are possible because the Idea of freedom makes me a member of an intelligible world. This being so, if I were solely a member of the intelligible world, all my actions *would* invariably accord with the autonomy of the will; but because I intuit myself at the same time as a member of the sensible world, they *ought* so to accord. This *categorical* "ought" presents us with a synthetic *a priori* proposition, since to my will as affected by sensuous desires there is added the Idea of the same will, viewed, however, as a pure will belonging to the intelligible world and active on its own account—a will which contains the supreme condition of the former will, so far as reason is concerned. This is roughly like the way in which concepts of the understanding, which by themselves signify nothing but the form of law in general, are added to intuitions of the sensible world and so make synthetic *a priori* propositions possible on which all our knowledge of nature is based.
>
> The practical use of ordinary human reason confirms the rightness of this deduction. . . . The moral "I ought" is thus an "I will" for man as a member of the intelligible world; and it is conceived by him as an "I ought" only in so far as he considers himself at the same time to be a member of the sensible world.

158. See Aristotle, *Nicomachean Ethics*, 1094 b; Bekker, II, p. 1094; *Works*, IX: "For even if the end is the same for a single man and for a state, that of the state seems at all events something greater and more complete whether to attain or to preserve; though it is worth while to attain the end merely for one man, it is finer and more godlike to attain it for a nation or for city-states. These, then, are the ends at which our inquiry aims, since it is political science, in one sense of that term."

159. With reference to the remainder of the sentence, see Supplement, p. 384 (*Pap*. IV A 234).

160. See Hebrews 9:27; Romans 2:16; II Corinthians 5:10.

161. See Horace, *Epistles*, I, 11, 29; *Opera*, p. 580; Loeb, pp. 324-25.

162. See, for example, Augustin Eugène Scribe, *To Aar efter Bryllup, Familien Riquebourg, Aurelia, Enten elskes eller døe, Repertoire* (1831) 32, (1832) 40, (1834) 65, (1835) 100.

163. See, for example, Sirach 7:36.

164. Cf. Hesiod, *Works and Days*, 289-90; *Hesiod The Homeric Hymns and Homerica*, tr. Hugh G. Evelyn-White (Loeb, New York: Macmillan), p. 25.

165. With reference to the remainder of the sentence, see Supplement, p. 385 (*Pap*. X² A 115).

166. With reference to the close of the section, see Supplement, p. 385 (*Pap*. III B 191:15).

ULTIMATUM [A FINAL WORD]

1. Adam Gottlob Oehlenschläger, *Ludlams Hule*, V; *Oehlenschlägers Digterværker*, I-XVIII (Copenhagen: 1844-49), VIII, p. 177.

2. See Supplement, p. 385 (*Pap*. IV A 255).

3. With reference to the remainder of the paragraph, see Supplement, p. 385 (*Pap*. III B 183).

4. Corresponds to the grade of C.

5. With reference to the remainder of the text, see Supplement, p. 386 (*Pap*. III C 5). See also "The Gospel of Suffering," *Upbuilding Discourses in Various Spirits, KW* XV (*SV* VIII 350-69).

6. See Supplement, pp. 386-87 (*Pap*. IV A 56, 256).

7. The text for Sunday, August 15, 1841, and July 31, 1842.

8. Cf. Genesis 18:20-32.

9. See Exodus 20:5.

10. See Luke 13:1-4.

11. See Matthew 5:45.

12. See Genesis 32:24-26.

13. See Job 40:2.

14. See Romans 12:11.

15. Cf. Matthew 7:7.

16. See I Corinthians 3:7.

17. With reference to the following five sentences, see Supplement, p. 384 (*Pap*. IV A 234).

18. See Supplement, pp. 361, 306-07 (*Pap*. I A 75; IV A 42; VIII¹ A 465); *Either/Or*, I, Supplement, p. 505 (*Pap*. IV A 216); *Postscript, KW* XII (*SV* VII 105, 157-211).

SUPPLEMENT

1. See *Either/Or*, I, Supplement, pp. 453-59, *KW* III (*Pap*. I A 72). The two letters are ostensibly addressed to Peter Wilhelm Lund (1801-1880). Emanuel Hirsch regards both letters as part of the fictive "Faustian Letters."

2. See p. 354.

3. See *JP* V 5101 (*Pap*. I A 76).

4. See *JP* V 5104 (*Pap*. I A 79).

5. A game (*Forundringsstolen*, also, but rarely, named *Beundringsstolen*), sometimes called the wonder stool or wonder game, in which one person sits

blindfolded on a stool in the middle of a circle while another goes around quietly asking others what they wonder about the person who is "it." Upon being told what others had wondered about him, he tries to guess the source in each instance. See *Fragments*, p. 52, *KW* VII (*SV* IV 219); *Sickness unto Death*, p. 5, *KW* XIX (*SV* XI 117); "To Mr. Orla Lehmann," *Early Polemical Writings, KW* I (*SV* XIII 28).

6. See *From the Papers of One Still Living, KW* I (*SV* XIII 28).

7. Kierkegaard's first reference to Socrates. His dissertation, *The Concept of Irony, with Continual Reference to Socrates,* was published in 1841.

8. See, for example, *Either/Or,* I, p. 25, *KW* III (*SV* I 9-10); *Repetition,* p. 173, *KW* VI (*SV* III 211); *Anxiety,* p. 99, *KW* VIII (*SV* IV 369).

9. See *JP* V 5105 (*Pap.* I A 80).

10. Pythagoras, Greek philosopher (6 c. B.C.). Cf. Diogenes Laertius, *Lives of Eminent Philosophers,* VIII, 10; *Diogenis Laertii de vitis Philosophorum,* I-II (Leipzig: 1833; *ASKB* 1109), II, p. 94; *Diogen Laërtses filosofiske Historie,* I-II, tr. Børge Riisbrigh (Copenhagen: 1812; *ASKB* 1110-11), I, p. 368; *Lives of Eminent Philosophers,* I-II, tr. R. D. Hicks (Loeb, New York: Putnam, 1925), II, p. 329:

> He divides man's life into four quarters thus: "Twenty years a boy, twenty years a youth, twenty years a young man, twenty years an old man; and these four periods correspond to the four seasons, the boy to spring, the youth to summer, the young man to autumn, and the old man to winter," meaning by youth one not yet grown up and by a young man a man of mature age. According to Timaeus, he was the first to say, "Friends have all things in common" and "Friendship is equality"; indeed, his disciples did put all their possessions into one common stock. For five whole years they had to keep silence, merely listening to his discourses without seeing him, until they passed an examination, and thenceforward they were admitted to his house and allowed to see him.

11. See Matthew 5:45.

12. J. G. Fichte (1762-1814), German philosopher. Kierkegaard had *Johann Gottlieb Fichte's sämmtliche Werke,* I-XI (Berlin, Bonn: 1834-36; *ASKB* 489-99), and *Die Bestimmung des Menschen* (Berlin: 1838; *ASKB* 500).

13. Novalis (Friedrich v. Hardenberg), *Heinrich von Ofterdingen Novalis Schriften,* I-II, ed. Ludwig Tieck and Friedrich v. Schlegel (Berlin: 1826; *ASKB* 1776); *Henry von Ofterdingen,* tr. Palmer Hilty (New York: Ungar, 1964), p. 110.

14. Cf. *Either/Or,* I, p. 27, *KW* III (*SV* I 11-12).

15. See *Fragments,* p. 37, *KW* VII (*SV* IV 204); *JP* III 3598 (*Pap.* II A 763); *Pap.* IX B 68, p. 393.

16. See *Figaros Givtermaal eller Den gale Dag,* tr. Niels Thoroup Bruun (Copenhagen: 1817), IV, 14, pp. 138-42; *Le Nozze di Figaro* (*The Marriage of Figaro*), tr. Ruth and Thomas Martin (New York: Schirmer, 1951), pp. 445-58.

17. See *Either/Or,* I, p. 28, *KW* III (*SV* I 12).

18. Cf. p. 14.

19. Johan August Musäus, "*Legenden von Rübezahl,*" *Volksmärchen der Deutschen,* I-V (Vienna: 1815; *ASKB* 1434-38), II, p. 26; *Musæus' Folkeæventyr,* I-III, tr. Frederik Schaldemose (Copenhagen: 1840), II, pp. 24-25.

20. On the term "reality," see p. 12 and note 13.

21. Diogenes Laertius, I, 91; *Vitis,* I, p. 43; Riisbrigh, I, p. 41; Loeb, I, p. 95.

22. See Christoph Friedrich Bretzner, *Sovedrikken,* adapted by Adam Oehlenschläger (Copenhagen: 1808), p. 19.

23. The Danish rix-dollar was worth about $5.00 in 1973 money.

24. Marquise de Prie, in Alexandre Dumas (*père*), *Gabrielle de Belle-Isle,* tr. Theodor Overskou, I, 1; *Det Kongelige Theaters Repertoire* (1841), 132, p. 2.

25. See *Either/Or,* I, p. 27, *KW* III (*SV* I 11).

26. Johann Wolfgang von Goethe, *Faust,* I, 20; *Goethe's Werke. Vollständige Ausgabe letzter Hand,* I-LX (Stuttgart, Tübingen: 1828-42; *ASKB* 1641-68 [I-LV]), XII, p. 199; *Faust,* tr. Bayard Taylor (New York: Random House, 1950), p. 146.

27. Karl Rosenkrantz, *Kritische Erläuterungen des Hegel'schen Systems* (Königsberg: 1840; *ASKB* 745). The pages cited are a discussion of marriage in ch. 4, "*Gunther's und Pabst's Katholische Polemik gegen Hegel. 1831.*"

28. Wilhelm Gottlieb Tennemann, *Geschichte der Philosophie,* I-XI (Leipzig: 1798-1819; *ASKB* 815-26).

29. See *For Self-Examination, KW* XXI (*SV* XII 333-34).

30. Hegel, *Phänomenologie des Geistes, Georg Wilhelm Friedrich Hegel's Werke. Vollständige Ausgabe,* I-XVIII, ed. Philipp Marheineke et al. (Berlin: 1832-45; *ASKB* 549-65), II, pp. 63-64; *Jubiläumsausgabe* [*J.A.*], I-XXVI, ed. Herman Glockner (Stuttgart: 1927-40), II, pp. 71-72; *The Phenomenology of Mind* (tr. of *P.G.*, 3 ed., 1841; Kierkegaard had 2 ed., 1832), tr. J. B. Baillie (New York: Harper, 1967), pp. 135-36:

Natural consciousness will prove itself to be only knowledge in principle or not real knowledge. Since, however, it immediately takes itself to be the real and genuine knowledge, this pathway has a negative significance for it; what is a realization of the notion of knowledge means for it rather the ruin and overthrow of itself; for on this road it loses its own truth. Because of that, the road can be looked on as the path of doubt, or more properly a highway of despair. For what happens there is not what is usually understood by doubting, a jostling against this or that supposed truth, the outcome of which is again a disappearance in due course of the doubt and a return to the former truth, so that at the end the matter is taken as it was before. On the contrary, that pathway is the conscious insight into the untruth of the phenomenal knowledge, for which that is the most real which is after all only the unrealized notion. On that account, too, this thoroughgoing scepticism is not what doubtless earnest zeal for truth and science fancies it has equipped itself with in order to be ready to deal with them—viz. the *resolve,* in science, not to deliver itself over to the thoughts of others on their mere authority, but to examine everything for itself, and only follow its own conviction, or, still better, to produce everything itself and hold only its own act for true.

31. In Æschylus's *Agamemnon* and Homer's *Iliad*, Agamemnon is a Mycenæan king, leader of the Greeks in the Trojan War. In Homer's *Iliad*, Thersites is an ugly, scurrilous Greek.

32. See Diogenes Laertius, VII, 160; *Vitis*, II, pp. 69-70; Riisbrigh, I, pp. 344-45; Loeb, II, pp. 263-65: "Ariston the Bald, of Chios, who was also called the Siren, declared the end of action to be a life of perfect indifference to everything which is neither virtue nor vice; recognizing no distinction whatever in things indifferent, but treating them all alike. The wise man he compared to a good actor, who, if called upon to take the part of a Thersites or of an Agamemnon, will impersonate them both becomingly."

33. See Diogenes Laertius, VII, 85; *Vitis*, II, p. 38; Riisbrigh, I, pp. 312-13; Loeb, II, pp. 193-95:

An animal's first impulse, say the Stoics, is to self-preservation, because nature from the outset endears it to itself, as Chrysippus affirms in the first book of his work *On Ends*: his words are, "The dearest thing to every animal is its own constitution and its consciousness thereof"; for it was not likely that nature should estrange the living thing from itself or that she should leave the creature she has made without either estrangement from or affection for its own constitution. We are forced then to conclude that nature in constituting the animal made it near and dear to itself; for so it comes to repel all that is injurious and give free access to all that is serviceable or akin to it.

As for the assertion made by some people that pleasure is the object to which the first impulse of animals is directed, it is shown by the Stoics to be false. For pleasure, if it is really felt, they declare to be a by-product, which never comes until nature by itself has sought and found the means suitable to the animal's existence or constitution; it is an aftermath comparable to the condition of animals thriving and plants in full bloom.

See also Cicero, *De finibus bonorum et malorum*, III, 5; *M. Tullii Ciceronis opera omnia*, I-IV and index, ed. Johann August Ernesti (Halle: 1756-57; *ASKB* 1224-29), IV, pp. 170-71; *Cicero De finibus bonorum et malorum*, tr. H. Rackham (Loeb, New York: Macmillan, 1914), pp. 233-35:

He [Cato] began: "It is the view of those whose system I adopt, that immediately upon birth (for that is the proper point to start from) a living creature feels an attachment for itself, and an impulse to preserve itself and to feel affection for its own constitution and for those things which tend to preserve that constitution; while on the other hand it conceives an antipathy to destruction and to those things which appear to threaten destruction. In proof of this opinion they urge that infants desire things conducive to their health and reject things that are the opposite before they have ever felt pleasure or pain; this would not be the case, unless they felt an affection for their own constitution and were afraid of destruction. But it would be impossible that they should feel desire at all unless they possessed self-consciousness, and consequently felt affection for themselves. This leads to the conclusion that it is love of self which supplies the primary impulse to action. Pleasure on the contrary, according to most Stoics, is not to be reckoned among the primary objects of natural impulse; and I very strongly agree with them, for fear lest many immoral consequences would follow if we held that nature has placed pleasure among the earliest objects of desire."

34. Goethe, *"Freisinn," West-östlicher Divan, Werke,* V, p. 7.

35. W.M.L. de Wette, *Lærebog i den christelige Sædelære,* tr. C. E. Scharling (Copenhagen: 1835; *ASKB* 871).

36. See *Stages, KW* XI (*SV* VI 189-90); *JP* I 745 (*Pap.* V A 33).

37. Tennemann refers to Seneca, *Epistles,* 94; "On the Value of Advice," *Seneca ad Lucilium epistulae morales,* I-III, tr. Richard M. Gummere (Loeb, Cambridge: Harvard University Press, 1917-25), III, pp. 11-13:

> That department of philosophy which supplies precepts appropriate to the individual case, instead of framing them for mankind at large—which, for instance, advises how a husband should conduct himself towards his wife, or how a father should bring up his children, or how a master should rule his slaves—this department of philosophy, I say, is accepted by some as the only significant part, while the other departments are rejected on the ground that they stray beyond the sphere of practical needs—as if any man could give advice concerning a portion of life without having first gained a knowledge of the sum of life as a whole!
>
> But Aristo the Stoic, on the contrary, believes the above-mentioned department to be of slight import: he holds that it does not sink into the mind, having in it nothing but old wives' precepts, and that the greatest benefit is derived from the actual dogmas of philosophy and from the definition of the Supreme Good. When a man has gained a complete understanding of this definition and has thoroughly learned it, he can frame for himself a precept directing what is to be done in a given case.

38. See *JP* 1244 (*Pap.* IV C 60).

39. See *Fear and Trembling,* p. 123, *KW* VI (*SV* III 168); *Postscript, KW* XII (*SV* VII 267-68 fn.).

40. Cf. Aristotle, *Metaphysics,* 986 a; *Aristoteles graece,* I-II, ed. Immanuel Bekker (Berlin: 1831; *ASKB* 1074-75), II, p. 986; *The Works of Aristotle,* I-XII, ed. J. A. Smith and W. D. Ross (Oxford: Oxford University Press, 1908-52), X:

> Evidently, then, these thinkers [Pythagoreans] also consider that number is the principle both as matter for things and as forming both their modifications and their permanent states, and hold that the elements of number are the even and the odd, and that of these the latter is limited, and the former unlimited; and that the One proceeds from both of these (for it is both even

and odd), and number from the One; and that the whole heaven, as has been said, is numbers.

See also *Fear and Trembling*, pp. 62, 69, *KW* VI (*SV* III 112, 118).

41. *Der Koran. Aus dem Arabischen wortgetreu neu übersetzt, und mit erläuternden Anmerkungen versehen von Dr. L. Ullmann* (Crefeld: 1840; *ASKB* 603).

42. See *Fragments, KW* VII (*SV* IV 205-06).

43. See Martin Luther, *En christelig Postille*, tr. Jørgen Thisted, I-II (Copenhagen: 1828; *ASKB* 283), I, p. 17, p. 16.

44. "Public Confession," *Fædrelandet*, 904, June 12, 1842; see *The Corsair Affair and Articles Related to the Writings*, pp. 3-12, *KW* XIII (*SV* XIII 397-406).

45. Ibid., p. 5 (399).

46. "Literary Quicksilver Or a Venture in the Higher Lunacy," *Ny Portefeuille*, I, 7, February 12, 1843, col. 198-216; see Corsair *Affair*, pp. 73-86, *KW* XIII (*SV* XIII 471-86).

47. "*A Letter*," "*Another Letter*," 33, 35, February 5, 7, 1843; see Corsair *Affair*, pp. 63-68, *KW* XIII (*SV* XIII 460-66).

48. No. 1143, February 8, 1843; see Corsair *Affair*, pp. 69, 72, *KW* XIII (*SV* XIII 69-72).

49. Advertised in *Adresseavisen*, 43, February 20, 1843.

50. Cf. Jean Paul, *Des Feldpredigers Schmelze Reise nach Flätz, Sämmtliche Werke*, I-LX (Berlin: 1827; *ASKB* 1777-99), L, p. 33; *Stages, KW* XI (*SV* VI 40).

51. A play on a line in J. L. Heiberg's review of *Either/Or*. See "A Word of Thanks to Professor Heiberg," Corsair *Affair*, p. 17 and note 40, *KW* XIII.

52. See *Either/Or*, I, p. 12, *KW* III (*SV* I xiv).

53. In *From the Papers of One Still Living, KW* I (*SV* XIII 72 fn.), Kierkegaard criticized the view in a novel by Hans Christian Andersen that "genius is an egg, that needs warmth for the fertilization of good fortune; otherwise it becomes a wind-egg." H. C. Andersen, *Kun en Spillemand*, I-III (Copenhagen: 1837; *ASKB* 1503), I, p. 161 (ed. tr.). Cf. *Only a Fiddler*, tr. anon. (Boston: Houghton Mifflin, 1908), p. 110.

54. Kierkegaard, as a cover for his pseudonymous writing and to eliminate the appearance of authority, promoted this impression not only by being an assiduous peripatetic and conversationalist on the streets of Copenhagen, as well as a frequenter of cafés and the theater, but also by contriving to be seen during the intermission of events he did not attend. See *Point of View, KW* XXII (*SV* XIII 544-48).

55. Johan Ludvig Heiberg, "*Litterær Vintersæd*," *Intelligensblade*, 24, March 1, 1843 (*ASKB* U 56), p. 290.

56. See *Berlingske Tidende* (ed. Mendel Levin Nathanson), 56, March 1, 1843.

57. See Bruun, *Figaros Givtermaal*, III, 6, p. 93. The scene is not in Martin; see III, 4, pp. 96-97.

58. See Hans Peter Holst, "*Tutti-Frutti*," *Ny Portefeuille*, I, 9, February 26, 1843, col. 279.

59. Cf. *Anxiety*, p. 8, *KW* VIII (*SV* IV 280).

60. Cf. Johan Ludvig Heiberg, *Recensenten og Dyret* (Copenhagen: 1827), 14, p. 42; *Skuespil*, I-VII (Copenhagen: 1833-41; *ASKB* 1553-59), III, p. 234.

61. See Supplement, pp. 388-90 (*Pap.* IV B 19) and notes.

62. See *Fædrelandet*, 1143, February 8, 1843; *Berlingske Tidende*, 35, February 7, 1843; Corsair *Affair*, pp. 66-72, *KW* XIII (*SV* XIII 463-70).

63. See *Fear and Trembling*, p. 7, *KW* VI (*SV* III 59).

64. See J. L. Heiberg, "Litterær Vintersæd," *Intelligensblade*, 24, March 1, 1843, p. 288; "A Word of Thanks to Professor Heiberg," Corsair *Affair*, p. 17 and note 40, *KW* XIII (*SV* XIII 412).

65. See Herodotus, *History*, VII, 100; *Die Geschichten des Herodotus*, I-II, tr. Friedrich Lange (Berlin: 1811; *ASKB* 1117), II, p. 183; *Herodotus*, I-IV, tr. A. D. Godley (Loeb, New York: Putnam, 1921-24), p. 403.

66. See J. L. Heiberg, "Litterær Vintersæd," *Intelligensblade*, 24, March 1, 1843, p. 291; "A Word of Thanks to Professor Heiberg," Corsair *Affair*, p. 17 and note 39, *KW* XIII (*SV* XIII 412).

67. Ibid.

68. The first number of J. L. Heiberg's journal appeared March 15, 1842.

69. See note 66 above.

70. See note 64 above.

71. See H. L. Martensen's review of J. L. Heiberg, *En Sjæl efter Døden. En apocalyptisk Comedie, Nye Digte* (Copenhagen: 1841; *ASKB* 1562), in *Fædrelandet*, 398, January 10, 1841, col. 3209-11.

72. Ibid. See *Prefaces*, *KW* II (*SV* V 29).

73. J. L. Heiberg, *Intelligensblade*, 24, March 1, 1843, pp. 285-92.

74. Ibid., pp. 291-92.

75. See Jens Baggesen, *Jens Baggesens danske Værker*, I-XII (Copenhagen: 1827-32; *ASKB* 1509-20), I, p. 282; *Fear and Trembling*, p. 106, *KW* VI (*SV* III 153).

76. J. L. Heiberg, *Intelligensblade*, 24, March 1, 1843, pp. 289-91.

77. Hans Peter Holst (1811-1893), editor of *Ny Portefeuille* until April 1, 1843.

78. See *Prefaces*, *KW* IX (*SV* V 27).

79. See J. L. Heiberg, *Intelligensblade*, 24, March 1, 1843, p. 284.

80. An allusion to Hans Peter Holst, *Ude og hjemme. Reise-Erindringer* (Copenhagen: 1842; *ASKB* 1569).

81. See *Prefaces*, *KW* IX (*SV* V 28).

82. Johan Ludvig Heiberg (1791-1860) was not only the leading writer, literary critic, dramatist, and Danish Hegelian of the time, but he was also an amateur astronomer of considerable competence and had an observatory in his residence on Christianshavn.

83. J. L. Heiberg's *Syvsoverdag* (Copenhagen: 1840) was dedicated to King Christian VIII and Queen Caroline Amalie.

84. See *Prefaces*, *KW* IX (*SV* V 23).

85. See *Intelligensblade*, 24, March 1, 1843, p. 289.

86. *The Concept of Irony, with Continual Reference to Socrates*, published September 16, 1841.

87. "Silhouettes" was completed July 25, 1842; the preface was completed in November 1842. See *Point of View, KW* XXII (*SV* XIII 526).

88. Ibid. (527).

89. See *Either/Or*, I, pp. 153-64, *KW* III (*SV* I 130-41).

90. See *Stages, KW* XI (*SV* VI 236-37).

91. See *Either/Or*, I, p. 13, *KW* III (*SV* I xv).

92. See p. 354.

93. See *Point of View, KW* XXII (*SV* XIII 526).

94. Cf. *Prefaces, KW* IX (*SV* V 24).

95. "*Kirkelig Polemik*," *Intelligensblade*, 41-42, January 1, 1844, pp. 97-114, especially p. 111. The article was prompted by a comment in Kofoed Hansen's review of *Either/Or* in the *Fyenske Fjerdingaarsskrift for Literatur og Kritik*, IV, 1, 1843, pp. 384-85.

96. The pseudonym of Bishop Jacob (Jakob) Peter Mynster, formed from the middle letter in each of his three names.

97. See Andreas Frederik Beck, "*Plump Usandhed*," *Kjøbenhavnsposten*, 4, January 4, 1844.

98. Cf. *Either/Or*, I, p. 27, *KW* III (*SV* I 11).

99. Propertius, II, 10, 6.

100. See J. L. Heiberg, "*Litterær Vintersæd*," *Intelligensblade*, 24, March 1, 1843, p. 292: ". . . and finally perhaps some one of the individuals will lay before the public this view" (of the meaning of *Either/Or*).

101. See p. 118; *Either/Or*, I, p. 235, *KW* III (*SV* I 209). See also Jakob Ludwig Karl and Wilhelm Karl Grimm, "*Sechse Kommen durch die ganze Welt*," *Kinder- und Haus-Märchen, gesammelt durch die Brüder Grimm*, I-III (Berlin: 1819-22; *ASKB* 1425-27), 71, I, p. 379; *The Complete Grimm's Fairy Tales*, tr. Margaret Hunt and James Stern (New York: Pantheon, 1972), p. 345; *Letters*, Letter 195, pp. 278-79, *KW* XXV.

102. See Anon., "*Fragmenter af en Brevvexling*," *Forposten*, 11-15, March 12, 19, 26, April 2, 9, 1843, pp. 41-43, 45-48, 49-51, 57-59. See also *Either/Or*, I, Supplement, pp. 552-53, *KW* III (*Pap.* IV 231).

103. Johan Frederik Hagen, *Fædrelandet*, 1227, 1228, 1234, May 7, 14, 21, 1843, col. 9845-60, 9901-08, 9957-64.

104. See note 95 above.

105. The following phrase of eight words is written in the margin at the end of J. L. Heiberg, "*Litterær Vintersæd*," *Intelligensblade*, 24, March 1, 1843, p. 292.

106. An allusion to J. L. Heiberg, "*At orientere sig*," *Intelligensblade*, 32, July 1, 1843, pp. 169-92, especially p. 187.

107. See "A Word of Thanks to Professor Heiberg," *Corsair Affair*, pp. 17-21, *KW* XIII (*SV* XIII 411-15).

108. See, for example, Hans Lassen Martensen, *Den christelige Daab betragtet med Hensyn paa det baptiske Spørgsmaal* (Copenhagen: 1843), pp. 2-3.

109. Eugène Scribe, *Den første Kjærlighed*, tr. J. L. Heiberg, 12; *Repertoire* (1832), 43, p. 9.

110. In Greek mythology, the title of Aphrodite rising from the sea.

111. See Ludvig Holberg, *Don Ranudo de Colibrados, eller Fattigdom og Hof-færdighed*, I, 4, III, 6, IV, 9, *Den Danske Skue-Plads*, I-VII (Copenhagen: 1788; *ASKB* 1566-67), VI, no pagination.

112. See p. 403 (*Pap.* IV B 46, p. 202).

113. In the text of *Either/Or*, I, A and B are printed without a period.

114. See *Either/Or*, I, pp. 41, 530-31, *KW* III (*SV* III 126; *Pap.* I A 169).

115. See *Either/Or*, I, p. 243, *KW* III (*SV* I 216).

116. *Fædrelandet*, 1227-28, May 7, 1843, col. 9855.

117. Island(s) far off the coast of Chile and by some considered to have been the location of the wreck and rescue of Alexander Selkirk (Robinson Crusoe).

118. Bianco Luno Press. See *JP* V 5871 (*Pap.* VII¹ A 2).

119. *Stages, KW* XI (*SV* VI 175-459).

120. *Stages, KW* XI (*SV* VI 291).

121. See Supplement, pp. 410-11 (*Pap.* IV A 215).

122. See, for example, *JP* V 5661, 5662, 5663 (*Pap.* IV B 140, 141, 142), entries written in preparation of *Stages*.

123. For expressions of hospitality toward Swedish and Norwegian Students of the Scandinavian Student Association meeting in Copenhagen and information on a projected loan fund for artisans, see *Kjøbenhavnsposten*, 135, 142, June 14, 23, 1845; *Fædrelandet*, 1914, 1915, 1920, 1921, 1922, 1923, 1924, 1925, 1926, 1927, June 16, 17, 23, 24, 26, 27, 28, 30, July 1, 2, 1845.

124. See *Either/Or*, I, p. 287, *KW* III (*SV* I 259).

125. See *Postscript, KW* XII (*SV* VII 252-57).

126. Ibid. (256).

127. Ibid. (255).

128. Ibid. (256).

129. Ibid. (253).

130. Ibid. (249).

131. On Kierkegaard's relation to *Corsaren*, see Historical Introduction, *Corsair Affair*, pp. vii-xxxiii, *KW* XIII, and pertinent sections of the text and supplement.

132. See Supplement, pp. 428-29 (*Pap.* IV B 59, p. 225).

133. See *Point of View, KW* XXII (*SV* XIII 569-70 fn.).

134. Cf. *Works of Love, KW* XVI (*SV* IX 233).

135. Christian Molbech (1783-1857), historian, linguist, literary critic, named Councilor of State, June 28, 1845.

136. See *KW* XII (*SV* VII 548).

137. Carl Reitzel (1789-1853), the leading bookseller, publisher, and printer in Copenhagen at the time. See *Letters*, Letter 157, *KW* XXV.

138. *The Book on Adler*, which was not published by Kierkegaard. See *Pap.* VII¹ B 235.

139. Jens Finsteen Gi(j)ødwad (1811-1891), editor of *Kjøbenhavnsposten* 1837-39, co-publisher of *Fædrelandet* from December 1839 and editor 1844-45. He was Kierkegaard's middleman with the printer and bookseller of the pseudonymous works.

140. On the relation between Kierkegaard and Peter Ludvig Møller, see Historical Introduction, Corsair *Affair*, pp. x-xxix, *KW* XIII.

141. See *Christian Discourses, KW* XVII (*SV* X 163).

142. See Philippians 2:12.

143. Published June 12, 1842. See Corsair *Affair*, pp. 3-12, *KW* XIII (*SV* XIII 397-406).

144. Published pseudonymously (*Inter et Inter*) in *Fædrelandet*, 188-91, July 24-27, 1848. See *Christian Discourses, KW* XVII (*SV* X 319-44).

145. Johanne Luise Pätges Heiberg (1812-1890), wife of Johan Ludvig Heiberg and the leading Danish actress at the time.

146. Anna Helene Brenøe Nielsen (1803-1856), Danish actress famous particularly as the foremost portrayer of Oehlenschläger's heroines. See *Stages, KW* XI (*SV* VI 126-27 fn.); *JP* I 152 (*Pap*. VI A 118).

147. See note 139 above.

148. *Crisis*. See Supplement, pp. 437-38 (*Pap*. IX A 175), and note 139.

149. Ibid.

150. Ibid.

151. Rasmus Nielsen (1809-1844), professor of philosophy, University of Copenhagen. For a time it seemed as if Nielsen would be allowed to become in a sense Kierkegaard's successor. See, for example, *JP* 6239, 6246, 6301, 6302, 6341, 6342, 6402-06, 6574 (*Pap*. IX A 229, 258; X[1] A 14, 15, 110, 111, 343; X[6] B 83-86, 121); *Letters*, Letter 257, *KW* XXV.

152. See note 151 above.

153. *Crisis*. See Supplement, pp. 437-38 (*Pap*. IX A 175), and note 144.

154. See *Stages, KW* XI (*SV* VI 175-459).

155. The envisioned work "A Cycle of Ethical-Religious Essays" originally had the following parts (see *Papirer* IX B 1-6): Preface; no. 1, "Something on What Might Be Called 'Premise-Authors' "; no. 2, "The Dialectical Relations: the Universal, the Single Individual, the Special Individual"; no. 3, "Has a Man the Right to Let Himself Be Put to Death for the Truth?"; no. 4, "A Revelation in the Situation of the Present Age"; no. 5, "A Psychological Interpretation of Magister Adler as a Phenomenon and as a Satire upon Hegelian Philosophy and the Present Age"; and no. 6, "On the Difference between a Genius and an Apostle." *Two Minor Ethical-Religious Essays*, by H. H., published May 19, 1849, contains a preface and no. 3 and 6 of the above. "The Book on Adler," which remained in manuscript form, included a preface (Kierkegaard wrote eight different prefaces for it), no. 1, no. 2, and no. 5 of the above.

156. Adolph Peter Adler (1812-1869), Danish philosopher and theologian, was a student of Hegel's philosophy and later, prompted by visions, a kind of modern gnostic.

157. See note 155 above.

158. See note 155 above. The "Three Notes Concerning My Work as an Author" intended as appendices to "The Point of View" were: (1) "Concerning the Dedication to 'That Single Individual' "; (2) "A Word on the Relation of My Work as an Author to 'That Single Individual' "; and (3) "Preface to the 'Friday Discourses.' " Eventually no. 3 was omitted. See *Point of View, KW* XXII (*SV* XIII 585-99). A shortened version of no. 3 was used as the preface to *Two Discourses at the Communion on Fridays* (1851), *KW* XVIII (*SV* XII 263-90).

159. Published April 26, 1848.

160. See *Letters*, Letters 154, 156, 157, *KW* XXV.

161. See *Armed Neutrality, KW* XXII (*Pap.* X⁵ B 106, 107).

162. *Christian Discourses* and *Crisis*, published April 26, July 24-27; *Point of View*, "as good as finished" (*JP* VI 6258; *Pap.* IX A 293); *Armed Neutrality*, "written toward the end of 1848 and the beginning of 1849" (*Pap.* X⁵ B 105); drafts of *The Lily of the Field and the Bird of the Air* and of *Practice in Christianity*, I, written; "Herr Phister as Captain Scipio," completed.

163. The second edition of *Either/Or* was issued on May 14, 1849. On the same day *The Lily of the Field and the Bird of the Air* was published, and on May 19 *Two Minor Ethical-Religious Essays*, by H. H.

164. This idea was not carried out.

165. The two preceding titles became Parts II and III (of three) of *Practice in Christianity*, published September 25, 1850.

166. See *JP* VI 6337 (*Pap.* X¹ A 95).

167. See note 163 above.

168. The reference is to Regine Olsen, Kierkegaard's fiancée.

169. *Postscript, KW* XII (*SV* VII 120-21 fn.).

170. *Two Upbuilding Discourses* was published May 5 (Kierkegaard's birthday), 1843. See *Eighteen Discourses, KW* V (*SV* III 11).

171. Adam Gottlob Oehlenschläger (1779-1850); Rasmus Villads Christian Winther (1796-1876); Henrik Hertz (1797-1870).

172. See note 151 above.

173. Jacob (Jakob) Peter Mynster (1775-1854), Bishop of Sjælland (1834-54).

174. See note 168 above.

175. P. 11, *KW* VI (*SV* III 64).

176. Ibid., 15-16 (68-69).

177. This entry was the proposed title of Kierkegaard's last work. Kierkegaard considered *Either/Or* as the first work in the authorship proper. The proposed title indicates that he regarded Either/Or, *mutatis mutandis*, as the appropriate rubric for the entire authorship. See *JP* VI 6945-47 (*Pap.* XI³ 55-57).

178. See note 173 above.

BIBLIOGRAPHICAL NOTE

For general bibliographies of Kierkegaard studies, see:

Jens Himmelstrup, *Søren Kierkegaard International Bibliografi*. Copenhagen: Nyt Nordisk Forlag Arnold Busck, 1962.

Aage Jørgensen, *Søren Kierkegaard-litteratur 1961-1970, 1971-1980*. Aarhus: Akademisk Boghandel, 1971; *Kierkegaardiana*, XII, 1982.

François H. Lapointe, *Sören Kierkegaard and His Critics: An International Bibliography of Criticism*. Westport, Connecticut: Greenwood Press, 1980.

Kierkegaard: A Collection of Critical Essays, ed. Josiah Thompson. New York: Doubleday (Anchor Books), 1972.

Søren Kierkegaard's Journals and Papers, I, ed. and tr. Howard V. Hong and Edna H. Hong, assisted by Gregor Malantschuk. Bloomington, Indiana: Indiana University Press, 1967.

For topical bibliographies of Kierkegaard studies, see *Søren Kierkegaards's Journals and Papers*, I-IV, 1967-75.

INDEX

518   Index

ADVISORY BOARD

KIERKEGAARD'S WRITINGS

Library of Congress Cataloging-in-Publication Data
(Rev. for vol. 2)

Kierkegaard, Søren, 1813-1855.
  Either/or.

  (Kierkegaard's writings, 3-4)
  Translation of: Enten-eller.
  Includes bibliographies and indexes.
  I. Hong, Howard Vincent, 1912- . II. Hong, Edna Hatlestad, 1913- . III.
Series. IV. Series: Kierkegaard, Søren, 1813-1855. Works. English. 1978; 3-4.
PT8142.E57E5 1987   198'.9   86-25516
ISBN 0-691-07315-5 (v. 1 : alk. paper)
ISBN 0-691-02041-8 (v. 1 : pbk.)
ISBN 0-691-07316-3 (v. 2 : alk. paper)
ISBN 0-691-02042-6 (v. 2 : pbk.)